Democracies in Peril

T0384981

Globalization is triggering a "revenue shock" in developing economies. International trade taxes – once the primary source of government revenue – have been cut drastically in response to trade liberalization. Bastiaens and Rudra make the novel argument that regime type is a major determinant of revenue-raising capacity once free trade policies have been adopted. Specifically, policymakers in democracies confront greater challenges than their authoritarian counterparts when implementing tax reforms to offset liberalization's revenue shocks. The repercussions are significant: while the poor bear the brunt of this revenue shortfall in democracies, authoritarian regimes are better off overall. Paradoxically, then, citizens of democracies suffer precisely because their freer political culture constrains governmental ability to tax and redistribute under globalization. This important contribution on the battle between open societies and the ability of governments to help their people prosper under globalization is essential reading for students and scholars of political economy, development studies, and comparative politics.

Ida Bastiaens is Assistant Professor of Political Science at Fordham University. Her research analyzes questions on the political determinants of integration in the global economy, the impact of international integration on fiscal and social welfare in developing countries, and citizen preferences for global capital flows. She has published in *International Interactions, Journal of European Public Policy*, and *Review of International Political Economy*.

Nita Rudra is Professor of Government at Georgetown University. Her research focuses on the problems of economic development, democracy, globalization, inequality, and redistribution in the developing world. Her work appears in *British Journal of Political Science, Journal of Politics, American Journal of Political Science, Comparative Political Studies*, and *International Organization*.

Democracies in Peril

Taxation and Redistribution in Globalizing Economies

Ida Bastiaens

Fordham University, New York

Nita Rudra

Georgetown University, Washington DC

CAMBRIDGE
UNIVERSITY PRESS

University Printing House, Cambridge CB2 8BS, United Kingdom

One Liberty Plaza, 20th Floor, New York, NY 10006, USA

477 Williamstown Road, Port Melbourne, VIC 3207, Australia

314–321, 3rd Floor, Plot 3, Splendor Forum, Jasola District Centre,
New Delhi – 110025, India

79 Anson Road, #06-04/06, Singapore 079906

Cambridge University Press is part of the University of Cambridge.

It furthers the University's mission by disseminating knowledge in the pursuit of
education, learning, and research at the highest international levels of excellence.

www.cambridge.org
Information on this title: www.cambridge.org/9781108470483
DOI: 10.1017/9781108556668

First published 2018

Printed and bound in Great Britain by Clays Ltd, Elcograf S.p.A.

A catalogue record for this publication is available from the British Library.

Library of Congress Cataloging-in-Publication Data
Names: Bastiaens, Ida, author. | Rudra, Nita, author.
Title: Democracies in peril : taxation and redistribution in the global economy /
Ida Bastiaens, Fordham University, New York, Nita Rudra, Georgetown
University, Washington DC.
Description: Cambridge, United Kingdom; New York, NY: Cambridge
University Press, 2018. | Includes bibliographical references and index.
Identifiers: LCCN 2018013737 | ISBN 9781108470483 (hardback)
Subjects: LCSH: Taxation – Developing countries. | Democracy –
Developing countries. | Free enterprise – Developing countries. |
Finance, Public – Developing countries. | Developing countries – Politics
and government. | Developing countries – Economic conditions.
Classification: LCC HJ2351.7.B37 2018 | DDC 336.09172/4–dc23
LC record available at https://lccn.loc.gov/2018013737

ISBN 978-1-108-47048-3 Hardback
ISBN 978-1-108-45488-9 Paperback

For Amma and Opa

Contents

Figures

Tables

Preface

A backlash against liberal institutions is brewing. Our book is not meant to add fuel to the fire. Instead, we hope our findings lend insight into how developing countries can better harness globalization's tremendous benefits. In our analysis, we take a critical eye to both democracy and free trade, pushing our readers to look at the unconventional or underemphasized challenges both face. We ultimately find that democracies are struggling to effectively implement tax reforms in the face of drops in government revenue at the onset of trade liberalization. Just as many critics of liberalism and globalization contend, elite interests and corporate demands inhibit democracies' progress, creating an environment of low confidence. In our book, we find such disappointments are hurting elected politicians' ability to convince voters the tax bargain is in their favor. Breaking this vicious cycle of low confidence–low revenue is critical – especially in developing countries – as they struggle to provide basic public goods for their large impoverished populations. We are thus also driven by social justice concerns: the longstanding stability and success of our cherished liberal institutions, democracy and free trade, as well as the well-being of those most in need among us.

This project started at the University of Pittsburgh as a research article that we quickly realized – with a gentle nudge from Ed Mansfield – needed more space to be developed fully. We thus began the process of transforming our thesis into a book manuscript. All along the way, we received invaluable feedback from our colleagues. Whether they helped with a small detail on statistical coding or larger theoretical framings, we owe them a debt of gratitude. We presented drafts of our argument and findings at: American Political Science Association 2013 and 2017, College of William and Mary, Columbia University, Georgetown University, Heidelberg University, International Political Economy Society 2012, International Studies Association 2012, Johns Hopkins University, London School of Economics, McGill University, Princeton University, University of Colorado Boulder, University of Connecticut, University of Pennsylvania, University of Pittsburgh, University of

Southern California, University of Texas at Austin, University of Washington, and University of Wisconsin-Madison. We thank all the participants, discussants, and audience members for their questions and insights. We also extend our gratitude to Faisal Ahmed, Barry Ames, Andy Baker, Sarah Bauerle Danzman, Marc Busch, Jerry Cohen, Daniela Donno, Steven Finkel, Jennifer Gandhi, Jack Gerstein, Michael Goodhart, Jude Hays, Charles King, Marko Klansjo, Edward Mansfield, Dmitri Melhorn, Victor Menaldo, Helen Milner, Kevin Morrison, John Odell, Stephanie Rickard, Michael Ross, Carina Schmitt, Joel Simmons, Dan Tirone, James Vreeland, and Stephen Weymouth for their extensive comments and suggestions. Very special thanks to Dennis Quinn for his unwavering support and amazing wherewithal to read countless drafts, and engage in endless dialogue about the arguments in the book. Dennis, you are an amazing colleague. Research assistants at Georgetown University, Griffin Cohen, Rabea Kirmani, Florian Munch, and Kristen Skillman, helped with data collection, case research, and references. We wish to recognize both Fordham University and Georgetown University for financial support for research assistance, survey research, and professional editing.

Our book manuscript endured extensive revisions and rewrites, each one intended to greatly improve our draft. The final product would not be what it is without Cassandra Thomas. She read and reread our manuscript countless times, providing invaluable edits. Her creativity brought intrigue and appeal to our (boring) academic writing style. She was able to see the forest through the trees, but also paid a tremendous attention to detail. Thank you, Cass. We will also be eternally grateful to her husband and Nita's dear friend, Seth Miller, for motivating us with his enthusiasm for the book's argument, his mega-intelligent wit, and most of all, for inspiring "Subodh."

Our book workshop, hosted at Georgetown University with sponsorship from Georgetown University's Mortara Center for International Studies and Fordham University, was also absolutely critical to the development of this book. We deeply and sincerely thank our panelists – Jeffry Frieden, Judith Goldstein, Kenneth Scheve, Erik Wibbels, Kristen Looney, Irfan Nooruddin, and Joseph Sassoon – as well as the additional participants – Despina Alexiadou, Miles Kahler, George Shambaugh, and Jennifer Tobin – at the workshop. Our panelists took time out of their busy schedules to carefully read our draft and their feedback was instrumental in transforming our ideas and challenging us to develop a stronger and more coherent manuscript. We were inspired to sharpen and strengthen our puzzle, logic, and evidence because of the hard questions and comments we received at the workshop. Thank you. All errors are our own.

Last, but not least, we are indebted to our families and friends for their unfailing support throughout the writing of this book. Our parents, Leo and Devra Bastiaens, Brad and Regina Navia, Lina and Sujit Rudra, and Siva and Vasantha Sundaram, siblings, Jesse Bastiaens, Jonathan Navia, Krish Sundaram, and Ana Valdez, partners, Jason Navia and Ravi Sundaram, Ida's grandmother, Oma, and Nita's sweet daughter, Diya, as well as countless friends kept us sane when the sentences began to blur together. Their energy, encouragement, and love underlie every word we wrote.

We dedicate this book to Amma and Opa.

Amma is Ravi's mother, and Opa is Ida's grandfather, two of the most beautiful souls in this universe. They passed during the writing of this book. By dedicating this book to them, we are not just paying homage to their kindness. Through Amma and Opa, we are dedicating this book to the future generation who, we hope, like Amma and Opa, will improve liberal institutions with their hard work, good will, and sense of humanity: Laylah Conde, Maya Juanita Georgina Garcetti, Lydia Roberto, Diya Rudra Sundaram, Kareena Soheli Rudra, Jackson Snead, Reese Fritz, Natalie Snead, Rahul Rudra, Natasha Fritz, Tommy Adamski, Natasha Adamski, Alessandro Navia, Edith Bezdek, Beatrice Lawson, Felix Neskey, Annabel McIntosh, Lyanna Bridges, Henry Neitznick, Louie Decesar, Mary Zeanah Barley, Oscar Neskey, and Puja Monica Rudra.

Introduction

"So it has come to this," Subodh Reddy thought, as he sat tapping the retracted tip of his ballpoint pen on his sal wood desk, alone in his office on the second floor of the Andhra Pradesh State Assembly building.

"We are taxing cow urine."

It was late, and most of the other staffers had gone home to their families. His college friends were probably relaxing with a Kingfisher beer at a club in the financial district. There would be music, dancing, tipsy revelers bursting into laughter on the broken sidewalk outside.

And here he was, staring into space and listening to the creaking of his blowing fan, trying to think how, exactly, to start the draft of a bill to establish Andhra Pradesh's newest tax. Should he get right to the point, and put cow urine, "Gomutra," in the bill's title? Perhaps he should find a euphemism to disguise the ridiculousness of the demand? Or should he have listened to his pestering parents, and just become a cardiologist instead of getting a master's in Commerce?

He had heard that the state wasn't always this cash-strapped. Twenty-five years ago, when his biggest pastime was playing cricket with his young classmates, Andhra Pradesh was a very different place. But, in 1991, India had finally accepted that higher import and export taxes were putting them at a genuine disadvantage against multinational corporations, and liberalized its once-protected industries. And there were real, immediate benefits from these changes. So many more things you could buy. The government proudly touted increased growth rates. Indian giants like Tata Steel were given incentive to go conquer the globe. And conquer they did, building manufacturing plants in Europe and East Asia, and becoming one of the lowest-cost producers in the world. Every right-thinking economics student believed that globalization was, without question, a good thing for India.

Yet, Andhra Pradesh's finances were a constant anxiety for Subodh.

His state has always banked on its share of central government taxes to fund the bulk of its spending needs. Now they are facing over Rs. 15,000 crore revenue deficit. But the Indian government cannot seem to fill its coffers, and this had been true for a long time – over the last two decades, ever since they could no longer tax trade. This new tax was not the first that the government had imposed since liberalizing – to many people's dismay, a value added tax (VAT) was added in 2005 all across India. In Andhra Pradesh, finished goods were taxed at what most grumbled was a ridiculous rate of 14.5 percent. Foodgrains and materials like steel were taxed at a rate of 5 percent.

Still, government revenues barely sputtered; the money never seemed to come in, and the good times never came along. The government was now in dire need of new sources of income. And Subodh had been tasked with writing a bill to tax one of the few materials that was left out of the VAT discussions. The one industrial sector that had not – at least yet – pushed back against the government's reach.

It was time to tax cow urine.

Subodh inhaled deeply to focus his mind on writing. The only thing that disheartened him even more than the indignity of taxing cow urine was that this tax bill might not even solve the problem. Would local firms be willing to pay this tax? Could his fellow bureaucrats enforce and collect this tax? How would they bring in the money required for all the many projects Subodh had dreamed of when he entered government: better healthcare, education, roads, and infrastructure? Perhaps someday, he could tell his family of the glories of his days as a staffer in the State Assembly. But sadly, not today.

Subodh, our character in the story above, is a work of fiction. But the Andhra Pradesh (AP) tax on cow urine is real. Gomutra is used in many traditional Indian medicines, as well as in a wide range of hygiene and cleaning products. To understand why AP was forced to search for inventive ways to tax – and why governments throughout India and the developing world are struggling to find revenue for their treasuries – we have to step back from seemingly isolated local challenges and take a hard look at that great good of modern economics, globalization.

Could globalization in fact be the cause of these issues?

Stubbornly low – and still dwindling – government tax revenues are not a minor problem. The great philosopher and economist Adam Smith maintained that, alongside peace and justice, taxation is key to a successful society. Tax revenues enable government spending – spending that supports public goods that help reduce inequality and support sustainable growth. There is little doubt that states across the developing world are desperate for new sources of tax revenue to pursue such critical goals. In this book, we argue that the forces of globalization and free trade, in particular, are proving crippling to the finances of developing nations that allow political freedoms to flourish. In stark contrast, some of the world's most repressive regimes are having little problem filling public coffers alongside expanding globalization.

Our book thus finds the following: globalization is *not* the crux of the problem. As more and more citizens today bemoan globalization, we take a step back and ask why it does not seem to be working as anticipated for such large numbers. Our central finding is that trade and economic openness is good for the majority if and when governments can tax and redistribute to those who are falling behind. Somewhat paradoxically, citizens of democracies in the developing world suffer precisely because countervailing political pressures impede the government's ability to tax and redistribute under the auspices of globalization. Essentially, as these democracies open up, they are ill-equipped to address some of the distributional consequences that threaten to make free trade less palatable to the masses.

The Problem

Is globalization – or a side effect of it – triggering a largely unrecognized revenue crisis in a substantial portion of the developing world? The heart of the issue lies in how the governments of developing economies that joined the third wave of globalization, or the "late liberalizing" countries, raised their money prior to the 1990s.[1] Revenues were collected, in large part, from taxes on imports and exports. Specifically, tariffs on consumer goods, particularly luxury goods and intermediate goods produced domestically, as well as agricultural exports, led to high trade tax revenues. These tax revenues accounted for, on average, 40 percent of all total tax receipts in low-income economies, and 35 percent in lower-middle-income countries.[2] Altogether, they comprised almost one-third of tax revenues in the full sample of developing economies (see Figure 0.1).

Reliance on trade taxes persisted through the early 1990s, in large part because they are "easy to collect." This class of taxes includes import duties, export duties, profits of export or import monopolies, exchange profits, and exchange taxes. They are straightforward to monitor and solicit at a centralized location, such as border areas, and do not require a complex administration to manage. However, there are many

---

[1] Scholars and policymakers have identified three waves of globalization (via reduction in trade barriers and large flows of trade, capital, and migration): (1) 1870–1914, (2) 1945–79, and (3) 1980–today (Collier and Dollar 2002). Collar and Dollar (2002) use the term "new globalizers" to signify integration of developing countries in the third wave.

[2] Khattry and Rao 2002.

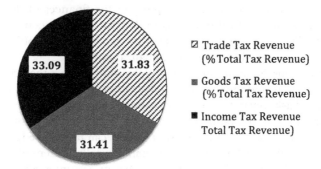

Figure 0.1 Tax Composition of Developing Countries – Early Liberalization Begins (1990)

Note: All tax revenue data taken from the World Bank in this book refers to central government tax revenue.

Data source: World Bank 2016a

arguments – some grounded in sound economic theory and others in market fundamentalism – against the extensive use of trade taxes.

From the late 1980s and into the 1990s, after the Latin American debt crisis, there was a shift toward more open international markets. The substantial lowering of tariffs was the critical component of this opening of markets, including membership in the World Trade Organization (WTO) and the provision of structural adjustment packages. With a general adoption of a more liberal stance towards trade, these "late liberalizers" ostensibly lost permanent access to a primary source of tax revenue.[3]

In effect, liberalizing trade translated into a large and rapid loss of money – i.e., trade tax revenues – for governments across the developing world. We label this a "revenue shock" because it is an event, often triggered in large part by exogenous factors, that produces a relatively sudden drop in government revenues. The repercussions are significant. Overall revenue levels in developing economies have always been far below those of advanced industrialized countries, and in spite of frequent, and sometimes extensive deficit spending, the provision of public goods is inadequate in many late liberalizing countries.

Developing nations thus must urgently replace almost a third of their already low tax revenue base with "hard to collect" domestic taxes. This is no easy undertaking. These reforms include increasing income

---

[3] Import taxes constituted 85 percent of trade tax revenues in 1990 in developing countries.

taxes on individuals and corporate entities, as well as implementing the
value-added tax (VAT). Goods taxes such as the VAT are complicated,
involving fees at various levels of production. Broadening income taxes
is no less arduous a task, given that a large percentage of citizens (and
firms) in poor economies are logistically difficult to tax. Weak bureaucracies, staff, and technologies amplify these problems.[4] In addition, with
liberalization, governments are in a conundrum: they face rising political
pressures to keep domestic taxes low so that less productive firms can
survive in the face of international market competition and, at the same
time, more productive exporting firms are demanding even lower tariffs.
Tax reform in the liberalizing environment is a challenge for all of these
reasons – both in passage and implementation.

The Puzzle

For many, it was expected that trade itself would be the solution. Despite
its recent unpopularity in some circles, free trade is frequently touted as
one of the keys to economic prosperity. Economists have long considered
it a central component of growth and development. As increased trade
and capital flows spur growth, the loss in trade tax revenues should
be easily replaced with the taxes collected from a more dynamic private sector. Trade liberalization in the developing world has thus been
heralded as a necessary step in the path to development success.

Yet, despite this rosy view, many developing countries have been facing
formidable challenges recovering from the revenue shock and substituting
their lost trade tax revenues with domestic taxes. Cross-national data over
the last 22 years shows that a great many developing economies have
experienced lackluster improvements in government tax revenues particularly *after* adopting free trade policies, and revenues have even fallen
over time in some countries. Nevertheless, this is certainly not the case for
all late liberalizing countries. Indeed, a certain subset of countries appears
to be performing just as conventional wisdom would expect: government
tax revenues are steadily expanding concomitant with trade liberalization.

What accounts for these differing patterns? Why are some governments
able to successfully increase domestic taxes and replace the lost trade
tax revenue, while others clearly are not? Academic studies up to this
point have not been able to explain this divergence. International financial institutions (IFIs) anticipated – at least initially – the domestic tax
reforms they recommended would more or less immediately follow

---

[4] IMF 2011a; Tanzi and Zee 2001.

liberalization. Perhaps the explanation lies more in politics than economics. The question in this book is, then, whether and to what extent *political* factors can play a role, either in making the situation better or worse. Why have only certain governments managed to ensure that the early- to mid-1990s revenue shock did not have long-lasting effects by raising – and collecting – taxes on individuals and capital?

The Challenge For "Late Liberalizing" Democracies

Subodh's problem is far from unique.

But it turns out to be far more common in democracies than nondemocracies.

We argue that, while the turn towards greater trade openness initially disrupted the ability of all late liberalizing countries to gather tax revenue, only in the case of democracies has it resulted in a lasting low-revenue trap. We differentiate late liberalizing democracies from advanced industrialized democracies by focusing on countries that embrace political and civil freedoms, but liberalized in the third wave of globalization with relatively low bureaucratic capacity. For a country to recover from revenue shocks in the global economy, history has shown that policymakers have two critical means to enact successful domestic tax reforms: compulsory and voluntary (or quasi-voluntary) tax compliance. Compulsory compliance depends on a government's willingness to use some form of force to impose its will on its own citizens, while quasi-voluntary compliance derives from citizen perceptions that the tax system is "fair," i.e., that the state is providing sufficient public goods in exchange for tax payments. Late liberalizing democracies fall short on both counts.

Institutional features of democracies limit the use of (extrajudicial) tools for compulsory compliance. By design, democracies are constrained from imposing tax reforms by fiat, and from soliciting tax payments from citizens through fear. The unfortunate result is that evasion is comparatively easy and costless; local businesses struggling to survive in a competitive global economy are even more likely to take advantage of this institutional feature. At the same time, quasi-voluntary compliance is being undermined, first by business hostility to higher taxes as global competition intensifies, and second, by low voter confidence in the fairness of the new tax proposals. Both groups lack confidence that the tax bargain under liberalization is beneficial, not believing their contributions will help them or society at large. For instance, less productive firms – particularly those linked to once-protected industries – lobby for lower domestic taxes as they struggle to compete in national markets with imports. The most productive firms are exporters, and they demand both lower taxes *and* lower tariffs, although they are more likely to privilege the latter. This is perhaps why democracies tend to liberalize faster *and* have lower domestic tax revenues. Fundamentally, hostility from voters and firms creates strong impediments to tax reforms. Such resistance is a deal breaker in late liberalizing democracies, where elected officials rely disproportionately on elite interest groups to stay in power.

Authoritarian leaders, in contrast, are more easily able to generate government tax revenues in response to the liberalization-induced revenue shock. They use different combinations of institutionalized coercion and quasi-voluntary compliance to collect taxes that can compensate for – and perhaps even surpass – the dramatic loss in trade taxes. Though all authoritarian regimes are *not* the same, and various authoritarian subtypes use different strategies to pursue unpopular tax reforms, they share certain traits. Reliance on a smaller subset of the population (and firms) for support and the ability to use extrajudicial force to mobilize tax revenues are two of the main commonalities. And both of these factors make tax reform in the face of a revenue shock far easier to implement.

In order to be certain that it is indeed regime types that vary in their responses to globalization and revenue mobilization, our book investigates whether other factors, such as weak state capacity and low gross domestic income, are responsible for the difficulties of revenue generation post-shock. But contrary to expectations, neither of these alternative explanations helps shed light on our puzzle. Instead, it appears the crux of the matter lies in the politics of liberalizing and freer societies. This is why democracies may find it more challenging to harness the benefits of free trade and globalization, while autocracies are forging ahead.

Why Should We Care?

In some parts of the world, then, the unintended consequence of globalization is stubbornly low government revenues. But the real problem is not globalization; it is how the political constraints of democracies are undermining the positive impacts of globalization. While many assume that democratic governments improve the prosperity of their country and the health and well-being of their citizens, none of these things are possible without the money to provide them. The catch is that, as globalization and free trade expands, democracies are finding it harder to raise money for the provision of critical public goods, such as adequate healthcare, clean water, a working infrastructure, and a school system capable of educating the populace to take advantage of the economic opportunities of the twenty-first century. Put simply, with globalization, political support for liberalization and political resistance to taxation is building in much of the developing world. This is a greater problem in democracies, where such opposition has more power to influence the direction of the country. In essence, this book is about an unfolding confrontation in the globalizing world; a battle between political freedoms and the ability of governments and their people to prosper – a fight that, in the current circumstances, neither can win.

This book is ultimately a reminder that it is time to get serious about understanding the distributional impacts of globalization. As of late, academics, the media, and international institutions have been grappling with an anti-globalization backlash. The unexpected success of Brexit and Donald Trump, thousands protesting against the Trans Pacific Partnership across both the developed and developing world, the rise of far-right nationalist-cum-protectionist movements everywhere, growing global frustration with the rising gap between the haves and have-nots, and increasingly violent anti-immigrant sentiments have set alarm bells ringing. In a great many countries, the general public is beginning to question the benefits of a flatter, more interconnected world. In effect, the voices of pro-globalization urban elites are progressively becoming faint amidst the angry protests of the many who see themselves as "losers" of globalization, despite the very real improvements it may have brought to their lives. And, as a result, international organizations are calling for "urgent action" to address the current discontents and perceived problems of globalization, such as rising disparities in income and wealth.[5] Our analysis can help inform the international community about a heretofore-overlooked reason why globalization may not be working for the average citizen, especially in democratic regimes, and what can be done about it.

India and AP's stubborn revenue crisis and our fictitious Subodh's very real tax dilemma are not what the architects of the post-war multilateral trade system ever anticipated. Indeed, expanding trade *has* raised incomes around the world, and both academics and policy elites have been particularly sanguine about how much citizens of developing countries (among others) benefit from the global economy. For these capital-scarce economies, following the theory of comparative advantage is touted as the best way to bring the much-needed influx of jobs, greater supply and diversity of affordable consumer goods, access to cutting-edge technology, boosts in income, and the path to sustainable growth that has been tried and tested by rich countries. Unfortunately, although this might be true, some of the challenges of distributing such benefits of globalization more widely – especially in developing countries – are

---

[5] Rowley 2017; Welle 2017.

still coming to light. This book focuses on one that has been grossly overlooked: democracies are finding it much harder to overcome revenue shocks in a global economy. Should the problem continue to be disregarded, it has the potential to both undermine international markets and further weaken fragile democracies. The bottom line is that free trade creates relative winners and losers, alongside the many improvements it brings; but the really big question is if and how democracies can navigate current political labyrinths to help the latter. Pro-globalization advocates and developing country policymakers should address this issue now, while overall public support for free trade is still higher than it is in rich, industrialized countries.

Focus and Plan of the Book

Our central argument is as follows: in an expanding global economy, late liberalizing democracies have greater difficulty recovering from revenue shocks than nondemocracies. To begin, the first section of the book provides a detailed look at the revenue challenge in the current era of globalization and how developing countries are confronting them. We look at why the revenue benefits of globalization are being undermined in democracies in particular. In later chapters, we look at the broader implications of this issue, and conclude by examining several case studies to get a more comprehensive perspective on the problem and its ramifications for developing nations.

Our first chapter presents the puzzle. Why does a pattern of divergence in revenue recovery persist across the liberalizing developing world? We also present a brief overview of previous research on this problem. Next, Chapter 2 provides the theoretical foundation for our argument that the trade-revenue shock is particularly problematic for democracies. It goes into more detail on the institutional differences and contrasting government incentive structures in democracies and authoritarian regimes, and why these impact recovery. Here we also identify two distinct types of authoritarian regimes ("liberal" and "conservative") and their contrasting taxation strategies in the global economy. A close examination of the data on tax revenue, the trends in different regime types, and consideration of alternative hypotheses is found in Chapter 3.

The next two chapters deal with the resistance to tax reform, particularly in democracies. In Chapter 4 we employ survey evidence to explore if and why citizens and economic elites are resisting domestic tax reform in democracies. Chapter 5 examines the role of firms – previously protected ones in particular – in lobbying the government for lower corporate tax rates. Although the focus of this book is on trade liberalization, this chapter briefly compares and contrasts the impacts of financial liberalization on tax revenue mobilization. We show how democracies are responding to these elite interests and seeing unimpressive corporate income tax revenues as a result.

Chapter 6 addresses the "so what" question, and explores the broader implications of post-trade-reform low-revenue traps. Do these empirical findings confirm doomsday predictions that lower government tax revenue is detrimental to development in democracies? How does the loss of tax revenue affect the poor in democracies? Could lower tax payments perhaps be good for the economy and citizenry? Turning to authoritarian regimes, we ask if political elites are using revenues from successful domestic tax reform to provide public goods or enrich themselves.

The last section of the book (Chapters 7, 8, and 9) presents in-depth, illustrative case studies. We look at examples of different regime types: conservative China; democratic India; as well as Jordan and Tunisia, both liberal authoritarian regimes with slightly more political freedom. We chose regionally important countries that relied on easy-to-collect taxes until they faced significant outside pressures to maintain lower tariffs and implement domestic tax reform. This approach allows us to trace the political forces underlying how and why policymakers in authoritarian regimes have been far more successful at implementing domestic tax reform and overcoming revenue shocks, while democracies such as India have not. The final chapter explores the broader consequences of low revenues in democracies. We ponder if democracies are in peril post-liberalization and suggest policies to modify this tension. Ultimately, this chapter lends insight into how open economies and open societies can be mutually beneficial.

Anyone who is concerned about development and bettering the lives of citizens in the developing world should be attentive to the implications of this book. The problems occasioned by revenue shocks are neither minor nor isolated. And the ramifications of such problems go beyond the immediate crisis of revenue we are discussing here. Citizen dissatisfaction with government and its provision of inadequate public goods leads to even less willingness to pay taxes, which only reinforces the inability of democracies to recover from revenue shocks. This vicious circle could lead to a rejection of trade liberalization, and thus threaten the progress of globalization and, perhaps worse, the validity of democratic governments. These are not problems to be taken lightly.

1 The Problem and Puzzle

We are under great financial stress. To put simply, we have no money.
Either God or GoI [Government of India] should help us.[1]
Senior Finance Department official
Andhra Pradesh, India
January 22, 2015

The cash-strapped government of the Indian state of Andhra Pradesh (AP)
is indeed in trouble. It is reeling under the revenue crisis, and both our character Subodh and his real-life counterparts – such as AP's Senior Finance
Department official above – have run out of hope that the national government can help them. Like much of the developing world, AP's subnational
government has more autonomy in expenditure than taxation, causing
them to rely heavily on central government revenue transfers.[2] But the
Indian central government is said to be "tight fisted" since they themselves
have been struggling to mobilize revenue since liberalization in 1991.[3]

This chapter provides a more in-depth look at why revenue shocks are
a serious issue for developing countries in today's global economy. To
assess this, we explore how a particular kind of revenue shock associated
with globalization – trade liberalization and the associated rapid reduction in trade taxes – has rattled large parts of the developing world with
its immediate effects on government revenues. Yet some countries are
recovering, while others are not.

Trade Liberalization and the Revenue Shock

With the adoption of the trade liberalization agenda, developing countries
gained much, but one important thing that they lost was a key source of
tax revenue for many of their governments. In the late 1980s/early 1990s,
structural adjustment packages from international financial institutions

[1] Nichenametia 2015.
[2] Bird 2010; Purfield 2004.
[3] Nichenametia 2015.

(IFIs), such as the World Bank and the International Monetary Fund (IMF), mandated that the liberalization of markets begin. Membership in the World Trade Organization (WTO) demanded the same. Once lower (bound) tariffs had been negotiated, increasing import tariffs was a clear violation of WTO rules.[4] And since liberalizing, productive firms have strengthened their opposition to high tariffs and any government efforts to reverse the course of trade liberalization. As a result, applied tariff rates have markedly decreased over time.

With market liberalization, constraints on the ability to tax trade have resulted in significant losses in government tax revenue. As part and parcel of deliberate trade liberalization policies led by IFIs, trade tax revenues rapidly decreased over the last three decades.[5] Indeed, Collier and Dollar (2002: 55) posit, "absolute reductions in tariff rates in developing countries have been much higher than in industrial countries." Recall from the introduction the great extent to which a large number of these nations relied on trade tax revenues. It is not surprising, then, that considerable empirical evidence confirms that trade liberalization is correlated with both exogenous pressures, from International Organizations and richer trading partners, such as the United States, and the erosion of the tax base in many developing countries.[6] We hereafter use large reductions in trade taxes as a proxy for "revenue shocks" and interchangeably refer to the overall steady decline in trade taxes thereafter with "trade liberalization." These shocks have been ongoing but were particularly severe the first five to seven years into the early 1990s, a period that includes the commencement of the WTO. Perhaps even greater problems come after the initial revenue shock; developing nations are now more exposed to a competitive market environment, which dampens the willingness of private actors to pay domestic taxes that could compensate for the revenue losses.

---

[4] The maximum tariff levels permitted by the WTO are bound tariff rates. In practice, most countries follow the "applied rate" rather than the bound rate on imported goods. The applied tariff rate is typically less than or equal to the bound rate. A tariff overhang (gap between a higher bound and lower applied rate) provides countries with flexibility to set their tariff levels (see Beshkar, Bond, and Rho 2015; Busch and Pelc 2014). If a country's applied tariff rate is above the bound rate, it could be taken to the WTO dispute settlement panel.

[5] See also Keen and Simone (2004).

[6] See Finger and Nogues (2002), Gallagher (2008), and Saner and Guilherme (2007) for analyses of external pressures for liberalization. Dean (2017) finds that US pressure is associated with decreases in average tariff levels in the targeted developing country. Aizenman and Jimjarak (2009), Baunsgaard and Keen (2010), and Khattry and Rao (2002) discuss the correlation between trade liberalization, trade taxes, and the overall revenue decline in many developing countries.

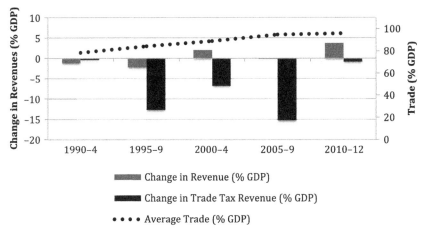

Figure 1.1 Revenue Shock in Developing Countries
Data source: World Bank 2016a

The trade-liberalization-induced revenue shock we focus upon in this book has an additional component: it rather permanently reduces the supply of revenue from a longstanding source (i.e., tariffs), creating a critical need to raise additional public money in the process.[7] As expected, the first big shock for developing countries occurred in the mid to late 1990s, at the heels of initial trade reforms and WTO accession (see Figure 1.1). We focus in this book on the countries that made major advances towards free trade in the early 1990s, and that the prestigious Organisation of Economic Co-operation and Development (OECD) nations did not deem an "economically more advanced nation."[8] On average, as trade tax revenues fell by 40 percent between 1990 and 2010, the level of trade increased by 24 percent. Figure 1.1 suggests some government revenue recovery starting in the early 2000s in response to this steady increase in trade and secular decline trade tax revenues. Is it sufficient? The figure masks whether individual countries were able to successfully replace the *total* loss in trade tax revenues with other domestic tax revenues.

Regardless, the trade-liberalization revenue shock poses serious challenges for developing economies. Adding to the dilemma of losing access to a critical tax revenue source, overall revenue levels in developing

---

[7] Burnside, Eichenbaum, and Fischer 2004; Tanzi 1986.
[8] In other words, we include any country that is non-OECD *during any year(s)* of our analysis (e.g., Chile, Czech Republic, South Korea). We include Turkey because it is a middle-income country.

economies have always been suboptimal. They have hovered at levels far below that of advanced industrialized countries (22 percent of GDP in developing countries, compared with 33 percent in developed countries); despite often resorting to extensive deficit spending as a consequence, public goods quality has generally been low.[9] The United Nation Conference on Trade and Development (UNCTAD 2016) estimates that achieving the Sustainable Development Goals (SDG) requires low-income countries to raise their current tax–GDP ratios by close to 4 percentage points. Along with the United Nations, the World Bank and the IMF both report that the need for revenue mobilization in many developing economies is substantial. IMF President Christine Lagarde declared:

A strong revenue base is imperative if developing countries are to be able to finance the spending they need on public services, social support and infrastructure.[10]

Likewise, World Bank Group President Jim Yong Kim says:

We very much want to help developing countries raise more revenues through taxes because this can lead to more children receiving a good education and more families having access to quality health care … If everyone pays their fair share, developing countries can close their financing gaps and promote inclusive growth.[11]

Conventional wisdom points to trade expansion as the answer to developing countries' long-term development. Economists, in particular, argue that economic growth from trade would automatically yield greater tax collections from a productive private sector. Yet, contrary to expectations, government revenues have, in fact, actually fallen or remained relatively constant in a large number of developing countries after adopting liberalization policies. This overall slight downward trend between trade openness and total government revenues is illustrated in Figure 1.2.[12]

Countries such as the Philippines, India, and Nicaragua have made great strides in global market expansion, but minimal improvements, if any, in government revenue. Looking more closely at the lower-right quadrant, it becomes clear that these countries are among a sizeable group of nations that follow this pattern. However, not all developing countries have suffered. Among a second set of countries, the outcome is different. Government revenues appear to be flourishing post-liberalization in

---

[9] World Bank 2016a.
[10] IMF 2015a.
[11] IMF 2015a.
[12] Government revenue includes cash receipts from taxes, social contribution, and other revenues such as fines, fees, rent, and income from property or sales; grants are not included (World Bank 2016a). The trends hold in samples excluding Eastern European and former Soviet countries or oil-rich countries.

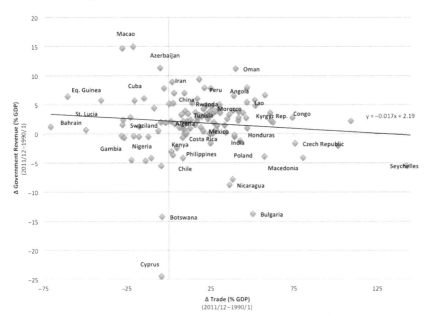

Figure 1.2 Trade and Revenue (Percent of GDP) in Developing Countries
Note: To avoid overcrowding in the figures throughout this chapter, we do not label all data points. We use Amelia II (Honaker, King, and Blackwell 2015) to impute all tax revenue data in this chapter so that missing observations do not skew the overall trends.
Data source: World Bank 2016a

countries such as China, Tunisia, and Morocco. This group shows positive improvements in trade *and* total revenue.

What explains the difference in post-liberalization revenues across these countries? Clearly, a subset of nations is following conventional wisdom and recovering from the revenue shocks. On average, tax revenue comprises nearly three-quarters of total government revenue across the developing world. Recovering from a liberalization-induced revenue shock thus requires successfully generating domestic revenues equal to or above the loss in trade taxes. How well are the late liberalizing economies doing on this front?

A Deeper Look at the Puzzle: Trade Liberalization and Domestic Tax Reforms

The revenue shock, which struck hardest in the 1990s, demanded that governments immediately replenish their treasuries. Recall that a third (or

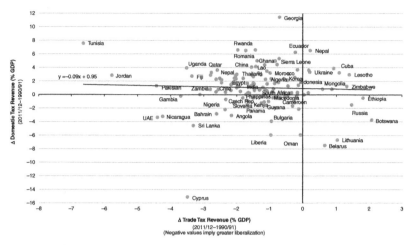

Figure 1.3 Trade Tax and Domestic Tax Revenue (Percent of GDP) in
Developing Countries
Note: Domestic tax revenue is calculated as total tax revenue minus
taxes on international trade.
Data source: OECD 2017; World Bank 2016a

more) of a vast many developing countries' revenue base was lost with
market reforms. If free trade is not itself the answer to the problem it
creates, what is? The obvious answer is domestic tax reform. Yet, many late
liberalizing countries have been facing formidable obstacles substituting
their lost trade tax revenues with domestic taxes. Figure 1.3 looks more
closely at this issue, now substituting changes in overall trade with changes
in trade tax revenues (i.e., shocks), our proxy for trade liberalization, and
domestic tax revenues (total tax revenue minus trade tax revenue) for total
government revenue. Movement left on the x-axis signifies greater declines
in trade tax revenues and movement upward on the y-axis indicates larger
increases in domestic tax revenues between 1990 and 2012. Countries that
are successfully implementing domestic tax reforms upon liberalization –
as anticipated by many international trade economists – are located in the
top-left quadrant (e.g., China, Morocco, Rwanda, Tunisia, Uganda).

Yet, again, as seen in Figure 1.2, it appears a large number of developing
countries are struggling to improve their revenue base alongside trade
liberalization and the concomitant losses in trade tax revenue (lower-left
quadrant – e.g., Nicaragua, Panama, Philippines). On average, low- and
lower- middle-income countries lost 2.83 percent of GDP in trade tax
revenue over time and gained only 2.4 percent of GDP in revenues from
other domestic taxes. Nearly 50 percent of the full sample experienced

a decrease or at most 1 percent improvement in domestic tax revenues over the last two decades.

Considering the last two figures together, the slight positive (and sometimes negative) changes in domestic revenues in Figure 1.3 suggest that the marginal increases in domestic taxes in many developing economies have been unable to offset the loss of trade taxes over time, resulting in disappointing total revenue growth overall (Figure 1.2).

IFIs are on full alert, and, as a result, much of their operational lending and research is currently focused on this issue.[13] They fully anticipated revenue loss with the implementation of trade liberalization programs, and packages include recommendations for domestic tax reform. As summarized by the IMF deputy managing director (2003–6), Agustín Carstens: "Given heavy dependence on trade taxes in many developing countries, tariff reductions are likely to lead to significant revenue losses ... Early measures to offset potential revenue losses are needed, such as strengthening tax administration, or reinforcing the consumption and income tax systems."[14] Standard policy advice from IFIs holds that the revenue loss from trade tax reductions must be offset with taxes such as the value-added tax (VAT), and a broader income tax base that includes more businesses and a larger public.[15] However, unforeseen difficulties involved with implementing new taxes, and the "superficial" nature of the tax policy recommendations in the early 1990s, all too often resulted in delays or indefinite postponement.[16] In response, tax reform has become an integral aspect of current "second generation reforms."[17]

At the onset, such reforms are technically challenging. Untrained and uneducated staff, insufficient data and technology, and poorly designed operational systems commonly plague developing country tax efforts.[18] Added to this, a large percentage of citizens in poor economies are either

---

[13] Carstens 2005; Cottarelli 2011; World Bank 2015a.
[14] Carstens 2005.
[15] Bastiaens and Rudra 2016; World Bank 2007. Other forms of advice and assistance from IFIs include technical support (i.e., computerization or information technology resources), staff training platforms, organizational and personnel infrastructure reform services, taxpayer education programs, operational trainings (for auditing, collection operations), and the development of codes to harmonize filing and payment procedures (Barbone et al. 1999; Cottarelli 2011; IMF 2011b).
[16] Rajaram 1992.
[17] Naim 1994; Navia and Velasco 2003. First generation IFI programs included macroeconomic reforms such as privatization, liberalization, and deregulation (see IMF 1989). The second stage involves more complex state reforms linked to improving political and institutional development (see Naim 1994 and Navia and Velasco 2003). Examples are reforms related to civil service, labor market, delivery of public services, and tax collection.
[18] IMF 2011a; Tanzi and Zee 2001.

not formally employed and/or geographically dispersed, and are therefore logistically difficult to tax. As a result, the middle and upper quintiles that participate in the formal sector have been bearing the overwhelming burden of income taxes.[19] Goods taxes, such as the VAT, are also complex and costly to administer and monitor relative to other types of taxes.[20] They involve both taxes and deductions (on taxed inputs) at multiple stages of production, leading to high administrative and compliance costs. Even developed economies have been struggling to raise government revenue via the VAT.[21] According to a recent United Nations Report: "Significant additional public resources will be necessary to realize sustainable development and achieve the sustainable development goals (SDGs). Towards that end we are committed to bolstering government revenues as needed while improving the efficiency of our expenditures ... Our efforts will include broadening the tax base."[22] Increasing revenue through higher domestic taxes requires more developed administrative structures and strong political incentives to implement *and* collect taxes.[23]

The developing world has historically had difficulties building bureaucratic capacity (and, correspondingly, the ability to successfully implement tax reforms). Developing countries continue to rank far below their developed counterparts on this measure.[24] Perhaps more surprising, existing data suggests minimal improvements in bureaucratic quality over the last two decades of trade liberalization.[25] Policymakers must thus make a concerted *political* effort to prioritize tax reform both *de jure* and *de facto*. By successful "tax reform," in this analysis, we refer to the adoption of, and compliance with, new tax policies, ultimately resulting in higher revenue mobilization.

Herein lies the challenge for governments of developing nations: faced with the more competitive pressures of globalization, can they possibly convince the populace to comply with higher domestic taxes? Figures 1.1 through 1.3 suggest that a subset of nations have been successfully

---

[19] Auriol and Warlters 2005.
[20] Bird and Gendron 2007; Keen 2013; Le 2003.
[21] Keen 2013.
[22] United Nations 2015a.
[23] Aizenman and Jinjarak 2009.
[24] Data from the International Country Risk Guide defines bureaucratic quality as "the institutional strength and quality of the bureaucracy ... high points are given to countries where the bureaucracy has the strength and expertise to govern without drastic changes in policy or interruptions in government services ... and day-to-day administrative functions." It is coded 1 (low quality) through 4 (high quality). A t-test indicates a statistically significant difference in average bureaucratic quality scores across developed and developing countries throughout the 1980s, 1990s, and today.
[25] Since 1990, the average annual change in bureaucratic quality has been 0.008 for the sample of 115 developing countries.

meeting this challenge while a comparably large group of late liberalizing developing nations have not. We turn to existing research to find an answer to this puzzle.

Existing Research and Unanswered Questions

Scholars in international political economy (IPE) have looked closely at the globalization–tax relationship, but their research provides limited clues to explain the pattern in Figures 1.1–1.3. Much of IPE research focuses on the impacts of *financial* liberalization on taxes, and analyzes only a small sample of advanced industrialized democracies.[26] Throughout the 1980s and 1990s, scholars made dire predictions about the decreasing ability of policymakers in rich economies to tax mobile asset holders and increase revenues in a global economy.[27] However, following Quinn (1997), multiple studies have produced evidence that governments retain significant ability to tax, despite increasing globalization.[28] In a nutshell, the impact of financial liberalization on changes in the tax rate are revenue neutral, due to one or more of the following reasons: (1) increasing taxes on capital; (2) governments raising alternative revenue from capital; (3) increasing labor taxes; and/or (4) type of domestic institutions. Overall, differences in revenue outcomes now boil down to which *domestic* factors drive this outcome, but these disagreements are relatively minor given the emerging consensus that globalization – and financial liberalization in particular – has limited revenue impacts.[29]

Wibbels and Arce (2003) is an important exception that explores this question in Latin America and finds that capital flows do exert a downward pressure on capital taxation. Hallerberg and Scartascini (2017), in contrast, recently demonstrated that Latin American countries can improve their revenue base by implementing tax reform during a banking crisis, although these reforms are contingent on the availability of non-tax revenue and electoral cycles. During election years, Latin American countries fail to increase taxes, even when facing revenue shortfalls.

Scholars are now turning to analyzing the impacts of transfer pricing and/or tax havens on revenues in developed countries; the results

---

[26] The analytic focus of most IPE scholarship in this vein is on capital mobility, though some do include trade openness in their tax models (Plumper, Troeger, and Winner 2009; Swank and Steinmo 2002).

[27] Gill and Law 1989; Lee and McKenzie 1989; Razin 1990; Wilson 1985.

[28] Garrett and Mitchell 2001; Neumann, Holman, and Alm 2009; Swank and Steinmo 2002.

[29] Basinger and Hallerberg 2004; Hays 2003; Plumper, Troeger and Winner 2009; Quinn 1997; Slemrod 2004; Swank and Steinmo 2002.

are mixed thus far.[30] A few scholars have begun to question – but not yet test – if or how transfer pricing might impact revenue in developing countries.[31] The bottom line is that low revenues are a critical concern for developing economies, particularly as multinational corporations face greater options for tax avoidance, such as transfer pricing.

Research on *trade liberalization* and taxes in developing economies has been limited and far more optimistic. Trade economists generally agree that trade liberalization will bring in much-needed government revenue.[32] Their forecasts are based on international economic theories that predict that trade increases growth and income which, in turn, increase revenue. For example, Bhagwati and Panagariya (2013: 95) discuss how trade "facilitates additional poverty reduction by generating revenues that enable the financing of redistributive programs." The basic contention in this literature is that government coffers will automatically increase alongside trade-induced economic growth. This has yet to be tested. This literature predicts a positive trend between trade liberalization and revenue growth.

Yet Figures 1.1 through 1.3 suggest the assumption of the positive revenue impacts of trade liberalization requires more careful scrutiny. Recall that a small number of studies reveal a negative correlation between trade liberalization and the tax base in developing countries. This is precisely why domestic tax reforms, such as the VAT and more broad-based income taxes, have become urgent upon liberalization, despite being on the agenda for a quite a while. The puzzle of why only some countries have been successful at making this revenue transition has yet to be solved.

To summarize, previous scholarship on globalization and taxation has failed to provide an adequate explanation for why only some developing country governments have increased domestic taxes in the liberalizing environment and replaced the lost trade tax revenue. Moving forward, we take our cue from IPE research on the globalization–tax debate and question whether and to what extent *political* factors can mitigate the relatively sudden loss of the tax base upon liberalization. What enables some governments to manage the effects of the trade liberalization shock by raising and collecting taxes on individuals and capital? And what, in particular, is holding others back, giving rise to long-lasting damage?

By exploring the impacts of major revenue shocks in developing countries through disentangling the links between trade liberalization, tax revenue mobilization, and politics, this book contributes to several

---

[30] Bartelsman and Beetsma 2003; Hines 2004; Zucman 2014.
[31] Keen and Mansour 2010; Malesky 2015
[32] See, for examples, Bhagwati and Panagariya 2013; Krueger 1998; Reimer 2002; Viet 2015; Winters and Martuscelli 2014; Winters, McCulloch, and McKay 2004.

pivotal debates in political science. First, it adds to research on the fiscal implications of international market expansion by being among the first to examine the redistributive consequences of declining international trade tax revenue.[33] Although we consider the impacts of financial liberalization in succeeding chapters, our focus is on the revenue impacts of trade liberalization. Second, many studies analyzing the impacts of openness on welfare spending ignore supply-side dynamics, i.e., revenue mobilization.[34] Third, scholars have deliberated if and how politics affects revenue generation, but little research addresses how this dynamic may be affected by conditions of economic globalization, particularly in countries with weak tax administration systems.[35] We predict that regime type in particular matters for revenue mobilization in developing countries *after* the liberalization process has begun. Finally, as more and more scholars question the conventional wisdom that democracy helps the poor, this analysis offers new insights on this debate by taking into account developing democracies' political challenges of revenue expansion in an era of global markets.[36]

Why Developing Economies Are in a Unique Situation

Our findings that a group of "late liberalizing" countries are facing lower revenue growth upon liberalizing are unexpected, given current scholarship, and disquieting. But these developing countries are facing an entirely different set of circumstances than their predecessors. Today's advanced industrialized democracies confronted a vastly different state of affairs when they abandoned heavy trade taxes in the nineteenth century. These "early liberalizers" had greater latitude to embrace tax reforms – both domestically and internationally oriented – and could do so when politically expedient. In other words, they liberalized and adopted tax reforms primarily in response to domestic calculations, rather than external pressures from other nations. Also of great import, early liberalizers already had strong state capacity, both a more developed tax bureaucracy and a decent supply of public goods preceded liberalization.[37]

---

[33] Wibbels and Arce 2003.
[34] Nooruddin and Simmons 2009; Rickard 2012; Rudra 2008.
[35] See, for examples, Bates and Lien 1985; Boix 2001; Cheibub 1998; Fairfield 2015; Levi 1988; Meltzer and Richard 1981.
[36] Keefer and Khemani 2005; Ross 2006.
[37] Aidt and Jensen 2009. Barnes (2010) finds that trade is associated with greater direct taxation in Western Europe in late 1800s–early 1900s. See Cardoso and Lains (2013) on public goods.

Another distinction is that today's industrialized nations also had strong state capacity to tax *before* democratizing. This empirical observation calls into caution the generalization that high taxation necessarily follows more representative governments – one that influenced a generation of scholars such as Robert Bates, Douglass North, Mancur Olson, and Charles Tilly. Rather, in pre-modern Europe, it is often overlooked that the means to impose *and* enforce tax compliance from powerful resource holders emerged *before* the consolidation of representative institutions.[38] In a sense, then, state capacity to tax the powerful existed prior to effective bargaining over democratic representation in advanced economies. This is a quite different scenario from developing democracies (and nondemocracies) that are liberalizing while ramping up efforts to mobilize domestic taxes, all in the face of low state capacity. In this scenario, our analysis suggests taxpayers forced to pay more before democratizing may pay less afterwards.

The problem of revenue shocks in developing countries goes beyond the crisis of the trade liberalization-induced one we focus upon in this book. As markets continue to expand, and developing countries become more integrated with the global economy, external forces, such as the global financial crisis in 2008, the Eurozone crisis in 2009, and the East Asian financial crisis in 1997, cause immediate decreases in government receipts. Our book analyzes and follows in detail the impacts of one of the biggest revenue shocks developing countries have faced in recent history. We contend that these other revenue shocks are likely to have similarly contrasting effects in developing country democracies and nondemocracies. In the next chapter, we turn to discussion of domestic tax reforms, the different types, and why they are so necessary and so challenging to implement, particularly for democracies in a globalizing economy.

---

[38] Boucoyannis 2015.

If there is a loophole, we will always take it. Traditionally, going back to the British Raj and the rulers before that, tax has been used to punish people. There's still no faith in government or banks among normal people here, so there is no desire to pay income tax.[1]

Undeclared income, or "black money," is costing India billions of dollars. The informal economy, which is paid all or mostly in cash, is extensive and hard to tax. In 2016, in an attempt to recover lost revenue from unpaid taxes, the government launched not one, but two tax amnesty schemes, in addition to a widely criticized "demonitization," in which 500 and 1,000 rupee notes were removed from circulation with little to no warning, all in an effort to uncover this untaxed income.

In the first amnesty, according to the government, nearly 700,000 people suspected of tax evasion were contacted and offered immunity if they came forward and paid their taxes and a penalty. India's finance minister, Arun Jaitley, said that 64,275 declarations were made in the four months of that amnesty. A group of street food vendors in Mumbai alone, for example, declared nearly $7.5 million in untaxed assets. All told, the first amnesty unearthed $9.5 billion in undeclared income and assets. A second was promptly announced the next month.[2] Given the size of India's black economy, however, this is a drop in the bucket.[3]

Weak and inefficient tax administration systems plague all of the late liberalizing countries. India's issues are just one illustration of a fundamental problem confronting many developing countries. Monitoring and enforcing goods, services, and income tax policies are a colossal

---

[1] "Rahul," an aviation industry employee, quoted in "The Drive to Rid India of Black Money" (2017).

[2] "India Tax Evasion Amnesty Uncovers Hidden Billions" 2016; Singh 2016; "The Drive to Rid India of Black Money" 2017.

[3] Estimates on the size of India's black economy vary. One report suggests it is 23 percent of its GDP, totaling over 270 billion dollars ("Can India's Currency Ban Really Curb the Black Economy?" 2016). However, Kumar (2002) estimates it is closer to 40 percent of GDP.

challenge. Informal entrepreneurial activities and agriculture are sectors that loom large in developing economies, and exacerbate their revenue challenges because they are hard to reach.[4]

Trade taxes, long relied on by developing countries for the bulk of their tax revenue, had low administration and capacity demands since they were easy to monitor and collect at cross-border locations. Additionally, these "easy to collect" taxes were (initially) less politically contentious. They are less visible and have a lower perceived impact on citizens than both direct taxes, like an income tax, and indirect taxes, such as the VAT.[5] Dependence on trade taxes thus helped keep tax reform from becoming a central political issue in both democracies and nondemocracies.[6] Even when overall levels of public revenues were wanting, the steady supply of trade tax revenues provided some degree of fiscal stability. But now, after liberalization, increasing domestic revenues is a pressing need. Tax reform involves designing appropriate tax legislation, broadening the base (e.g., reducing rates and exemptions, taxing the self-employed), strengthening tax administrations and enforcement capabilities, and/or simplifying the tax code.[7] We maintain that the ultimate metric for tax reform success in any, or all, of these areas is whether government revenue has concomitantly increased.[8]

Similar to our fictional Subodh's dilemma in AP, developing countries across the world are faced with the dual challenge of recovering their revenue losses and expanding their tax revenue base after losing their ability to impose high tariffs. Advances in administration and bureaucratic capacity have generally been slow. Officials must unduly rely on citizen "willingness" to pay taxes, or voluntary compliance, and they need quality government services to do this. Contrast our initial

---

[4] See for example, Avi-Yonah and Margalioth 2007/8; Fuest and Riedel 2010; IMF 2005; Keen and Simone 2004. Imposing and monitoring taxes in the informal sector is particularly challenging because business operations are unregistered, difficult to detect, and conducted in cash.

[5] See Adam 2009 and Katsimi and Moutos 2010. Consumption taxes on the whole made up a small proportion of the revenue base in LDCs pre-liberalization (see Tanzi and Zee 2000: 304), while agricultural export taxes were "easy to collect" and collected indirectly (offering farmers below world market prices) by state marketing boards (Bates 1981). The lack of transparency in the design and implementation of these price interventions contributed to a lack of public awareness of how they were being taxed (see Valdes 1996: vii).

[6] Cottarelli (2011: 19) notes that it was not until the 1990s – the post-liberalization era – that tax reforms were "more earnestly" pursued in developing countries.

[7] Arnold 2012; Bogetic and Hassan 1993; IMF 2011a; Stotsky 1995.

[8] Bastiaens and Rudra 2016. Bird and Gendron (2007) highlight the importance of assessing revenue as a metric for success – lowering the threshold of the VAT (i.e., one way of broadening the base) can result in administrative efficiency losses and low revenue gains because of the incorporation of many small taxpayers in the tax system.

example of India's rampant tax evasion to the attitudes expressed on a tax hike in Singapore in 2015, the first increase in the highest marginal personal tax rate in 30 years. While some expressed doubts about competitiveness, others were confident that it would not put a damper on willingness to live and work in Singapore – not to mention pay taxes. It appears that Singapore's more advanced tax administration system was not the critical factor driving compliance. According to an expatriate lawyer in the top income bracket, quoted by CNBC, "You get tons of great services from the government – it's safe, clean, good public transport, good public hospitals and schools so at least the money is going somewhere useful."[9]

Under what political-economic contexts will citizens react in one way versus another – resist or comply? What does it take to make tax reform efforts successful? This is a critical question, particularly in the current globalizing environment where taxpayers – both individuals and businesses – have an ever-increasing array of loopholes, tax shelters, and other tricks available to them, along with international economic pressures to keep taxes at a minimum. This chapter takes a closer look at how and why democracies and nondemocracies have different levels of success in raising money in today's global economy. We investigate why the loss of trade taxes has resulted in a low-revenue trap only in the case of democracies, and not in authoritarian regimes.

Why Democracies Face Greater Resistance to Tax Reform Post-Liberalization

We contend that regime type is a critical factor impacting tax revenue mobilization post-shock. A broadly accepted premise in political science is that all political leaders are incentivized to stay in power. What differs across regime types is the groups they depend on to stay in power while pursuing their goals, such as implementing unpopular tax reforms in the globalizing environment. Executives in democratic countries rely on voters and special interest groups, who are frequently vociferous opponents of tax reform.[10] Nondemocratic leaders need primarily to satisfy a small group of loyalists, which they can do with tax breaks and exemptions.[11] At the same time, authoritarian regimes must prevent the

---

[9] Harjani 2015.
[10] Grossman and Helpman 1994.
[11] Bueno de Mesquita et al. 2005; Magaloni 2008. Autocrats must provide select benefits to individuals in their small ruling coalition to ensure their loyalty and prevent defection (Bueno de Mesquita et al. 2005).

larger population who resist these reforms from rebelling, and they do so using various strategies depending on the *type* of dictatorship.[12]

Building on Levi (1988) and a wealth of supporting theoretical and empirical evidence, we determine that leaders have two main strategies (S) in which they can overcome resistance to taxes from those they depend on for power: (S1) quasi-voluntary compliance; and/or (S2) coercion.[13] Levi (1988: 52–53) establishes that rulers best mobilize revenues through quasi-voluntary compliance, wherein taxpayers "choose to pay" based on perceptions that "the tax system is fair." Their confidence is derived from the ruler's delivery of promised benefits, such as – but not limited to – competent infrastructure and public goods provision, in exchange for taxes (i.e., the fiscal bargain).[14] Put simply, citizens support higher taxes when they receive commensurate government services, irrespective of regime type. It is *quasi*-voluntary because willingness to comply is backed up by enforcement and/or expectations that others will also comply.[15] Although public goods provision per se may be less of a factor in business tax compliance, confidence that government will use existing tax policies to benefit them still plays a role in their decision matrix. S2 refers to the fear of serious sanctions that evaders face, if caught.[16]

In the liberalizing environment, democratic policymakers fall short on both counts, while nondemocracies concentrate their efforts on the latter or rely on a mix of the two to enact tax reforms. We divide authoritarian regimes into two broad categories following Gandhi (2008): institutionalized authoritarian regimes and underinstitutionalized authoritarian regimes, which we re-label as "liberal" and "conservative," respectively. The primary distinction is that, contrary to conservative authoritarian regimes (ConservAuth), dictators in more liberal authoritarian regimes (LibAuth) allow *some* power-sharing with opposition groups and thereby provide some social benefits in exchange for tax

---

[12] Gandhi 2008; Gandhi and Przeworski 2006; Svolik 2012.

[13] Alm, Jackson, and McKee 1993; Bodea and LeBas 2016; Cheibub 1998; Dell'Anno 2009; Fjeldstad 2001; Glaser and Hildreth 1999; Ross 2004. Barone and Mocetti (2011), Levi, Sacks, and Tyler (2009), and Glaser and Hildreth (1999) provide empirical support for link between tax compliance and public good satisfaction.

[14] Material incentives of quasi-voluntary compliance "include but are wider than financial rewards, standard of living and working conditions ... they include sanctions, incentives, and reciprocity practices that produce social order and conditional cooperation" (Levi 1988: 68).

[15] Levi 1988: 52.

[16] Note that Levi (1988) includes technologies for monitoring and enforcement as tools of compulsory compliance, in addition to fear of sanctions. We emphasize the latter since we focus on countries with weak tax monitoring systems; whereas Levi (1988) is based on developed economies.

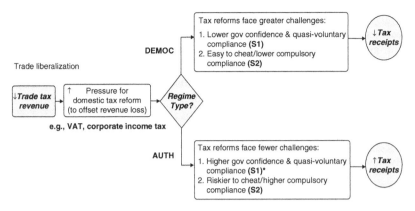

Figure 2.1 Argument
* Liberal Authoritarian (LibAuth) regimes only

reform support to mobilize revenues post-shock. Dictators in liberal regimes hereby favor the strategy of coopting opposition groups with the provision of social benefits in exchange for higher taxes post-liberalization. This institutional arrangement, somewhat paradoxically, results in higher citizen confidence that LibAuth rulers will keep their fiscal bargains (quasi-voluntary compliance). Leaders of conservative regimes, however, cooperate less with the opposition and rely disproportionately on coercion to prevent rebellion and solicit (compulsory) compliance.

Based on these regime dynamics, we predict that the revenue-raising capacity of policymakers in democracies is significantly encumbered in the aftermath of the liberalization-induced revenue shock, while nondemocratic leaders proceed unhindered. Figure 2.1 outlines our argument; we present this in more detail in the next section.

Liberalizing Democracies and Tax Revenue Challenges: S1 and S2

Interest groups that represent the priorities of business elites wield considerable influence over tax policies and even voter preferences in developing world democracies. According to Grossman and Helpman (1994), democracies often face a trade-off between maximizing public welfare and appeasing special interest groups. Indeed, business interests maintain disproportionate political power in developing country democracies marked by capital scarcity *and* high-income inequality.[17] Elected

---

[17] Acemoglu et al. 2014; Fairfield 2015; World Bank 2006.

officials rely on them for campaign financing, government revenues, investment, information, and, often, personal enrichment. Grossman and Helpman (1994) further argue that vested interests win (usually uninformed) voter sympathy by collecting and publicizing information that supports their argument. This is why industry groups can wield considerable influence over tax policies and voter preferences in democracies.

Accordingly, if businesses feel confident that the fiscal contract is fair, and it is reasonable to support the fiscal contract, both firms and voters may be convinced to follow. This quasi-voluntary compliance is more likely to have occurred in developing countries *prior* to liberalization. Governments provided large firms with a host of subsidies in exchange for taxation: protectionism, cash grants, loans, and selective exchange rates. And, as predicted by Grossman and Helpman (1994), these elite economic groups helped convince voters that this exchange was good for public welfare, despite the fact that public goods suffered as a consequence in many democracies.[18] Incumbents exacerbated the latter trend. Motivated by electoral competition and short time horizons, they invest in highly visible, "pork barrel" projects that are quick and cheap, especially pre-election.[19] Robinson and Torvik (2005) maintain that incumbents in developing countries are incentivized to build inefficient social projects that only they can control – and not the opposing politician – so they can win voter support. We are thus not surprised that an increasing number of empirical studies have rejected the popular notion that democracies supply more public goods.[20] In effect, citizens uphold a pre-liberalization fiscal contract associated with protectionist benefits (for business) and the lure of higher – and more secure – job and wage provision (for voters), despite substandard infrastructure and services.

---

[18] Protectionism was pitched as offering low prices ("Brazilians See Austerity Breaking Development" 1982) and jobs ("Thousands Protest Trade Pact in India" 1994). Yet, prior to liberalization, export subsidies directly competed with anti-poverty programs in democracies, such as India and pre-Chavez Venezuela (Buxton 2014; Kohli 2012), leading to "truncated welfare states" (Diaz-Cayeros, Estevez, and Magaloni 2016) and a neglect of human development (Nazmi 1995).

[19] Drazen and Eslava 2010; Vergne 2009: 66.

[20] Acemoglu et al. 2014; De La O 2014; Keefer 2007; Keefer and Khemani 2005; McGuire 2010; Mohtadi and Roe 2003; Robinson and Torvik 2005. See Keefer (2007) and Weingast's (2009: 286) discussion on how politicians in developing country democracies often confront political credibility problems and have incentive to engage in clientelistic, myopic policies with immediate payoffs. Acemoglu et al. (2016) is a recent exception, but they do not account for the tendency of elite capture in democracies – which they discuss in their earlier work (Robinson and Acemoglu 2008, see also Acemoglu et al. 2014; Albertus and Menaldo 2014) – and whether the public goods outcomes disproportionately serve more privileged groups (Nelson 2007; Ross 2006). As they themselves contend, democracy may not be "pro-citizen"; elites have incentives to limit redistribution by increasing their *de facto* political power in democracy (Robinson and Acemoglu 2008: 269).

Quasi-voluntary compliance unravels when (actual and potential) taxpayers feel the new tax bargain is no longer in their favor.[21] In the late 1980s and early 1990s, the fiscal contract was radically altered; governments simultaneously withdrew protections for domestic firms and attempted to levy new taxes and tax practices on businesses. But now, with greater exposure to global competition and international tax havens, businesses are well positioned to demand that the government *cut* taxes.[22] Less productive firms have particularly strong incentives to do so. Resistance from various business groups holds powerful political persuasion where elected officials depend heavily on elite loyalties for reelection.[23]

Voters are also less willing to pay taxes in this new economic environment. First, it is not hard for businesses to convince voters of the perils associated with imposition of the VAT and corporate income taxes in a global economy, and they do; local businesses spread information that such reforms will reduce overall investment, drive small firms to close and large ones to relocate, lower wages, and slow growth.[24] Even technical reforms (e.g., computerization) can be politically contentious in democracies.[25] Second, the pattern of poor public goods provision is apt to become a touchstone issue for ordinary voters in light of the new fiscal contract. Although there is variation across democracies, recall studies show that, on average, they are not delivering quality public goods. Quasi-voluntary compliance of ordinary citizens is more critical post-liberalization because the new taxes are more visible (e.g., income taxes, VAT) and a good portion is levied on the broader public.

As anticipated, the new tax reforms aimed at broadening the income tax base and implementing the VAT have met with protest across the

---

[21] Levi and Sacks 2009; Ross 2004.
[22] "Bandh Against VAT Planned" 2005; "Guatemalans Join Forces to Fight Tax Rises" 2001; "Thousands Protest in Ukraine over Tax Reform" 2010.
[23] Empirical research suggests that low-income groups have even less influence on policies in countries with high levels of poverty and inequality, which are salient characteristics of developing world democracies. See Acemoglu et al. 2014; Bartels 2008; World Bank 2006. Bartels (2008) finds that policymakers in the USA, a country with high inequality, are virtually unresponsive to low-income groups. Both the gini (income inequality) index (World Bank 2016a) and post-transfer gini index (Solt 2016) in late liberalizing democracies are *higher* on average than nondemocracies **and** advanced industrialized democracies between 1990 and 2013, and they continue to confront significant poverty challenges (Mkandawire 2006; Varshney 2000).
[24] See Mateo 2014; Moseti 2015; "Valley Traders Demand Rollback of Taxes" 2016.
[25] "KTF Revolts Against New VAT Form" 2011; " 'Total Solution Project' Will Affect Small Businesses, Say Traders" 2016. Technical reform to improve administrative infrastructures includes computerization and information technology resources, training platforms for staff, and getting expert advice to increase efficiency, automation, and information management systems (Barbone et al. 1999; Cottarelli 2011; IMF 2011a).

developing world, often calling for tax increases on the rich instead.[26] For example, in a recent nationwide protest against the rising tax burden in Brazil, one protestor summarized it best: "We pay too much in taxes and we get bad services in exchange, bad hospitals, bad public education, public transportation is terrible."[27] Low business and voter confidence in government is raising the challenges of mobilizing domestic tax revenue post-shock (i.e., strategy 1 in Figure 2.1).

State coercion, which includes extrajudicial force, is an alternative means by which developing country governments could implement domestic tax reforms and force recovery from the revenue shock (see strategy 2 in Figure 2.1).[28] In nations with weak tax monitoring and enforcement systems, coercion can take the specific forms of passing tax laws by executive decree, the use of arbitrary and extreme punishments to increase tax compliance, and/or the presence of exceptionally harsh penalties for tax evaders and collectors (if detected).[29] But democracies have limits in the use of these institutional tools (especially compared to authoritarian countries), creating greater opportunities for evasion.[30] Previously protected business sectors struggling to compete internationally can then more easily engage in tax evasion, while rewarding politicians who avoid cracking down on it.[31]

Authoritarian Regimes: Successful Tax Revenue Mobilization

In the absence of electoral accountability, autocratic leaders have great flexibility in selecting tax rates and ignoring demands from interest groups outside their small winning coalition.[32] However, the *loss* of government revenue from initial trade liberalization threatens to disrupt the status quo, regardless of whether resources are being allocated for self-enrichment purposes, buying off a smallish group of loyalists, or securing social stability and preventing revolution. Policymakers in authoritarian regimes thus face comparable pressures to implement domestic tax reform post-shock.

In contrast to democracies, autocrats need only the support of their small ruling coalition for the new tax proposals, but they must

[26] See "A Rum Do" 2012; Rippee 2013; "Thousands at May Day Rally against GST" 2014.
[27] "Brazil: Protesters Angry with Poor Services and High Taxes Keep Up Pressure at Sao Paulo March" 2013.
[28] Levi 1988.
[29] For example, tax collectors have been executed for taking bribes for tax evasion in in China. See Jingqiong 2011.
[30] Kenny and Winer 2006; Levitsky and Way 2002.
[31] Goerke and Runkel 2011.
[32] See Meltzer and Richard 1981. Haggard and Kaufman (1995) and Przeworski (1991) discuss how authoritarian countries can more easily implement economic reforms.

avoid rebellion while imposing them on the opposition. Ruling coalition members may be easily appeased with select privileges such as tax concessions, loopholes, and exemptions. However, it is *politically* too costly for autocrats to provide these same exceptions to those who are not allied with the ruling clique, including rich members of the business community.[33] Industry groups do not sway the masses (for or against fiscal contracts) and influence policy outcomes in the same way that they do in democracies. Many economic elites lie outside the autocrat's loyalist coalition and, as members of the opposition, risk severe punishment for tax evasion.[34] Famous examples are the serious punitive measures for corporate tax evasion levied on elite members of the opposition in Russia and China.[35] Media and academic reports also highlight the use of heavy force in tax collection in other liberal and conservative authoritarian regimes such as Vietnam, Belarus, Uzbekistan, Tanzania, and Ethiopia.[36] Since the loyalist coaltion is small and a subset of economic elites is always part of the opposition, autocrats have access to a larger base of potential taxpayers.

But how do autocrats increase taxes on members outside ruling coalition post-shock without risking revolt? Tactics for preventing revolution in this scenario varies among different regime types, especially since history has shown that taxation without representation can cause violent upheaval. Recall that previous empirical studies demonstrate that citizens can be willing to tolerate higher taxes as long as commensurate services are provided in exchange, regardless of regime type. Gandhi (2008) presents the most systematic discussion of how different regime types use different strategies to placate the opposition.

Conservative Post-Shock Tax Revenue Strategy: S2

Conservative regimes (ConservAuth) rely primarily on coercion to thwart potential revolution while mobilizing revenues from tax reforms

---

[33] Bueno de Mesquita et al. 2005.
[34] Easter (2002), Lim (1998), and Satpaev (2007) present examples of economic elites outside the autocrats' winning circle. Quinn (2003) discusses stronger capital controls in autocracies. Saudi Arabia, for example, recently arrested eleven princes, including a billionaire (Kirkpatrick 2017).
[35] See "Chinese Dissident's Firm Challenges Tax Evasion Allegations" (2011) and Weir (2003).
[36] For example, in Vietnam: "The ministry called on the heads of provincial and city tax departments to use coercive measures to reclaim the unpaid taxes in accordance with the Law on Tax Management" ("Tax Evaders Pay Up to $32 Million to Vietnam Gov't." 2015). In Uzbekistan, forced or compulsory labor is a legal punishment for tax evasion (US Department of State n.d.). See also "Heavy Riot Policy Presence in Minsk Following Crackdown" 2017. Liberal authoritarian regimes such as Tanzania and Ethiopia are also notorious for excessive punishments for tax evasion (Fjeldstad 2001; Prichard 2015).

(i.e., strategy 2 in authoritarian branch – Figure 2.1).[37] Common coercive tax-collection efforts include excessive fines, physical coercion and punishment, and sometimes even death. While noncompliance inevitably occurs, in the instance that both democracies and nondemocracies have equally inefficient tax administration systems, the severe penalties for evasion in the latter – even if the risk of detection is slight – make it *relatively* more likely citizens will comply.

ConservAuth regimes tend to be overly optimistic or stubborn in deeming that the opposition can be managed through force.[38] ConservAuth regimes can include personalist dictators and kleptocrats known to be more risk accepting as well as one-party states. They rely on coercion more so than quasi-voluntary compliance, imposing punitive rates of taxation on any citizen who wants to depose the existing regime.[39] The trade-off for this chosen tactic is lower legitimacy, shorter regime durability, and economic volatility.[40]

China, for example, a conservative regime, has enjoyed increased revenues and effective tax reform alongside its liberalization policies directed at increasing trade and reducing the role of state-owned enterprises. China relies primarily on an iron fist to impose and collect taxes with a "strong-armed police force" that enforces tax collection.[41] After China gained entry to the WTO and reduced tariffs, concerns of foregone revenue have led Chinese officials to target high-income earners for "special scrutiny."[42] Individuals – including government legal and tax officials – have been executed for tax fraud in China.[43]

Liberal Post-Shock Tax Revenue Strategy: S1 and S2

Although all authoritarian leaders have the power to use coercion to implement post-shock tax reforms, first by fiat, followed by fear, some authoritarian regimes simultaneously pursue softer measures to solicit cooperation from the opposition. According to Gandhi (2008), liberal

---

[37] Gandhi 2008: 76.
[38] Gandhi and Przeworski 2007: 1289.
[39] Acemoglu, Robinson, and Verdier 2004; Levi and Sacks 2009; Wintrobe 1998. ConservAuth examples are Belarus' Alexander Lukashenko and Libya's Muammar Gaddafi. In China, officials under former President Jiang Zemin beat peasants to death in response to tax evasion (Bernstein and Lu 2000: 746).
[40] Chandra and Rudra 2015; Levi 1988. Gandhi and Przeworski (2007) find that regimes that rule mostly by brute repression survive on average five years fewer than power-sharing authoritarian regimes.
[41] O'Neill 2000.
[42] Goodman 2002.
[43] Donohoe 2001.

authoritarian regimes (LibAuth) tend to mollify opposition groups with specific concessions, some of which can successfully support greater quasi-voluntary compliance with post-shock tax reforms (i.e., S1 and S2 in the authoritarian branch, Figure 2.1). LibAuths' general cooptation tactics include granting select civil liberties to the opposition, and supplying some public goods.[44] The last concession is critical to our analysis since it boosts the opposition's confidence that governments will use (and have used) tax revenues effectively. Indeed, IFIs have identified many LibAuths as exemplar countries for investing in public goods during the era of protectionism.[45] Urban industrialists in the opposition who lament the higher taxes and loss of protectionism can still justify the new fiscal contract based on better infrastructure and faster services.[46] The longer time horizon for liberal leaders increases their incentives to coopt the opposition with public goods.[47]

This tactic of providing select benefits alongside repression leads to quasi-voluntary compliance with tax reforms. Tax reforms such as the VAT, for instance, have been implemented without much fanfare in liberal regimes such as Singapore, Tunisia, and Jordan, countries also known for providing public goods.[48] Regardless of the different strategies employed, both authoritarian regimes are more successful than democracies at implementing tax reforms and mobilizing revenues after trade-related revenue shock.

Hypothesis

We anticipate that democracies will struggle to mobilize government tax revenues post-shock, far more than their authoritarian counterparts. In democracies, economic elites can further pressure governments for *lower*

---

[44] In authoritarian countries, for the role of political institutions see Conrad 2011; Gandhi and Przeworski 2006; Geddes 2003; Wright 2008; for civil liberties see Acemoglu and Robinson 2006; Gandhi 2008; Linz 2000; and for income redistribution see Bueno de Mesquita and Smith 2010; Miller 2015; Wintrobe 1998.

[45] The World Bank has called LibAuth countries such as Tunisia, Jordan, Singapore, and Malaysia "success stories" in regards to their inclusive growth and social safety nets prior to and at the start of liberalization (World Bank 1980; World Bank 2016c).

[46] See, for example, Harjani (2015).

[47] Leaders with longer time horizons avoid myopic efforts to control the opposition (e.g., private payoffs), and invest in public goods instead (see Wright 2008).

[48] Well-functioning public goods can also offset the adverse impact higher taxes can have on labor productivity and total tax receipts by encouraging better growth performance, and increasing the total body of taxable goods and services (see Angelopoulos, Economides, and Kammas 2007).

taxes in the competitive globalizing environment. We thus propose the following hypothesis:

H1: *Lost trade tax revenue will be accompanied by lower domestic tax revenues in democracies (a positive relationship); in authoritarian regimes, trade tax revenue losses will be followed by higher domestic tax revenue generation (a negative relationship) since tax reforms are likely to be successful.*

Liberal authoritarian regimes succeed through two distinct strategies: (S1) quasi-voluntary compliance and (S2) the use of fear and coercive tools. Conservatives prioritize S2, while developing country democracies can take advantage of neither. The observable implications of S1 and S2 are:

S1: *Citizens in liberal authoritarian regimes have more confidence in government relative to other regime types – i.e., democracies and ConservAuth regimes.*

S2: *Citizens in developing country democracies are more likely to evade taxes than their counterparts in authoritarian regimes – i.e., LibAuth and ConservAuth regimes.*

Summary

Democratic governments are, by definition, supposed to represent the will and thereby the best interests of their people. But they are, we contend, constrained by reality, both in the form of budgets and the influence of special interests (among other issues). The prosperity of their country and citizens cannot improve without sufficient money to do so, and globalization and free trade *coupled with democracies' own institutional and political constraints* are cutting into the budget. Put simply, we argue both citizen and interest-group resistance to taxation in much of the developing world is creating serious problems in democracies starved for revenues after liberalization.

It is remarkable that, under conditions of openness, authoritarian leaders may be finding it easier to fulfill their ruling mandates and implement domestic tax reform. We argue that liberal autocrats do so through a balance of compulsory and quasi-voluntary compliance, while more conservative authoritarian regimes lean more heavily on coercion. Regardless of the tactic employed, authoritarian leaders are expected to successfully increase taxes alongside trade liberalization. Our prediction challenges current one-size-fits-all prescriptions for tax reform post-liberalization. Fiscal policy reforms that involve local government efforts – particularly elected ones – need to be considered very carefully. Revenue generation upon liberalization is not as simple as many scholars and pundits have assumed, and failure to consider this reality may have implications for the very governments in need.

3   Empirical Assessment: Democracies in Peril

The tax collection department in Andhra Pradesh sent notices to Ayurvedic pharmaceutical companies demanding that they pay a value-added tax of 5 percent for the cow urine – or *Gomutra* – they use as a component of some of their products. *Gomutra* has a long history in India, particularly in Ayurvedic medicine, an ancient healthcare tradition that has been practiced in India for at least 5,000 years.

Is taxing *Gomutra* a solution? Will it work? Time will tell, but as with all AP's previous efforts to increase revenue, once-protected Indian industries protest, saying that higher taxes put them at a disadvantage with imports and multinational companies (MNCs).[1] In an interview, the president of Telangana Guashala Federation Mahesh Agarwal says: "If the government imposes a tax on cow urine, there can be nothing worse than this. I am not happy at all. We are going to agitate against this. There are several other ways to collect tax … If the government wants to generate revenue, they can impose higher taxes on milk and milk products manufactured by multinational companies."[2]

This is the heart of the issue. Interest groups representing less productive industries, such as the Ayurvedic firms that use *Gomutra* in herbal medicines, are resisting any new taxes. The AP government has little political or institutional leverage over such groups, and neither does the broader population want to step in to fill in the revenue gap created by the revenue shock. Both business elites and citizens throughout India lack confidence that the government can or will ensure that they benefit from paying higher taxes. This is a hard sell in the globalizing

---

[1] Prior to liberalization and India's acceptance into the World Trade Organization, the government heavily protected Ayurvedic and other traditional medicines with flexible patents, price controls, and tariffs (Perlitz 2008; Shaikh 2015). In India, firms that develop products using *Gomutra* (e.g., facial cleansers, soaps, disinfectants, and traditional medicines) are facing increased competition from foreign producers of herbal medicines and cleaning products (Author Interview with general manager of Gomutra Organics, "Himalaya, India's Booming Herbal Healthcare Company" 2013).
[2] "Cows Have Come to the Rescue of Cash-Strapped Indian States" 2016.

environment where exporters demand sustained liberalization (and thereby low tariffs), less productive local businesses face rising competition, and wealthier individuals and businesses can move their money or relocate to low-tax countries.[3] Neither does the central Indian or AP government have the institutional means to use fear as a tool to force them to pay taxes.

This chapter looks at the data to assess whether our primary contention that late liberalizing democracies – such as India – have greater difficulty recovering from revenue shocks than nondemocracies in an expanding global economy is true. If our predictions hold, we will observe that democracies exhibit a revenue pattern distinct from authoritarian regimes *after* advancing towards free trade. We also compare and contrast our findings with alternative hypotheses.

A Closer Look at the Raw Data on Regime Type

A prima facie look at the data suggests that regime type may indeed be a critical answer to the puzzle of which countries are effectively mobilizing revenue post-liberalization. We examine changes in domestic tax and trade tax revenues between 1990 and 2012 for 133 developing countries.[4] Figures 3.1a and 3.1b illustrate the contrast in domestic tax revenue collection between liberalizing democracies and authoritarian regimes. In the former (Figure 3.1a), the change in domestic tax revenues appears to stagnate and even slightly decline as democratic countries lose trade tax revenue (i.e., move left on the x-axis), while in nondemocracies (Figure 3.1b), domestic tax revenues are clearly increasing with liberalization.[5] But what explains this difference? Perhaps it is because authoritarian regimes are less open, and the loss in trade tax revenues is not as large overall? Figures 3.2 and 3.3 suggest that this is not at all the case.

Democracies and nondemocracies both suffered similar losses of trade tax revenue. The binding overhang (i.e., the difference between the bound and applied tariff rates), on average, appears to be similar for both regime types. Revenues from tariffs have been steadily declining in both regime types, although interestingly, the overall level of trade taxes has

---

[3] Kaul 2016.

[4] As in previous chapters, we use Amelia II (Honaker et al. 2015) to impute tax revenue data in the graphs in this chapter. Regime type is determined by Marshall and Gurr (2016).

[5] Note that these trends hold even when we drop possible outliers (nondemocratic Jordan, Tunisia, and Georgia, and democratic Nicaragua, Pakistan, Lithuania, Botswana, and Cyprus).

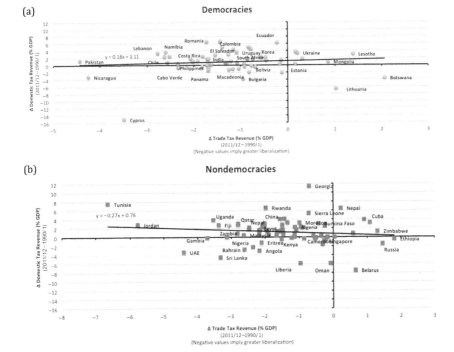

Figure 3.1a and 3.1b Liberalization-Revenue Shock by Regime Type
Data source: World Bank 2016a

been slightly lower (by 0.9 percent) in democracies. We would expect, then, that it would be democracies that find it easier to replace their lost trade tax revenues with domestic taxes, leaving *total* government revenues either unaffected or increasing overall, if the trade enthusiasts are in fact correct.

But Figure 3.4 shows us just the opposite; total government revenues have been decreasing or remaining relatively constant in late liberalizing democracies since the late 1990s, but steadily increasing in nondemocracies overall. Democracies have higher revenue levels initially (they are generally wealthier countries); however, by the end of the time period, their levels appear be converging with nondemocracies. Figure 3.5 further confirms that the five-year change in revenue in nondemocracies between 1990 and 2009 is positive and increasing, while this change is negative or close to zero in democracies. Since domestic taxes have minimally changed in democracies, and overall government revenues appear to be declining, these figures suggest two

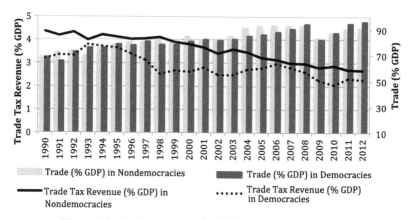

Figure 3.2 Trade (Percent of GDP) and Trade Tax Revenue (Percent of GDP) by Regime Type
Data source: World Bank 2016a

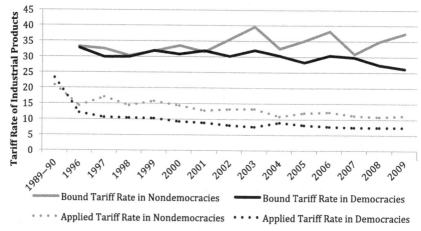

Figure 3.3 Tariff Rates by Regime Type
Data source: World Integrated Trade Solution (WITS) 2016

things: (1) the losses from trade tax reductions are outpacing domestic tax mobilization; and (2) governments are not using other means – fines, fees, or income from property sales – to make up for the revenue gap. In contrast, both figures suggest that authoritarian regimes are far outpacing poor democracies in revenue generation and will soon surpass them.

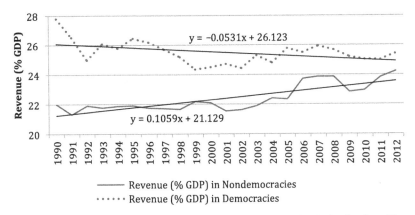

Figure 3.4 Government Revenue (Percent of GDP) by Regime Type
Data source: World Bank 2016a

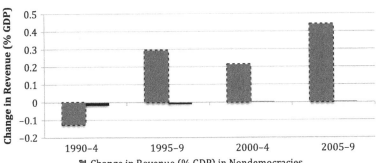

Figure 3.5 Five-Year Average Changes in Revenue (Percent of GDP) by Regime Type
Data source: World Bank 2016a

Alternative Explanations

Research by a small but influential group of scholars studying fiscal capacity – that is, the ability of governments to generate tax revenues – in developing countries generates possible alternative explanations for why tax revenues have not been increasing alongside trade liberalization in a large subset of countries. The most common explanation for weak fiscal performance is poor administrative quality.[6] Both

---

[6] Besley and Persson 2011; Brautigam, Fjeldstad, and Moore 2008; Tanzi and Zee 2000; Von Soest 2009.

Baunsgaard and Keen (2010) and Khattry and Rao (2002) predict that low-income countries will be least able to replace lost trade tax revenues, using low gross domestic product (GDP) per capita as a proxy for state capacity. Observing more recent time-series data, however, we see no systematic difference between richer and poorer developing nations' pattern of tax revenue mobilization. Government tax revenues in low-income countries have actually been *increasing* alongside liberalization, contrary to their predictions.[7] Figures 3.6 and 3.7 show larger reductions in trade taxes are associated with *higher* domestic tax revenues in poor countries, as well as low bureaucratic quality countries.[8] In other words, neither income levels (Figure 3.6) nor bureaucratic capacity (Figure 3.7) seem to explain why a sizeable group of countries have been experiencing lower revenues alongside liberalization, as seen in the puzzling pattern in Chapter 1. When countries are grouped according to their income levels (Figure 3.6) and bureaucratic capacity (Figure 3.7), trade is positively associated with tax revenue collection (i.e., lower values on the x-axis represent liberalization). This does not surprise us since, as noted earlier, we do not see much variation in their bureaucratic quality over time and not surprisingly, it pales in comparison to rich countries. It certainly appears that regime type might help explain the "puzzle" of this book, and signals that tax revenue generation continues unabated primarily in nondemocracies.

As another check, we assess the data to be sure that bureaucratic quality, economic growth, or state-owned enterprises (SOEs) are not driving the differences *between* regime types. In other words, is it the case that nondemocracies are better at overcoming revenue shocks because they have higher bureaucratic quality, higher economic growth, or SOEs? Table 3.1a indicates that, prior to liberalization in the 1980s and early 1990s, democracies and nondemocracies had comparable institutional capabilities. Post-liberalization democracies have a marginally better bureaucratic quality score, which only further contributes to the puzzle of why they are failing to generate necessary domestic tax revenues upon liberalizing. Economic growth is also not the cause of the inability of democracies to raise domestic revenues post-liberalization.

---

[7] A t-test reveals no statistically significant difference in domestic tax revenue of lower- and higher-income countries at the start of liberalization. Yet, the average annual change in domestic tax revenue between 1990 and 2009 of low- and low-middle-income countries was 0.2 in comparison to the average of −0.02 in upper-middle and high-income countries (p-value of 0.06).

[8] Income classification is determined by the World Bank Lending Groups.

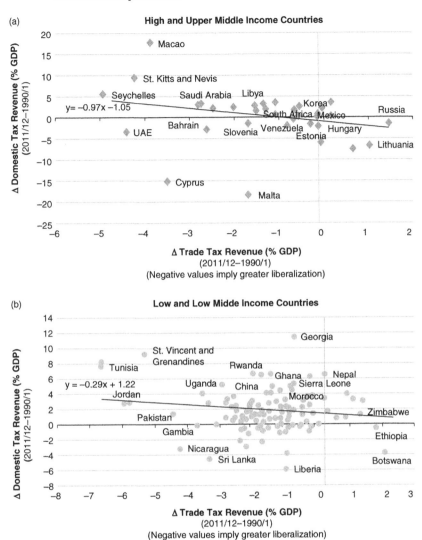

Figures 3.6a and 3.6b Liberalization-Revenue Shock by Income Classification
Data source: World Bank 2016a

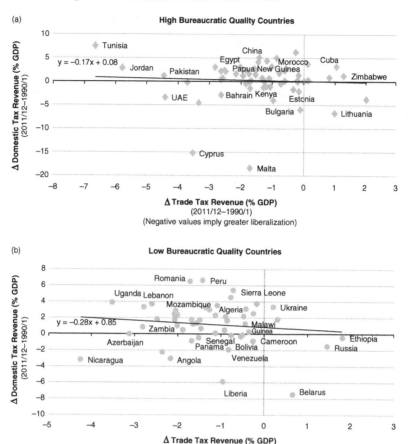

Figures 3.7a and 3.7b Liberalization-Revenue Shock by Bureaucratic Quality

Data source: International Country Risk Guide 2012; World Bank 2016a

Table 3.1b indicates that, overall, no systematic difference in growth rates by regimes exists over time.

Authoritarian regimes also do not disproportionately rely on revenues from SOEs, particularly in comparison to their democratic counterparts. SOE privatization and liberalization have gone hand-in-hand for most countries, including authoritarian ones.[9] Accession to the WTO includes

[9] Campos and Esfahani 1996; Van de Walle 1989.

Table 3.1a *Bureaucratic Quality (Scale 0–4)*
Pre- and Post-Liberalization by Regime Type

	Democracies	Nondemocracies	P-value of t-test by Regime
1985	1.9	1.5	0.116
1990	1.7	1.6	0.507
1995	2.0	1.8	0.199
2000	2.2	1.4	0.000
2005	2.1	1.4	0.000
2010	2.1	1.5	0.000

Data source: International Country Risk Guide 2012

Table 3.1b *GDP Growth Pre- and Post-Liberalization by Regime Type*

	Democracies	Nondemocracies	P-value of t-test by Regime
1985	1.2	3.5	0.088
1990	2.9	3.2	0.878
1995	4.4	3.5	0.380
2000	4.0	4.2	0.830
2005	5.1	6.7	0.018
2010	4.7	5.5	0.197

Data source: World Bank 2016a

reducing subsidies to state enterprises.[10] Further, pre-liberalization, most SOEs paid little in direct taxes.[11] And, post-liberalization, studies find the impact of their privatization on government revenue is ambiguous.[12] Data from World Bank's (1996) "Bureaucrats in Business" indicates that investment in SOEs (as a percent of GDP) – i.e., fixed capital formation in SOEs – was similar across democracies and nondemocracies pre-liberalization (and at the start of liberalization) (see Figure 3.8).

Finally, it is worth considering whether the Eastern European countries or oil-rich countries may be skewing the trends. The former are recently democratized countries with complex tax systems pre-liberalization, while the latter tend to be authoritarian nations that rely far less on tax revenues. Eastern European nations represent a unique set

[10] Bajona and Chu 2010.
[11] See Gray, Short, and Floyd (1984).
[12] McKinnon 1991; Van de Walle 1989.

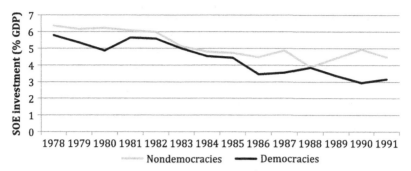

Figure 3.8 SOE Investment (Percent of GDP) by Regime Type
Data source: World Bank 1996

of countries that simultaneously embarked on extensive fiscal, market, and political reforms mandated by the IMF or European Union.[13] In effect, they differ from the larger developing country sample because their "big bang" transition included tax reform. As Appel (2006: 43, 56–57) contends, these reforms reflected "much less traditional domestic variables – like the strength of particular interest groups"; instead, "the East European cases ... ceded enormous control over indirect and most of the direct tax policymaking" to Brussels and central government policymakers.[14] Throughout this manuscript, we consider data trends and regression models both with and without the Eastern European and oil-rich nations. Our previous Figures 3.1a and 3.1b, for example, show trends in support of our argument upon excluding either set of countries. We note in the manuscript if and when our results are differentially impacted by the inclusion or exclusion of these countries.

Testing the Hypotheses

We now focus on rigorously evaluating our primary hypothesis (H1) by estimating statistical regressions on two revenue datasets. Our primary dataset is from the World Bank's World Development Indicators (World Bank 2016a). Our alternative dataset is the recently established International Centre for Tax and Development's (ICTD) Government Revenue Dataset (2017).[15] While the latter has the advantage of covering a longer time-series (1980–2013), our caution is that it combines data (and sometimes variable definitions) from different country sources,

[13] Appel 2006; Bruno 1992; Rodlauer 1995. Sachs and Woo (1994) provide evidence that the reform experience of the Eastern European countries is distinct from other formally communist states, such as China.
[14] Appel 2006: 43, 56–57.
[15] Prichard, Cobham, and Goodall 2014.

international organizations, and regional datasets, which in some cases lead to "imperfections owing to differences in methods and the occasionally subjective nature of data choices."[16] We also cannot be sure how to interpret declines in trade taxes in the early 1980s, since the great majority of developing countries did not start reducing trade taxes as part of their liberalization effort until the mid-to-late 1980s. As a compromise, we ran our models on both datasets, while placing greater emphasis on the WDI. The ICTD models and data descriptions are in Appendix B. Although the raw ICTD data suggests that domestic revenues in democracies appear to be increasing slightly more than they are in the WDI dataset, the statistical results are similar across the two datasets.[17]

Existing scholarship empirically confirms that the rather dramatic decline in trade taxes in the late 1980s and early 1990s is a direct consequence of trade liberalization,[18] and indeed, international development organizations such as the World Bank, United Nations, International Monetary Fund, and World Trade Organization are treating them as equivalent.[19] Using declines in trade tax revenue as proxy for trade liberalization is critical for our analysis, because we want to know precisely how much revenue loss was tied directly to liberalization.

Our revenue models cover 105 non-Organisation for Economic Co-operation and Development (OECD) countries, from 1990 to 2012. The panel data is unbalanced due to some missing observations. Our analysis begins in 1990, since this is the first year that the most reliable time-series data on government revenues is available.[20] This time frame is suitable to test our hypothesis, since trade liberalization did not begin until after the wave of economic crises in the late 1980s and early 1990s, with the resulting decline in trade tax revenue beginning mostly in the mid-1990s.[21]

We apply a fixed effects statistical regression. The general model specification is as follows:

$$Y_{i,t} = X_{i,t-1} {}^* \beta_0 + Z_i {}^* \beta_1 + D\partial + T\lambda + e_{i,t}$$

---

[16] Prichard et al. 2014.
[17] We checked if the revenue trends in the ICTD dataset are similar to the World Bank's revenue data. Some differences exist, but the puzzle in Figures 1.2 and 1.3 (Chapter 1) still holds among the sample of longstanding democratic and nondemocratic nations that depend on taxable income (rather than oil rents). As in the World Bank revenue data, for democracies, positive improvements in domestic revenues get smaller as countries lose trade tax revenue, while in the nondemocracies domestic revenues are increasing with liberalization.
[18] Aizenman and Jinjarak 2009; Khattry and Rao 2002.
[19] See, for examples, the World Trade Organization's Negotiating Group on Market Access (WTO 2003), the United Nation's African Trade Policy Centre (2004), and IMF Research by Abed et al. (1998).
[20] IMF 2011a.
[21] Aizenman and Jinjarak 2009.

In this equation, Y measures government revenues in country i at time t, and X and Z are vectors of the independent variables. We run models with and without country fixed-effects (D vector), but prefer the latter to address omitted variable bias.[22] All models include panel-corrected standard errors to address heteroskedasticity and serial correlation. We also control for time effects (T vector).

Our dependent variables proxy successful domestic tax reform in three ways: *domestic tax revenue, goods and service tax revenue,* and *income tax revenue*. Domestic revenue is defined as total tax revenue minus taxes on international trade. Taxes on goods and services refer to taxes on products and services, like the VAT. Income taxes include taxes on income, profits, and capital gains, and thereby include taxes on both individuals and corporations; however, in developing countries, *the bulk of the income tax revenue is from corporate taxes.*[23] Domestic tax revenue is thus our most critical dependent variable; if one type of reform (e.g., VAT) succeeds relative to another (e.g., income tax), net domestic revenues reveal whether tax revenues in the aggregate have compensated for the lost trade tax revenues. Goods and income tax revenue may *decline* alongside liberalization if businesses successfully pin blame on excessive tax burdens for their poor international performance. All revenue variables in our main models are measured as a percent of GDP, but we apply other measures – growth in tax revenue and revenue per capita – below and in the robustness checks. We focus on tax revenue collected by the central government, as subnational taxation is rare and often ineffective in the developing world.[24] Subnational tax revenue data is also of limited availability. Appendices C.1 and C.2 contain detailed variable descriptions and summary statistics. Appendices C.3 and C.4 list the countries in our sample.

Our model builds on Bueno de Mesquita et al.'s (2005) model of tax revenue, which includes population (logged) and GDP per capita (logged). Based on broader tax revenue literature, we add GDP growth, central government debt (percent of GDP), IMF credits (percent of GDP), aid (percent of GDP), fuel exports (as a percent of merchandise exports), and the degree of capital account openness. GDP per capita (logged) and growth capture the level and pace of economic development, which is positively associated with government revenue.[25] Government

---

[22] According to taxation literature in developing countries, time-insensitive country effects, such as the organizational cultures of the administration, cultural acceptance of corruption, and local work ethics, are critical to our models (Job, Stout, and Smith 2007; Richardson 2008).

[23] Cottarelli 2011.

[24] Bird 2010; DeMello 2000; Purfield 2004.

[25] Gupta 2007.

debt, aid flows, and IMF credits represent upward pressure on government tax revenues, while capital account openness may dampen it.[26] We originally included government expenditures but drop it because of endogeneity concerns; our results were unaffected regardless. Finally, developing nations that get their primary export revenues from fuels can rely on nontax revenues, and are thus far less dependent on domestic tax reforms. We lag all independent variables, as we do not expect a simultaneous impact of political or economic conditions on revenues.

The inclusion of government debt and capital account openness as controls are of particular importance. Since previous research suggests that some countries – democracies in particular – have easier access to debt markets, they may recover from revenue shocks more rapidly.[27] Existing international political economy (IPE) research has also focused on the impacts of financial liberalization on revenues because it becomes more difficult to tax mobile asset holders. We thus expect a positive coefficient for central government debt and a negative one for capital account openness.

The principal causal variable of interest in H1 is the interaction between trade tax revenues and regime type (***trade tax rev*polity***). We treat trade taxes as exogenous in these models since developing countries have had limited leverage negotiating tariffs under the World Bank and IMF agreements, but relax this assumption in selection models.[28] We expect a positive and statistically significant coefficient of the interaction terms (H1). This means, in democracies, declines in trade tax revenue upon liberalizing are associated with lower (or no change in) domestic tax revenue, a positive (or statistically insignificant) conditional coefficient. Conversely, in nondemocracies, liberalization and the simultaneous decline in trade tax revenue are associated with increases in domestic tax revenue (a negative conditional coefficient).

We use the continuous variable for polity in our main model, since our general expectation is that, the higher the polity score, the more voters and interest groups play a role in influencing incumbents to forgo tax reforms. In these models, post-shock revenue mobilization will *not* differ across authoritarian subtypes. Nonetheless, we reestimate our models using a

---

[26] Cheibub 1998, Schultz and Weingast 2003; Tanzi 1989.
[27] Schultz and Weingast 2003. As additional checks, we limit the sample to democracies only as well as control for several alternative measures of debt (total debt service and total external debt stocks to gross national income).
[28] We estimate a Heckman selection model, whereby we check if IFI pressures are driving both trade tax revenue declines and domestic tax revenue changes. We rely on WTO membership to predict a nation's commitment to drastic trade tax reductions. The model then estimates the impact of trade tax revenue*polity on domestic tax revenue. Our primary findings hold in the selection model.

Table 3.2 *Predicted Marginal Effects of* Declining *Trade Tax Revenue on* Domestic Tax Revenues

	Marginal Effect of a Decline in Trade Taxes (Conditional on Polity)*	Description	Interpretation
Dependent Variables: Domestic Tax Revenue (DR), Goods Tax Revenue (GR), Income Tax Revenue (IR)			
Democracies	+	A one-unit decrease in trade tax revenue leads to a one-unit decrease in DR/GR/IR.	Domestic tax reform has been unsuccessful in response to drops in trade taxes (i.e., liberalization and need for domestic taxes to replace lost trade tax revenues). Citizens resist higher (new) taxes, while elites demand *lower* taxes in the liberalizing environment, resulting in lower revenues.
Nondemocracies	–	A one-unit decrease in trade tax revenue leads to a one-unit increase in DR/GR/IR.	Domestic tax reform has been successful in generating higher revenues post-trade reforms. In response to drops in trade taxes, nondemocracies' domestic tax revenues are increasing.

* The trade tax revenue-polity interaction term itself is predicted to be positive and statistically significant.

democracy dummy variable, which are countries that score 6 or higher on the polity scale.[29] See Table 3.2 for a summary of the predicted effects.

We also employ a "trade tax revenue shock" variable as an independent variable of interest. This "trade tax shock" variable is calculated as the change in trade tax revenue (percent of GDP) between 1990–91 and 1996. This measure thus captures the total decline in trade tax revenue at the start of liberalization and the WTO. We also assess the impact of a six-year change in trade tax revenue (percent of GDP), since it takes an average of three to four years for domestic tax reforms to be enacted.[30]

[29] See Marshall and Gurr (2016). Note that results are robust to different cut-off points for democracy (polity≥ 4, 5, 6).
[30] See Michielse and Thuronyi (2010).

This variable thus corresponds to two cycles of domestic tax reform. Finally, we assess a model using the percent change of tax revenue.

We estimate both baseline and full models.[31] For ease of presentation, Table 3.3 presents the findings for our most critical dependent variable, net domestic taxes. Our primary independent variable – the interaction between trade tax revenue and polity – is positive and statistically significant. This suggests support for H1, which predicts that declines in trade tax revenues will be associated with declines in government revenue (and primary domestic taxes) in democracies. Appendices A.1–A.5 present the estimation results for our other dependent variables: income tax and goods tax revenue. Interestingly, capital account openness also appears to have a negative impact on tax revenues, although this finding does not hold across different models.

To provide some insight into the magnitude of these effects, Figure 3.9 evaluates the interaction across the full range of possible values for the conditioning variable polity, and uses the appropriate corrected standard errors to assess the significance of the conditional effects.[32] The histograms show the representation of countries at different values of polity in our dataset, underscoring that our sample of democracies tends to score below Polity = 10 (highest level of democracy). Figure 3.9 indicates that a 10 percent decrease in trade tax revenue in a democracy is associated with a 0.06 reduction in domestic tax revenue. This is not a small amount; within our full sample of countries, the average yearly change in domestic tax revenue is 0.096 points. In direct contrast, the same decrease in trade tax revenue in an authoritarian regime corresponds to an increase in domestic tax revenue by 0.07 points.[33]

This pattern is consistent with H1; in more authoritarian regimes, declines in trade tax revenue are associated with increases in government revenue (a negative relationship). We are less concerned about the predicted effects of *increasing trade tax* revenues since the select few countries that have been experiencing a steady increase in trade tax revenues post–1990s are mostly poor, resource-dependent, authoritarian, or small island regimes. In our sample, less than 5 percent of countries have more than a 1 percent increase in trade taxes between 1990 and 2000.

Calculating the marginal effects of trade tax revenue declines on the two domestic tax subcategories reveals an interesting pattern. Income tax

---

[31] Our second base model includes the most important foundations of revenue generation in developing economies: level of development; fuel exports (proxying for reliance on nontax revenue); and capital account openness.

[32] Brambor, Clark, and Golder 2006.

[33] Trade tax revenues decreased by 52 percent in our sample from 1990 to 2012.

Table 3.3 *Determinants of Domestic Tax Revenue (Percent of GDP)*

DV:	(1)	(2)	(3)	(4)	(5)	(6)
	Domestic Tax Revenue (% GDP)					% Δ Domestic Tax Revenue
Trade Tax Revenue (%GDP) $_{t-1}$	-0.184**	-0.189**	-0.0291			
	(0.0804)	(0.0751)	(0.112)			
Democracy Dummy $_{t-1}$ (1 = Dem; 0 = LibAuth or ConservAuth)	-0.371					
	(0.343)					
Trade Tax Revenue (% GDP)*Democracy Dummy $_{t-1}$ (1 = Dem; 0 = LibAuth or ConservAuth)	0.322***					
	(0.118)					
Polity $_{t-1}$		-0.0887**	-0.113***			0.275*
		(0.0412)	(0.0433)			(0.166)
Trade Tax Revenue (% GDP)*Polity $_{t-1}$		0.0561***	0.0643***			
		(0.0168)	(0.0196)			
Trade Tax Shock				1.338***		
				(0.492)		
Polity				0.0403	0.0777	
				(0.0450)	(0.0531)	
Trade Tax Shock*Polity				0.110**		
				(0.0490)		
ΔTrade Tax Revenue (% GDP)					-0.0146	
					(0.0110)	
ΔTrade Tax Revenue (% GDP)*Polity					0.00387**	
					(0.00178)	

50

%ΔTrade Tax Revenue (% GDP) $_{t-1}$						−0.0241
						(0.0164)
%ΔTrade Tax Revenue (% GDP)*Polity $_{t-1}$						0.00454**
						(0.00213)
GDP Per Capita (Logged) $_{t-1}$	0.962***	1.064***	1.197**	−0.536	−0.0497	−8.808***
	(0.316)	(0.319)	(0.601)	(0.514)	(0.905)	(2.927)
Fuel Exports $_{t-1}$	0.0431***	0.0456***	0.0617***	0.0569***	0.0595***	0.0856
	(0.0125)	(0.0127)	(0.0180)	(0.0139)	(0.0221)	(0.166)
Capital Account Openness $_{t-1}$	−0.175	−0.203	−0.0553	−0.0102	−0.648*	−1.647
	(0.144)	(0.144)	(0.156)	(0.120)	(0.342)	(1.099)
Debt (% GDP) $_{t-1}$			−0.0227***	−0.0190***	−0.0271***	−0.0579
			(0.00696)	(0.00544)	(0.0102)	(0.0555)
Population (Logged) $_{t-1}$			3.893	7.968***	−2.238	11.77
			(2.367)	(2.113)	(3.700)	(12.58)
GDP Growth $_{t-1}$			−0.00343	0.0407*	0.00477	0.371**
			(0.0258)	(0.0217)	(0.0353)	(0.179)
Aid (% GDP) $_{t-1}$			−0.0590	−0.000515	−0.00722	0.634***
			(0.0372)	(0.0196)	(0.0343)	(0.228)
IMF Credits (% GDP) $_{t-1}$			−0.0140	0.120	−0.228**	−0.304
			(0.0618)	(0.0732)	(0.0957)	(0.353)
Observations	1,057	1,057	338	204	203	310
R-squared	0.952	0.951	0.956	0.984	0.973	0.431
Number of Countries	105	105	45	21	33	43

Standard errors in parentheses

*** p<0.01, ** p<0.05, * p<0.1

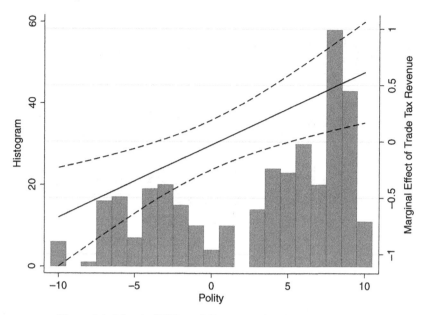

Figure 3.9 Marginal Effect of (Declining) Trade Tax Revenue (Percent of
GDP) on Domestic Tax Revenue (Percent of GDP) Conditional on Polity

revenues appear to suffer in democracies, but are generally unaffected by
declines in trade tax revenue in authoritarian regimes.[34] This suggests that
firms and elites in democratic regimes are more successful in lobbying
for lower income taxes. Authoritarian regimes also show consistent
improvement in goods and service tax revenues, compared to democracies. Altogether, authoritarian regimes seem to be doing far better than
democracies in replacing revenue losses from trade liberalization with
their total domestic tax revenues. Marginal effect graphs for income tax
and goods tax models are in Appendices A.3 and A.4.

These findings provide critical information for pundits and IFIs that
have been encouraging developing countries to implement the VAT and
other domestic taxes concomitant with trade liberalization; it appears
that, for the most part, authoritarian governments are heeding their
advice. In democracies, our results suggest that adoption and/or compliance with these reforms have been weak; revenue collection from taxes
on income has been sluggish after the adoption of trade liberalization

[34] While the conditional coefficient was often positive in democracies, in a few alternative
model specifications, income tax revenues were unresponsive (i.e., statistically insignificant) to liberalization.

policies. Tax reforms appear to confront serious resistance in the liber-alizing environment and, as our case studies will show, sometimes even technical improvements (such as computerization) can be politically contentious in democracies.

Sensitivity Analysis, Alternate Hypotheses, and Selection Models

We subjected these results to a wide battery of robustness checks (see Appendices A.6–A.14). First, we estimate models using a different measure of tax revenue (per capita), in case changes in GDP are affecting our revenue estimations. Second, we use a sampling strategy to minimize the effect of countries that switch regime types. In other words, we limit the sample to cases that are governed continuously by either authori-tarian or democratic leaders. Appendix C.4 lists the countries that do not change regime type in our sample. Third, we check to see if governments are using nontax means (income from fines, fees, licenses, rent, etc.) to compensate for the loss of trade taxes (and they are not) in Appendix A.8. Nontax revenue is calculated as total government revenue minus tax revenue. We also omit oil-rich countries and transitional states from our sample.

We employ an error-correction (EC) model to estimate both permanent and transitory relationships between tax reductions and total govern-ment revenue. The EC model includes both lagged levels and changes of all the independent variables. The parameters for the lagged variables are of key interest to our analysis, since we want to know whether trade tax reductions are related to long-term trends in government revenues. Since tariff rates were high pre-liberalization, reducing restrictions can immediately result in higher trade volumes. However, we expect that, in the long run, after further liberalization, additional reductions in taxes will not result in greater trade volumes to offset the lower tariff rate, and overall trade tax revenues will decrease in democracies.[35]

Next, we evaluate if *bureaucratic quality*[36] is a key explanatory variable that explains tax revenue changes, and renders regime type insignificant. It is telling that democracies, on average, have higher bureaucratic quality than nondemocracies, and yet, are less successful at increasing domestic tax revenues post-liberalization (see Table 3.4). We both include bur-eaucratic quality as a control and as a substitute for regime type (see Appendix A.12). We find support for our hypothesis; bureaucratic

---

[35] Khattry 2003.
[36] Besley and Persson 2011.

Table 3.4 *Bureaucratic Quality (Scale 0–4) across Regime Types*

	Mean	Median	Standard Deviation
Developing Democracies	1.80	2.00	1.11
Nondemocracies	1.47	1.56	0.97
OECD Democracies	3.71	4.00	0.59

Data source: International Country Risk Guide 2012

quality is not an alternative explanation for the puzzle in Chapter 1. It will be interesting to see (in the next section) if, as we expect, citizens are more likely to avoid paying (cheat on) taxes in democracies, despite having higher-quality bureaucracies.

Some critics might still be concerned that states nonrandomly select into trade liberalization and democratization. For instance, IFI pressures may explain government decisions to lower trade tax revenues and implement domestic tax reforms. To check this, we use a two-stage estimation approach. We rely on WTO membership and North–South Preferential Trade Agreement (NSPTA) participation to predict selection into high categories of our key independent variable. These variables have minimal direct effect on our dependent variable. Developing countries that participate in the WTO or NSPTAs may be more likely to implement drastic reductions in their trade taxes.[37] However, there is not a strong theoretical connection between WTO membership or NSPTAs and domestic tax reform. We also employ a two-stage estimation of selection into democracy. We instrument for democracy using lagged GDP per capita and regional diffusion of democracy.[38] See the results in Appendices A.13 and A.14, which are consistent with the pattern in Table 3.3.

To address missing observation concerns, we estimate our models on imputed data. We follow Honaker et al. (2015) and use Amelia II, which uses an "EMis" algorithm to generate datasets to account for missing observations. Table 3.5 details the estimation results. The pattern holds that nondemocracies outperform democracies on revenue generation post-liberalization.[39]

Although not reported here, we also ran the models with several additional changes: alternative regime specifications (i.e., Boix, Freedom

---

[37] Hoda 2001.
[38] See Acemoglu et al. (2016).
[39] One difference in these results is that the marginal effects indicate that democracies do see a small increase in domestic tax revenue (though smaller than nondemocracies); however, they still see lower total government revenues overall upon liberalizing trade.

Table 3.5 *Determinants of Domestic Tax Revenue (Percent of GDP): Multiple Imputation Estimations*

DV:	(1)	(2)	(3)
	Domestic Tax Revenue (% GDP)	Income Tax Revenue (% GDP)	Goods Tax Revenue (% GDP)
Trade Tax Revenue (%GDP) $_{t-1}$	**−0.186*****	**−0.0132**	**−0.189*****
	(0.0498)	**(0.0288)**	**(0.0454)**
Polity $_{t-1}$	**0.00333**	**−0.00391**	**0.00257**
	(0.0354)	**(0.0154)**	**(0.0226)**
Trade Tax Revenue (% GDP)*Polity $_{t-1}$	**0.00582***	**0.00375***	**0.00230**
	(0.00349)	**(0.00203)**	**(0.00277)**
GDP Per Capita (Logged) $_{t-1}$	0.403	0.249	0.181
	(0.305)	(0.204)	(0.149)
Debt (% GDP) $_{t-1}$	0.00742★	−0.00270	0.0110***
	(0.00437)	(0.00404)	(0.00232)
Capital Account Openness $_{t-1}$	−0.0620	−0.0826	0.0741
	(0.153)	(0.0821)	(0.0784)
Population (Logged) $_{t-1}$	−0.813	0.172	−1.376***
	(1.114)	(0.656)	(0.508)
GDP Growth $_{t-1}$	0.00650	−0.00102	0.00756
	(0.0116)	(0.00514)	(0.00675)
Aid (% GDP) $_{t-1}$	−0.000908	−0.00637	0.00414
	(0.0542)	(0.0276)	(0.0238)
Fuel Exports $_{t-1}$	−0.00351	0.0140**	−0.0180***
	(0.0114)	(0.00619)	(0.00696)
IMF Credits (% GDP) $_{t-1}$	0.0679	0.0113	0.0587**
	(0.0687)	(0.0328)	(0.0294)
Observations	4,075	4,075	4,075
Number of Countries	163	163	163

Standard errors in parentheses
*** p<0.01, ** p<0.05, * p<0.1

House, Albertus and Menaldo's gamed democracy); different samples (i.e., omitting failed states); alternative specifications of trade tax revenue (i.e., percent of total revenue); and additional controls (i.e., government expenditure, aid for tax reform).[40] Partisanship is often cited as a

[40] Including the following control variables did not change our main results: corruption, oil rents (percent of government revenue), and agricultural value added or exports (percent of GDP). Controlling for corruption, in particular, addresses Bergman's (2010) hypothesis that voluntary compliance depends on the tradition and culture of the rule of law.

determinant of fiscal policymaking in the OECD nations, but we do not include it as a primary control in our models.[41] Left–right coding is unreliable in developing countries, since parties across the political spectrum endorse both open markets and redistribution.[42]

Taken together, our primary findings hold in response to the changes listed below:

1. Three different measures of regime type
2. Additional controls (bureaucratic quality, government expenditure, aid for tax reform)
3. Sample in which countries maintain the same regime type over time
4. Sample that does *not* include failed, oil-rich, and transitional states
5. Selection into democracy and trade liberalization (driven by IFIs)
6. Different measures of tax revenue (*not* weighted by GDP)
7. Different model specifications.

After evaluating the findings from all the various models, as well as different model specifications, and taking all conditional coefficients of interaction terms into account, definite patterns emerge. In reaction to past revenue shocks, total government revenues in democracies have yet to recover, whereas government revenues in authoritarian regimes are relatively undeterred. Our findings also show that, in an era of declining trade taxes, total domestic taxes (e.g., taxes on goods, services, income added together) are decreasing in democracies, while increasing in nondemocracies. The latter group appears to be particularly successful in recovering from shocks with goods tax revenue. Income tax revenues, however, appear the hardest hit post-liberalization in both regime types; they decline in democracies, and remain relatively unchanged (statistically insignificant) in authoritarian countries. Altogether, our primary finding is that nondemocracies are outperforming democracies on total government revenue and domestic tax revenue mobilization efforts post-trade liberalization.

Conclusion

Globalization and trade liberalization handed developing countries a large problem in gathering sufficient money to keep afloat and make progress. And it turns out that politics, unsurprisingly, play a large role in how they can do this, and how successful they have been. Our findings

---

[41] Note, however, that our results remain the same when we use partisanship as a control (Keefer 2015).
[42] See Rudra and Tobin (2017).

in this chapter suggest that a country's type of government is one of the most significant factors in how trade liberalization will impact revenue. Interestingly, it appears that adopting free trade reforms appears to have a more consistent impact on tax revenues in developing economies than financial liberalization.

Democracies face a particularly uphill climb. Democratic politicians simply have fewer incentives and (extrajudicial) institutional resources to effectively implement tax reforms in the globalizing environment compared to their authoritarian counterparts. The wealthy represent small, but politically powerful, vested interest groups that create strong resistance to higher taxes and command the distribution of government revenues (tilted in their favor).

Conversely, authoritarian leaders appear to be much more effective at raising tax revenue in response to revenue shocks. We anticipated these findings because, unlike in democracies, authoritarian leaders have *relatively* more political autonomy from wealthy elites (as a whole) and can rely on fear and repression to implement and collect taxes on the masses. At the same time, alongside these coercive tactics, liberal authoritarian regimes are careful to "buy" confidence in leaders and ensure stability alongside the tax hikes. Chapter 4 turns to these underlying assumptions and uses survey data to assess their plausibility.

What happens when the government suddenly declares that the money in your pocket is worthless? The people of India found out at midnight on 8 November 2016, when Prime Minister Narendra Modi made a surprise television announcement to the effect that 500 and 1,000 rupee notes (worth about £6 and £12) were now illegal tender. Anyone holding undeclared money would either have to put it in a bank account to make it "legal," or destroy it. Predictably, chaos ensued.[1]

When India's Prime Minister Modi set his demonitization scheme into action, panic was universal, but hit harder for some than others. One businessman, the owner of several garment factories in a suburb outside of New Delhi, initially worried that the action might hurt him, since he held hundreds of thousands of rupees in untaxed cash. But – with the aid of a friend and a couple bottles of whisky – he fairly quickly came up with a strategy. Instead of declaring the cash himself, and thus pay taxes on his hidden gains, he pushed the burden down the line: he made large purchases – in cash consisting of 500 and 1,000 rupee notes – of fabric for his factory. Then he generously decided to give many of his employees, typically paid in cash, large advances on their salaries in the same denomination of currency notes.[2]

This businessman's unwillingness to declare his income or pay taxes on it is standard behavior in India, and, indeed, in many developing world democracies. Particularly, since democracies ended their reliance on trade taxes, they have had a great deal of trouble both in passing tax reform to include different sources of revenue, and in making any new taxes effective. But authoritarian regimes have less of a problem. Our research leads us to believe that there is a relationship between a regime's power structure and its ability to implement tax reform in the

---

[1] "The Drive to Rid India of Black Money" 2017.
[2] Nielsen 2017.

global economy. In the previous chapter, we identified two key strategies to mobilizing revenues: generating confidence in government, and coercion.

Authoritarian regimes have two main advantages in this game. First, they can impose reform on the populace by fiat, and enforce it by the threat of severe punishment upon those who defy the rules. Second, they do not need to generate confidence in the entire population; they must primarily protect and maintain the confidence of their relatively small group of loyalists, e.g., by providing loopholes or strategic exceptions in compliance. Some authoritarian governments, however, also coopt the opposition with targeted subsidies, and thus will buy support from outside groups as well. Regardless of who is coopted, those outside the small circle of power recognize they are at higher risk if they duck the government's mandate.

Democracies in emerging economies lack the means to use fear and intimidation to the same extent as their authoritarian peers and see a great deal of tax evasion and resistance to reform. They struggle to effectively raise revenue, are thus not able to fund public goods, and see confidence in government plummet. This sets up a vicious circle in which faith in government is undermined further, providing additional incentive to cheat and resist, which cuts into the government's ability to raise revenue, and thus to spend money benefitting the public. And so the problem persists.

Democracies in the developing world may ultimately be in a low confidence–low revenue trap if both real and potential taxpayers resist higher taxes because they do not believe governments will use their money in a beneficial way. Authoritarian regimes risk this outcome as well, but unlike democracies, they can compensate by using fear and coercion to intimidate citizens into complying with tax reforms. And, if such regimes deliver quality public goods to subvert rebellions, even the opposition is likely to accede to paying higher taxes. Ultimately, citizens of democracies – especially developing economies with less mature institutions – are expected to have low public confidence in government, and governments of democracies lack the institutional tool of coercion to make up for the public's resulting reluctance to cooperate. Government attempts to appease the population by catering to interest groups can often make this worse. As our factory owner puts it, "[Black money] is gonna return to the same amount. There are loopholes. In India, there is a loophole for everything."[3] Even when the government moves quickly, often the money moves quicker still.

---

[3] Nielsen 2017.

This chapter investigates how confidence in a government as well as coercion impacts the willingness of its citizens to cheat on taxes, and how different types of governments respond to overcome the problem (or fail to do so). To answer this question, we will take a closer look at the data, including survey responses from a broad sample of developing economies. Survey questions include measures of confidence in government and willingness to cheat on taxes. We analyze data using various statistical methods to establish the validity of our intuition, specifically whether democracies tend to have limited confidence in government and a higher propensity (and freedom) to cheat on taxes.

Evaluating Revenue Strategies

Drawing from Levi (1988), we identified two key strategies to mobilizing revenues in Chapter 3: confidence in government and coercion. We argued that democracies face far greater resistance in applying either strategy to mobilize revenues in the globalizing environment. The observable implications of our argument are as follows:

S1: *Confidence in government is low in democracies (and conservative authoritarian regimes), particularly in comparison to liberal authoritarian regimes.*

S2: *The propensity to cheat on taxes will be highest in democracies, relative to both liberal and conservative authoritarian regimes.*

We follow the efforts of Levi and Sacks (2009) to capture these important aspects of successful tax compliance and turn to public opinion data. We use data from an original survey conducted through Amazon's Mechanical Turk (MTurk)[4] and the World Values Survey (WVS) to assess our predicted correlations. Our goal in this chapter is to establish whether the strategies driving revenue mobilization vary between regime types, as well as *within* authoritarian regimes, in the directions we expect. Our intuition is that liberal authoritarian regimes – which tend to have longer time horizons – "buy" stability alongside tax reforms through continued investments in broad-based public goods. Conservative authoritarian regimes are relatively more risk-accepting and rely disproportionately on coercion to achieve their revenue goals. This chapter thus carefully defines the different authoritarian regime types and how they are classified.

---

[4] MTurk is an online survey platform to recruit and compensate individuals for completing tasks (e.g., surveys) available at Amazon.com. Detailed information on MTurk is available on Amazon's webpage (https://www.mturk.com/mturk/welcome) and in Berinsky, Huber, and Lenz (2012).

In order to evaluate our implications, then, we begin by more specifically classifying the three different regime types. Developing countries scoring 6 or higher on the polity scale are classified as democracies.[5] We classify liberal and conservative authoritarian regimes based on Gandhi (2008). We apply Gandhi (2008) rather than other recent classifications of nondemocracies because she presents the most systematic discussion of how and why different regime types use distinct strategies to placate the opposition. The challenge here is that Gandhi's (2008) measure of LibAuth is based on parties and election practices in the legislature.[6] Currently, however, an approximate 90 percent of authoritarian countries have multiple parties in their legislature. Scholars have also critiqued the mere presence of parties and/or legislatures in authoritarian regimes as window dressing and not real power-sharing with opposition groups that solicits actual cooptation.[7]

To address these concerns, we use polity's "political competition" (POLCOMP) to get a better sense of power-sharing and differentiate between LibAuths and ConservAuths. Higher POLCOMP scores, or the rules on political expression, organization, and activity, *within the broader sample of authoritarian regimes* reflect greater power-sharing, and thus cooptation. LibAuths are coded as "1" if the country's score is above the authoritarian mean of "higher institutional of political participation" and "lower government restrictions on political competition."[8] ConservAuths are coded "1" if they score below the authoritarian POLCOMP mean, and are thereby more apt to rely on coercive institutions to silence the opposition. We also logically include personalist dictators (or "vicious psychopaths"), since they rely disproportionately on repression to govern, according to Geddes (2003: 53) and Linz (2000).[9] In sum, this coding of POLCOMP captures variation in power-sharing *within* authoritarian regimes.

While POLCOMP and polity are very closely correlated (r = 0.9), POLCOMP provides a more nuanced and precise classification of the authoritarian subtypes. For example, regimes such as Bangladesh (2007–8), Morocco (1998–2009), and Bhutan (2005–7) are coded as

---

[5] See Marshall and Gurr (2016).
[6] The updated version of Gandhi's (2008) data is Cheibub, Gandhi, and Vreeland (2009).
[7] Chandra and Rudra 2015; Nijzink, Mozaffar, and Azevedo 2006; Pepinsky 2014; Truex 2017.
[8] POLCOMP scale is from 1, unregulated or no political organizations or oppositional activity, to 10, stable and enduring groups regularly competing for political influence (Marshall and Gurr 2016).
[9] Personalists are excessively repressive regimes that tend to "fight tooth and claw to hang on to power" (Geddes 2003: 53–66). See also Linz (2000: 150–153).

extremely authoritarian by polity (polity score less than −5 or "autocracies"), but are LibAuths according to POLCOMP (POLCOMP score greater than 2), and should be so because of their relatively greater – but still restricted – power-sharing.[10] Similarly, some regimes are coded as moderately authoritarian by polity (polity score between −5 and 5 or "anocracies"), but are actually ConservAuths according to POLCOMP (POLCOMP score less than 3), because they do not permit power-sharing.[11] POLCOMP and Cheibub et al.'s (2009) measure of legislature parties is correlated at 0.7.

Preliminary evidence indicates that LibAuth autocrats do indeed provide more broad-based public goods relative to democracies and ConservAuth autocrats.[12] Table 4.1 illustrates the variation in authoritarian regime types, with liberal authoritarian countries more heavily emphasizing the provision of public goods (i.e., primary education, which is so often neglected relative to university education in developing countries), higher POLCOMP, and relatively higher individual freedoms, or empowerment.[13] It is notable that democracies have a lower average level of primary education spending than the majority of liberal authoritarian countries.

Consistent with expectations, liberal authoritarian regimes provide some level of public goods compared to more substandard ones in democracies; and this government action may indeed be correlated with poor government confidence – we assess this question next.

Assessing Strategy 1: The Low Tax Revenue Trap

The next step is to use more rigorous statistical analysis to assess if survey respondents in LibAuths express more government confidence

---

[10] Morocco, Bhutan, and Bangladesh exhibited poverty reduction and strong public good provisions under the specified period (Achy 2010; Maddy-Weitzman and Zisenwine 2013; World Bank 2013) as well as power-sharing developments such as the introduction of political parties or electoral or constitutional reform (European Parliament 2014; Royal Government of Bhutan 2005; Shamrat 2016).

[11] Examples include Uganda under Musheveni (1993–2004), Pakistan under Musharraf (2002–6), and Gambia under Jammeh (1997–2009). Uganda, Pakistan, and Gambia failed to adequately invest in public goods and reduce poverty under the specified period (IMF 2011c; John 2009; World Bank 2012), while limiting political opposition or consolidating power in the executive (Borzello 2000; Rhode 2002; US Department of State 2002).

[12] Note that we code Singapore as LibAuth (though POLCOMP = 2) because of its "exceptionalism" in using good governance as part of its social contract (see Quah 2013; Rodan 2008).

[13] UNESCO Institute for Statistics 2011. The Empowerment Index (0–14 scale) is an additive index of foreign movement, domestic movement, freedom of speech, freedom of assembly and association, workers' rights, electoral self-determination, and freedom of religion (CIRI 2010).

Table 4.1 *Regime Type Comparisons (2000–9)*

	POLCOMP	Empowerment Index	Primary Edu Spending	Country Examples
Democracies	8.7	10.0	36.5	Argentina, Bulgaria, Costa Rica, El Salvador, Estonia, India, Kenya, Philippines, Zambia
LibAuth	5.8	6.0	41.9	Jordan, Malaysia, Morocco, Mozambique, Papua New Guinea, Singapore, Sri Lanka, Tanzania, Tunisia
ConservAuth	3.1	3.7	36.2	Azerbaijan, Belarus, Burkina Faso, China, Libya, Myanmar, Qatar, Syria, Vietnam

Note: POLCOMP ranges from 1 (repressed) to 5 (competitive).
Empowerment index ranges from 0 (no government respect) to 14 (full government respect).
Primary education spending is as a percent of total education spending.
Data source: CIRI 2010; UNESCO Institute for Statistics 2014

(S1) than their counterparts in democracies and ConservAuths. To analyze S1, we conducted an original survey using Amazon's Mechanical Turk (MTurk) platform. We surveyed close to 300 individuals in 50 countries of varying regime types during the winter of 2015–16. MTurk allows us to design a survey to confirm whether respondents' satisfaction with public goods provided by their government impacts their willingness to pay taxes. MTurk has the advantage of more country coverage (and regional diversity), but fewer respondents. For external validity, we gathered data from the World Value Survey (WVS) waves four through six (1999–2004, 2005–9, and 2010–14), which provides time-series data and a more secure survey environment.[14] Waves four–six allow us to assess "confidence" levels at a time when the great majority of developing countries are considerably liberalized. Appendix G.1 contains descriptions and summary statistics of all survey questions and variables in our MTurk analyses. Appendix G.2 lists the countries in the MTurk sample. Appendix G.3 contains the specific WVS survey questions and

---

[14] WVS conducts face-to-face interviews in the interviewee's environment and is supervised by academic researchers.

data descriptions. Appendix G.4 lists the countries in the WVS sample under each regime classification.

Assessing S1 is the extent to which citizens and elites view that governments deserve quasi-voluntary compliance. Applying Levi and Sacks (2009: 314), citizen willingness to support broader income tax and VAT reforms should hinge, first, on whether they perceive government is "engaging in serious efforts to meet its fiscal contract with constituents by delivering infrastructure and services." Hereby, we gauged respondents' level of public goods satisfaction (S1) in MTurk by randomly assigning them a question regarding: (a) quality of public primary schools; (b) quality of government hospitals; (c) supply of clean water; or (d) quality of roads. The scale of response is 1 to 5, from very dissatisfied to very satisfied.

Next, our MTurk survey questioned respondents on their willingness to pay taxes *after* they were primed with S1: "If the government needs more revenue, would you be willing to pay higher taxes?" Answer responses were from 1, definitely no, to 5, definitely yes. Here we are capturing quasi-voluntary compliance more than cheating, since internet surveys cannot protect respondents' privacy from governments. From the WVS, we collected survey data on "confidence in government" to proxy S1.[15]

Across all the models, we control for the respondents' income, age, gender, elite status, and their sense of overall government effectiveness.[16] The elite status variable should be statistically insignificant since we expect that elite compliance is conditional on regime type. At the country level, we control for GDP per capita (logged), unemployment (percent of total labor force), and the size of the illicit economy (percent of GDP). We include regional dummies. Building on Levi (1988), we also control for the average willingness to pay score in each country to account for the general norms on tax compliance in the respondent's home country.

In the estimations, we assess S1 by including both democracy and ConservAuth dummy variables, since we expect confidence and quasi-voluntary compliance in these regimes to be lower, relative to LibAuths (the base category). The democracy and ConservAuth coefficients should be negative, while the LibAuth dummy coefficient should be positive. We

---

[15] The "confidence in government" question asks respondents' confidence in "the government," with responses ranging from 1, "None at all," through 4, "A great deal."

[16] In MTurk, to control for government effectiveness we asked: "How much of this tax money do you think the government would use for improving your city and/or country?" Response options ranged from 1 (none of it) to 4 (all of it). In the WVS models, we include bureaucratic quality to proxy for government effectiveness (International Country Risk Guide 2012). In MTurk, we measure economic elites as full-time, university-educated workers (since large business owners or company controllers are not taking this survey). In the WVS, we code elite professions as business owners and highly skilled workers.

estimate ordered logit regressions (and multilevel models, see Appendix D.10) with robust standard errors clustered at the country level.

The models in Table 4.2 gauge whether regime type and confidence are *correlated*, rather than causally related. One potential drawback of using survey data is that citizens in authoritarian countries may fear reprisals and provide disingenuous responses to politically sensitive questions. If this were indeed the case, then we would expect citizens of conservative authoritarian regimes most fearful in reporting that they have low government confidence. Interestingly, responses in authoritarian regimes show almost as much variation as democracies. It is also noteworthy that the WVS Constitution is officially committed to providing a safe environment for interviewees, following "sound and ethical practice in the conduct of public opinion research". Ultimately, however, a negative coefficient for conservative authoritarian regimes – which rely primarily on repression – would mitigate concerns about reporting bias. Table 4.2 presents the estimation results.

The statistical pattern in Table 4.2 is consistent with our expectation that citizens in LibAuth countries are more satisfied with the government provision of public goods, relative to the other two regime types (S1, Table 4.2, columns 1–2). Respondents in developing country democracies are also less willing to pay higher taxes compared to respondents in LibAuth countries (Table 4.2, column 3 and 4). To elaborate, a respondent in a LibAuth country selected "satisfied" or "very satisfied" with public goods provision with 47 percent predicted probability, in comparison to 22 percent in democracies. The predicted probability of selecting "definitely yes" or "yes" to willingness to pay taxes was lower in democracies (15 percent) than in LibAuth regimes (19 percent). Interestingly, respondents from ConservAuth regimes responded that they were least satisfied with public goods (13 percent) and least willing to pay taxes (12 percent). Appendices D.1–D.6 graph the MTurk predicted probabilities from Table 4.2.

WVS findings in Table 4.2, column 5 and 6 further confirm S1: the democracy dummy coefficient is negative and statistically significant in predicting government confidence (S1). Appendices D.7–D.9 plot the WVS predicted probabilities. We take the negative coefficient on ConservAuths in the government confidence models as suggestive evidence that respondents are expressing their true opinions in authoritarian regimes.

Taken together, these results demonstrate that, in the developing world, more democratic countries are associated with weaker confidence in their governments. The next critical question is whether citizens in

Table 4.2 Ordered Logit Estimations of S1 (MTurk and World Values Survey)

DV	(1)	(2)	(3)	(4)	(5)	(6)
	Satisfaction Public Goods	Satisfaction Public Goods	Willingness Pay Taxes	Willingness Pay Taxes	Confidence in Govt	Confidence in Govt
Survey	MTurk	MTurk	MTurk	MTurk	WVS	WVS
Strategy	S1	S1	S1	S1	S1	S1
LibAuth	*1.193**** *(0.322)*		*0.284** *(0.160)*		*0.405** *(0.245)*	
Democracy		*-1.125**** *(0.318)*		*-0.263** *(0.157)*		*-0.543*** *(0.246)*
ConservAuth		*-1.879**** *(0.507)*		*-0.525*** *(0.221)*		*-0.0845* *(0.380)*
Income	-0.464* (0.263)	-0.383 (0.283)	0.886** (0.363)	0.905** (0.364)	-0.0483** (0.0197)	-0.0495** (0.0199)
Age	-0.0945 (0.186)	-0.116 (0.184)	-0.567*** (0.153)	-0.568*** (0.155)	0.00436*** (0.00157)	0.00461*** (0.00163)
Male	-0.00983 (0.299)	0.0756 (0.318)	0.131 (0.238)	0.161 (0.241)	-0.0550 (0.0406)	-0.0566 (0.0414)
Elite Status	0.324 (0.238)	0.348 (0.240)	0.147 (0.261)	0.156 (0.265)	-0.276*** (0.0628)	-0.264*** (0.0629)
Unemployment	-0.0238 (0.0239)	-0.0371 (0.0268)	-0.00431 (0.00885)	-0.00889 (0.00902)	-0.0161 (0.0149)	-0.0137 (0.0150)
GDP Per Capita (Logged)	0.927*** (0.196)	0.904*** (0.170)	0.102 (0.0987)	0.0926 (0.0921)	-0.259* (0.133)	-0.172 (0.146)

Govt Effectiveness	0.377	0.365	0.645**	0.645**	-0.278**	-0.252**
	(0.235)	(0.234)	(0.264)	(0.265)	(0.129)	(0.127)
Illicit Economy	-0.00342	0.000134	-0.00518	-0.00447	-0.0430***	-0.0394***
	(0.0124)	(0.0125)	(0.00863)	(0.00868)	(0.00943)	(0.0118)
Cheat Norm			2.076***	2.068***		
			(0.185)	(0.189)		
Region Dummies	Yes	Yes	Yes	Yes	Yes	Yes
Pseudo R-squared	0.087	0.090	0.18	0.18	0.047	0.047
Observations	272	272	272	272	58,884	57,403
Number of Countries	50	50	50	50	44	43

Standard errors in parentheses

*** $p<0.01$, ** $p<0.05$, * $p<0.1$

democracies are more likely to cheat on taxes, relative to their authoritarian counterparts, in the post-liberalization era.

Assessing Strategy 2: Regime Type and Coercion

First, we look at the data on cheating pre-liberalization. We argued that it was rational for businesses and the elite to engage in compliance pre-liberalization because they received industrial protections and did not face international market competition pressures. Fortunately, the WVS included the question on whether respondents feel it is justifiable to cheat on taxes in both the 1981–4 and 2010–14 survey waves. We use the WVS question entitled, "Justifiable: Cheating on Taxes," to assess whether citizens of democracies are more likely to cheat on taxes than their counterparts in nondemocracies. The dependent variable is a dummy equal to 1 if respondents indicate it is "never justifiable to cheat on taxes," and 0 if otherwise.[17] Although the data in the pre-liberalization period (1981–4) is very limited, it lends some suggestive support to our claim. Table 4.3 illustrates that a higher percentage of elites – i.e., the primary taxpayers – respond in the survey that it is "never justifiable to cheat on taxes" in the 1980s than they do today.[18] Incidentally, we cannot rule out that cheating increased post-liberalization as many of these nations democratized.

Post-liberalization, we expect the cheating pattern to diverge based on regime type, since we predict citizens in democracies have a higher propensity to cheat on taxes (S2). In contrast, citizens in both authoritarian subtypes should have a lower propensity to cheat due to fear of the autocrats' coercive capabilities. The findings for respondents in ConservAuths are particularly relevant here because we expect ConservAuth leaders to rely primarily on fear to successfully increase tax revenues post-liberalization. If S2 is confirmed, liberal and conservative authoritarian regimes will be negatively associated with the likelihood to cheat on taxes.

Once again we estimate logit regressions (and multilevel models, see Appendix E.4) with robust standard errors clustered at the country level. The individual and country-level controls are the same as in Table 4.2. As previously, we also include the average cheating on taxes score in each country in these estimations testing S2.[19] In these models, we include

---

[17] We employ a binary operationalization because otherwise the gradations for cheating are too small.

[18] We measure elites as individuals who report an income of 9 or 10 on the income question scale from 1 to 10. The cheating on taxes question asks if "Cheating on taxes if you have a chance" is "Never Justifiable" (= 1) through "Always Justifiable" (=10).

[19] Levi 1988.

Table 4.3 *Cheating on Taxes, Elite Respondents (World Values Survey)*

Year	N indicating Never Justifiable to Cheat on Taxes	Total N	Percent
Wave 1981–4	101	184	54.89
Wave 2010–14	106	269	39.41

Note: Countries in sample (based on availability): South Korea, Mexico, and South Africa
Data source: World Values Survey 1981–4 and 2010–14

both ConservAuth and LibAuth regime type dummy variables in the WVS model predicting cheating on taxes, given our predictions that cheating will be higher in democracies (the base category). We expect negative coefficients for LibAuths and ConservAuths and a positive coefficient for democracies. Table 4.4 presents the estimation results.

Findings in all models in Table 4.4 provide support for our argument that *de facto* tax reform is less likely to be successful in democracies, because citizens of these nations are more likely to freely cheat on taxes (S2). This is telling; recall that democracies have higher bureaucratic quality scores on average compared to nondemocracies (see Table 3.1a). The predicted probability of responding that cheating on taxes is justified is over 40 percent in democracies, but 28 and 29 percent in LibAuths and ConservAuths, respectively (see Appendices E.1–E.3 for predicted probabilities). Interestingly, elite status is significant in WVS models (only), but not in the expected direction. Next, we explore this further and ask whether elite positions are conditional on regime type.

Are Economic Elites Resisting Taxes Post-Shock (S1 and S2)?

We expect that compulsory and quasi-voluntary compliance for economic elites wanes in democracies in light of increased international market competition, and alongside prevailing disappointments in government services. As in previous models, we estimate an ordered logit of government confidence and a logit of cheating on taxes, controlling for individual and country-level variables (see Appendix F.3 for multilevel model estimation results). Here, however, we limit our sample to better-off respondents with taxable assets (i.e., business owners and highly skilled workers).[20]

[20] Economic elites are defined as "Employer/manager of establishment with 10 or more employed" and "non-manual officer workers" (World Values Survey).

Table 4.4 *Logit Estimations of S2 (World Values Survey)*

DV	(1)	(2)
	Cheating on Taxes	Cheating on Taxes
Strategy	S2	S2
LibAuth	*−0.538***	
	(0.263)	
Democracy		*0.505***
		(0.235)
ConservAuth	*−0.488**	
	(0.275)	
Income	−0.0547	−0.0561
	(0.0361)	(0.0360)
Age	−0.00935***	−0.00926***
	(0.00179)	(0.00176)
Male	0.104***	0.107***
	(0.0367)	(0.0360)
Elite Status	−0.0874*	−0.0860*
	(0.0469)	(0.0462)
Unemployment	−0.0480**	−0.0478**
	(0.0212)	(0.0207)
GDP per capita (logged)	0.309**	0.309**
	(0.126)	(0.124)
Govt Effectiveness	−0.308*	−0.310*
	(0.173)	(0.173)
Illicit Economy	0.0108	0.0114*
	(0.00774)	(0.00628)
Cheat Norm	0.668***	0.666***
	(0.158)	(0.159)
Region Dummies	Yes	Yes
Pseudo R-squared	0.084	0.082
Observations	62,538	64,039
Number of Countries	44	45

Standard errors in parentheses
*** p<0.01, ** p<0.05, * p<0.1

We anticipate government confidence for this group is influenced by their disappointment with an interventionist government that no longer protects their economic interests as it once did in a less open economy. We thus add trade tax revenue (percent of GDP) to these elite models. We

Table 4.5 *Logit and Ordered Logit Estimations of S1 and S2 among Elites (World Values Survey)*

DV	(1)	(2)	(3)	(4)
	Confidence in Govt	Confidence in Govt	Cheating on Taxes	Cheating on Taxes
Strategy	S1	S1	S2	S2
LibAuth	*0.758***	*1.097***		
	(0.251)	*(0.440)*		
Democracy			*0.157*	*0.437***
			(0.154)	*(0.206)*
Trade Tax (% GDP)	*0.0991**	*0.122***	*−0.142***	*0.0295*
	(0.0573)	*(0.0588)*	*(0.0485)*	*(0.115)*
Trade Tax (% GDP) *LibAuth*		*−0.159*		
		(0.242)		
Trade Tax (% GDP) *Democracy*				*−0.234***
				(0.118)
Region Dummies	Yes	Yes	Yes	Yes
Pseudo R-squared	0.028	0.029	0.082	0.084
Observations	7,891	7,891	8,927	8,927
Number of Countries	34	34	36	36

Standard errors in parentheses

*** p<0.01, ** p<0.05, * p<0.1

Note: Controls are: respondent's income, age, gender, average cheating in country, unemployment, GDP per capita, size of illicit economy, and government effectiveness. Complete regression results (and multilevel models) are presented in Appendices F.1–F.3.

estimate the impact of regime type interacted with trade taxes on S1 and S2 among elites (as well as a baseline model that includes trade tax revenue as a control). Lower trade taxes (more liberalization) should increase the elite's propensity for tax evasion in democracies; we thus expect a negative coefficient on the interaction of trade taxes*democracy in the cheating model. We are theoretically ambivalent, however, whether elites in democracies will have less government confidence in more open economies, relative to elites in ConservAuths (see Table 4.5). Interestingly, elite respondents in LibAuths report more government confidence than other regime types independent of the level of trade taxes (Table 4.5, column 1). The full estimation results are in Appendices F.1 and F.2.

We find support for S1 and S2 among elite respondents. Liberalization (lower trade taxes) is associated with lower elite confidence in all developing countries, regardless of regime type (Table 4.5, column 1). But only elites in democracies report higher tax evasion with liberalization (relative to both nondemocracies); trade tax revenue*democracy is negative and statistically significant in the cheating models (Table 4.5, column 4). Put another way, while liberalization is associated with lower elite confidence in all regimes, it appears to impact their propensity for cheating in democracies only. More specifically, in democracies with an average level of trade tax revenue, the predicted probability of selecting cheating on taxes is close to 40 percent – nearly ten percentage points higher than respondents in nondemocracies.

In sum, taken together, findings in this chapter provide suggestive support for S1 and S2: leaders in ConservAuth regimes rely primarily on fear of coercion to extract tax revenue, while leaders in liberal authoritarian regimes rely on both public goods *and* fear to successfully implement tax reform. Somewhat ironically, then, quasi-voluntary compliance with new tax reforms is more likely to occur in LibAuth than in democracies of the developing world.

Conclusion

This chapter presents some telling data on democracies and the reasons why their publics are likely to resist higher taxes post-liberalization. Lack of confidence in the government and the inability to use coercion to impose tax reform play a key role. Citizens in democracies are less likely to be happy with the public goods being provided – in terms of how they work and whom they serve – and that is reflected in their opinion on government and their faith in its ability to spend their money effectively. And both citizens and firms are likely to simultaneously resist tax reform and dodge the actual taxes.

Our data and analysis suggest that citizens of liberal authoritarian regimes perceive that their government provides more socially efficient public goods than other regime types. This confidence plays a key role in the government's ability to extract revenue from its population with relatively greater ease. Conservative authoritarian regimes rely on arguably riskier means (i.e., coercion) to collect revenue, perhaps compromising social stability (and regime legitimacy) in the process. And yet, the evidence suggests that their revenue-raising capacity, at least, is not being compromised.

5   Why Firms Resist

> The monies don't come from bringing in the small guys. You have to be talking about the upper-income categories. That's where you'll get the big money from.[1]

Could one logical solution for democracies be taxing large corporations? After all, they are relatively easy to locate and subject to public reporting requirements. The economy of developing countries tends to be dominated by small producers operating outside the formal sector. It is therefore common for governments to rely on large corporations for tax revenue. This is especially the case post-liberalization, when tariffs become less viable sources of revenue. International financial institutions (IFIs), such as the World Bank and the IMF, insist that corporate tax contributions are vital to ensuring a stable revenue base for developing countries.[2] Indeed, corporate income taxes generally yield two-thirds of all income taxes in developing economies; in rich countries, it is only one-fourth. It makes sense that developing world democracies might lean on corporations to help overcome the revenue shock.

In line with this rationale, recall how policymakers from Andhra Pradesh hope to boost sluggish government revenues by imposing taxes on companies that use cow urine. But this is not an easy endeavor. Large Ayurvedic companies that use cow urine in the production of their products share a history of receiving generous government subsidies, which include a variety of tax concessions. For example, products with "Ayurvedic Proprietary Medicine" labels had lower levies (8 percent) compared with similar products without this label (20 percent).[3] For decades, it was common practice for the government to provide a host of economic incentives (e.g., tariff protections, tax rebates, lower duties, credits) to manufacturing industries – such as India's biomedical

---

[1] Kavita Rao, an economist at the National Institute of Public Finance and Policy, quoted in McCarthy (2017).
[2] Lagarde 2016; Oxfam 2016; UNCTAD 2015; World Bank 2016b.
[3] Bode 2006.

manufacturing sector – targeted for development during the protectionist era.[4] In the 1950s and 1960s, the Indian government gave "financial dispensations" to Ayurvedic medical producers because it was "an affordable alternative for western drugs ... [and] a matter of national pride."[5]

With increased market competition, Ayurvedic domestic sales and exports have slowed down, which is a sharp departure from previous annual growth rates of 10–12 percent. They are facing intense competition from more productive alternative medicine and herbal product firms such as Dabur and Himalaya. Formerly protected Ayurvedic manufacturing firms are now pressing the Indian government hard for lower tax rates, and the government is responding.[6] These firms appear to be taking advantage of the rent-seeking relationship with the Indian government – arguably developed during the protectionist era – to successfully obtain lower tax payments.[7]

Once again, India is not unique. Corporate tax revenues have been slow to increase across many democracies. To broaden the revenue base post-shock, the World Bank and IMF have been advising developing countries to lower their corporate tax rates, while closing tax loopholes and other types of special exemptions.[8] The conventional logic is that lower corporate tax rates increase revenues by increasing incentives for tax compliance, encouraging the emergence of new firms, and attracting foreign capital.[9] The challenge to all governments, however, is three-fold. First, firms – especially the more numerous, less productive ones (such as India's Ayurvedic firms) – are demanding lower tax rates and loopholes so that they can better compete in both import and export markets;

---

[4] See Shaikh (2015) and Warrier (2011). India's government assistance has long aimed to "encourage the indigenous manufacture of bulk drugs" (Shaikh 2015: 2).

[5] Bode 2006: 229.

[6] Reports that Ayurvedic industries experience reduced tax burdens are many (See, for examples, Kunnathoor 2013 and "Withdrawal of Excise Duty Demanded" 2014). The large Ayurvedic firm Patanjali Ayurved's chief executive officer recently demanded that the government "keep ayurveda at the lower end of the tax rate" in the recent tax reform negotiations ("There Should Be Minimum Tax on Ayurvedic Products: Acharya Balkrishna" 2016).

[7] State and central government officials have "gone out of the way" to offer tax concessions to Ayurvedic industrial firms in order to "promote the traditional system of medicine" ("Patanjali to Invest Rs 500 Crore for Food Processing Unit in Madhya Pradesh" 2016 and "Tax Concession on Ayurveda Medicines?" 2012). Some examples include corporate income tax concessions for herbal drug investments in the 2003 national budget and a 100 percent corporate tax exemption for five years in Himachal Pradesh ("Herb Today, Gone Tomorrow Seems to be the Name of the Game" 2003 and "Punjab Hit by HP Tax Concessions" 2006).

[8] World Bank 2005.

[9] IMF structural reform agendas typically include both reductions in and simplifications of corporate tax rates (see Vreeland 2006).

second, simultaneously occuring financial liberalization provides mobile asset holders greater opportunities to avoid taxation; and finally, more productive exporting firms resist higher tariffs, which could mitigate the revenue shocks.

Developing countries are heeding IFI advice and lowering corporate tax rates; the problem is that in many developing countries, revenue generation has not risen in tandem. The revenue base has instead become narrower, *not* broader.[10] This raises concerns: since democracies are more sensitive to lobbying from a wide range of formal firms, lower corporate tax rates *and* lack of compliance (via loopholes, exemptions, and evasion) are likely to occur. This chapter will look at the role of firms in tax reform, and how the history of import substitution industrialization impacts today's political and economic incentives for industry.

Increased Competition and Business Elites

Large firms are less likely to engage in voluntary or compulsory compliance with higher taxes post-liberalization in democracies, especially in comparison to nondemocracies. In addition to disappointment with public goods, businesses have added reason for low government confidence post-liberalization: greater international market competition. Recall that the tax bargain prior to liberalization was beneficial to large domestic industrialists: these firms enjoyed import protection and other economic subsidies in exchange for (albeit still low) tax payments. After liberalization, firms from the once-protected sectors have lower confidence that the government's new tax bargain (i.e., higher taxes alongside lower import protections) will benefit them.[11]

We propose that democracies are experiencing a relatively rapid decline in corporate taxation rates and revenues in response to demands from a key interest group: *less productive firms*. This is a distinct departure from current explanations, which contend that large, more productive exporting firms are the main lobbyists for declining corporate taxes in a global economy.[12] We posit, instead, that once-protected firms, now struggling to compete in the globalizing environment, tend to dominate the economic landscape of developing countries, and have the lowest confidence that the new tax proposals

---

[10] Mascagni, Moore, and McCluskey 2014; United Nations 2002.
[11] Trust in political institutions is critical for affluent actors to support taxation (Berens and von Schiller 2016).
[12] Dür 2007; Krishna and Mitra 2005; Yasar 2013.

benefit them. They demand lower taxes and concessions as compensation for the greater import and export competition, while ostensibly providing their support of liberalization in exchange. Their successful resistance has roots in the strong political coalitions that were formed with governments during the protectionist era. In contrast, while less productive firms in authoritarian regimes may experience the same drop in government confidence post-shock for similar reasons, their lobbying does not have the same influence on policymakers. The use of coercion and harsh punitive measures for tax violations are added tools that authoritarian regimes threaten to employ to solicit corporate tax compliance. In contrast, low corporate taxes are likely to be a lower priority for larger, more productive firms since they have more options to route around local taxes.

The logic of this chapter is as follows. We first analyze the decline of corporate tax rates (CTRs) in developing economies. Since our focus is on if and how vested interests are lobbying governments in democracies, it is instructive to focus on both how tax *policies* and revenues aimed at firms are changing across regime types. We then turn to firm-level data from the World Bank's World Business Environment Survey to assess our intuition that less productive firms are key interest groups successfully driving lower corporate taxes in democracies, but *not* in authoritarian regimes. Our final section employs a difference-in-difference estimation to assess if indeed these critical vested interests are driving lower corporate tax revenues post-shock in developing world democracies.

Existing Research and Declining Corporate Taxation in the Developing World

While CTRs have been steadily declining in countries all over the world, this trend appears to be particularly acute in developing economies. This should be good news, since low CTRs can lead to higher compliance and entry of new firms. However, studies note the disappointing growth in income tax revenues in developing countries over the last few decades.[13] We also know, from Chapters 1 and 2, that some countries are facing unique challenges in mobilizing income tax revenues post-shock. Declining CTRs is thus a problem worthy of investigation, since shortfalls in corporate tax revenues in many developing nations are producing significant losses to society as a whole. Yet most of the empirical research on corporate taxation per se has generally focused on rich countries. Only in recent years has the literature turned to developing economies.

---

[13] Carnahan 2015; Mascagni et al. 2014; World Bank 2005.

The scholarly consensus is that CTRs are declining globally.[14] Studies find that capital-scarce poor nations are more inclined to use tax incentives (tax holidays, free trade zones, loopholes, lower tax rates) to lure businesses.[15] Developing countries also struggle to introduce transfer-pricing legislation and monitor the tax compliance of multinational firms, which is quite complex and costly.[16] It is estimated that almost half of all foreign direct investment to developing countries flows through tax havens.[17] In consequence, rather than lower corporate rates contributing to a broader tax base and filling bare government coffers, growth in income tax revenues has been disappointing.[18]

Studies of CTRs have thus been helpful in terms of showing the steady decline of taxes on capital, and identifying the susceptibility of developing economies to this trend. However, with the exception of Fairfield (2010, 2015), Hart (2010), and von Schiller (2016), they do little to help us understand the actors and political context driving this trend. Many scholars assume that large exporting firms are behind falling CTRs; they can successfully pressure the government for lower taxes because of the government's perceived threats of lower profits and disinvestment if they behave otherwise.[19] This assumption may be problematic. First, it has not been put to any kind of empirical test in developing economies. Second, lobbying for low tax rates may be less of a priority for large, more productive firms that are focusing on pursuing lower tariffs.[20] These firms already have extensive options for tax avoidance, such as transfer pricing. However, large, less productive firms struggling to compete in both local and/or export markets care about tax rates, and they have the advantage – in developing democracies, at least – of being high in numbers.

This is precisely why it is imperative to explore which corporate interests are politically active on tax policies, and have direct connections to the government. Many urban industrialists, who are part of historically strong political coalitions formed during the protectionist period, have great incentive to lobby for lower business taxes.[21] Scholars often wrongly

---

[14] Overesch and Rincke 2009; Zodrow 2010.
[15] Queralt (2017) finds that states with weak fiscal capacity protect declining industries in exchange for tariff protections. However, note that developing countries' discretion to use trade barriers has become increasingly difficult since structural adjustment policies in the late 1980s and WTO membership in the 1990s.
[16] Cooper et al. 2016; Malesky 2015.
[17] Malesky 2015.
[18] Abbas and Klemm 2012; Abramovsky, Klemm, and Phillips 2014; Crivelli, De Mooij and Keen 2015.
[19] For example, Dür (2007), Krishna and Mitra (2005), Yasar (2013).
[20] Helpman, Melitz, and Yeaple 2004; Melitz 2003.
[21] Some scholars do consider how politics impacts CTRs (Hart 2010; Genschel, Lierse, and Seelkopf 2016), but the historical political legacies linked to the import substitution industrialization era are neglected.

assume that domestic industrialists that thrived during the import substitution industrialization (ISI) era have become less viable post-liberalization. Instead, studies show these groups continue to maintain both political *and* economic influence on governments and extract benefits.[22] Many of these leading domestic industrialists from once-protected sectors can successfully demand rents – such as lower taxes – in exchange for their support of free trade policies, especially in countries that have a history of strong ISI policies.[23] We consider this possibility in the next section.

Less Productive Firms, Democracies, and Low Corporate Tax Rates

We contend that large, less productive firms can hold strong political sway over governments in tax negotiations. As Kurtz and Brooks (2008: 245–247) explain, such firms are likely part of strong political coalitions that emerged during the protectionist period.[24] This is especially true in nations where import substitution was once most advanced. Urban industrialists thrived in strong ISI legacy countries, benefitting from sharp increases in growth for the first few decades, rapid industrialization, infrastructure improvements, and the development of a relatively strong manufacturing sector. ISI was also a political bargain wherein urban industrialists worked in concert with governments to protect them from groups that could threaten them: foreign exporters, unskilled labor, and rural producers.

Democratic governments are likely to respond to the interest of these less productive firms with lower tax rates for two reasons. First, a wide range of empirical studies in economics and political science find that "losers" from globalization receive more government compensation.[25] As trade economists have been observing, liberalization spurs heterogeneous firm-level responses; since exporting involves costs (e.g., transportation, information, marketing, distribution), it is the larger, more productive firms that can more easily enter international markets (i.e., the "winners").[26] Studies show that firms that invest in new technologies, labor productivity, and product quality have a higher probability of survival in export markets.[27] Less productive large domestic-oriented firms

---

[22] Kurtz and Brooks 2008; Schamis 1999; Zhou 2008.

[23] See Etchemendy (2001), Kingstone (1999), and Murillo (2001).

[24] Note that Kurtz and Brooks (2008) refer to potentially competitive firms.

[25] Adsera and Boix 2002; Baldwin and Robert-Nicoud 2007; Kurtz and Brooks 2008; Rodrik 1997; Walter 2010.

[26] Bernard et al. 2007; Melitz 2003; Melitz and Redding 2014.

[27] Lileeva and Trefler 2010.

that were created and sustained under heavy protectionism (ISI) may have more difficulty entering export markets (i.e., the "losers"), and thus be the most threatened by more productive foreign competitors.[28]

Second, the literature on globalization suggests these demands will be most effective in countries where the losers are organized and have political clout.[29] Once-protected large, less productive domestic firms fall precisely into this category. The political coalitions they formed during the import substitution period continue to endure under the new market environment.[30] In consequence, they now receive government compensation to "level the playing field with companies in nations with more efficient credit markets and more developed infrastructure."[31] Less productive large-scale firms hereby may stay economically and politically viable by providing their tacit support of liberalization in exchange for government subsidies, such as provision of skills, access to finance, low taxes, and tax exemptions. These firms, particularly because they are relatively large in size and play a critical role in creating employment, are well positioned to lobby the government and demand compensation in the form of lower taxes. We ultimately expect these vested interests to wield strong political influence in democracies, which depend on a broad coalition of economic elites for campaign financing and electoral support.[32]

In Brazil, for example, we see that large beneficiaries of ISI are still key political players and, not surprisingly, often recipients of generous tax concessions. The 1956–61 Plano de Metas and other government policies throughout the 1970s supported manufacturing industries, such as automobiles, petrochemicals, and steel, through subsidies, tariffs, and credit.[33] Government procurement (upwards of 80–100 percent) further financed these sectors.[34] With liberalization, previously protected less productive sectors, such as Brazil's chemical industry, are struggling to be more globally competitive, slowly increasing their exports by 10 percent per year since the 1990s.[35] The Brazilian government continues to

---

[28] See Barkey (1989), Chen (1987), and Krueger (2002).
[29] De Figueiredo and Richter 2014; Rudra 2008.
[30] Kurtz and Brooks 2008.
[31] Kurtz and Brooks 2008: 247.
[32] See Weymouth (2012).
[33] Amann 2000.
[34] Amann 2000.
[35] Pinto 2011. The chemical industry now exports close to 9 percent – $9 billion in 2009 – of its sales (Pinto 2011). This contrasts with Brazil's cell phone industry, whose exports increased 900 fold between 1994 and 2006 from 0.3 billion to close to 3 billion dollars (Bonelli and Pinheiro 2008). It now exports 8 percent of the world's cell phones (Bonelli and Pinheiro 2008). Unlike the aforementioned sectors, the cell phone industry took off only in the 1990s with Motorola and Ericsson investing in Brazil (Bonelli and Pinheiro 2008).

compensate these and other previously protected manufacturing firms with large tax breaks and incentives.[36] As anticipated, Brazil's corporate income tax revenues have been stagnant since the mid-2000s. Corporate tax evasion is rampant in Brazil – among both small and large corporations.[37]

The interests of more productive firms may be less unified in terms of spending resources lobbying for lower tax rates. On the one hand, they may have good incentives to demand lower taxes from governments in response to cost constraints and variations in market power over time. At the same time, exporters are already operating above the export productivity threshold (i.e., fixed and variable costs of exporting cut-off) and through self-selection, both participate in export markets and invest in future productivity (such as research and development), further reinforcing the selection effect.[38] These firms already have extensive options to route around corporate taxation, such as access to export processing zones, exporter tax exemptions and loopholes, transfer pricing.[39]

More productive firms may also be willing to pay *domestic* taxes in the new global economic environment if they believe, in equilibrium, it will result in greater productivity or lower costs, i.e., government financing of public goods such as skill development, healthcare, and infrastructure. We have no reason to assume that the correlation between public goods and the willingness to pay taxes does not apply to corporations. Empirical research suggests, for instance, that foreign firms are willing to accept higher tax rates if they are associated with public goods provision.[40] In another example, when asked about Singapore's 2016 budget, President Chew of Fujitsu Singapore – a Fortune Global 500 firm – indicated that, "It was great to see that the 2016 Budget

---

[36] "Brazil to Extend Tax Breaks to All Manufacturers" 2013; Farah 2013.

[37] The number of businesses involved in Brazil's informal economy is quite large: only 120 out of 6,000 firms with more than 250 employees are listed and traded on the Sao Paulo Stock Exchange (Kenyon 2008). Further, large firms typically conceal a quarter of their sales from tax authorities (Kenyon 2008).

[38] Aw, Roberts, and Xu 2011.

[39] Tax avoidance is common for MNCs in the form of transfer pricing (Conover and Nichols 2000; Bernard, Jensen, and Schott 2006; Taylor, Richardson, and Lanis 2015), and large exporters who tend to populate export processing zones that offer a host of tax concessions (e.g., Abidoye, Orazem, and Vodopivec 2014). Granting low CTR and loopholes for exporters is historically common in developing countries. For example, Brazil's recently reinstated Reintegra program grants corporations income tax credits equivalent to 0.3 percent of their export value (Soto 2014). India, as well, has several policies to promote exports such as free trade zones, technology parks, customs, income tax, and excise duty exemptions, refunds, or rebates for manufactured exports (see Pillay 2011 and www.indianindustry.com/trade-information/export-incentives.html).

[40] Benassy-Quere, Fontagne, and Lahreche-Revil 2005: 591.

included educational programmes to help develop a stronger workforce."[41] Other executives in this survey pointed to the importance of government investment in other public goods such as infrastructure, healthcare, and family care. The difference is that the stakes of paying higher taxes may be more costly for less productive firms and incentivize them to more actively mobilize.[42] Overall, more productive firms may uniformly view lower tariffs as beneficial, but show less unanimity on lobbying for lower CTRs.

In democracies, this is a death knell for raising CTRs. Interest groups commonly compete for influence over government policies, and those who have both the government connections and highest stake in the policy outcome (i.e., less productive firms) win.[43] Less productive firms represent the majority of businesses in developing economies (70 percent of firms, on average) and can form strong interest groups.[44] In both types of nondemocratic regimes, however, we expect to see greater government success in pressuring corporations for more taxes, since not all economic elites are included in their loyalist coalition. Firms connected to the ISI legacy may or may not be part of the loyalist coalition.

We thus explore the following hypothesis:

H1: In the liberalizing environment, businesses are more successful resisting taxes in democracies than they are in authoritarian regimes.

Because we anticipate that it is the influence of large, less productive industrialists – particularly those that received protections during the ISI period – who are behind this resistance in democracies, we also propose the following:

H2: The decline in corporate taxes will be more acute in democracies with strong ISI legacies.

Tax Policies in Democracies and Nondemocracies: Country-Level Data

To assess H1, we begin by analyzing the decline of CTRs in developing countries. We focus on CTRs in this chapter to in order to more closely

---

[41] Bittleston 2016.
[42] Interestingly, Fairfield (2015) distinguishes between firms with structural (or investment) power and instrumental (or political) power. She explains, "structural power requires no organization ... instead, market signals coordinate their behavior ... instrumental power entails engagement within the political arena and deliberate actions to influence policy such as lobbying" (Fairfield 2015: 2).
[43] Baldwin and Robert-Nicoud 2007; Bertrand, Bombardini, and Trebbi 2014.
[44] Baldwin and Robert-Nicoud 2007. See also Yackee and Yackee (2006).

assess how interest groups are directly impacting government *policy*, which is distinct from Chapter 3's revenue models. We expect that democracies will experience steeper declines in CTRs than authoritarian regimes because they are more susceptible to demands by less productive firms, as well as large exporters.

In general, cross-national tax policy data in developing economies is extremely complex and has limited availability.[45] However, Genschel et al. (2016) built the largest, newly compiled dataset on CTRs covering developing countries for close to 18 years. The CTR is the statutory rate collected from the KPMG corporate tax survey. We employ both the rate of change and level of CTR as dependent variables. Once critical control variables are included, our models cover 37 developing countries between 1995 and 2010.[46]

To begin, we check if IFI expectations that lower tax rates will be accompanied by greater compliance and thereby, higher corporate tax revenues. Table 5.1 suggests that low CTRs are generally associated with low revenues in democracies (i.e., a positive correlation). A sample of low- and middle-income nondemocracies seem to be an exception. Even then, low correlations overall suggest CTRs are not perfect indicators of how good the government is at raising revenues. For our purposes, however, it is a useful proxy of political bargaining: lower tax rates may reflect government responsiveness to business pressures – allowing at least some corporations to pay fewer taxes and access loopholes so they can better compete in the global economy.

CTRs have been declining over time in both democracies and nondemocracies. However, the average rate of CTR reductions in nondemocracies is slower (1 percent annually) than it is in democracies (2 percent annually). Democracies are also experiencing slower growth in corporate income tax revenue. In the 2000s, for instance, corporate income tax revenues grew rapidly in middle-income nondemocracies (2.4 percent annually) compared to democracies (a reduction of 0.002 percent). Taken together, this suggests nondemocracies are reducing CTRs *and* broadening their tax base, consistent with IFI predictions.

Next, we focus on the impact of the trade liberalization revenue shock on CTRs in democracies and nondemocracies. Our primary independent variable is, once again, *trade taxes*polity*, and we use both a continuous

---

[45] Bahl and Bird 2008.

[46] Note that Swank (2016) has also recently put together an excellent dataset on CTR that includes developing countries. This dataset is 0.90 correlated with Genschel et al. (2016) and incorporates slightly fewer countries. We run our models using both datasets, and there is little variation in our primary findings. We focus on Genschel et al. (2016) because we maintain the maximum of observations when adding necessary controls.

Table 5.1 *Correlation between CTRs and Corporate Tax Revenues in Democracies and Nondemocracies, 1995–2011*

	Low- and Middle-Income Countries	All Developing Countries
Democracies	0.16	0.09
	(0.004)	(0.06)
	N = 309	N = 472
Nondemocracies	−0.27	−0.01
	(0.001)	(0.85)
	N = 164	N = 200

Note: P-values in parentheses
Data source: Genschel et al. 2016; Prichard et al. 2014

measure (polity) as well as a democracy dummy. Recall that, when the democracy dummy is equal to 1, ConservAuths and LibAuths are equal to 0. We focus on this democracy dummy in the estimations because we have no prior expectations for why LibAuths and ConservAuths may systematically differ in their ability to set CTRs. We predict a positive coefficient on this interaction; as trade tax revenue decreases (suggesting that liberalization is expanding), CTRs also decrease in democracies. We also estimate the impact of capital account openness on CTRs since governments of all regime types face incentives to compete for international investment by reducing the corporate tax burden. This coefficient should be negative.

Following Chapter 3, we apply a fixed effects statistical model. All models include panel-corrected standard errors to address heteroskedasticity and serial correlation. For model specification, we build on Chapter 3's revenue models and recent academic work on corporate taxation in developing countries, specifically Genschel et al. (2016) and Wibbels and Arce (2003). We first estimate a simple model controlling for the key variables of IMF credits (percent of GDP), the World Bank's investment profile, and portfolio investment inflows (percent of GDP). IMF credits capture the extent to which IFIs, through their market-oriented loan conditions and policy advice, are influencing tax policy.[47] A country's investment profile can have a major impact on their CTR as politicians seek to attract capital in risky environments with lower tax rates.[48] Finally, net portfolio

---

[47] See also Wibbels and Arce (2003).
[48] See Genschel et al. (2016). More precisely, the investment profile measures investment risk associated with contracts, profit and payment (scale from 0 to 12 with higher values indicating lower risk) (ICRG 2012).

investment inflows (percent of GDP), which measures the importance of liquid investments on national policymaking,[49] should increase the power of capital relative to labor and be associated with lower CTRs.[50] Portfolio investors are expected to have a relatively strong influence on politicians, in comparison to foreign direct investment, because of the mobility of these assets. We also include country dummies and control for time effects.

Appendix H details the additional control variables in the full model: GDP per capita, GDP growth, fuel exports (percent of exports), population (logged), foreign direct investment inflows (percent of GDP), government spending (percent of GDP), agricultural employment (percent of total employment), and regime durability, and the regression results, respectively.[51] Appendix H.1 presents the full model estimation results. Appendix H.2 contains the results for the rate of change of CTR. The baseline model results in Table 5.2 lend support to H1.

In democracies, an increase in openness (measured as the reduction in trade taxes) is associated with declines in CTRs. This is true regardless of how democracy is measured. Figure 5.1 highlights the marginal effect of decreases in trade tax revenue on CTRs in democracies and nondemocracies. For example, in a democracy (polity = 10), a 10 percent decrease in trade tax revenue is associated with 0.10 decline in the CTR. To put this in perspective, given that the average trade tax revenue decline across developing world democracies was 57 percent between 1997 and 2011 (from 3.3 percent of GDP to 1.4 percent of GDP), our model predicts CTRs would decline over this same period from an average of 31 percent to 13 percent.[52] In contrast, declines in trade tax revenue in authoritarian regimes have no statistically significant impact on changes in CTR. Interestingly, capital account openness, once again, appears to have less of an impact on tax rates than trade. This finding for capital account openness is broadly consistent with patterns found by scholars analyzing financial liberalization and corporate taxation in the OECD countries.[53]

This statistically insignificant effect in authoritarian regimes is not surprising because it is likely that tax reforms – such as lowering the CTR – were implemented soon after the initial trade tax revenue shock; but henceforth, we do not anticipate that there will be a more rapid decline in tax rates in response to further increases in openness

---

[49] World Bank 2016a.
[50] Wibbels and Arce 2003.
[51] Results are robust to excluding the oil rich economies.
[52] The average CTR for democracies was 31 percent in 1997 and 23 percent in 2011 (a 26 percent decline).
[53] See, for example, Garrett and Michell (2001) and Takashima (2007).

Table 5.2 *Determinants of CTRs*

DV	(1)	(2)
	CTR	CTR
Trade Tax Revenue (% GDP)$_{t-1}$	−0.167	0.172
	(0.229)	(0.196)
Democracy Dummy $_{t-1}$	−1.610**	
(1 = Dem; 0 = LibAuth or ConservAuth)		
	(0.678)	
Trade Tax Revenue (% GDP)*	0.976***	
Democracy Dummy $_{t-1}$		
(1 = Dem; 0 = LibAuth or ConservAuth)		
	(0.316)	
Polity $_{t-1}$		−0.180**
		(0.0723)
Trade Tax Revenue (% GDP)'**Polity** $_{t-1}$		0.0816***
		(0.0309)
Capital Account Openness $_{t-1}$	−0.322	−0.383
	(0.322)	(0.315)
Investment Profile $_{t-1}$	−0.200**	−0.197**
	(0.0896)	(0.0863)
Portfolio Flows (% GDP) $_{t-1}$	0.0156	0.0104
	(0.0372)	(0.0367)
IMF Credits (% GDP) $_{t-1}$	0.0701*	0.0531
	(0.0401)	(0.0399)
Observations	280	280
R-squared	0.982	0.984
Number of Countries	37	37

*** $p<0.01$, ** $p<0.05$, * $p<0.1$
Standard errors in parentheses

since nondemocracies are less susceptible to interest group pressures. To check this, we reran the models by splitting the sample and comparing CTRs in the 1990s, which is the decade that most tax reforms were first introduced, to the 2000s.[54] As expected, despite the reduction in sample size, trade tax changes showed a positive and statistically significant relationship with CTRs in the early decades of liberalization, but not thereafter. Trade tax revenue in democracies, on the other hand, had a consistently positive and significant impact on CTRs.

---

[54] We estimated a fixed effects regression of trade tax revenue (percent of GDP) on CTRs across a sample in the 1990s and then the 2000s.

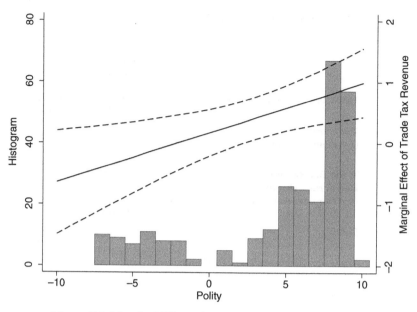

Figure 5.1 Marginal Effect of (Declining) Trade Tax Revenue (Percent of GDP) on CTRs Conditional on Polity

Less Productive Firms: Firm-Level Data

We need firm-level data to assess H2, which focuses on vested interests that emerged from strong IFI legacies. We ask if *less productive firms* have critical influence on the tax bargain post-liberalization. Turning to the World Bank's Enterprise Surveys (ES) data between 2006 and 2015, we select the most objective question on taxation, i.e., the number of tax inspections, as our dependent variable to proxy firms' ability to avoid government taxation.[55] We expect that, in democracies, less productive large firms will have fewer tax inspections (i.e., greatest tax avoidance) because of their relative bargaining position vis-à-vis the government. The variable of interest is: "Over the last 12 months, was this establishment visited and/or inspected by tax officials (value of: 1 if there was a visit, 0 if no visit)?" Although local governments have some autonomy in this domain, it is important to emphasize that national agencies are primarily responsible for tax enforcement and

[55] We do not use the ES questions on whether the tax administration or tax rate is a "major constraint" because they are subjective measures.

Table 5.3 *Number of Productive and Unproductive Firms across Developing Countries*

	Large Productive Firms (Percent of Total)	*Large* Less Productive Firms (Percent of Total)
All Countries	23%	77%
	(N = 4,739)	(N = 15,718)
Democracies	24%	76%
	(N = 3,039)	(N = 9,382)
Nondemocracies	22%	78%
	(N = 1,465)	(N = 5,219)

Note: Sample includes large, domestic, private firms only. Large firms have 100 or more employees (see Ayyagari, Demirguc-Kunt, and Maksimovic 2015).
Data source: ES 2016

inspections, with local branches reporting directly to central government bodies.[56]

We operationalize less productive firms using the ES variable: "In fiscal year X, what percent of this establishment's sales were: direct exports?" Following ES coding, exporting firms maintain 10 percent or more of sales from exports. We thus code "less productive firms" as firms that have 10 percent or less direct exports, while productive "export oriented" have more than 10 percent sales from exports. Firms with 10 percent or less of sales as direct exports are considered "less productive" as they primarily serve the domestic market.[57]

We first compare the numbers of productive to less productive large firms in the different regime types. We limit our sample to large firms because these firms are the easiest to monitor and tax in developing economies, and they have the resources and capacity to influence politicians. According to Table 5.3, both democracies and authoritarian regimes have similar numbers of productive (about 25 percent) and less productive large firms (about 75 percent). The difference is that we predict that the sizeable population of large, less productive firms is likely to have greater political importance in democracies.

If our intuition is correct, we would find that the average number of tax inspection visits for less productive firms is lower in democracies than it is in authoritarian regimes.[58] We also compare the treatment of

[56] Blanc 2012.
[57] Following World Bank research, exporting firms have 10 percent or more of sales from exports (Dinh, Mavridis, and Nguyen 2010).
[58] We focus on domestically owned, private firms, rather than government-owned ones, as a hard test of our prediction that large less productive firms have undue influence

Table 5.4 *Tax Inspections of Domestic, Private Firms in Democracies and Nondemocracies*

Firms in Sample	Firm Size	Countries in Sample	Democracies	Nondemocracies	P-value of t-test
All	All	All	0.54	0.67	0.00
All	All	Low & MI	0.59	0.71	0.00
Less Productive	Large	All	0.63	0.71	0.00
Less Productive	Large	Low & MI	0.63	0.73	0.00
Export-Oriented	Large	All	0.66	0.73	0.00
Export-Oriented	Large	Low & MI	0.64	0.72	0.00

Data source: ES 2016

less productive firms with more productive firms in both regimes types, exploring whether government officials in democracies will be more "forgiving" to less productive firms, as we predict. We also drop the high-income countries so that the included countries are more comparable with each other.[59] Interestingly, firms in democracies experienced a lower rate of tax inspections than nondemocracies across all samples (Table 5.4).

But perhaps more interestingly for our analysis, we find that large, less productive firms in democracies consistently receive fewer tax inspections than export-oriented firms (Table 5.5). There appears to be minimal difference in tax inspections across these firms within the sample of nondemocracies. This pattern holds in samples that include foreign-owned firms, government-owned firms, and manufacturing firms only.

To further assess our argument, we estimate a logit model on the ES survey data. Our dependent variable is the same: tax inspections (1 = visited by an official in the past year, 0 = not visited). Our independent variable of interest is democracy. As before, we operationalize democracy using a democracy dummy as well as polity. In Appendix I.1, we also include regressions with liberal and conservative regimes (with democracy as the base category) to assess if there is a difference in tax inspections of LibAuths or ConservAuths relative to democracies. Finally, we interact democracy dummy with firms that

over tax policies and practices. Nonetheless, we compare the rate of tax inspections in samples including government-owned firms, excluding small firms (fewer than 100 employees), and excluding high-income countries.

[59] In Table 5.4, middle- and low-income countries have a GDP per capita below the sample mean.

Table 5.5 *Tax Inspections across Domestic, Private Firms in Democracies and Nondemocracies*

Firms in Sample	Countries in Sample	Less Productive Firms	Productive Firms	P-value of t-test
Large Firms	Democracies	0.63	0.66	0.00
Large Firms	Nondemocracies	0.71	0.73	0.19

Data source: ES 2016

have higher export sales to check if it is a conditional relationship. If democracy*export sales are positive and statistically significant, then this suggests less productive firms (firms with lower export sales) in democracies are experiencing fewer tax inspections, or pressures to pay taxes, than more competitive firms.

We control for GDP per capita and bureaucratic quality on the country level and firm size (log of total employment), and sales (log of total sales) on the firm level.[60] Statistical estimations also include a regional dummy variable and year dummies, and have robust standard errors clustered by country. Appendix I.5 contains the variable definitions and descriptive statistics for the ES dataset. Appendix I.6 lists the countries represented in the sample.

Table 5.6 presents the results of tax inspections in a sample of all domestic firms, which are consistent with our expectations. Democracy is negatively associated with tax inspections and the interaction is positive and statistically significant. Table 5.7 presents the predicted probabilities for the regression in Table 5.6, column 3.

Table 5.7 indicates that, as a firm's exporting capabilities (i.e., their competitiveness) increases, it is slightly more likely to receive tax inspections. Democratic governments thus appear to be compensating less productive firms with looser tax monitoring.

As robustness checks, we limit the sample to less productive firms, or those firms that export 10 percent or less of their annual sales, to test if they have greater political influence in democracies than nondemocracies. See Appendix I.2 and I.3. We also limit the sample to large firms to assess our contention that it is the large, less productive firms that are the key interest group driving the low tax rates and revenues in democracies. See Appendix I.4.

---

[60] Firm profit is not available in the ES dataset.

Table 5.6 *Determinants of Tax Inspections*

DV	(1)	(2)	(3)	(4)
	Tax Inspect.	Tax Inspect.	Tax Inspect.	Tax Inspect.
Democracy Dummy (1 = Dem; 0 = LibAuth or ConservAuth)	−0.597***	−0.459*	−0.517**	
	(0.146)	(0.265)	(0.261)	
Exports (% Sales)		−0.000316	−0.0101***	−0.005**
		(0.00155)	(0.00231)	(0.0023)
Exports (% Sales)*Democracy Dummy (1 = Dem; 0 = LibAuth or ConservAuth)			0.0135***	
			(0.00245)	
Polity				−0.0213
				(0.0270)
Polity*Exports (% Sales)				0.001**
				(0.000)
GDP Per Capita (Logged)		−0.244**	−0.259**	−0.2729*
		(0.124)	(0.122)	(0.1403)
Bureaucratic Quality		−0.0630	−0.0480	−0.1267
		(0.166)	(0.164)	(0.1673)
Sales (Logged)		0.00217	0.00279	0.0084
		(0.0363)	(0.0361)	(0.0379)
Employment (Logged)		0.264***	0.269***	0.2622***
		(0.0561)	(0.0549)	(0.0548)
Region Control	Yes	Yes	Yes	Yes
Year Dummies	Yes	Yes	Yes	Yes
Observations	94,039	42,675	42,675	42,675

*** $p<0.01$, ** $p<0.05$, * $p<0.1$
Standard errors in parentheses

Table 5.7 *Predicted Probabilities of a Tax Inspection in Democracies and Nondemocracies by Level of Exports (Table 5.6, Column 3)*

Exports (% Sales)	Predicted Probability of a Tax Inspection in	
	Democracies	Nondemocracies
0	0.55	0.68
5	0.56	0.66
10	0.56	0.65
25	0.57	0.62

As expected, in a sample of large firms, the democracy*export inter-action is positive and significant. In essence, in democracies, as large firms increase their exports, the likelihood of a tax inspection also increases. Looking at this another way, in a sample of less productive firms only, democracy is negatively associated with tax inspections.

Role of ISI Legacy on Tax Revenues: Country-Level Data and Difference-in-Difference Estimations

The intuition behind H2 is that less productive firms formed during the import substitution period have both the greatest incentive and political resources to lobby democratic governments for a favorable tax bargain. Following Brooks and Kurtz (2008), we measure ISI legacy as coun-tries with above the median manufacturing value added as a percent of GDP in 1980. Countries with more entrenched import substitution policies were associated with advanced capital-intensive manufacturing by the early 1980s. Indeed, amongst low- and middle-income democ-racies, those with a legacy of ISI have a higher percentage of large, pri-vate, unproductive firms (75 percent in our sample) in comparison with similar democracies with a weaker ISI legacy (68 percent). Next, we use the ES to observe the average number of tax inspections in *democracies* with and without an ISI legacy. We focus on large, domestically owned, private firms. Table 5.8 shows that tax inspections are indeed lowest (0.61) for less productive firms in democracies with a strong ISI legacy; but this is not the case in authoritarian regimes.

The findings thus far complement the statistical pattern uncovered in Chapter 4, which was that citizens and elite resistance to tax reform hampers revenue recovery post-shock in democracies. If this is true, then democracies with strong ISI legacies – or those with large, politically powerful less productive firms – will be most vulnerable to a revenue trap post-liberalization.

As a harder test of this logic, we now use a difference-in-difference modeling strategy on a sample of democracies to determine the effect of a trade revenue shock on corporate income and total domestic tax *revenues*, respectively, in a "treatment" group and a "control" group. The treatment group – the strong ISI legacy countries – should be highly sus-ceptible to liberalization shocks. This means that countries with strong ISI legacies had higher tariffs (especially on manufactured goods) and thus experience more intensive revenue shocks upon liberalizing. The control group – countries with a weak ISI legacy – had lower tariffs prior to liberalization and are relatively more insulated from the effects of the shock. Countries in this category should have weaker vested interests, a

Table 5.8 *Tax Inspections of Large, Domestic, Private Firms in ISI and Non-ISI Legacy Democracies and Nondemocracies*

Firms in Sample	Countries in Sample	ISI Legacy Countries	Weak ISI Legacy Countries	P-value of t-test
Less Productive Firms	Democracies	0.61	0.70	0.00
Less Productive Firms	Nondemocracies	0.72	0.74	0.20

Data source: ES 2016

smaller manufacturing base (pre-liberalization), and, thus, relative to the treatment group, less successful resistance to revenue mobilization post-shock. Unfortunately, we could not estimate difference-in-difference models using CTRs because of limited data availability (pre-WTO, which is our measure for "shock" in these models) for a large number of countries; the Genschel et al. (2016) dataset starts in 1995. However, if our results from these models confirm our predictions, the broader pattern (from all the models taken together) suggests that lower CTRs are indeed associated with declining, rather than increasing corporate tax revenues.

Ultimately, the control group in a difference-in-difference estimation can assess whether democracies would still have faced grave problems mobilizing revenue in the absence of large trade tax shocks. If such shocks are indeed driving a downward trend in revenue generation, then we should observe a statistically significant difference in tax revenues in the treatment and control groups. Our treatment group, or countries that are relatively more vulnerable to a negative trade tax shock, are democracies with a historical legacy of import substitution industrialization. Our intuition is that previously protected large, less productive firms in democracies with a strong ISI legacy will successfully oppose the higher taxes necessary to recover from the shock for three reasons: (1) vulnerability to import competition; (2) pressure to become more competitive exporters; and (3) the rent-seeking behavior sustained from the import substitution era. We thus apply "ISI legacy" to proxy for the presence of organized interests that have long colluded with policymaking elites (for tax subsidies in particular). We argue that firms in strong ISI legacy countries have long held deep political connections with the regime, and thereby have leverage to effectively advance widespread tax concessions and privileges, resulting in comparatively lower tax revenues.

We assess the difference in corporate tax revenues between the treatment and control groups (i.e., ISI and non-ISI legacy countries) across two time periods: pre- and post-trade tax revenue shock.[61] In these models, we identify the years before a country's date of entry into the World Trade Organization (WTO) as pre-shock. We also employ income tax revenue and domestic tax revenue as dependent variables.[62] In effect, we are comparing ISI and non-ISI country tax revenue differences before and after WTO participation. The difference-in-difference model is:

$$\Delta \text{Tax Revenue}_{it} = \beta_0 + \beta_1 \text{WTO}_{it} + \beta_2 \text{ISI Legacy}_{it}$$

$$+ \beta_3 \text{WTO} \star \text{ISI Legacy}_{it} + \beta \text{ Controls}_{i,t-1} + \varepsilon_{it}$$

In this model, β_1 represents the effect of the revenue shock in the "control" group and β_3 in the "treatment" group. We control for the same controls as the revenue models in Chapter 3: GDP per capita (logged); capital account openness; total population (logged); GDP growth; aid (percent of GDP); fuel exports (percent of exports); IMF credits (percent of GDP); and central government debt (percent of GDP). We run our model on a sample of late liberalizing democracies. To address missing observation concerns and ensure we have sufficient observations before and after the treatment, we estimate our models on imputed data. We follow Honaker et al. 2015 and use Amelia II, which uses an "EMis" algorithm to generate datasets to account for missing observations.

One challenge with this strategy is that we may not be comparing groups (democratic countries) with similar probabilities of having a treatment effect – a strong ISI legacy. Strong ISI legacies may be the result of confounding variables, such as country size or resource endowments, which could drive the difference in outcome (tax revenues), rather than ISI per se.[63] Selection into the treatment group is thus a concern. We need a statistical strategy that allows us to determine – with some level of confidence – that lower government revenues are associated with ISI democracies that have a history of strong, rent-seeking interest groups, rather than its size and/or its natural resource endowments. We can do so by matching a treatment group member democracy (with an ISI legacy) with a control group member democracy (with no ISI legacy) where the two countries have similar (natural resource or population) profiles. In other words, applying matching techniques to eliminate systematic differences between the treatment and control groups may be

---

[61] Prichard et al. 2014.
[62] World Bank 2016a.
[63] Country size (population or wealth per capita) and resource endowments are often cited as important determinants of ISI; smaller and resource-poor countries have been historically more export oriented (e.g., South Korea) (McGuire 1994; Nomi 1997). Foreign aid and IMF assistance are also critical components of the import-export orientation of developing countries because of (1) the liberal policies promoted by Bretton Woods

Table 5.9 *Difference in Corporate Income Tax Revenues Pre- and Post-WTO for ISI and Non-ISI Legacy Democracies*

	Pre-WTO Corporate Income Tax Revenue	Post-WTO Corporate Income Tax Revenue	Diff-in-Diff
Difference (Treated-Control)	−0.018	−1.658***	−1.640***
SE	(0.174)	(0.322)	(0.366)

critical.[64] We expect that ISI legacy democracies will generate less corporate tax revenue post-liberalization than non-ISI legacy democracies and the resulting difference-in-difference will be negative and statistically significant.

Table 5.9 presents the results of the difference-in-difference (diff-in-diff) kernel propensity score estimation for a sample of democracies. We find that democracies with ISI legacies have lower corporate tax revenues post-liberalization: the difference-in-difference is negative and statistically significant. Essentially, the "treatment" group has lower revenue levels than the control group after joining the WTO. Appendices J.1 and J.2 present the results for domestic and income tax revenue, which further support the results in Table 5.9.

Pre-liberalization, ISI legacy countries did not bring in a statistically significant difference in corporate income tax revenue than non-ISI legacy countries. Post-liberalization, ISI legacy countries have more difficulty taxing once-protected sectors, thus generating less corporate income tax revenue. Overall domestic tax revenue suffers. In particular, post-liberalization, the difference in corporate tax revenue in ISI legacy democracies compared to non-ISI legacy countries was −1.7 units. The

institutions and (2) the need for foreign exchange by the recipient country (Nomi 1997). Capital account openness is associated with trade policymaking of developing countries (Biglaiser and Brown 2005; Nomi 1997): because relative capital abundance is often associated with more export capacity and less ISI. Countries may also engage in structural reform (i.e., less ISI) to attract more capital. Debt and growth are macroeconomic variables that are associated with government need for structural reform (Biglaiser and Brown 2005).

[64] We employ kernel propensity score matching in our difference-in-difference estimation, calculated by a probit regression of the covariates on the treatment. By limiting the sample to include treatment and control countries that fall within a range of similar propensity scores, the model makes inferences on treated democracies only if a comparison (i.e., "matched") control country is also in the sample. This matching of the covariates across countries that did and did not receive the treatment, allows us to more effectively isolate the effect of the treatment on the final outcome.

standard deviation of corporate income tax is 2.2, thus this difference is nearly three-quarters of a standard deviation. And, the difference across the time periods is statistically significant: corporate tax revenue pre-liberalization in ISI vs. non-ISI democracies minus post-liberalization corporate tax revenue in ISI vs. non-ISI democracies is −1.64 units.

Conclusion

This chapter focuses on the role that strong corporate interests can play in resisting efforts by democratic governments to implement tax reforms post-shock. We look closely at corporate income tax revenue and corporate tax rates, since this has been a critical area of tax reform, and, at least in a technical sense, easier to implement than the VAT.[65] In democracies, we argue that powerful urban industrialists that received generous government support during the protectionist period will be the strongest advocates of lower taxes in the global economy. Given their political ties to the government, they can negotiate support for liberalization policies in exchange for tax concessions that will help them compete in the new global environment.

We explore data on corporate tax rates and revenues and government tax policy to assess our intuition. Our findings support the contention that democratic nations with strong legacies of import substitution industrialization are particularly susceptible to revenue shocks. Existing research assumes – but does not actually test – that governments are responding to large exporters' demands for lower taxes. In contrast, our findings suggest that the impetus comes from less productive firms that emerged during the import substitution period. Although, the possibility exists that these firms may form broader coalitions with exporters in their resistance to tax reforms.

Democratic policymakers are thus in a bind with globalization. As we show in this chapter, less productive – yet still relatively large – firms are likely to successfully lobby for lower taxes. It is increasingly common for such businesses to pressure the government for lower corporate income taxes to reduce their "disadvantage" in the global economy. At the same time, more productive firms demand low tariffs. The Philippines, for example, is currently lowering its corporate tax rate in response to business demands that the government set the rate "equal to the

[65] The VAT involves higher compliance, monitoring, and administration expenses relative to other types of taxes because the VAT involves both taxes and deductions (on taxed inputs) at multiple stages of production (Keen 2013). Even developed economies have been struggling to raise government revenue vis-à-vis the VAT (Keen 2013).

current corporate income tax rate of China, Indonesia, Malaysia, and Myanmar" and make the Philippines "a desirable place to do business."[66] Tariff rates were also reduced in response to industry lobbying to "help manufacturers grow their competitiveness by reducing the cost of their inputs."[67] Ultimately, democracies can neither easily resort to increasing domestic taxes nor rely as before on greater tariff revenues to fill government coffers.

[66] Cacho 2016.
[67] Vera 2014.

6   The Repercussions: Who Suffers?

Is it possible that policymakers' angst about low government revenues in Andra Pradesh (AP) is overblown? Is their desperate search for creative taxes and effort to target businesses an unnecessary endeavor? After all, AP has never done particularly well in spending its existing revenues wisely. Schools, hospitals, water, and sanitation departments continue to offer mediocre services and serve as a constant reminder of their government's ineptitude.[1] As the former Special Chief Secretary to the AP government recently asserted:

Both the Centre and State governments are spending the least amount on public health and a majority of the money is being paid to corporates. The State government is diluting the government health systems and nullifying the public schemes.[2]

It also cannot be ignored that international financial institutions (IFIs) such as the IMF have been treating taxes as both "good" and "bad" policy. Perhaps emphasizing tax reform to mobilize revenue post-shock is not a good strategy for developing countries after all.

Up to this point, we have discussed the conundrum that democracies are stuck in a revenue trap exacerbated by the loss of trade taxes. This seems like an unequivocal misfortune, since so many developing countries have substantial revenue requirements. Our findings thus far *assume* that they are now harder pressed to increase investments in much-needed infrastructure, health, education, and other development needs. On the other hand, authoritarian regimes have successfully recovered revenue, so there is an assumption that such investment on their part – if any – is unharmed. Is the conclusion truly that simple, in either case?

Put another way, we ask how trade liberalization, specifically via the loss of critical government revenues in democracies, transforms public

---

[1] See for examples "Andhra Pradesh Has Less Than 10 Percent Sewerage Treatment Capacity" (2016) and Prasadi (2016, 2017).

[2] "Andhra Government Expenditure on Healthcare Very Poor: Ex-Chief Secretary" 2017.

welfare in these nations. Are public goods, such as social benefits, infrastructure, and national defense, left inadequately funded? Will governments cut support for the poor? How does this compare to the changes in authoritarian regimes?

This chapter focuses on whether lower tax revenues post-shock have any real impact on developing countries. We investigate our driving assumption throughout the book thus far that lower revenues are problematic for developing economies. How has spending *actually* changed, in both democracies and authoritarian regimes? Could limited budgets in democracies in fact generate more efficient spending? Similarly, could additional revenue in nondemocracies actually damage efficiency, perhaps leading to additional rewards to favored groups at the expense of others? And how have the poorest segments of society fared in these different circumstances? Is inequality rising in liberalized democracies? This chapter seeks to answer these questions.

Could Lower Revenue Be a Blessing in Disguise?

The analyses in Chapters 3–5 are predicated on inefficient government spending in developing world democracies, and how it fuels low public confidence. Critics may justly contend that a lower revenue equilibrium, precisely because it "forces" lower spending, is a boon for developing countries. Indeed, many economists, including those at IFIs, have long been advocating for small government. The argument is that big government and the associated tax burden hurts growth, distorts allocation of resources in the economy, changes producer and consumer behavior, and creates sclerotic bureaucracies.[3] The current revenue predicament identified in this book may thus be a blessing in disguise. Take for instance, this recent report by the World Bank:

> [T]he excess burden of tax increases disproportionately with the tax rate … Likewise, the scope for self-interested bureaucracies becomes larger as the government channels more resources. At the same time, the core functions of government, such as enforcing property rights, rule of law and economic openness, can be accomplished by small governments. *All this suggests that as government gets bigger, it becomes more likely that the negative impact of government might dominate its positive impact* [emphasis ours].[4]

While development scholars might lament the loss of government revenue and its potential use for improving poverty, some economists might

---

[3] Bergh and Karlsson 2010.
[4] Gill and Raiser 2012: 363.

celebrate "small" government and the retrenchment of spending (and taxes) that were inefficiently distributed. Clearly, a tension exists in the IFI approach. On the one hand, they recognize that raising tax revenues is necessary for governments to recover the losses from trade taxes and serve their development needs; at the same time, they have long been supporting small government in the developing world, sensitive to the reality that higher taxes can adversely impact market outcomes.

In this chapter we analyze the impacts of changing revenues post-liberalization. At the heart of the issue is whether the loss of trade taxes is of any real consequence in developing economies. In other words, how does the loss of revenues in democracies, actually impact public welfare in these countries? We begin by exploring previous analyses of the distributional impacts of trade liberalization, particularly with respect to the poor and overall inequality. Scholarship on the extent to which the domestic political conditions can mediate the impacts of trade on public coffers and pro-poor spending is limited. Our analysis tries to remedy this by investigating if and how revenue shocks may be a critical aspect of the trade–poverty relationship, specifically by looking at how revenue losses from trade liberalization affect public goods, with an eye towards uncovering the manner in which government support for the poor in particular is changed.

In this process, we discover that once again, regime type is a key factor conditioning how trade affects the well-being of the poor. As democracies struggle to recover from revenue shocks, the poor may suffer the consequences of concomitant reduction of government services. In effect, while the poor may have been receiving meager public benefits before trade liberalization, such services are likely to get even worse after the adoption of significant trade reforms, and exacerbate pre-existing inequalities.

Liberal authoritarian regimes, on the other hand, appear to marshal their revenue success post-liberalization towards strengthening their ruling mandates. Our findings reveal that policymakers in this regime type use their post-liberalization domestic revenues to increase investments in critical public goods, bolstering their ability to sustain public confidence and social stability (as seen in Chapter 4). Inequality appears to be declining in liberal authoritarian regimes. Data on conservative authoritarian regimes, however, suggests that they are directing their surplus revenues for other purposes, such as, possibly, increasing rewards to their small ruling clique and/or enriching themselves.

Next, we provide, in more detail, the theoretical context and empirical support for the argument that regime type is a critical variable mediating the distributional impact of declining trade taxes in the developing world. Original survey data and cross-national data from the World Bank support the controversial finding that liberal authoritarian countries are indeed outperforming both democratic and conservative authoritarian countries in their poverty reduction post-liberalization.

What We Know about Trade and Poverty

Research on the distributional impacts of trade, particularly as it affects the vast populations of poor citizens in developing countries, is not as prevalent as one might expect. Two sets of scholarship explore the issue, one based in international economics (IE), and the other in international political economy (IPE). In IE, empirical research on the relationship between globalization and poverty has produced mixed results. Some studies claim that globalization has improved economic growth and thereby brought significant economic benefits to the poor over the past few decades,[5] while others contest the existence of a positive correlation between the two phenomena.[6] Still other scholars have tried to bridge the two sides of the debate, arguing that the effect of globalization on the poor is dependent on a multitude of factors – including institutions, policies, and initial conditions – and thus can vary both across and within countries.[7]

This literature also varies in its scope; some assess a collection of case studies or focus on a particular region; some present purely theoretical models; and still others conduct rigorous statistical analysis of cross-country data or microlevel data.[8] While each approach has its merits, the bottom line is that IE scholars have failed to reach a consensus on the relationship between globalization and poverty. Added to this, more recent research is needed. Most empirical studies analyze the 1980s and 1990s, which is when most developing economies had just begun liberalizing.

More relevant to our analysis, the vast majority of IE studies look mainly at the effects of globalization on overall growth, or on absolute measures of poverty, and not at broader concepts of poverty. The development community has long encouraged scholars to turn away from the

[5] Bhalla 2002; Dollar 2001; Dollar and Kraay 2002; Dollar and Kraay 2004; Hasan, Mitra, and Ural 2006; Porto 2003.
[6] Goldberg and Pavcnik 2007; Rodriguez and Rodrik 2001; Rodrik, Subramanian, and Trebbi 2002; Wade 2004.
[7] Agenor 2002; Amiti and Davis 2011; Harrison 2006; Ravallion 2001.
[8] Agenor 2002; Alfaro et al. 2004; Basu 2006; Dollar and Kraay 2004; Ghosh 2002; Maertens and Swinnen 2009; Nicita 2009; Porto 2006; Rao and Qaim 2011; Seshan 2014; Wade 2004; Wacziarg and Wallack 2004.

standard measures of growth, inequality, and income to assess progress in human development.[9] Overall, as renowned economist Ann Harrison laments, "there is surprisingly little evidence on this question ... Most works focus on the distributional consequences of globalization, rather than poverty."[10]

The literature in IPE has approached this question in another way, taking domestic political conditions into account and asking how it might affect the trade–poverty relationship. Using public welfare expenditures as the dependent variable, IPE scholars empirically explore if and how trade and capital flows impact government spending decisions on the poor. Unlike the IE literature, this (smallish) group of scholars seem to generally agree that developing economies are reducing spending on safety nets alongside greater exposure to international markets and competition.[11] They reason that developing country governments are striving to keep labor costs low in an effort to promote firms' export competitiveness and attract foreign capital.

Despite this emerging consensus in IPE, we still know little about how trade liberalization is correlated with spending and resources intended for the poor. Most of the dependent variables employed (e.g., social security, total education spending, Human Development Index) focus on programs that disproportionately benefit the better off in developing economies, not the poor.[12] It is also critical to emphasize that this strand of research has neglected analyzing the supply-side of the fiscal equation, which is how liberalization affects government revenues that have been directed towards helping the poor.

While findings in this chapter are suggestive and would benefit from further research, it begins to help fill critical gaps in both IE and IPE. First, by exploring how trade liberalization – once again operationalized

---

[9] See Nussbaum and Sen (1993).
[10] Harrison 2006: 1.
[11] Garrett and Mitchell 2001; Kaufman and Segura-Ubiergo 2001; Mosley 2003; Nooruddin and Simmons 2009; Rudra 2002; Rudra 2008; Wibbels 2006; Wibbels and Arce 2003. Note that Kosack and Tobin (2006) fits within this body of literature, but focuses on the negative impacts of FDI on human development (rather than welfare spending) in developing countries. Haggard and Kaufman (2008) observe variations in social policy across liberalizing developing countries. Avelino, Brown, and Hunter (2005), Kaplan (2013), and McBride (2015) are exceptions. Avelino et al. (2005) find trade openness to be positively associated with education and social security spending in Latin America. However, since social security spending tends to be targeted towards the better off in Latin America, the Avelino et al. (2005) findings would not indicate that trade is associated with greater pro-poor spending. Kaplan (2013) and McBride (2015) focus on financial, not trade, liberalization.
[12] Rudra 2008. See Rudra (2009) for a discussion of the nonpoor bias of the Human Development Index.

as the reduction in trade taxes – impacts broader measures of poverty, we underscore the importance of considering how revenue changes impact the well-being of the poor. This includes public goods such as infrastructure and defense, which arguably affect living conditions of both the poor and the nonpoor. Second, we explore how the impacts of trade liberalization might be conditional on our key political variable: regime type. In effect, our analysis adds to both the IE and IPE literatures by exploring if and how the loss of trade tax revenues is associated with government spending in various political environments, particularly those programs that more directly target the poor.

Trade Liberalization Revenue Shock, Politics, and Social Welfare

The theoretical foundations for the analysis in this chapter are based on the "starve the beast" literature – that reductions in government spending tend to follow decreases in taxes.[13] For precisely this reason, IFIs often advise developing countries to improve their tax ratio to fight poverty.[14] Recall that Chapters 3 and 5 establish that developing world democracies face greater revenue constraints after their adoption of trade liberalization than do authoritarian regimes. We anticipate that the dramatic cut in trade taxes in democracies is adversely impacting government programs aimed at improving public welfare, particularly those that disproportionately serve marginalized populations. If this is true, then pro-poor programs – such as social assistance or public works projects – that were already suffering from inefficiencies and leakages, may be getting even worse post-liberalization.

The poor are likely to be the most heavily penalized by the shortage of fiscal resources because of their inferior bargaining position relative to strong, organized elites. As political battles ensue over the distribution of now even more scarce government revenue, the less organized and least powerful interest groups in democratic nations are apt to lose.[15] Put simply, elected officials have even greater incentive to retrench pro-poor spending in the face of budget reductions, while protecting socially inefficient programs that benefit the better off. As Nooruddin and Simmons (2006: 1010) put it, explicitly pro-poor programs are "politically easy

---

[13] See Manage and Marlow (1986) and Ram (1988). While there is some variation on this hypothesis in the literature, the critical point for our analysis is that the predominant causal flow is from revenue to expenditure, at the federal level in particular (see also Romer and Romer 2009 and Talvi and Vegh 2005).

[14] Cottarelli 2011; IDB 1998: 7.

[15] See Nooruddin and Simmons (2006).

targets" since, "while certainly unpopular with citizens, [they are] less likely to hurt policymakers than cutting programs that are associated with well-organized and powerful lobbies."

As such, we expect the supply of public goods that disproportionately benefit the poor to be negatively impacted by declining trade tax revenues; politicians are more likely to use scarce government resources to protect powerful interests. It is also possible that government spending on politically high-priority programs may even increase despite tax reductions.[16] According to Nooruddin and Rudra (2014), governments necessarily increase spending on programs benefitting the more organized, better-off citizens as the risks and uncertainties of globalization intensify. And, while conditional cash transfer programs have proliferated across democracies, questions remain about the long-run impacts of these programs on chronic poverty.[17] Inequality should then increase post-liberalization in democracies.

Take, for instance, the case of now-democratic Liberia; the country is experiencing revenue shortfalls in part because its Economic Partnership Agreements with the European Union mandate substantial trade tax reduction.[18] In a purported effort to safeguard the poor, President Ellen Johnson Sirleaf declared cuts in inefficient government programs that benefit the better off (e.g., travel expenses and other benefits of government officials) alongside increased spending on development needs. And yet, shortly afterwards, Liberia's finance minister (Amara Konneh) reported on the regressive nature of public spending:

[T]he government of Liberia is spending [the] bulk of the revenue generated, about 60 percent, on administration which includes salaries and other incentives to government employees ... the Ministry has collected US$3.1 billion in revenue but 60 percent of this amount has been spent on government administration which represents just 40,000 people of the total population of Liberia.[19]

Another editorial in a major African newspaper entitled "Selling Democracy as an Endangered Demon to the Poor" reports:

To get a graphic picture of the unbalance, the fiscal budget is a hand-to-mouth document for the government and its officials because 80 percent of it is recurrent, which means money spent on the government and its officials, while

---

[16] Romer and Romer 2009.
[17] See, for instance, the Lomelí (2008) and Rawlings and Rubio (2005) discussion on the long-run impacts of conditional cash transfers on intergenerational poverty reduction.
[18] See Bilal, Dalleau, and Lui (2012).
[19] Fallah 2015.

20 percent is long-term, which suggests projects for redevelopments. Even in the latter, the kickbacks may as well go to recurrent.[20]

Thailand's new government faced a similar crisis of funding post-liberalization as a result of revenue loss followed by unsuccessful efforts at domestic tax reform. One newspaper reported, "Increases in VAT, excise duty and inheritance tax would not generate sufficient income to pay for populist projects."[21] According to the report, politicians shy away from implementing these taxes and, instead, actively lower both tariffs and taxes to please the corporate sector. Despite some increases in corporate tax revenues, Thailand's total government revenue as a percent of GDP has stayed constant throughout the 2000s; between 2003 and 2012, Thailand saw only a 0.02 percent growth in revenue.

In sum, these cases illustrate the broader theoretical point that, in democracies, when it comes to political battles between the less organized poor and the more organized elites over constrained fiscal budgets, the latter tend to prevail. A key implication is that inequality is expected to increase in liberalized democracies.

Our primary hypothesis is thus:

H1: In response to revenue shock, democracies will protect programs that serve the better off and spend less on the poor.

In contrast, we are ambivalent about the impact that declining trade tax revenues will have on the poor (and nonpoor) in authoritarian regimes. Recall that declining tax revenues are not of major fiscal consequence in this regime type; authoritarian leaders appear to be far more successful at raising domestic taxes as a substitute for the lost trade tax revenues. Of the two authoritarian regime types, liberal authoritarian (LibAuth) regimes are more likely to use expanding revenues to increase investment in some level of public goods, since this is key to their ruling mandate, which is to maintain social stability alongside higher taxes. Inequality should correspondingly be on the decline in these countries.

In Jordan for example, the prime minister stated his aim to direct government spending towards improving public welfare after higher projected revenues provided opportunity to engage in an "expansionary fiscal stance":

The government will respond by preparing a medium-term budget that will be ready for examination by the upcoming Parliament and government. As we draft the budget, we will observe the highest standards of fiscal discipline ... The criterion we will adopt is not populism, but justice manifested in sharing

[20] Kamara 2012.
[21] "New Government Will Face Early Crisis of Funding" 2011.

responsibility with the future generations and the fair distribution of economic burdens in a way that ensures a decent living for all. After thorough study, the government will build on efforts by previous governments to work out a mechanism to redirect subsidies to those who deserve them ... Our responsibility here is to ... address fiscal imbalances and direct resources to productive projects and sectors that add value and reflect positively on our economy and on all classes, especially the middle class and the limited and low-income segments.[22]

Of course, this could just be political pandering directed towards pacifying the masses; ruling elites in liberal authoritarian regimes may have little incentive to systematically *increase* redistribution in response to liberalization, since they are already maintaining some critical public goods that mitigate social instability concerns (as seen in Chapter 4).

We anticipate that conservative authoritarian (ConservAuth) autocrats will be less likely than their LibAuth counterparts to use post-liberalization revenues to improve public goods provision, since they tend to rely primarily on repression to govern. In China, for instance, the government introduced tax rate cuts in response to greater tax revenues post-liberalization. Upon achieving a smaller budget deficit and buoyant tax revenue, China announced more tax cuts and lower borrowing.[23] This lower tax rate may indirectly benefit low-income individuals, but will have no progressive impact on public goods or projects.

Is it possible that declining trade tax revenues might adversely impact the poor in authoritarian regimes, similar to what we expect in democracies? We contend that it is feasible that, although an authoritarian government's overall revenue-raising capacity is relatively unaffected by trade reform, it still may use this instance to penalize the poor. Budgets are still tight, and spending priorities still matter. For example, in the presence of limited electoral pressures, transparency, and accountability, both authoritarian regime types might use "extra" tax revenues to enrich the political elites and/or those in their ruling clique.[24] Take, for instance, the budget measures proposed in Dar es Salaam, Tanzania. Unlike democracies, policymakers did not make an effort to disguise their elite spending priorities at the expense of the poor: "The Council of Ministers in its decision on Austerity measures approved an average monthly spending of SSP 650Million for the remainder of 2011/2012, it also protected the salaries of all public employees and introduced cutting of operating and capital budgets by 50 percent for most agencies and the States transfer were to be cut by 10 percent."[25] Likewise, in ConservAuth

[22] "Fair, Free Elections Government's Top Political Priority – PM" 2012.
[23] O'Neill 2006.
[24] McGuire and Olson 1996.
[25] Goch and Panchol 2012.

Uganda, the government prioritized the House and Defense budget over the delivery of health services:

The government has slashed budget allocations to several ministries and referral hospitals so as to raise Shs300 billion *to pay for supplementary expenditure in State House and Defence*. News of budgets cuts in an already poorly funded health sector would be the latest indication yet that the NRM [National Resistance Movement] government is betraying its 2011–2016 manifesto promise to deliver adequate healthcare to all Ugandans. The NRM government had, in its manifesto, committed to spend more towards delivery of health services, including equipping all health units, scaling up supply of medicines, provision of housing, improved welfare for health workers and elimination of theft of medicines… [Members of the Parliament] Amos Lugoloobi (Ntenjeru North) and Judith Franca Akello (Agago Woman) expressed concerns that departments "notorious" for large spending like State House and defence don't suffer budget cuts [emphasis ours].[26]

To summarize, while we have relatively clear expectations regarding how poor democratic governments are likely to react in response to the loss of trade tax revenues, the response of more authoritarian regimes is difficult to predict a priori and must be subject to an empirical test. Our only expectation is that liberal authoritarian regimes are more likely than conservative ones to increase pro-poor spending (as is consistent with their ruling strategy) in response to trade liberalization. This may, in large part, be related to their effort to coopt opposition groups and maintain social stability in an uncertain global economic environment.

A Look at the Data

We now examine how the loss of trade tax revenues impacts public goods provision across the different regime types. If our intuitions are correct, we should observe declining trade tax revenues associated with cutbacks in government programs, particularly those aimed at the poor. It is important to note that poverty-related data, in general, tends to be sparse. The empirical observations in this chapter emphasize correlations, and reveal suggestive trends; they should not be treated as causal inferences leading to conclusive evidence.

To begin, Table 6.1 reports basic descriptive statistics on improvements (or lack thereof) in several pro-poor public goods across regime types. We focus on poverty outcome variables for two reasons: (1) cross-country data on pro-poor public goods spending is extremely limited; and (2) they serve as a rough proxy for the level of government efficiency in the vast

[26] Mugerwa 2013.

Table 6.1 *Comparing Public Goods Provision across Regime Types*

| | | Change between 1990–1 and 2011–12 | | |
		Post-Tax Inequality	Infant Mortality	Primary and Secondary Education Spending
Country Average	Nondemocracies	2.5	−33.66	−1.11
	ConservAuth	9.62	−33.53	−0.22
	LibAuth	−5.51	−33.89	−2.43
	Democracies	0.92	−20.96	−3.78

Note: The level of inequality is on a scale from 0 to 100; the negative values for the change in post-tax inequality suggest inequality reduction.
Data source: Solt 2016; World Bank 2016a

array of pro-poor public programs and policies. We also emphasize inequality as a key variable of interest capturing the benefits of the elite versus the poor. We include a post-tax inequality indicator in Table 6.1 to assess how income tax policies affect income distribution, i.e., the effect of taxes and transfers on inequality.[27] In each case, democracies do worse than the other regime types in their efforts to improve welfare outcomes for the poor; the rate of poverty improvement is even slightly lower than ConservAuth regimes. Liberal authoritarian regimes show the highest progress in all three categories.

Here again, we must use caution evaluating this data, given all its limitations. One option for cross-checking this information is to observe subjective perceptions of poverty by citizens living within these nations. What is the variation in the perception of public goods provision across democratic, LibAuth, and ConservAuth countries? We use data from our original survey, conducted in Amazon's Mechanical Turk (see Chapter 4), to answer this question. Recall that we assessed the survey respondent's satisfaction with public goods provision by randomly assigning them questions regarding: (a) quality of public primary schools; (b) quality of government hospitals; (c) supply of clean water; or (d) quality of roads. The scale of response is 1 to 5, from very dissatisfied to very satisfied. Figure 6.1 presents the average satisfaction with public goods in the low- and middle-income

[27] Solt 2016.

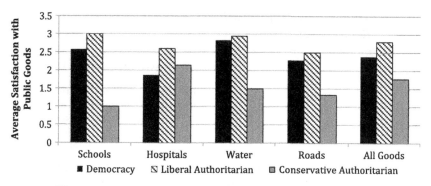

Figure 6.1 Satisfaction with Public Goods Provision among Low- and Middle-Income Developing Countries*

* Algeria, Bangladesh, Bolivia, Brazil, Bulgaria, Colombia, Costa Rica, Dominican Republic, Ecuador, Egypt, Ethiopia, Georgia, Ghana, India, Indonesia, Ivory Coast, Jamaica, Jordan, Kazakhstan, Kenya, Macedonia, Malaysia, Mauritius, Mexico, Moldova, Morocco, Nigeria, Pakistan, Peru, Philippines, Romania, Serbia, South Africa, Sri Lanka, Thailand, Tunisia, Turkey, Ukraine, Zambia

Data source: MTurk Survey

countries across the three regime types. Respondents in liberal authoritarian countries indicated higher average satisfaction with all public goods, suggesting that public goods provision is superior in this regime type and *corroborating the trends emerging from the objective poverty/inequality data*.

Next, to more rigorously test our primary hypothesis, we estimate a series of OLS models predicting poverty and broader social welfare outcomes. The unit of analysis is country-year, and the sample consists of all developing countries for which data is available from 1990 to 2013. Our primary dependent variables include a mix of both spending and outcome variables (as the data allows) to get a sense of levels and effectiveness of government spending. We make an effort to differentiate between spending on public goods that disproportionately benefit the poor and those that are geared towards the better off, since our analysis suggests that governing elites will protect the latter in the face of revenue shortfalls. This is not an easy challenge, since many social spending variables that are commonly assumed to be favorable to marginalized populations (e.g., social security) actually benefit middle- and upper-income groups that represent stronger vested interests in developing countries. It is also possible that some public goods, such as infrastructure and defense, benefit both rich and poor.

To address this, we draw from existing literature to differentiate between public goods that are mostly directed towards (1) pro-poor social benefits; (2) nonpoor social benefits; (3) infrastructure; and (4) defense. Our model takes this basic form following the poverty and spending models of Ross (2006) and Wibbels (2006), respectively:

$$Y_{i,t} = X_{i,t-1} * \beta_k + X_{i,t-1} * \beta_j + D\partial + T\lambda + e_{i,t}$$

In this model, Y measures the social welfare spending or outcomes in country i at time t, and X is the vector of independent variables lagged by one year. The model contains country fixed-effects (D vector) to address omitted variable bias. We also control for time effects (T vector) with year dummies. We include panel-corrected standard errors to address heteroskedasticity and serial correlation.

Our primary independent variable is the interaction variable: trade tax revenues and regime type. We focus on trade taxes reductions to proxy the revenue shocks per se, rather than the trade revenue shock variable from Chapter 3, which results in a tremendous loss of observations in our poverty models. If our predictions are correct, then the trade tax revenue*democracy interaction variable will be positive and significant for pro-poor benefits, and negative and significant for nonpoor benefits. In other words, in the face of revenue losses from trade liberalization, governments in democracies are more likely to cut pro-poor spending while protecting nonpoor benefits. We expect that as trade taxes decline, inequality will worsen in democracies (negative relationship). We are ambivalent about the expected sign and significance of the trade tax revenue*LibAuth and trade tax revenue*ConservAuth interaction terms. However, we concede that it is plausible that liberal authoritarian countries are investing greater resources in pro-poor public goods after engaging in (successful) domestic tax reform post-liberalization. Thus, it is hypothesized that, as trade taxes decline in liberal authoritarian countries, inequality levels should decline.

We treat insignificant results with particular caution. On the one hand, they could suggest that governments are protecting the status quo for these programs, neither increasing nor decreasing budgetary resources in the face of trade liberalization. At the same time, however, we cannot reject the possibility that the statistically insignificant effect is due to the relatively small sample size. Table 6.2 summarizes our expectations.

Variables that represent "pro-poor" spending are primary and secondary education spending, reductions in infant mortality, reductions in poverty, and female literacy. We also include inequality as a dependent variable to capture the extent to which public goods and government spending are reaching the poor in relation to the rich. Next, we compare

Table 6.2 *Predicted Marginal Effects of Declining Trade Tax Revenue on Social Benefits*

	Marginal Effect of Decline in Trade Taxes (Conditional on Regime Type)	Description	Interpretation
DV: Social Benefits for Poor			
Democracies	+	A one-unit decrease in trade tax revenue is associated with a one-unit decrease in social benefits for poor in democracies.	Revenue shocks in democracies are associated with welfare retrenchment for goods and services for poor.
LibAuth and ConservAuth	+/−/insignificant	If +, a one-unit decrease in trade tax revenue is associated with a one-unit decrease in social benefits for poor in nondemocracies. If −, a one-unit decrease in trade tax revenue is associated with a one-unit increase in social benefits for poor in nondemocracies. If insignificant, a one-unit decrease in trade tax revenue is not associated with social benefits for poor in nondemocracies	We are ambivalent about the impact of revenue shocks (which are replaced with domestic tax revenues) on social benefits in nondemocracies. Although, we leave open the possibility that liberal authoritarian regimes *increase* spending on the poor post-shock (a negative coefficient)
Dependent Variable: Social Benefits for Non-Poor			
Democracies	−/insignificant	A one-unit decrease in trade tax revenue is associated with a one-unit decrease in social benefits for nonpoor in democracies.	Revenue shocks in democracies do not translate into welfare retrenchment for goods and services for nonpoor.
LibAuth and ConservAuth	−/insignificant	If −, a one-unit decrease in trade tax revenue is associated with a one-unit increase in social benefits for nonpoor in nondemocracies. If insignificant, a one- unit decrease in trade tax revenue is not associated with social benefits for nonpoor in nondemocracies	We are ambivalent about the impact of revenue shocks (which are replaced with domestic tax revenues) on social benefits for nonpoor in nondemocracies.

these with how much declining trade tax revenues affect government resources allocated to higher income groups. These allocations would include social security spending (percent of GDP) and public employment spending (percent of GDP), as these are typically resources enjoyed by the upper and middle classes in developing countries.[28]

Finally, we assess whether democracies are increasing investments in public goods that conceivably benefit both rich and poor – infrastructure and defense – in response to liberalization. Infrastructure includes railroads, air transport, internet users, and access to water and sanitation. Defense spending is operationalized as armed forces personnel and military spending (percent of GDP). Certainly, it is possible that these public goods disproportionately favor the nonpoor. For example, air transport and internet can benefit elite groups who can afford and lobby for the provision of these goods in areas where the poor have limited access. Likewise, the elite may also be benefitting disproportionately from defense spending because of their larger employment presence in the armed forces. However, since this is virtually impossible to determine on a cross-national basis, we treat them here as potentially benefitting both rich and poor.

We include the standard controls of GDP per capita (logged), economic growth, and population (logged), as in Ross (2006). We also control for capital account openness, trade (percent of GDP), aid (percent of GDP), IMF credits (percent of GDP), debt (percent of GDP), and fuel exports, following our previous empirical estimations in Chapter 3.[29] Appendix K.1 presents descriptive statistics of all the key variables.

Table 6.3 summarizes the key regression results of trade tax revenue*regime type on various dependent variables related to social benefits for the poor, social benefits for the nonpoor, infrastructure, and military goods. It indicates where a statistical effect was found for the impact of declining trade taxes and for the interaction terms between this variable and regime type. Complete regression results are in Appendix K.

The results in Table 6.3 favor our primary hypothesis; in democracies, a decline in pro-poor benefits is associated with revenue shocks: lower primary/secondary education spending; higher poverty headcount; higher poverty gap; and lower female literacy rates. Table 6.3 further suggests that democracies are *increasing* nonpoor benefits such as social security alongside trade liberalization. Democracies also continue to invest in some military goods (i.e., armed forces personnel) alongside trade liberalization.

In an interesting contrast to democracies, liberal authoritarian regimes seem to witness improvements in social benefits for the poor alongside

[28] Huber and Solt 2004; Nooruddin and Rudra 2014.
[29] See also Wibbels (2006).

Table 6.3 *Poverty Regression Results Summary Table*

What is the marginal effect of declining trade taxes in each regime?			
	Democracies	LibAuth	ConservAuth
Social Benefits for Poor			
Primary and Secondary Education Spending	Decrease*	n.s.	Increase***
Infant Mortality	n.s.	n.s.	Decrease***
Poverty Headcount	Increase**	Decrease***	n.s.
Female Literacy	Decrease***	Increase*	Decrease**
Gini Index	n.s.	Decrease***	Increase***
Poverty Gap	Increase**	Decrease***	Increase***
Infrastructure			
Railroads	Decrease***	Increase***	n.s.
Air Transport	Decrease**	Increase**	n.s.
Internet Users	n.s.	Increase**	n.s.
Water	n.s.	n.s.	Increase*
Sanitation	n.s.	n.s.	n.s.
Social Benefits for Nonpoor			
Social Security	Increase***	n.s.	Decrease**
Public Sector Employee Compensation	n.s.	Decrease*	Increase**
Military Goods			
Armed Forces Personnel	Increase**	Decrease**	n.s.
Military spending	n.s.	Decrease*	Increase**

n.s. denotes not statistically significant; *** $p<0.01$; ** $p<0.05$; * $p<0.1$
Increase indicates a negative coefficient (negative relationship between declining trade taxes and dependent variable); Decrease indicates a positive coefficient (positive relationship between declining trade taxes and dependent variable).
Light shaded cells indicate an improvement in social benefits and **Dark shaded cells** indicate a reduction in social benefits.

trade liberalization. This is consistent with their ruling mandate, which is to maintain public confidence and stability by investing in public goods. Post-liberalization liberal authoritarian regimes show improvements in many poverty indicators: lower inequality, higher female literacy, lower poverty gap, and a lower poverty headcount. The data also suggests that infrastructure development – such as internet, railway, and airway – is also improving with liberalization. In contrast, military spending and public sector employee compensation (a mostly nonpoor benefit) are declining with reductions in trade tax revenue. Taken together, these results suggest that, in the liberalizing environment, liberal authoritarian countries are spending more on pro-poor programs and/or infrastructure, possibly at the expense of nonpoor benefits (e.g., public employee compensation). Inequality is correspondingly decreasing in these regimes.

The findings for conservative authoritarian regimes are intriguing. Governing elites appear to cut back both poor and nonpoor spending with trade liberalization, as suggested by the correlation between lower trade tax revenue and lower social security spending, lower female literacy, higher inequality, and a higher poverty gap. This may be for economic reasons (to improve export competitiveness, attract capital flows, and/or maintain healthy fiscal budgets) or for political ones (to enrich the ruling elites). We do see some improvement in primary/secondary education spending, access to water, and infant mortality rates. It is not inconceivable that ConservAuth rulers allocate some revenue surplus towards the poor, since all authoritarian leaders seek to prevent revolution, maintain stability, and require some level of political legitimacy, particularly in a more uncertain globalizing environment.[30] Nonetheless, the statistical pattern suggests that ConservAuth governments are reluctant to spend as much on public goods as their LibAuth counterparts. The exception is higher military spending and public sector employees. One likely possibility is that conservative authoritarian regimes are using their domestic tax revenues for political gains amongst their small ruling elite.

In sum, the estimation results in Table 6.3 and Appendix K reveal that the unintended consequence of openness (i.e., lower revenues) is that it further undermines the capacity of democracies to provide public goods and redistribute. In direct contrast to democracies, it seems policy elites in liberal authoritarian regimes are making concerted efforts to ensure that the poor are protected, while ConservAuth regimes appear to be minimizing public goods spending altogether.

Concluding Remarks

Previous research presents mixed findings on the impact of globalization on the poor. But our analysis suggests that the poor may indeed be harmed by lower revenues in the liberalizing environment, specifically in democracies and conservative authoritarian regimes. We find that trade revenue shocks in democracies are associated with contractions in goods and services to the poor: the pace of improvements in primary education completion, infant mortality, literacy, and poverty levels appear to slacken. At the same time, democratic governments tend to be reluctant to cut services to the better-off for example, formal sector-related social security benefits. Inequality is more likely to increase in liberalizing democracies.

---

[30] See Bueno de Mesquita and Smith (2010) and Desai et al. (2009).

In contrast, liberal authoritarian countries continue pro-poor spending (e.g., primary education and health spending) as well as spending on infrastructure projects post-liberalization. Inequality also appears to be decreasing. In conservative authoritarian countries that rely mostly on coercion to raise revenues, we find limited support for increasing poor and/or nonpoor benefits with trade liberalization. We suspect leaders in these regimes are using additional revenues to enrich themselves or their inner circle.

Findings in this chapter highlight that developing world democracies may be caught in a vicious cycle. As failings in public goods provisions underscore disenchantment with government, and cheating continues unabated, policymakers find it that much more difficult to increase taxes, and government coffers are strained. Low tax compliance then breeds further financial challenges for democracies to provide public goods and, again, exacerbates citizen disgruntlement. Brazil is a good example of this conundrum. As one (unemployed) protestor put it at a public demonstration: "We don't have good schools for our kids. Our hospitals are in awful shape. Corruption is rife. These protests will make history ... *We're massacred by the government's taxes ... This is a communal cry saying: 'We're not satisfied'* [emphasis ours]."[31]

Whether higher revenues in democracies would improve public good provision is a question that stands. Would effective domestic tax reform trickle down to the poor in democracies? While we can't test this counterfactual here, we can say that combining domestic tax reform with measures to boost confidence in government is essential for democracies trying to successfully raise revenues and provide for all their peoples.

The trends in this chapter are curious: How can governments in globalizing democracies continue to fall short on revenues and ignore the broader needs of society, far more than their nondemocratic counterparts? While the poor may have less confidence in their democratic leaders, it seems unlikely that they would stage a wholesale revolt against the system, given the protection of core civil liberties in democracies.[32] Added to this, "white elephant" projects in democracies are not just to impress the rich; temporary assistance programs targeted for the poor, such as public works, might "buy" hope and public support, even if they do little to improve their current situation.[33] All in all, we wonder how long democratically elected leaders in the globalizing environment can ride on the coattails of (often unfulfilled) promises of voice and change. We return to this puzzle in our concluding chapter.

---

[31] Gayathri 2013. Brazil's tax revenues were stagnant in the 1990s, increased in the early 2000s, and have been declining since the mid-2000s (World Bank 2016a). As Brazilian firms engage in high tax evasion (Pinto, Lisboa, and Batista 2013; Rapoza 2004), the Brazilian public ends up with the heaviest tax burden in Latin America (Ondetti 2015). In fact, the tax burden is heavier on lower-income groups than upper-income ones (Baer and Galvao 2008).

[32] Bueno de Mesquita et al. 2005; Sen 1999.

[33] Lal et al. 2010.

> I feel no problem if the government or any social leader makes a call for
> people to rise up and fight a problem for the nation. But that is condi-
> tional upon one basic thing. It should solve the problem.[1]

India represents a paradigmatic example of the challenges developing
world democracies face in their efforts to replace lost trade tax revenue
post-liberalization. It has faced struggles to raise revenues. Attempts to
reform the tax system have been met with resistance all around, and
implementation of what reform has passed has proved equally difficult.

Following India's balance of payment crisis in 1991, policymakers
embraced economic openness and began moving towards implementing
rapid reductions in trade taxes. Once this revenue shock hit, the Indian
government immediately placed domestic tax reform at the top of its
political agenda. However, implementing income and goods and service
tax reforms in response to the shock met both technical difficulties and
intense political resistance.

India's technologically weak tax administrative system includes a complex tax structure, high tax rates, and poor monitoring and enforcement
capacity. As is typical in developing economies, the tax system operates
with inept information systems and low levels of automation; such that
collections and audits rely on the whims of poorly equipped (and trained)
personnel. In addition, the majority of India's workers are employed in
rural areas or the urban informal sector. Efforts to collect taxes in these
hard-to-reach areas have been limited, resulting in an exceptionally
narrow tax base.

Politically, tax reform proved unpopular, to say the least. Businesses,
once protected, demanded lower taxes to compete in the global market.
Citizens proclaimed goods and service taxes unfair, and income taxes too
high a burden. In addition, the revenue problems generated by the shock

---

[1] Suyash Rai, a senior consultant at the National Institute of Public Finance and Policy,
quoted in Nielsen (2017).

115

proved harmful to already inefficient public goods. And with the population increasingly unsatisfied with how the government was spending their money, resistance to taxes and tax evasion increased. Devika Dhingra, a young analyst at PricewaterhouseCoopers in Gurgaon, near Delhi, feels paying taxes is her civic duty, but most of her peers tell her, "Paying taxes is of no use to us because the government won't do anything for us." For them, she says, it is like pouring money "down a drain."[2] In effect, India is struggling to achieve both voluntary and compulsory compliance to the tax reforms proposed after liberalization began, similar to other developing democracies.

Tax Structure and Administration

India's pre-liberalization tax system was, as a former chief economic advisor to the Indian government put it, "pretty miserable."[3] Taxpayers shunned a tax structure marked by remarkable complexity and excessively high rates. Multiple taxes on taxes had cascading effects that accumulated across the production-distribution chain.[4] Excise duties were complicated, spread across 24 different rates ranging between 2 and 100 percent.[5] Income tax structures were similarly dense; 11 different income tax brackets existed in the early seventies, with rates ranging from 10 to 85 percent, alongside wide-ranging incentives and exemptions.[6] At the same time, because of India's socialist history and emphasis on equity, income tax rates have been remarkably high. The marginal tax rate was effectively over 94 percent in the seventies, creating enormous incentives for evasion and avoidance.[7] It is no wonder that India's tax system was described as opaque and arbitrary.

India has a strong history of import substitution industrialization (ISI), which reinforced its reliance on trade taxes. Since the 1940s, Indian policymakers have protected "strategic" sectors such coal, steel, aircrafts, shipbuilding, power generation.[8] They also privileged public sector infrastructure, manufacturing, and industries such as automobiles and pharmaceuticals.[9] The Indian government became famous for being

---

[2] McCarthy 2017.
[3] Acharya 2005: 2061.
[4] Rao 2000. Inputs were routinely taxes, while credits on these taxed inputs were rare.
[5] Acharya 2005.
[6] Cnossen 2013; Das-Gupta, Ghosh, and Mookherjee 2004; Tax Administration Reform Commission 2014.
[7] Rao 2000.
[8] Armijo 1997: 203.
[9] Armijo 1997; Singh 2014.

the "License Raj," a reference to the complex and elaborate system of licenses, regulations, and bureaucratic hurdles set up to run, maintain, control, and protect certain businesses during its long period of protectionism, from 1947 through 1990.

Various administrations made concerted efforts to reform the tax system in the seventies and early 1980s, with limited success. As a result, the government's disproportional reliance on trade taxes continued until the early 1990s.[10] Just prior to liberalization, the 1980s marked the decade of highest central government tax revenue generation, spurred by trade taxes, as shown in Figure 7.1. Trade taxes were low in the 1970s in response to import quotas imposed shortly after independence to reflect India's longstanding commitment to autarchy.[11] By the late 1970s and early 1980s, the Indian government began embracing efforts to boost exports by loosening select import controls, resulting in high and differentiated tariff rates.[12] The weighted average tariff rate increased from 38 percent in 1980–1 to 87 percent in 1990.[13] The peak rate was 400 percent in 1990. This complex tariff structure resulted in varying effective rates of protection, and provided little incentive to be efficient. Regardless, trade tax revenues rose steadily, well into the late 1980s.

Liberalization and Domestic Tax Reforms

Shortly after liberalization in 1991 and the immediate reduction in trade taxes, the new Congress government, led by Narasimha Rao, elevated domestic tax reforms as a political priority. And indeed the tax reform agenda was critical for revenue (re)generation. Figure 7.2 shows the extent to which the Indian government took liberalization and their 1995 WTO commitment to reduce tariffs seriously.

The IMF facilitated India's liberalization process in the early 1990s by providing structural adjustment loans (SALs) and mandating "rapid and comprehensive" tariff reform.[14] In terms of revenue generation, IFIs called for decreases in trade taxes, reductions of major tax rates, VAT

[10] Burgess and Stern 1994; Rao and Rao 2006.
[11] Burgess and Stern 1994.
[12] According to Burgess and Stern (1994), four main factors stimulated export growth: greater subsidies and concessions to exporters; creation of a diversified industrial base; depreciation of the rupee; and a shift towards export markets in developing and centrally planned economies.
[13] Rao and Rao 2006.
[14] Topalova 2004. See also IMF (1998) and Panagariya (2004) for the role of the IMF in India's trade liberalization in the early 1990s. Maximum tariff rates, for example, were lowered from 400 percent in 1991 to 40 percent in 1997 (IMF 1998).

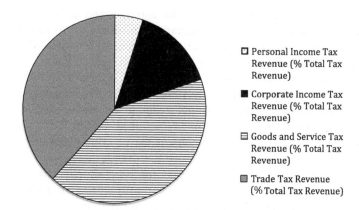

Figure 7.1 Tax Revenue Distribution in India Pre-Liberalization, 1980
Data source: Reserve Bank of India, Central Government Revenue Data

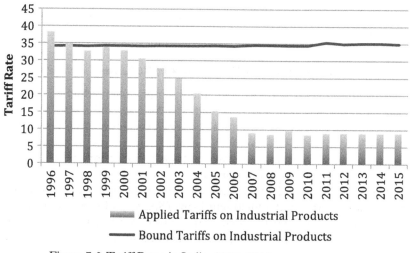

Figure 7.2 Tariff Rates in India, 1996–2015
Data source: World Integrated Trade Solution (WITS) 2016

reforms, and modernization of the tax administration system. A 1991 World Bank report states, "Tax reform is needed, most importantly to shift the incidence of taxation from tariffs (now about half of tax revenue) to domestic taxes since this will facilitate much needed tariff reductions."[15] Suggested tax administration reforms included addressing the audit process, strengthening of risk assessments, and training staff in computer operations.[16] The World Bank, Asian Development Bank (ADB), and the IMF thus emphasized three much-needed areas of tax reform in India: (1) designing VAT regulations; (2) reducing corporate income tax exemptions; and (3) providing technical assistance with tax reforms.[17]

In response, the Rao government promptly established the Tax Reform Committee (TRC), headed by senior economist Raja Chelliah. Three volumes of the TRC report (1991–3) constituted the first systematic effort of post-independence tax reform and "the finest treatment of tax policy and reform issues in India in the past 30 years."[18] Export taxes were largely abolished by 1992, except for select items such as tea and some minerals.[19] For the first time in decades, the 1991–2 budget included a significant reduction of import duties. This emphasis on low import duties continued through successive administrations, underscoring the widespread political acceptance of trade liberalization. As a result of such liberalization, trade tax revenue steadily declined, from 48 percent of total tax revenue in 1990 to 15 percent in 2014.

The majority of India's tax collection is conducted by the central government through income and trade taxes. The states' dominant source of revenue is the sales tax, but they also have the power to tax agriculture and other (relatively minor) goods and services, such as motor vehicles. Goods and service taxes are collected by both the central government and states (this relationship is discussed in depth later in the chapter). However, it is the central government that is the target of the much-needed tax reform efforts in India; the Government of India (GOI) collects roughly double the direct and indirect tax revenues (as a percent of GDP) of the states. The latter are thus dependent on central government revenues to fund public goods (e.g., education) for which they are mandated to provide by the Constitution.[20]

The TRC aimed to reform all the major domestic taxes: personal income tax (PIT); corporate income tax (CIT); and the goods and services taxes. The Committee's goal was to substitute for the lost revenue

---

[15] World Bank 1991.
[16] ADB 2009; Rao and Chakraborty 2007.
[17] ADB 2004; IMF 2015b; IMF 2016a; World Bank 2004.
[18] Acharya 2005.
[19] IMF 2002.
[20] States are primarily responsible for public health, while the states and central government are concurrently responsible for education, transportation, and social insurance (Rao and Singh 2007).

from trade taxes in three interrelated ways: broaden the tax base; simplify the tax structure; and reduce evasion. To achieve these goals, goods and service tax reform involved: (1) imposing a service tax; and (2) converting the excise tax into a value-added tax (VAT). A service tax was introduced for the first time in 1994, which was of critical importance since the service economy was rapidly expanding in India post-liberalization. In 1996–7, goods tax reform involved the "modified VAT," or MODVAT, levying indirect taxes on a large number of commodities.[21] In 2000, the MODVAT was converted to the single-rate CENVAT, or centralized VAT. In 2005, the VAT involved separate taxes by states and the central government on goods.

Personal income tax revisions aimed to achieve the main reform goals by simultaneously increasing the exemption limit and reducing the tax rates. The first set of direct tax reforms occurred in the early 1990s, to be followed by more in 1997–9. The Rao government proposed a new, simplified, three-tier personal income tax structure, with an entry rate of 20 percent and a top rate of 40 percent.[22] The maximum rate of the wealth tax was reduced to 1 percent, and the exemption limit continued to increase through different administrations post-1991.[23]

The primary change in revenue sources came from corporate income tax reforms. By the 2000s, the corporate income tax rate was reduced to 33 percent, but with significant exemptions; other corporate taxes included a 12.75 percent tax on dividend distribution, a minimum alternative tax on profits, a tax on fringe benefits, and various withholding taxes on interest, royalties, etc.[24] This rate reduction contributed to fast corporate income tax revenue growth in the 1990s, tripling as a percentage of GDP, from 0.91 percent in 1990–1 to 2.73 percent in 2009–10. The manufacturing sector contributed to the majority of corporate tax collections, though these collections have been declining since 2004–5 (see Figure 7.3).[25]

Despite this major overhaul of the tax system and some revenue success of corporate income taxation, however, overall government revenue generation has been disappointing (see Figure 7.4). After some initial success, revenue generation from domestic tax reforms began to taper in the mid-2000s. None of the individual taxes has been able to generate the same level of revenues as trade taxes in

[21] De 2012. Note that MODVAT was first introduced in 1986 on a limited number of commodities.
[22] Acharya 2005.
[23] De 2012.
[24] Poirson 2006.
[25] Rao and Rao 2006.

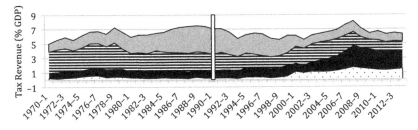

Figure 7.3 Tax Revenue (Percent of GDP) in India, 1970–2013
Data source: Reserve Bank of India

the 1980s. Despite improvement in the 2000s, the GOI laments the slow growth in the tax-to-GDP ratio. India's high GDP growth is small consolation in this context. As Indian tax specialist Govinda Rao put it:

The ratio is critical [to the Indian government] because if India's GDP is increasing and taxes aren't keeping up, there is huge amount of GDP that is not included in calculations. [It suggests a] huge amount of evasion taking place ... *India has failed to make up for revenue loss on account of phasing out customs duties, and this is because of lackluster tax reform* [emphasis ours].[26]

Similar concerns were reflected in the most recent Tax Administration Reform Commission (TARC) solicited by the Ministry of Finance in 2013. According to the Commission, India has one of the lowest tax–GDP ratios among comparable countries.[27] Even excise taxes – the primary revenue source in the 1970s – show a declining trend, primarily because of the continued use of widespread exemptions and the slow growth of the manufacturing sector (vis-à-vis the service sector).[28]

In the end, the TARC produced a scathing report of the progress of India's tax reforms, concluding that India's tax administration is "in a vulnerable position due to its static structure."[29] India's efforts to expand the tax base and reduce exemptions and reductions have fallen short of government goals, with the wealthiest Indians and largest companies

[26] Rao 2015.
[27] TARC 2014.
[28] Rao and Rao 2006.
[29] TARC 2014.

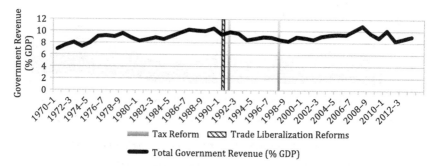

Figure 7.4 Total Government Revenue (Percent of GDP) in India, 1970–2013
Data source: Reserve Bank of India

paying the lowest amount of taxes.[30] The harsh reality is that the effective tax rate has barely improved post-liberalization, and pressures on (and resistance from) existing taxpayers have increased as a result.[31]

Political Resistance to Taxes in Globalizing Environment

Why have the Indian government's top-down efforts at tax reform had such disappointing results? The bottom line is that taxpayers have little confidence that the Indian government will use their tax dollars for the public good, giving rise to intense political resistance towards the government's new tax mobilization efforts. Despite widespread consensus that India is in need of major tax reforms, there has been increasing political opposition, alongside widespread tax avoidance and evasion. For middle-class voters, the key issue is that the current revenue system – in terms of both taxation and spending – privileges the wealthy and large business owners. At the same time, the wealthy elite – which include previous beneficiaries of the ISI system – lament India's high tax rates and complex system in light of poor government performance and their own efforts to conduct business in the more competitive globalizing environment. Rao and Rao (2006) attribute special interests' lobbying to the widespread exemptions throughout India's tax code. These politically charged constituencies are placing the Indian government in a problematic position as their drive to mobilize much-needed public revenue continues.

[30] Ghosh and Kumar 2012; TARC 2014.
[31] Poirson 2006; TARC 2014.

Mass protests towards the post-liberalization tax reforms are based on claims that the Indian government has been hosting tax policies that privilege business and deprive the nation of much-needed revenues.[32] This grievance spurred the Anti-Corruption crusade that galvanized the nation in 2011. In addition to Anna Hazare's hunger strike protesting political corruption, Baba Ramdev led national demands for the repatriation of black money from foreign banks.[33] Leftist parties accused the government's tax policies of "shamelessly supporting capitalists and corporates" by implementing unreasonable hikes in service taxes, eliminating property taxes, and providing heavy tax rebates for large businesses.[34]

Claims that India's tax system favors the wealthiest groups are not without merit; smaller businesses in India pay taxes disproportionate to their income, and contribute the bulk of tax revenue. As TARC reports in 2008–9, the numbers of corporate taxpayers in the lower income tax bracket (Rs. 0–100 crore) was 463,507, and those in the high-income slab (above Rs. 500 crore) numbered just 186 taxpayers. Banerjee and Piketty (2005) show that the top marginal income tax rate in India has been dramatically declining since 1991, concomitant with a rising income share of the top 1 percent. Public outcries for the government to stop the expanding opportunities for powerful groups to avoid taxation through loopholes and exemptions have gained momentum since the 2011 Anti-Corruption movement.[35] Despite reform efforts and protests to broaden the tax base, existing data suggests that the income tax base continues to be very narrow, adversely affecting tax buoyancy.

This low public confidence in government is exacerbated by longstanding frustrations that public spending has made minimal improvements in poor citizens' quality of life. Despite India's successful – and relatively rapid – reduction in *absolute* poverty,[36] policy analysts and Indian scholars alike publicly bemoan the government's failure to improve the living standard of the bottom strata. Despite decades of public planning, the provision of public goods such as effective quality primary education, public health, and clean drinking water still falls short.[37] Several empirical studies convincingly demonstrate that public education, health, and development-type spending in India have had minimal impact on (publicly) targeted

---

[32] Mehta 2010; Virmani 2014.
[33] Black money refers to "factor incomes which should have been reported to income-tax authorities but are not" (Kumar 2002: 9).
[34] "Left Parties Protest Centre's Alleged Anti-Poor Policies" 2015.
[35] Burke and Kumar 2011; Kannan 2011; Randolph 2011.
[36] United Nations 2015b.
[37] Bhagwati 2004; Drèze and Sen 2013; Virmani 2006.

groups.[38] Organizations representing marginalized populations frequently protest poorly functioning public goods, lamenting that they see little government improvement in response.[39] Neglect of social services for the poor is one big reason why India's center-left (and historically dominant) Congress Party, which campaigns as the "Party of the Poor," has fared poorly in recent elections.

Interestingly, while public survey evidence reveals that India's rapid growth has helped boost satisfaction with *economic conditions* in the last two years, confidence in the GOI's ability to improve public goods still wanes. As the 2015 Pew Global Report reports:

> Nevertheless, Indians believe their country still faces myriad challenges. More than eight-in-ten say crime, jobs, inflation and corruption are *very* big problems. Concern about air pollution is up 22 points in just the past year, complaints about poor-quality schools are up 20 points and worry about health care is up 15 points … Despite widespread satisfaction with their economy, their institutions and Modi, Indians nonetheless believe they face a range of very serious problems. And, in some cases, their concern is on the rise.

The World Values Survey further confirms the low and stagnant government confidence levels in India throughout the 2000s; it ranks lower than other middle-income nondemocracies, such as Jordan, which is a liberal authoritarian regime.[40]

It is thus not surprising that nationwide protests emerged against tax reforms, maintaining that the benefits of the proposed VAT in 2005, the new service tax, and other taxes (e.g., toll tax) are not directed towards average wage earners.[41] For instance, the public resisted the imposition of the toll tax as "unfair to commuters" because "roads are in poor shape and attendant facilities are sub-standard."[42] The Confederation of All India Traders (CAIT), which is an organization that advocates for small traders and businesses, took out a "VAT funeral procession" against the new taxes. The National Secretary of CAIT, Praveen Khandelwal, maintained, "we are continuing our strike against VAT, which will keep prices high and affect the poor."[43] Similarly, the Ministry of Finance

---

[38] Bhalotra 2007; Drèze and Sen 2013; Gangopadhyay and Nath 2001.

[39] "Authorities Get a Wake Up Call on the State of Roads" 2012; "Cong Gherao Against 'Poor' Healthcare in Nabarangpur" 2012; "Poor Suffer the Brunt of Doctor Shortage in Bhadrak" 2011; "Shiv Sena Protest over Water, Power Supply in Jammu" 2015.

[40] In India, survey respondents reveal an average of 2.6 on a government confidence scale of 0–4 (highest). Jordan's average score is 3.1.

[41] "Mumbai Eateries Go on Strike Against New Service Tax" 2013; "VAT: Traders to Appeal to President" 2005.

[42] Chaturvedi 2014.

[43] "VAT Implemented in 20 States Today" 2005.

reports that, "Indirect tax policy in India tends to be constantly battered by special interest groups that find it to their interest to have the structure cater to their particular benefit."[44]

An even greater challenge for the Indian government is posed by the fact that politically powerful wealthy groups, identified by the public as the beneficiaries of tax reform, are just as disenchanted with the administration's tax efforts. Large corporations have lobbied against India's new taxes, arguing that they are prohibiting their ability to effectively conduct business in international markets.[45] Their major objection is that, despite the lowering of India's tax rates post-liberalization, they are still too high compared to other nations, incentivizing them (and other investors) to favor alternate low-tax destinations.[46]

Indeed, India's corporate tax rate is among the highest globally.[47] One editorial review notes that, "lower tax rates would encourage companies to consider India as an important business hub and this would be in conformity with Prime Minister Narendra Modi's call to companies to 'Make in India!' "[48] Labor-intensive industries at the state level are concerned that high taxes would reduce their comparative advantage within India as well, possibly unleashing a "race to the bottom" across Indian states. Textile and garment workers in Odishu, for example, mobilized against a higher VAT in their state relative to its neighbors.[49]

The unfortunate consequence is that, as the Indian government attempts to balance the need for revenues with a response to business demands, India's tax structure has become even more complex. Indian businesses continue to lobby against "mindboggling layers of taxation."[50] This is why many – though not all – Indian businesses actively lobbied for the Goods and Services Tax (GST), which simplifies the VAT by posing one rate between the Center and states.[51] Fear of revenue loss, however, played a critical role in delaying its passing for over 15 years from the date when discussions first began, and still continues to be a concern.

Lackluster confidence in governance adds to business resistance towards paying taxes. As one New Delhi businessman put it, while

---

[44] Government of India 2004: 54.
[45] Mandal 2009; "Readymade Garment Dealers Stage One-Day Strike" 2015.
[46] Carter 2014; PricewaterhouseCoopers and World Bank Group 2014; Ramanujam 2002. See the Appendix of PricewaterhouseCoopers and World Bank Group (2014) joint Report on Paying Taxes: India is 158 on tax rankings and the Total Tax Rate in India is 62.8 percent.
[47] "India's Corporate Tax Rates among Highest Globally: World Bank Report" 2013.
[48] Vasal and Jain 2014.
[49] "Voice Against Tax Shriller" 2012.
[50] "Indian Business Owners Protest Against New Tax" 2013.
[51] "Indian Business Owners Protest Against New Tax" 2013.

admitting to breaking the tax laws: "Why should I pay my taxes while the politicians are getting richer and richer every day?"[52] High taxes, alongside ineffective public goods provision, particularly in infrastructure, contribute to the resistance by the rich to tax reforms, further encouraging both foreign and domestic businesses to invest outside of India.[53]

Globalization has also enabled other forms of tax avoidance, such as signing more bilateral tax treaties, which allow taxpayers to take advantage of tax havens abroad. In an effort to increase both foreign investment and trade, the Indian government has signed the Double Tax Avoidance Treaty (DTAT) with up to 88 countries, with 85 currently in force.[54] This treaty avoids taxes levied on two or more districts on the same (personal and corporate) income. Scholars argue that DTAT has allowed taxpayers to redirect domestic investment through certain countries, Singapore and Mauritius in particular, so that they can avoid paying taxes in India.[55] The World Bank estimates that such practices have contributed to a "black (nontaxable) economy" that is equal to a fifth of GDP, adding to public ire against wealthy businesses taking advantage of such practices.[56]

Adding to India's large "black economy" is India's large and persistent informal sector. Scholars argue that India's complex tax system, alongside the growth of trade, has contributed to the growth of this sector.[57] India's informal sector now accounts for almost 58 percent of GDP, and is only increasing with globalization.[58] Such large underground or informal sectors represent the large pool of resources that the Indian government fails to effectively tax.

Tax evasion takes various forms, including direct avoidance, underreporting, and taking advantage of loopholes. It is a known and acceptable practice in India. To date, tax evasion is not treated as a criminal offense punishable by law.[59] As Sonu Iyer, a tax expert at Ernst & Young in New Delhi put it, "The reality is simple: There are very few

---

[52] "Tax Evasion 'Rampant' among India's Wealthy" 2013.
[53] Giriprakash 2015; "Poor Infrastructure, High Taxes Deter Foreign Airlines from Investing: IATA" 2015.
[54] Nandy 2014.
[55] "Mauritius Overtakes Singapore as India's Top Source of FDI" 2014; "Singapore Replaces Mauritius as Top Source of FDI in India" 2014.
[56] "India's Shadow Economy: Evasive Action" 2013; Mehra 2014; Schneider, Buehn, and Montenegro 2010.
[57] Ghani, Kerr, and Segura 2015.
[58] Rada 2010.
[59] The Indian Supreme Court has only recently been considering tax evasion as a criminal offense, but only for the wealthy engaging in over 50 lakhs of tax evasion "to prevent any hardship to salaried and small tax payers" (Choudhary and Mahapatra 2015).

people who are paying taxes ... and tax dodging is everywhere. It's rampant – rampant."[60] But, it is not just the rich evading their taxes. Fewer than 3 percent of Indians file income tax returns at all, and officials claim only about 1.5 million taxpayers claim they earn more than one million rupees per year.[61] Empirical studies confirm that tax enforcement has been weak.[62] It is no wonder that India's overall tax compliance rates have appreciably declined since the mid-1960s, despite post-liberalization tax reforms geared directly at addressing this issue.[63]

In order to gain acceptance for the VAT when it was first implemented in the mid-2000s, policymakers immediately began granting exemptions. The government excluded a large number of products from the VAT, such as computers, bicycles, tableware, toys, and tractors, often "without good reason."[64] In fact, the public has labeled the current government the "exemption raj."[65] Empirical assessments of post-liberalization tax reform reveal its revenue impact has been minimal, and even negative in some states.[66] Large-scale evasion and weakness in VAT administration added to a disappointing revenue performance.[67]

Prime Minister Atul Vajpayee first initiated discussions in 2000 aimed to simplify the VAT by merging most of the existing indirect taxes levied by the Center and states into a single system of taxation, or what is now labeled the Goods and Services Tax (GST). The Indian National Congress party finally presented the GST to Parliament in 2011, finally passing in August 2016 under the reign of the Bharatiya Janata Party (BJP). The GST is meant to serve as "a taxation system that is economically efficient, neutral in its implication, simple to administer, encourages voluntary compliance and, most importantly, integrates India to a single common market."[68] The BJP fought hard for reform, arguing that GST would make the tax system more predictable and transparent, attract investment, and increase revenues. Many manufacturers also advocated for the tax bill because it would simplify the tax code and reduce business costs through recovery of the GST incurred on input costs via tax credits.

While the success of the Goods and Services Tax is laudable, and it is a much-needed improvement to India's complex tax system, all positive

---

[60] "Tax Evasion 'Rampant' among India's Wealthy" 2013.
[61] "Tax Evasion 'Rampant' among India's Wealthy" 2013.
[62] Das-Gupta, Lahiri, and Mookherjee 1995.
[63] Das-Gupta et al. 1995.
[64] Acharya 2005.
[65] Bagchi 2002.
[66] Das-Gupta 2012.
[67] Das-Gupta 2012.
[68] Chandran 2016.

revenue projections are based on a "flawless" GST that will be put in place.[69] But skeptics are numerous. The opposition contends that the BJP's tax reform efforts are "all carrot policy to traders."[70] There is concern that the GST – set at a rate aimed at improving industry competitiveness in the global marketplace[71] – will fail to boost revenues, particularly since it is lower than the recommended "revenue neutral rate."[72] India's businesses are already lobbying for exemptions and lower rates under the GST.[73] This is why *The Economist* laments the ongoing politically motivated exemptions negotiated in the GST, and its ultimate failure to prevent tax evasion, concluding that:

[I]t is disappointing that negotiations under way this week seem likely to result in a tax so complicated and multi-tiered that many of the benefits it offers will be bickered away before it is launched.[74]

Result: Low Government Revenues

As anticipated, political resistance from vested interests and the general public has successfully disrupted revenue mobilization post-liberalization, culminating in a low tax–GDP ratio. A vast array of exemptions, reductions, and loopholes have thwarted the three interrelated goals of tax reform: the tax base remains narrow; tax structure continues to be complex; and cheating is, by some measures, shown to be increasing.[75] The government has been accused of "meek surrender on tax reform," turning a blind eye to tax evasion and signing DTAT.[76]

Increasing corporate tax revenues is indeed one of the government's biggest tax challenges. To achieve this, GOI has proposed phasing out tax exemptions while simultaneously decreasing the tax rate. But this is no easy task. While passing the new GST has been a contentious political struggle, shifting the burden to direct taxes may be even more difficult, since it involves taking on powerful entrenched interests. Indeed, in the 2015–16 Budget, Finance Minister Arun Jaitley proposed the bold reform of reducing the corporate tax rate from 30 percent to 25 percent, while reducing exemptions and concessions. As expected, corporations

---

[69] Vaishnav 2016.
[70] Ashar 2016.
[71] Banerjee 2016.
[72] Dedhia 2016. The revenue neutral rate is the "single rate which preserves revenue at desired (current) levels" (Government of India 2015: 15).
[73] Ray and Jaipuria 2016.
[74] "Taxation in India: Take it Easy" 2016.
[75] Das-Gupta et al. 1995.
[76] Nayyar 2010; Vikraman 2016.

embraced the former proposal, but resisted the latter. The Confederation of Indian Industries (CII) is lobbying for an even lower tax rate of 18 percent, while both the bigger and the smaller companies in India continue to gain benefits from tax concessions.[77] For instance, in the 2016–17 Budget, large businesses (that host "large workforces") – many of which enjoyed significant subsidies during the protectionist era (e.g., manufacturing, textiles, gems, and jewelry) – will benefit from an increased basic exemption limit.[78] Not surprisingly, the revenue foregone as a result of tax incentives and exemptions in 2014–15 grew almost 8 percent per year, according to government statements.[79] This is, in large part, why the contribution of direct taxes to total tax revenue of the central government has fallen from 61 percent in 2009–10 to 51 percent in 2015–16 (provisional).[80]

Successive governments continue to respond to pressures from wealthy businesses by lowering the marginal tax rate and expanding the number of exemptions and loopholes. In the 2004–5 budget, the government abolished taxes on equity capital gains. The rates for short-term capital gains were reduced to a flat 10 percent, and the income tax exemption limit was raised, once again, in the 2014–15 budget. The many exemptions for company and personal income taxes persist, despite the recommendations of the recent GOI's Kelkar Task Force (KTF) report to phase them out. The newly elected Modi government once again raised the exemption and investment limit in 2014–15.[81]

The government's multifaceted challenge is that it must balance global market pressures for low taxes, appease conflicting demands from pressure groups (e.g., paying low taxes and wanting better infrastructure), and successfully implement domestic tax reforms. The bargaining power of wealthy groups has increased in response to the greater exit options in the globalizing environment; the Indian government is responding by granting a maze of deductions and exemptions. This strategy may certainly have boosted some sectors, but they have simultaneously created ambiguity and opportunities for more cheating and rent seeking.[82] At the same time, the majority of the population remains outside of a continually shrinking income tax bracket (recall that only 3 percent of Indians pay taxes, and the exemption limit keeps increasing). As Rao commented

[77] Magazine 2016.
[78] Surana 2017.
[79] Srivastava 2015.
[80] Allam 2016.
[81] "Income Tax Exemption Limit 2014–15 Increased" 2014.
[82] Nayyar 2015.

in a recent interview, the Indian government responds to public opinion, and the masses clearly do not want to pay higher taxes.[83]

With their backs against the wall, the Indian government has been accused of resorting to ad hoc and ineffective tactics ("tax terrorism") to raise much-needed government revenue.[84] "Tax terrorism" not only deters foreign investment and creates prolonged, expensive legal battles, it also generates little revenue for the government. Another ineffective, ad hoc tax instrument employed by the GOI is the minimum alternative tax, which stipulates a minimum income rate a corporation must pay regardless of exemptions or deductions. While the minimum alternative tax was introduced for domestic businesses in 1997, recent court cases have found foreign companies are subject to the tax as well.[85] Confusion on the applicability, consistency, and legality of the minimum alternative tax makes it a source of great tension among businesses in India.

So What?

The question remains whether India's disappointing revenue growth in response to big liberalization revenue shocks has had any real impacts on its citizens. After all, given that India's GDP growth has been impressive post-liberalization, it may well be that the low tax ratio and stagnant revenues are of no real consequence to the public. Recall, however, that our theoretical priors are that budget shortfalls will impact the poor more than vested groups who have the political muscle to safeguard the public programs and subsidies they favor. This is critical for a rapidly emerging nation, like India, that continues to struggle with widespread poverty and rising inequality. It was precisely this issue that gave rise to heated public debates during India's most recent election between two world-famous economists – Amartya Sen and Jagdish Bhagwati – and their conflicting views on why liberalization and concomitant GDP growth has not helped improve the lives of the poor.[86] Indian tax specialist Govinda Rao put it succinctly,

We should be in a position to generate at least 3 percentage points to GDP [currently spent on industrial subsidies] to release adequate resources for infrastructure, education, healthcare. We have amongst the lowest spending on healthcare. It is feasible and should be done ... *Expenditures on human development have been seriously constrained because of the low level of taxes that we have.*[87]

---

[83] Rao 2015.
[84] Nayyar 2015.
[85] Crabtree 2015.
[86] Bhagwati and Panagariya 2013; Drèze and Sen 2013; Harris 2013.
[87] Rao 2015. Emphasis ours.

Trends in spending cuts suggest that the revenue crisis is indeed adversely impacting the poorest sectors of the population, while programs and subsidies serving more privileged groups remain relatively unscathed. This is not entirely surprising, since public spending in India has a history of favoring public projects that benefit wealthier groups.[88] Rather, the critical point is that stagnant revenues post-liberalization are contributing to the widening gap between the rich and poor. The Indian finance ministry recently reported that government subsidies to rich industrialists, in the form of various tax exemptions and incentives, are approximately three times the amount spent on subsidies to the poor and farmers.[89]

By 2013, the center-left coalition government United Progressive Alliance responded to the shortfall of government tax revenues by enacting massive cuts to rural development schemes, such as the Mahatma Gandhi National Rural Employment Guarantee Scheme – India's largest pro-poor social program.[90] Then-Union Minister for Rural Development Jairam Ramesh protested the cuts as "savage" and "unproductive."[91] Cuts in both elementary and higher education were also proposed, and the Ministry of Human Resource Development did reduce spending on elementary and secondary education between 2014 and 2015. Likewise, the current Modi government is facing accusations that it is allowing critical poverty programs such as the National Food Security Act (proposed in 2013) and the Public Distribution Scheme (which dates back to the late 1930s) to languish in the face of revenue shortfalls.[92]

As our analysis anticipates, when revenue setbacks occur, spending cuts on the poor are prioritized over subsidies for privileged groups. Figure 7.5 indicates that tertiary education – which disproportionately benefits wealthy elites – has increased, despite proposed budget cuts, while primary spending has steadily decreased. Between 1999 and 2012, government expenditure on primary education peaked at 1.6 percent of GDP in 2000, and then steadily decreased to a low of 0.8 percent of GDP in 2010. Tertiary education spending, on the other hand, increased from 0.8 percent of GDP in 1999 to 1.5 percent in 2012.

Health spending has been taking a particularly hard hit. The current government is slashing social sector allocation in sectors such as health

---

[88] Keefer and Khemani 2005.
[89] "Tax Exemptions for Rich Costs Government Rs 4.6L cr" 2011.
[90] Ghosh 2015.
[91] Mehra and Shivakumar 2013.
[92] Patnaik 2015.

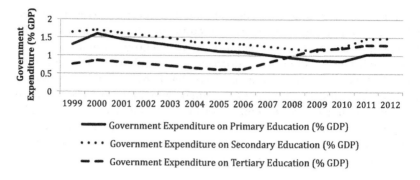

Figure 7.5 Government Expenditure on Education (Percent of GDP) in India, 1999–2012
Data source: UNESCO Institute for Statistics

even further.[93] In a country whose public health spending is already among the lowest in the world, the Indian government is putting key disease control initiatives at risk by ordering a cut of nearly 20 percent in its 2014–15 healthcare budget, due to fiscal strains.[94] Since the rich in India tend to resort to private healthcare, this is less of an issue.[95] Figure 7.6 depicts the government expenditure on healthcare between 1985 and 2012 using two different sources to maximize the time frame under analysis (data from India Stat [1985–97] is shown by the solid black line, while the dotted black line represents Ministry of Finance data [1996–2012]). Health spending declined from close to 1.5 percent of GDP in the mid-1980s, to approximately 1 percent of GDP in 2012. In particular, the GOI cut health spending significantly in the late 1980s and early 1990s, and subsequent spending (between 1995 and 2012) remained stagnant.

These trends shed some insights on why recent empirical studies have failed to find a positive relationship between India's liberalization efforts and poverty reduction. One study, for instance, found evidence that trade liberalization has failed to improve food security for the poor,[96] while others found that greater exposure to free trade increased (or failed to help) incidences of poverty in India.[97] Drèze and Sen (2013) best describe India's current paradox of liberalization:

[93] Nagarajan 2014.
[94] Kalra 2014.
[95] Drèze and Sen 2013.
[96] Panda and Kumar-Ganesh 2009.
[97] Jha 2000; Topalova 2007.

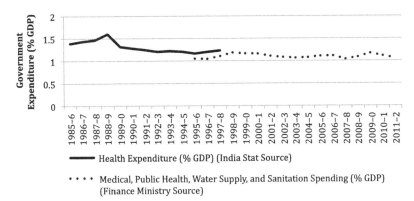

Figure 7.6 Government Expenditure on Health (Percent of GDP) in India, 1985–2012
Data source: Government of India Ministry of Finance, India Stat

The living standards of the middle classes (which tends to mean the top 20 percent or so of the population by income) have improved well beyond what was expected – or could be anticipated – in the previous decades. But the story is more complex for many others such as the rickshaw puller, domestic worker, or brick-kiln laborer. For them, and other underprivileged groups, the reform period has not been so exciting. It is not that their lives have not improved at all, but the pace of change has been excruciatingly slow and has barely altered their abysmal living conditions.[98]

Free trade may thus be responsible for helping India dramatically improve its growth rates and reduce absolute poverty, but the disappointing revenue growth which has also occurred likely explains why India has yet to improve the type of public goods provision that could boost its relative poverty rates. Our analysis provides one piece of the missing puzzle of why this is India's reality post-liberalization; it lies in the revenue challenges a developing world democracy faces in a rapidly expanding global economy.

Summary

The Indian case exemplifies the challenges of a democracy in raising revenues in response to trade-tax revenue shock. Similar to other democracies in this analysis, India is facing greater challenges because its tax administration structures are too inefficient to serve the needs of the

[98] Drèze and Sen 2013: 29.

broader public. Additionally, as a democracy, it cannot rely on coercion to pass reforms. Further, a relatively recent global study rated India as a "weak democracy" because of its corruption and "lack of accountability in its public institutions."[99]

Prior to openness, trade taxes were a critical source of revenue during India's import substitution industrialization period. After India's commitment to rapidly reduce tariffs following liberalization and IMF intervention in 1991, governing officials immediately began scrambling to implement domestic tax reforms.[100] Yet, in spite of the official commitment to raise revenues among the higher echelons of the governing elites, political challenges consistently plagued reform implementation in practice, particularly among state and local policymakers. Low government confidence and the absence of effective administration or enforcement generate mass opposition – both explicitly, through protests, and informally, through cheating and evasion. India's wealthy business elites are powerful vested interest groups that emerged from the import substitution industrialization era – the Birla, Tata, and Reliance industries for example – and international market openness has only added to their ability to avoid taxes.[101] These are India's central political challenges.

These political challenges even affect efforts at technical reform of the tax system. India is the largest borrower from the Asian Development Bank (ADB), which played a major role in facilitating tax reform, such as the adoption of the VAT. The Bank attempted to help build capacity to manage the tax, although generally not very efficiently. Afterwards, the ADB rated technical assistance towards VAT legislation (from 1996 to 2003) only "partially successful."[102] Traders in India, for example, have resisted computerization of taxation: "It will require a small shopkeeper in a village to keep a computer, which is not possible."[103] The programs were effective in improving legislative and regulatory frameworks, as well as administration systems and procedures, including automating tax administration and preparing for the introduction of VAT. Corporate tax revenues have certainly improved since liberalization, but overall revenue generation is still sputtering along. Ultimately, the report rated its program as not "successful," but "relevant."[104] In fact, a recent IMF report indicates, "India's revenue-to-GDP ratio remains considerably

---

[99] Global Integrity 2004; "Study Sees India as Weak Democracy" 2004.
[100] IMF 1998; Panagariya 2004.
[101] Kohli 2006.
[102] ADB 2004.
[103] "'Total Solution Project' Will Affect Small Businesses, Say Traders" 2016.
[104] ADB 2007. Even in the 1990s, the IMF (1998) indicated, "India's disappointing revenue performance so far reflects the partial nature of the reforms."

below its emerging market peers" and "Efforts to improve tax administration ... should be stepped up as the scope for revenue gains is large."[105]

The Indian government is thus in a conundrum; despite badly needed revenues, it must cater to powerful elite groups demanding lower taxes and exercising (and in many cases following through on) exit threats. That their democratic freedoms allow these groups to influence tax policy in this way is not unique to India. The challenge is that the trade-offs are far starker in democracies. And it is the poor who suffer the most because of it.

[105] IMF 2016b.

8   Conservative Authoritarian Country
       Example: China

> [There is] palpable fear that the "New Silk Road" will end up produ-
> cing a scattering of large, abandoned "white elephant" projects.[1]

In stark contrast to democratic regimes like India, China has made
impressive advancements in overcoming the revenue challenges of
liberalization. China's achievements in reforming "hard to collect"
domestic taxes are even more impressive given the inherent difficulties of
implementing such reforms. This is not to underestimate the tax mobilization challenges that China has yet to overcome. Rather, our central
point is that a conservative authoritarian regime such as China has been
more successful in overcoming revenue shocks – despite growing market
competition and global opportunities for tax evasion – in comparison to
its democratic counterparts.

Trade liberalization – which occurred in two major phases in the
early 1980s and early 1990s – introduced a revenue shock which
placed great pressures on China's two key revenue sources, which
were "easy to collect": (1) state-owned enterprises (SOEs); and
(2) trade taxes. It was only after China pursued its second round of
major tax reforms in 1994 that revenue collection was able to keep
pace with the spectacular GDP growth that began as far back as the
early 1980s.[2]

China faced considerable political resistance to tax reforms after the
onset of liberalization. Unlike India, however, tax protests did little to
hinder ongoing reforms, and the central government steadfastly improved
compliance and revenue generation. Coercion played a fundamental role
in the success of these reforms in the liberalizing environment, despite a
lack of pro-poor public goods spending (pre-reform).

---

[1] Broadman 2017.
[2] Rumbaugh and Blancher (2004) show that China's exports and imports grew faster than
world trade starting in the early 1980s. See Zhu (2012) for detailed discussion of China's
GDP growth post-1978.

Tax Structure and Administration

The central government in China holds the power to make policies, including taxes, but, unlike India, local governments are responsible for major tax collection efforts. This is because China's longtime strategy has been to place the burden of revenue collection on local authorities in order to compensate for its weak tax administration system and inadequate central fiscal capacity.[3] Fiscal decentralization also had strategic aims; central politicians could negotiate particularistic contracts (e.g., subsidies, tax arrangements) with provincial governments (that are members of their loyalist group) in exchange for political support.[4]

At the same time, the Constitution mandates that local governments hold limited powers of taxation. At least initially, a large majority of local taxes were remitted to the central government (i.e., "the Center").[5] This intergovernmental fiscal system has been fraught with poor administrative accountability mechanisms for local tax collection efforts and transfers. Additionally, a distinct urban bias – that places disproportionate tax burdens on rural areas – marks decades of inefficient financing and expenditure.[6] Even today, the Center continues to be dependent on local governments to collect taxes.

Prior to the 1980s liberalization reforms, China's public revenues were based on its communist economic model, which focused on collecting agriculture, trade, and industry taxes. Agriculture taxes levied on peasant families were the main source of government revenue during the centuries of imperial rule.[7] However, as the Communist Party of China came to power in 1949 and set up the command economy, the formal agricultural tax, which was already low (approximately 10 percent of grain output), began to steadily decline.[8] Figure 8.2 indicates that, at the dawn of trade liberalization, land taxes constituted 5.5 percent of total tax revenue. Agricultural taxes were completely abolished by 2006.[9]

---

[3] Bernstein and Lu 2000.
[4] Shirk 1993.
[5] Tsai 2004. More specifically, local governments cannot set tax rates, change bases of collection, or introduce new taxes (see Wong 2000). They can retain only a portion of the profits of selected local enterprises (Wong 1992)
[6] Wong 2009.
[7] Bernstein and Lu 2003. Wong (2000) argues these were relatively "easy to collect" since they involved only 50,000 communes (versus the current tax base, which includes 200 million households and millions of township and village enterprises).
[8] Lin and Liu 2007. Rather, the larger source of government revenue came from informal taxes on agriculture through price scissors, which increased the price of agricultural inputs (such as fertilizer, pesticides, water), while depressing agricultural output prices (Imai 2000).
[9] Kennedy 2007.

Trade taxes constituted one of the largest sources of revenue in the nineteenth century, and the second largest source of revenue during the command economy. China relied heavily on trade taxes (40 percent of revenues) from the late 1800s through the early 1940s, when it lost control of its ports to war.[10] By the late 1950s, the central government took full control of commerce, through planning and nationalization of all firms engaged in trade.[11] Tariff revenue collection accelerated again in the early 1980s *after* initial tariff reductions were instituted. As the Laffer Curve suggests, trade tax revenues may initially increase after tariff reduction. During this period, trade tax revenues accounted for 13–15 percent of total central government revenue.[12]

Finally, prior to liberalization, "industrial taxes" comprised the largest form of revenue; this was a direct tax or profit remittance from SOEs. The taxes and profits from SOEs represented up to 90 percent of government revenues by the early 1980s. Not only were the government-supervised state-owned industries profitable, but indirect taxes levied on their turnover (*gongshang*) generated significant revenue.[13] These taxes were product-specific and highly differentiated, with the lowest rates on products that were encouraged by the government, and the highest on luxury goods. Taxes ranged from 0 percent to 317 percent.[14] Figure 8.1 illustrates that, at the brink of liberalization reforms, profit revenue from SOEs constituted 51 percent of total revenue, while taxes on state-owned industries made up the bulk of "total tax revenue" (see categorical breakdown of "tax revenue" in Figure 8.2).

Like trade taxes, SOE taxes and profits were also "easy to collect." The government could monitor the relatively small number of SOEs under the command economy, despite its underdeveloped tax bureaucracy.[15] Administrative expediency resulted from the intermingling of profit expropriation and tax collection and the state ownership of the means of production.[16] As a result, public revenue growth between 1953 and 1979 (7.3 percent) outpaced income growth (6 percent).[17]

To summarize, as Wong (2000: 4) put it in a World Bank report, China's tax system was "simple and crude"; personal, corporate, or income taxes did not exist. There were relatively few taxpayers, and mostly they were

---

[10] Goetzmann, Ukhov, and Zhu 2007.
[11] Lardy 1992.
[12] Wang and Zhai 1997.
[13] Wong 1992.
[14] Wong 1992.
[15] Lardy 2003; Prasad 2004.
[16] Wong 1992.
[17] Wong 1992.

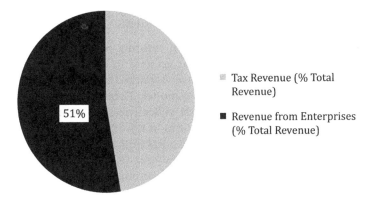

Figure 8.1 Government Revenue Distribution in China Pre-Liberalization, 1978
Data source: China Historical Statistical Yearbook

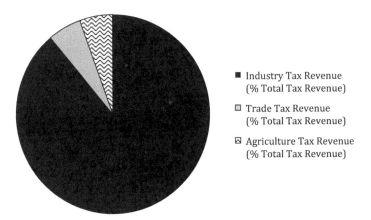

Figure 8.2 Tax Revenue Distribution in China Pre-Liberalization, 1978
Data source: China Historical Statistical Yearbook

SOEs, which were easy to monitor. The other source of revenue was trade taxes, which were also easy to collect. China's government revenue collection pre-liberalization was above the average of low-income countries.[18]

---

[18] The average tax revenue (for trade, income, and goods taxes) for low-income countries between 1975 and 1979 was 12.3 percent of GDP; China's total tax revenue in 1978 was 14.2 percent of GDP (Khattry and Rao 2002).

Liberalization and Domestic Tax Reforms

China's most significant trade liberalization reforms occurred in two phases, first in the early 1980s, followed by reforms in the early 1990s. The year 1978 was a watershed for China as it marked the beginning of efforts to reform its communist economic model. These early reforms, however, were aimed primarily at the de-collectivization of its rural economy.[19] The first phase of trade liberalization reforms, from 1980 to 1985, focused on promoting imports and exports through: (1) removing restrictions on creating foreign trade corporations; (2) opening special economic zones; (3) dismantling government planning of foreign trade; (4) pricing reforms of traded goods; (5) tariff reductions and export tax rebates; and (6) increasing SOE manager autonomy. The second phase of reforms in 1992 more specifically targeted the privatization of SOEs and the implementation of major tariff reductions.[20] Tariff rates fell to below 40 percent, which is considered a critical threshold for trade liberalization.[21]

China also engaged in "substantial" reductions in its bound and applied tariffs upon joining the WTO in 2001 (see Figure 8.3).[22] Tariffs on manufactured products, for example, were reduced from 24 percent in 1995 to 7 percent after WTO accession.[23] Interestingly, unlike India, the gap between applied and bound tariffs is minimal. This gap may reflect the leverage that exporters have over (democratic) governments, such as India.[24] China's revenue from tariffs (as a percent of GDP) peaked in 2001 and then declined in subsequent years.[25]

In comparison to India, China faced additional challenges while transitioning to a more liberalized economy. Developing an export-oriented trade regime went hand-in-hand with promoting the efficiency of SOEs, which dominated the economic landscape.[26] With

---

[19] Lin and Liu 2007. For instance, the collective production teams were disbanded, and individual households were incentivized to work sections of collective lands (Lipton and Zhang 2007). Other agricultural reforms included increases in procurement prices for major crops (negative effective protection reduced) and decreases in the amount of procurement in total agricultural production (Lipton and Zhang 2007).

[20] Takeuchi 2013; Zheng 2013. Trade reforms accelerated in the early 1990s as China applied for General Agreement on Tariffs and Trade (GATT) membership, eliminated central export subsidies, and increased local retention of foreign exchange (Gelb, Jefferson, and Singh 1992).

[21] Sachs and Warner 1995.

[22] Martin, Bhattasali, and Li 2004. See also European Union (2003).

[23] Ianchovichina and Martin 2001.

[24] Beshkar et al. 2015.

[25] Mohsin 2016.

[26] Branstetter and Feenstra 2002; Panagariya 1991; Takeuchi 2013.

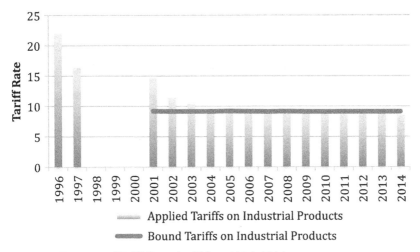

Applied Tariffs on Industrial Products

Bound Tariffs on Industrial Products

Figure 8.3 Tariff Rates in China, 1996–2014
Data source: World Integrated Trade Solution (WITS) 2016

trade liberalization, Chinese policymakers wished to enhance local industries' ability to compete on the global market. Trade reforms in the early 1980s immediately exposed SOEs to increasing competition from entrepreneurial local governments, collectives, private firms, and foreign investors.[27] Inefficient SOEs were thus seen as a major obstacle to China's ability to expand exports. Despite policy measures that were taken to improve incentives and raise SOE productivity, its decline in the first reform period was dramatic.[28]

The early 1990s reforms more aggressively targeted SOE efficiency by embracing privatization alongside major tariff reductions.[29] In both liberalization phases, the decline of SOE tax revenues and trade tax revenues dropped in tandem, as can be seen in Figure 8.4. The first major drop in both SOE and trade tax revenues occurred in 1984–5, followed by a second major reduction – albeit not as big – spurred by liberalization reforms in 1992–3. Reform of core public sectors was slow, however, and only gathered momentum in the mid-to-late 1990s.[30]

The trade liberalization revenue shock thus placed great strain on central government coffers as it involved major structural transformations from a centralized (command) system to a more (international)

---

[27] Li 1997.
[28] See Hofman and Yusuf (1995) and Wong (1991).
[29] Naughton 2007; Takeuchi 2013.
[30] Gallagher 2011.

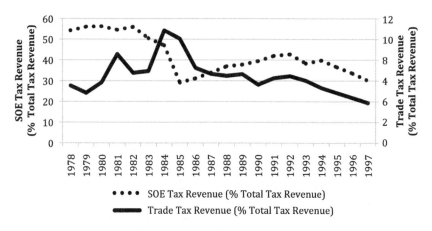

Figure 8.4 SOE and Trade Tax Revenue (Percent of Tax Revenue) in China, 1978–97*
* Based on data availability; SOE tax revenue not reported after 1997.
Data source: China Statistical Yearbook

market-oriented one. As Nicholas Lardy confirmed in an interview for this project, "the 1980s was the decade when trade expanded rapidly, but government revenue went down."[31] Indeed, in an effort to make up for the drastic revenue losses, each revenue shock was immediately accompanied by radical tax reforms. The first set of domestic tax reforms following the first liberalization shock in the 1980s began with the implementation of "enterprise taxes." Rather than remitting all their profits to the government, Chinese governing elites implemented the *Li gai shui* principle, or tax-for-profit, requiring SOEs to pay corporate income tax rate on profits at 55 percent.[32] In 1984, the implementation of the VAT, business tax, and product tax followed tax-for-profit reforms. Both the VAT and product tax were levied on industries,[33] while the business tax was imposed on services. The personal income tax (PIT) was introduced in 1980, but the exemption limit was too high to generate any significant revenue.[34]

[31] Lardy 2015.
[32] Shu-ki and Yuk-shing 1994.
[33] Product tax was imposed on the gross value of sold goods, while the VAT was levied only on net value (gross sales minus input price) of the goods. During the initial reform phase, the product tax was the primary revenue generator (see Shu-ki and Yuk-shing [1994] for details).
[34] Arsenault 2013.

One of the most critical aspects of the early 1980s fiscal reforms was the introduction of a revenue-sharing system with the local government. The objective was to give local governments greater incentives to collect taxes and balance their budgets. Three categories of revenues were created: (1) central; (2) local; and (3) shared. In an effort to improve equity amongst the provinces, the poorer provinces were able to retain a higher portion of shared receipts, while the wealthier ones were required to remit a portion of their surplus receipts to the center.[35] After the vast majority of enterprises were transferred to local governments by 1983,[36] local cadres began collecting corporate income tax (CIT) in their jurisdiction, part of which was remitted to the central government.

Despite these radical tax policy changes, the steady decline in fiscal revenues continued in the 1980s. Interestingly, much of the issues with China's new tax system in the 1980s mirrored the challenges India is currently facing with its tax reforms. These were, for example, the complicated and "cascading" tax structures caused by the large number of tax classifications (with only a small number yielding substantial revenue), coupled with the high number of tax rates (21 rates for product tax, 12 for VAT, and 4 for business tax).[37] As in India, the new tax system caused confusion among businesses and fueled concerns of paying dual taxes. A World Bank report in 1993 concluded that the "complicated rate structure remains a barrier to an equitable and efficient system."[38] The central-local fiscal reforms were also problematic, because wealthier provinces had limited incentive to collect revenues. Dependence on trade taxes as a key source of revenue thus persisted until the next set of domestic tax reforms.[39]

In an effort to return government revenues to their pre-liberalization levels (and above), China implemented another round of drastic domestic tax reforms in 1994. Critical to this analysis, this set of reforms followed sharp reduction in trade taxes in 1992.[40] The main objectives of this set of reforms were similar to India's post-1991 domestic tax reforms: simplify the tax structure, broaden the tax base, and reduce evasion. The tax structure was greatly simplified; more uniform VAT rates were adopted; the indirect tax system was revamped by using a standardized VAT (set now to 17 percent) to replace the product tax and the business tax (with

---

[35] Tsai 2004. This effort was not always successful and wealthier provinces gained more from reform (Shirk 1993).
[36] Groves et al. 1994.
[37] Shu-ki and Yuk-shing 1994; Toh and Lin 2005.
[38] World Bank 1993: viii.
[39] Wang and Zhai 1997.
[40] Zheng 2013.

pilot projects in 2012 and subsequent nationalization), and the rate structures were streamlined – all domestic enterprises were now on the same tax schedule, with the top rate reduced from 55 to 33 percent.[41] To expand the tax base, tax privileges for foreign companies were reduced;[42] and pilot projects for VAT on services expanded nationally.[43] Evasion was targeted by issuing a strong criminal code, increasing police enforcement, and implementing several anti-tax avoidance efforts, such as new general anti-avoidance rules (GAAR).[44]

Finally, the 1994 tax reforms sought to recentralize fiscal revenues by reforming the tax-sharing system. Only the PIT and VAT remained a shared tax, while all other taxes were classified as either central or local taxes. Revenue from the shared taxes was then redistributed among local governments.[45] This change, called the tax-for-fee reform, attempted to apply a standardized tax system to replace the vast array of taxes, fees, and levies that village leaders and upper-level officials had previously imposed on farmers (most often through harsh intimidation or coercion techniques).[46]

The tax trends in Figure 8.5 clearly illustrate that China has been successful in replacing – and even surpassing – the lost tax revenue from the two phases of trade liberalization, particularly after the 1994 fiscal reforms. Figure 8.5 once again shows the decline in SOE and trade taxes that reflect the first liberalization revenue shock (in the early 1980s), which continue through the second phase of reforms in the early 1990s. The VAT (or goods and services tax) represents the largest source of revenue growth post-1990s liberalization. CIT appears to be the second major source of revenue. Corporate taxes initially dropped, concomitant with the decline of SOE profitability, until the 1990s trade liberalization reforms promoted the privatization of SOEs. After reaching a low of 0.9 percent of GDP, corporate tax revenues begin rapidly and steadily increasing after the remarkable expansion of China's export growth, post-WTO accession in 2001.[47] The PIT still does not raise much revenue – it does cover more wage earners than in the 1980s and 1990s, but still only a small amount of the total population (8 percent).[48] As Figure 8.6 illustrates, consistent with Wong's (2000: 9) observation, the "seventeen-year decline [in revenue/GDP ratio] was finally reversed in 1996."

---

[41] Wong 2000.
[42] Riccardi 2013.
[43] Cui 2014.
[44] Farrell and Mui 2013.
[45] Tsai 2004.
[46] Luo et al. 2007.
[47] Yang, Zhang, and Zhou 2012.
[48] Ford 2011.

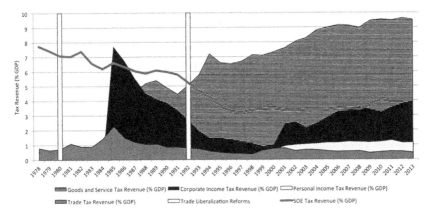

Figure 8.5 Tax Revenue (Percent of GDP) in China, 1978–2013

Note: SOE tax revenue 1978–97 calculated as Total Profit minus Total Profit after Taxes.

SOE tax revenue 1998–2012 calculated as sum of tax and extra charges on the principal business and value-added tax payable. Tax revenue includes both central and local taxes.

Data source: China Statistical Yearbook

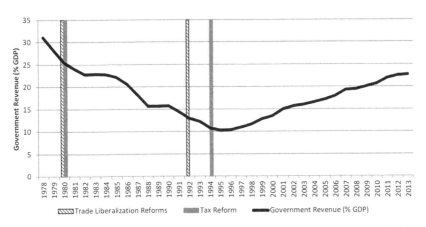

Figure 8.6 Total Government Revenue (Percent of GDP) in China, 1978–2013

Data source: China Statistical Yearbook

Political Resistance to Taxes in a Globalizing Environment

Despite the repressive nature of the Chinese government and China's history of coercion to implement tax laws,[49] post-liberalization tax reforms did not occur amidst political quiescence. The primary source of political discontent about the new tax laws and collections procedures has been located in rural areas, where the majority of the population in China resides.[50] Although China's regressive tax system has long overburdened its rural population, the last set of fiscal reforms exacerbated their discontent. The 1994 reforms to the tax sharing system (*fenshuizhi*) successfully increased the flow of central government revenues, but at great cost to rural sectors, particularly the poorest peasants. In the presence of poorly functioning basic public goods, protests linked to the increasing tax burdens have been rising, only to be met with brutal force and repression.

The institutional roots of the problem predate the 1994 reforms. In the absence of any autonomy in implementing taxes, local governments were held responsible for both the financing of and expenditures on nearly all public goods provisions in their jurisdiction (including the most vital and costliest public services such as infrastructure, education, health, and welfare). Expenditures have outstripped subsidies from higher levels of government for decades now.[51] To balance their budgets, local governments had little recourse but to raise "off budget" revenues (fees, licensing, fines, etc.), which did not have to be remitted to the Center.[52] Taxes from land sales and land use – which also make up a significant portion of business tax income related to real estate transactions – account for a large portion of revenue (30 percent or higher) at the local level.[53] Both these formal and informal modes of tax collection occurred amidst great repression and intimidation. Urban areas were spared for two reasons: first, they were paying lower taxes relative to their income; and second, high enterprise taxes comprised the bulk of urban revenues.[54]

The post-liberalization tax reforms of 1994 have exacerbated this urban bias; local governments are having more difficulty balancing their

---

[49] Wong 2001.
[50] Protests against taxes in urban areas also occur (see Lewis 2011).
[51] Tsai 2004.
[52] Bernstein and Lu 2000.
[53] Xu and Cui 2011. Note that estimates on revenue from land sales and use tend to vary widely (see, for example, Jinglian and Guochuan [2016] and Whiting [2011]).
[54] Chen 2008; Wang and Piesse 2010.

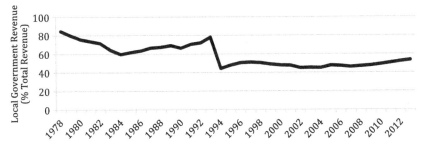

Figure 8.7 Local Government Revenue (Percent of Total Revenue) in China, 1978–2013
Data source: Chinese Statistical Yearbook

budgets and, as a consequence, tax burdens on peasants have been increasing. Recall that these reforms put the VAT as the main shared tax; this put great stress on local governments because the VAT was one of the key ways that local governments funded expenditures pre-reform. Accordingly, while the reforms boosted the Center's revenues, local government revenues simultaneously plummeted and then remained stagnant after the 1994 reforms (see Figure 8.7).[55] The strain on local revenues forced local townships to squeeze peasants harder to pay taxes *and* fees to finance local expenditures.[56]

Adding to their political discontent, rural citizens do not feel they are receiving public goods benefits commensurate with the extra costs of paying taxes. Neither does it seem that the increased central government revenue – some of which appears to have been directed towards the poor in recent years – has served to address their discontent. Similar to India, a storm of media and public criticism has been aimed at the quality of basic public goods provision.[57] The common view is that the central government prioritizes white elephants – large infrastructure project in particular – rather than investing in social welfare. As an example, public

[55] Local government revenue, as a percent of GDP, shows a slight increasing trend post-1994. However, the gap between local government revenue (percent of GDP) and expenditure (percent of GDP) suddenly and continually widened with the 1994 tax reform, and local expenditures continued to exceed revenues afterwards. See Appendix L.1.
[56] Bernstein and Lu 2000; An Chen 2008; Lin and Liu 2007.
[57] "China's Poor Rural Areas Said in Urgent Need of Teachers" 2008; "Official Says West China Sees Increasing Public Health Emergencies" 2006; "'Voices of the People Don't Speak for Masses" 2005.

healthcare experienced a dramatic decline between 1975 and 2005. According to Michelson (2012), "the proportion of rural residents with access to free community based health care dropped from 85 percent to 10 percent ... rural health care insurance coverage declined from 80 percent to 7 percent between 1980 and 1998."[58] Public infrastructure, drinking water provisions, and primary education are following similar downward trajectories and exacerbating urban–rural disparities.[59]

Public surveys on citizen attitudes in China confirm this discontent. One study, which conducted over 3,000 interviews of rural Chinese citizens in 2002 and 2010, indicated that confidence in local governments is impacted by the poor conditions of basic public goods, as we would expect.[60] Not surprisingly, overall confidence in local government is extremely low.[61] Another survey, of almost 4,000 Chinese citizens from 2003 to 2005, suggests that social welfare provision is among the chief areas of dissatisfaction.[62] More recently, Li (2016) finds, "popular trust in the Chinese central government is significantly weaker than five national surveys suggest."[63]

Widespread resistance to the post-1994 reforms has thus intensified. Local populations have resorted to massive protests, both peaceful (sit-ins) and violent. Local officials have responded to protests by collecting taxes through further intimidation and physical coercion. According to Bernstein and Lu (2000), local cadres use "means of dictatorship" to handle the instability, including forcible collections of funds, the use of tear gas, and paid responses by law enforcement agencies such as the People's Armed Police.[64] Local media reports confirm that scores of peasants have been beaten to death or committed suicide because of their overwhelming tax burdens and the brutal means of enforcement.[65] One source estimates that, right after tax reforms were implemented in 1994, at least 47 peasants died during tax and fee collection.[66] Tensions are also flaring over "land grabs." Local authorities are generating revenue by forcibly seizing private land at minuscule prices and selling to

---

[58] Michelson 2012: 133.
[59] Fu 2005; Jiang 2009; Song 2012; Wu 2010.
[60] Michelson (2012) finds that in the six counties he surveyed nonrandomly, perceptions of local goods provision improved. He notes, however, that his findings are not intended to be representative of rural China as a whole (Michelson 2012: 139).
[61] See Bernstein and Lu (2000).
[62] See Saich (2008).
[63] Li 2016: 100.
[64] Bernstein and Lu 2000: 758.
[65] Bernstein and Lu 2000.
[66] Cai 2008.

developers at exorbitant prices.[67] These officials are effectively selling as much as land as possible during their terms in office, "blinded by the prospect of this additional revenue."[68]

In this scenario, central government officials play a key – albeit complicated – mediating role that has thus far, on balance, favored the status quo. The Center is duly concerned that tax reforms fueling rural political discontent may be destabilizing to the regime.[69] The post-liberalization policy converting fees to taxes (i.e., tax-for-fee reform) was a conscientious attempt to address this issue, while improving the intergovernmental fiscal transfer system. Yet, the reforms have directly undercut this goal by increasing fees and overall tax burdens on local peasants. Both scholars and journalists further argue that the Center has actually served to embolden protestors by appearing sympathetic to their plight.[70]

The central government is thus caught in a conundrum; it is at once dependent on the local government to fulfill upper-level policy mandates and generate central government revenues, while still concerned with how harsh tax policies can fuel social instability that can threaten regime order. Local officials have been understandably confused by the unpredictability of central government support for their tax efforts.[71] At the same time, they are incentivized to maintain peasant tax burdens as their promotion by the central government depends on local socioeconomic development.[72] For now, the rural sector continues to shoulder excess tax burdens, while force and intimidation continue to support the post-liberalization tax reforms.

Result: High Government Revenues

In addition to using heavy-handed tactics, China appears to be gaining compliance to post-liberalization reforms by aggressively tackling tax evasion, and strictly limiting the number of exemptions to the CIT and VAT. In stark contrast to India, tax evasion is punishable by law and considered a criminal offense.[73] Harsh consequences for tax evasion persist, even after China removed tax avoidance from the list of offenses punishable by death in response to international human rights concerns.[74]

---

[67] Jianrong 2007.
[68] Cho and Choi 2014: 582.
[69] Bernstein and Lu 2000; An Chen 2008.
[70] Chan and Conachy 1999.
[71] Bernstein and Lu 2000.
[72] An Chen 2008.
[73] Li 1991; People's Republic of China 2015.
[74] McMaster 2011.

Now punishment ranges from fines to life imprisonment. This contrasts with the Indian government's treatment of tax offenses, which is far more minimal (seven years maximum). At the same time, blanket coercion is not the most (constantly) effective or foolproof means for mobilizing revenue; the Center's abolishment of agricultural taxes in 2004 was in response to a long history of massive rural unrest.

Officials are thus mobilizing revenue against a backdrop of discontent with the government. As one local resident put it, "People's living conditions are much lower than before. The grain price has gone down, but the taxes have not changed. People are discontented."[75] Disputes with tax authorities and plans to more strictly enforce taxes are often a source of discontent and protests.[76] Such practices bring local governments huge profits, enabling them to generate some tax revenue while liberally enriching themselves.

As indicated by the previous Figure 8.5, the VAT (under the "goods and service taxes" category) and CIT comprise the largest increase in revenues post-liberalization. While tax evasion is an issue in China[77] – as it is in most countries with weak tax administration systems – governing officials appear to be getting more aggressive in addressing it. China is mitigating cross-border tax avoidance alongside the new domestic taxes by adopting the GAAR and "look-through" policies, which involve more stringent checks to determine the true residence of the firm.[78] Corporate officials view cracking down on tax avoidance as an emerging trend in China.[79] For example, a tax partner at PricewaterhouseCoopers Services observes with respect to the "look through" approach in China:

Tax authorities are applying a "look through" approach, when it comes to the disposal of local shares. A well-trodden strategy used to be to make an investment through an offshore vehicle, either in what one might call a treaty friendly jurisdiction or in a tax haven. The idea would be that when the time came to dispose of the investment, this could be affected by selling the offshore entity rather than the local one, which would otherwise attract local tax.[80]

As a consequence, despite signing more DTATs (double tax avoidance treaties) than India (99), tax evasion seems to be comparatively less in

---

[75] Rennie 2000.
[76] For example, in Huzhou city, a dispute between tax authorities and a shop owner snowballed into a massive protest (Taylor 2012). See also "New Tax Plan Sparks China Protest" (2009).
[77] Fisman and Wei 2004; Sharkey 2004.
[78] Cheung 2012; Li 2010; PricewaterhouseCoopers 2015a; Shih 2015a.
[79] See also Shih (2015b).
[80] "Sealing off Tax Loopholes" 2009.

China.[81] The Chinese media has been heavily reporting the Mainland authorities' aggressive efforts at targeting tax evasion.[82]

China has taken several additional measures to increase compliance with reforms, particularly those aimed at political foes. First, tax officials have unleashed a "shock and awe" campaign in their battle against cross-border tax evasion. As noted in a statement by the State Administration of Taxation, "We will strengthen our combined investigation of major industries across borders, focusing on a series of major tax evasion cases, for the purpose of creating shock and awe in our anti-tax-avoidance efforts."[83] This crackdown applies not just to tax evaders but tax agents as well. For instance, 500 officials from taxation departments were sanctioned over illegal connections with tax agents in 2015 as part of this broader anti-corruption campaign.[84] Those outside of the central government's loyalist group get particular scrutiny – sometimes justly, sometimes not. Current President Xi Jinping has commonly used scandals involving accumulated wealth, dummy companies, and tax havens as weapons with which to attack political opponents.[85] Many politically contentious figures have been charged with tax evasion, including the internationally famous case of artist and government critic Ai Weiwei.[86]

Second, both compliance with the CIT and PIT have increased, albeit for differing reasons. The number of CIT exemptions has been significantly limited since 1980.[87] Table 8.1 contrasts the higher tax rates and vastly lower exemptions of China with India. The PIT revenue has certainly been increasing at a much more rapid rate in China, despite increasing exemption limits. According to Piketty and Qian (2010: 52), "Chinese income tax has become a mass tax during the 1990s, while it has remained an elite tax in India." Thus, despite increasing PIT exemptions in China, the number of exemptions is still lower than India's. In China, the threshold is below the median urban income; whereas, in India, the threshold is two to three times above it.[88]

---

[81] Devonshire-Ellis 2014; "Strict Tax Enforcement to Push China's Tax Revenue to New High" 2006. For example, according to the World Values Survey's Wave in 2000, "Please tell me for each of the following statements whether you think cheating on taxes if you have a chance can always be justified [10], never be justified [1], or something in between," the average response was 1.57 in China and 2.14 in India (World Values Survey 2015).

[82] "Beijing Targeting Tax Evasion by Multinationals" 2015; "Foreign Firms under Microscope" 2002; Shih 2014; Xiang 2013.

[83] Shih 2015b.

[84] "China: 533 Officials Punished for Ties with Tax Agents" 2015.

[85] Nakazawa 2016.

[86] See also Xu Zhiyong's arrest in Demick (2009).

[87] Piketty and Qian 2010.

[88] Piketty and Qian 2010.

Table 8.1 *Tax Rates in China and India*

	VAT	CIT	PIT
China	17% Exemptions or rate reductions available for certain primary products, medications, R&D products, small businesses, water, fuel, and exports.	25% Exemptions or rate reduction available for "New and High Technology" status firms, agricultural and environmental industries, and firms in special economic zones. Most exemptions and rate reductions are phased out after 2–5 years.	0%–45% Up to 42,000 yuan ($6,500) exempt. [Mean consumption per capita in 2010: $1,825** National income per capita in 2013: $5,500**] Percent of population subject to PIT in 2015 (estimated): 21.3%*
India	12.5%–15% Exemptions or rate reductions available for certain primary products, medications, information technology products, industrial inputs, fuel, books, and small businesses. All exports are exempt.	30%–40% Exemptions or rate reductions available for capital gains, dividends, R&D, hiring new workers, offshore banking, hotels and convention centers, export profit, infrastructure development, and for firms in specific regional locations.	0%–30% Up to 250,000 rupees ($3,800) exempt. [Mean consumption per capita in 2011: $730** National income per capita in 2013: $1,300**] Percent of population subject to PIT in 2015 (estimated): 2.9%*

*   The values in the table are projections by Piketty and Qian (2010). In 2000, Piketty and Qian (2010) calculated the percent of population subject to PIT was 9.4 percent and 2.9 percent for China and India, respectively.
**   World Bank 2016a
Data source: EY 2015; Hao 2011; KPMG 2012; KPMG 2014; Piketty and Qian 2010; PricewaterhouseCoopers 2015b; PricewaterhouseCoopers 2015c.

Tax Concessions to Loyalists

The discussion so far highlights how China's emerging tax system post-shocks has relied on coercive tactics targeting the broader population. To maintain this, it is just as critical for the government to dole out concessions to its loyalists, as discussed in Chapter 2. China's hesitation to levy land taxes is exactly the type of tax practice that is aimed at maintaining the loyalty of its winning coalition. Property taxes play a very limited role in the local public finance structure, despite being a more efficient, alternative source of revenue for local officials.[89] The biggest opponents of the tax are local government officials, followed by real estate investors and speculators.[90] This is in large part because the property tax would expose corrupt officials. As Ma and Adams (2013: 172) put it: "A property tax system, applying equally to all property-owners in China, would require records of who owns, who owes, and who paid. A 'sunshine' rule for property ownership would make corrupt officials more vulnerable to being exposed. Why would they want to do that to themselves?"

At the same time, all economic elites are not treated equally in China. The 1994 tax reforms, for example, were vehemently opposed by powerful SOEs. Recall that this reform focused on the VAT, but also placed more weight on the direct tax on corporate and individual income. In contrast to India, then, which tended to succumb to the practice of increasing the complexity of the tax system – in efforts to appease powerful interests – China "bravely" consolidated its five domestic enterprise income tax systems into one, promoting equity and rationality in the process.[91] The share of corporate income tax in China is still small, but steadily growing as a result. It is notable that these radical tax reforms took place with a critical eye towards maintaining ruling power. As the *South China Morning Post* (Hong Kong) reported at the onset of reforms: "the Central Committee will spell out ways to ensure the party's monopoly on power, in spite of its commitment to economic liberalization."[92] China continues to use lower tax rates to selectively reward certain firms, but not others.[93] The Aluminum Corporation of China Limited (Chalco) and China Petrochemical Corporation (Sinopec) are examples of productive firms identified as receiving special tax privileges.[94] China does give certain firms preferential treatment as they compete in the domestic and global market.[95] At the same time, they have demanded that these firms improve their global competitiveness.

In sum, using a combination of coercion and the "right" mix of tax policy changes, China has been able to recover from revenue shocks

[89] Cho and Choi 2014.
[90] Man 2012.
[91] Gensler 1995: 115.
[92] Lam 1993.
[93] Tubilewicz 2016.
[94] Sheng and Qian 2015; Tubilewicz 2016.
[95] Tubilewicz 2016.

post-liberalization. Before tax reforms, China's liberalization and high growth were not translating into higher government revenues. Numerous scholars concur that the 1994 tax reforms have been successful and sparked the increase in the tax–GDP ratio.[96]

So What?

The critical question is: How China has been making use of its improved revenue mobilization post-liberalization? Have governing officials been using these revenues to increase investment in basic public goods to help reduce urban–rural disparities and directly improve the livelihoods of the majority of its citizens? We identify two issues that suggest the bulk of its revenue success is not being shared amongst the masses, at least not directly. First, the 1994 post-liberalization tax reforms have made it even harder for local cadres to provide public goods, particularly in the poorest provinces. The second major indication is the Center's persistent tendency to prioritize development (e.g., infrastructure) expenses over basic public goods. However, more recently, we do see evidence that China is making more efforts to use revenue growth to improve basic services.

Recall that China's tax system has become more regressive because of the tax reforms. The direct consequence is that the quality of local public goods is worsening. The increase in central government revenues is not reaching the poor at local levels. With the 1994 reforms, the Center increased transfer payments to local governments to further ameliorate the burden on poor provinces. However, these funds are flowing into affluent lower-level regions and provincial governments.[97] Townships – the lowest (and poorest) level of administration in China – are facing the greatest challenge to public goods.[98] As one local newspaper summarized it: "The agitation over taxation levels is part of the wider resentment felt by the peasantry at declining living standards, perceived official corruption and the widening gap between rich and poor across rural China."[99] This is why China's biggest social challenge, to date, is to promote inclusive growth.[100] The regional disparities are stark and do not seem to be improving very rapidly.

---

[96] Kuijs and Xu 2008; Toh and Lin 2005; Tsai 2004; Wong 2000; Zhang 1999.
[97] An Chen 2008.
[98] Bernstein and Lu 2000; Lin and Liu 2007.
[99] Chan and Conachy 1999.
[100] IMF 2014.

Second, the Center's emphasis on economic development has not eased this inequity. Both journalists' and scholars' reports suggest that the tendency of Chinese officials to expend resources on large infra-structure projects ("white elephants") rather than investing in social welfare has persisted despite tax reform.[101] As Zhiwu Chen, an expert on China from Yale's School of Management, commented after a recent stimulus plan, "Indeed, while China's new stimulus plan overwhelm-ingly emphasizes infrastructure, it gives short shrift to social programs, such as health care and education ... This type of spending structure is nothing new to China."[102] Similarly, in response to questions on "Does China really need all this infrastructure? And what's going to happen when the bills come due?," Guo Tianyong, director of research for the Central University of Finance and Economics, commented in a recent media report, "'In China, we have an old saying: 'If it's medicine, it will have some poison inside.' '"[103]

In the last few years, however, there appears to be a favorable shift in spending patterns towards the poor. China continues to prioritize infra-structure projects but, at the same time, appears to be making efforts towards improving equity. Parts of the stimulus projects in 2014–15 include building affordable public housing alongside infrastructure projects.[104] As Nicholas Lardy commented in an interview, "China has a relatively weak record on increasing expenditure on social services, but they are recently doing better, such as their efforts to expand health insurance."[105]

The Center has indeed made concerted efforts towards improving health and education access. In 2007, the central government eliminated primary education fees – with emphasis on rural students – and began providing for the "nine-year compulsory education program" using minimal contributions from local governments.[106] Indeed, data from the Chinese Statistical Yearbook suggests that spending on key public goods – education and health – has been improving. The breakdown of education expenditure into primary, secondary, and tertiary levels

---

[101] Goh 2015.
[102] Zhiwu Chen 2008.
[103] Richburg 2010.
[104] Chang 2015; "China Puts Railways and Houses at Heart of New Stimulus Measures" 2014. Andrea and Zhan (2015: 2) are skeptical of such housing (and other migrant) initiatives in helping poverty or inequality as they "lure or force rural residents to leave land for the city and open up the countryside for agrarian capital."
[105] Lardy 2015.
[106] Xu and Cui 2011.

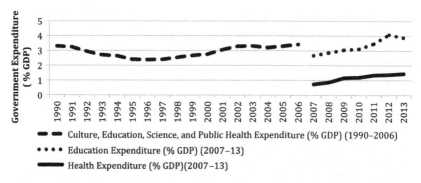

Figure 8.8 Government Expenditure on Health and Education (Percent of GDP) in China, 1990–2013
Note: Expenditure includes both central and local expenditure. Expenditure data trends exist from 1990 to 2006 and then 2007–13, due to different accounting measures by the Chinese Statistical Yearbook.
Data source: China Statistical Yearbook

is, unfortunately, not available. Health spending is improving and, according to our data, is one of the most rapidly expanding social welfare categories. This is largely because, in 2003, China, in response to growing health concerns and rural unrest, adopted a new health insurance system, the New Cooperative Medical Scheme (NCMS), which aims to provide universal health coverage.

While critical advancements in health and education have been made, empirical research finds challenges remain in addressing inequality, migrant needs, and higher quality care.[107] Education spending has seen improvements (see Figure 8.8). However, scholars argue that the level has been low compared to international standards and commensurate with China's GDP growth.[108] Both the level and quality of healthcare and education are still deteriorating in the countryside post-1994 reforms, while other administrative expenses of the township devoted to maintaining the bloated bureaucracy continue.[109]

More promising are recent efforts to expand the social insurance scheme to rural populations. China launched the National Rural Pension scheme in 2009. While scholars have long criticized the program for favoring urban residents,[110] it has succeeded in enrolling 326.4 million

[107] Chen and Jin 2011; Liu and Griffiths 2011; Meng et al. 2012; Wu and Zhang 2010.
[108] Dahlman, Zeng, and Wang 2007; Sheldon et al. 2011.
[109] Chen 2015.
[110] Saunders and Shang 2001; Ye 2011.

people in the rural sector.[111] In 2012, 55 percent of the adult population was covered by the social security old-age benefits program.[112]

Consequently, while China is devoting some of its government resources to quell social instability, the spending categories post-1994 with the largest growth rates are administration and social security. See Appendix L.2 for average annual growth rates for the various government spending categories. Lin and Wong (2012) conclude in one of the most recent studies evaluating the government's latest efforts in reducing inequality "at least in the early years of the new policy, the distribution of direct subsidies has not been able effectively to benefit the poor and protect disadvantaged groups."[113]

Summary

China's relatively successful experience with tax reforms in the liberalizing environment is a case illustration of conservative authoritarian regimes more generally. Of course, China is unique in certain aspects, including its pre-liberalization command economy model (and disproportional dependence on SOEs), large size, reliance on local government to collect tax revenues, and its export success followed by spectacular growth rates. Nonetheless, China exemplifies the broader approach used by ConservAuth regimes to increase domestic revenues when easy-to-collect taxes (on SOEs and trade) are no longer an option: coercion and taxing corporations.

This reliance on coercion was evidenced by the Center's imposition of the 1994 tax reforms despite popular resistance, the major re-centralization effort to redirect local revenues to the central government, the local government's brutal revenue collection techniques, and the harsh penalties implemented for tax evasion – both for individuals *and* corporations. That tax evasion often becomes a tool for targeting the political opposition heightens the public's risk perceptions related to noncompliance, even if the actual likelihood for discovery is still low. Recent tax reform in China has focused on getting "tough on corporate tax evasion" including collecting taxes from Alibaba.[114] A Chinese

---

[111] This program makes substantial progress over 1991 reforms in terms of loosening eligibility criteria, granting broader coverage, and, most importantly, providing substantial government subsidies to encourage the participation of the informal and rural sectors. The 1991 effort was based primarily on individual contributions (see Chen and Turner 2014; Hinz et al. 2013).
[112] Chen and Turner 2014.
[113] Lin and Wong 2012: 24.
[114] "China Plans to Get Tough on Corporate Tax Evasion" 2016; Yan 2015.

tax specialist even indicated, "the more high profile the company, the more likely that the government will have to make sure that taxes are collected."[115]

Overall, China's aggressive efforts to discourage tax evasion and reduce income tax exemptions suggest that international market pressures have not been as debilitating for revenue mobilization as they have been in India. However, challenges remain. The persistent urban–rural tax and spending divide, a still relatively narrow tax base, intergovernmental fiscal relations fraught with complexity (i.e., the mismatch between revenue responsibilities and expenditure assignment), and disproportional local reliance on land usage sales taxes are just a few examples. Although some of China's fiscal surplus has been redirected towards the poor, such as in health and education, the central government's redistributive efforts will continue to achieve limited success as long as these issues remain unresolved.

[115] Yan 2015.

9 Liberal Authoritarian Country Examples: Jordan and Tunisia

> Comprehensive fiscal and economic reform must protect the middle
> class and low-income people.
>
> Majesty King Abdullah II, Jordan
> October 10, 2017[1]

Jordan and Tunisia are examples of liberal authoritarian regimes. Each, while limiting political participation, do permit some political freedom, and put an emphasis on creating public goods to help coopt groups not included in the ruling elite. This puts them in a slightly different position in terms of reform than either India or China. Unlike India, they were able to use coercion, but unlike China, did not rely primarily on it as a driver of change. Instead, the Jordanian and Tunisian regimes more consistently pursued quasi-voluntary compliance as a key strategy.

Before liberalizing, Jordan and Tunisia both had high dependence on trade taxes and minimal reliance on direct taxation – typical of nations with weak domestic tax systems. With disproportional reliance on a mix of trade taxes and nontax resources, such as foreign aid, oil rents, and state-owned enterprises (SOEs), both Jordan and Tunisia hosted poorly functioning domestic tax systems in the early 1980s. Their challenges were similar to our other case examples and developing countries more broadly: frequent instances of double taxation;[2] complicated tax structures;[3] and a series of tax exemptions and loopholes.[4] In effect,

---

[1] "King: Fiscal Reform Must Protect Middle Class, Low-Income People" 2017.

[2] Transactions were often subject to taxes on both production and consumption in Tunisia (IMF 2000). Jordan had an excise duty on production, but did not have a domestic consumption tax in the early 1980s (Schroeder and Wasylenko 1986).

[3] IMF (2000) estimated 16 different tax rates on consumption taxes in Tunisia, pre-reform, ranging from 6.4 to 45.9 percent. Marginal rates on personal income taxes in Tunisia ranged from 10 to 80 percent (IMF 2000). Jordan's personal income taxes had five different maximum tax brackets (Schroeder and Wasylenko 1986).

[4] In Tunisia, each category of turnover tax had different rules and exemptions (IMF 2000). Jordan had a "generous system of deductions" for individuals and corporations (Schroeder and Wasylenko 1986: 15).

159

both Tunisia and Jordan had tax systems that were "complex, inefficient, and difficult to administer."[5] In order to overcome these challenges, Jordan and Tunisia relied on a degree of coercion, like China, but also emphasized national unity, and provided public goods that served a broad range of groups across the population, increasing the probability of quasi-voluntary compliance.

Tax Structure and Administration

As with India and China, Jordan and Tunisia have historically had weak tax administrations and limited instruments to raise tax revenues. All four cases ranked close to the developing country average of bureaucratic governance in the early 1980s.[6] In this sense, Jordan and Tunisia were fiscally similar to most developing countries, although, interestingly, their tax systems functioned better than their resource-rich regional peers.[7] Prior to liberalization, Jordan and Tunisia both depended mainly on trade taxes and used very little direct taxation. In fact, in comparison to the average developing country, Jordan and Tunisia had a much higher dependence on trade taxes, as revenue from tariffs at that time was close to 7 and 10 percent of GDP, respectively.

Figures 9.1 and 9.2 illustrate the composition of revenue, pre-liberalization. Trade tax revenue constituted 57 percent of tax revenue in Jordan and 31 percent in Tunisia. Jordan was able to rely on some foreign aid to boost revenues during this period, although it has been declining since 1980 (see Figure 9.3). Similarly, Tunisia's oil rents were high in the late 1970s and fell rapidly afterwards (see Figure 9.4). Direct taxes were predictably small in both nations due to narrow bases of collection,[8] while the General Sales Tax (GST) was a relatively larger component of the tax base in Tunisia. Tunisia's GST was composed of turnover taxes on production, consumption, and services, as well as an excise tax on luxury goods.[9] Jordan's indirect taxes in the early 1980s consisted of excise taxes and customs duties; it did not have a consumption tax.[10] SOEs were also a feature of Jordan and Tunisia's economies pre-liberalization, although

---

[5] Abed 1998; IMF 2000.
[6] In the early 1980s, China, India, Jordan, and Tunisia had a bureaucratic quality score of close to 2, on a scale from 0 to 4. The developing country average during this time was 1.4.
[7] Mansour (2015) discusses how the resource-rich Middle Eastern and North African countries have low institutional capacity for administering taxes, while nonresource-rich countries in this region have been successful in tax revenue mobilization.
[8] Nashashibi 2002; Schroeder and Wasylenko 1986.
[9] IMF 2000.
[10] Schroeder and Wasylenko 1986.

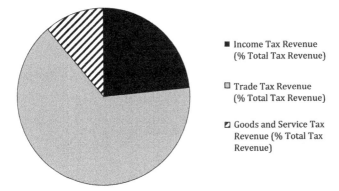

Figure 9.1 Tax Revenue Distribution in Jordan Pre-Liberalization, 1980

Note: All tax revenue data is provided by Rajeh A. Alkhdour, Head of the National Economy Division at the Central Bank of Jordan (Alkhdour 2015).

Data source: Central Bank of Jordan

not to the same extent as in China. In Jordan, SOEs were primarily concentrated in the mineral sector; the state was a major shareholder in the Jordan Phosphates Company, the Arab Potash Company, and the General Mining Company.[11] The Tunisian government maintained control and ownership of mining, transportation, and banking.[12] Overall, given relatively high levels of trade tax and nontax revenue, total government revenues pre-liberalization were larger in Jordan and Tunisia in comparison to our other case examples in this book.[13]

Liberalization and Domestic Tax Reforms

Both Jordan and Tunisia liberalized in the late 1980s due to balance of payments crises. The Hashemite Kingdom of Jordan adopted a liberalization program with IMF sponsorship in 1989, while the IMF introduced the structural adjustment program in Tunisia in 1986. Both of these economic decisions were driven by balance of payment problems and declining oil prices and remittances. With IMF assistance,

---

[11] Kanaan 2001. Jordan also had SOEs in electricity, transportation, and telecommunications (Kanaan 2001). The private sector was dominant in agriculture, construction, manufacturing, and services (Kanaan 2001).

[12] World Bank 2015b.

[13] See IMF (1995). China had similar levels of government revenue pre-liberalization due to its extensive SOE revenue to the state.

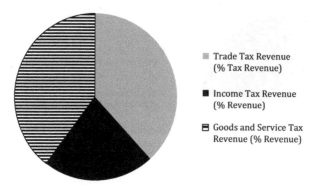

Figure 9.2 Tax Revenue Distribution in Tunisia Pre-Liberalization, 1975–80

Data source: IMF 1995

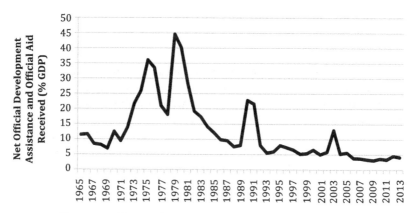

Figure 9.3 Nontax Revenue: Foreign Aid Flows (Percent of GDP) to Jordan, 1965–2013

Data source: World Bank 2016a

major steps were taken after the crises to reduce maximum tariff rates and liberalize the financial sectors. Additionally, both Tunisia and Jordan entered into several major free trade agreements with developed nations such as the European Union and United States and the broader global community that resulted in a mass drop in trade taxes.[14]

Tunisia and Jordan experienced a 37 and 54 percent change in average trade tax revenues, respectively, pre- and post-liberalization. India, in

[14] World Bank 2016a; IMF 2004b. Treaty examples include: Tunisia–EU 1995, Jordan–EU 2002, Jordan–US 2001, Tunisia–Pan-Arab Free Trade Area 1997, Jordan–Arab Free Trade Agreement 1998, Jordan–WTO 2000, and Tunisia–GATT 1990.

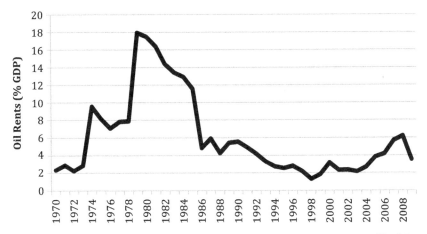

Figure 9.4 Nontax Revenue: Oil Rents (Percent of GDP) to Tunisia, 1970–2009

Data source: World Bank 2016a

comparison, saw a 34 percent decline. Further, Tunisia and Jordan's trade tax revenue started at a larger percent of GDP (close to 9 percent), while India and China's pre-liberalization trade tax revenue was closer to 3 percent (see Figure 9.5).

Although IMF and World Bank documents have deemed the liberalization process in both nations a "success," Tunisia still faces a far more complex tariff structure than Jordan. During the early stages of liberalization, tariff rates were reduced in Jordan in 1989, 1996, and 1999, from 300 percent to 35 percent.[15] As of 2008, the weighted mean of Jordan's tariffs was 5 percent.[16] While Tunisia has a relatively higher level of protection still in place,[17] the effective tariff (customs duties divided by import value) is low.[18] Applied tariff rates of both countries have been steadily decreasing since joining the WTO in 1995 (Tunisia) and 2000 (Jordan) (see Figures 9.6 and 9.7).

Regardless, Tunisia has seen strong economic progress with liberalization, doubling its exports in goods and services between 1996 and 2007. The international community corroborates Tunisia's successful global market integration. A recent World Bank report[19] and the Davos 2009

[15] IMF 2005. Maximum tariff rates pre-liberalization were quite high in the developing world. For example, Argentina and Colombia's maximum tariff rate were 400 and 521 percent, respectively (Berg and Krueger 2003).

[16] World Bank 2016a.

[17] Harrigan and El-Said 2010.

[18] Nashashibi 2002.

[19] World Bank 2009.

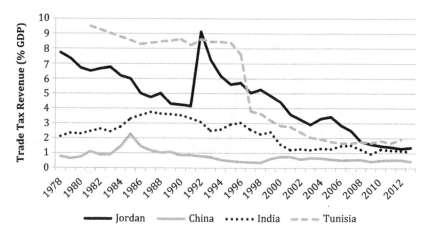

Figure 9.5 Trade Tax Revenue (Percent of GDP) Declines in China, India, Jordan, and Tunisia, 1978–2012
Data source: Central Bank of Jordan, Tunisia: IMF 1995 for years 1975–92 and World Bank 2016a for years 1993–2012, China Statistical Yearbook, Reserve Bank of India

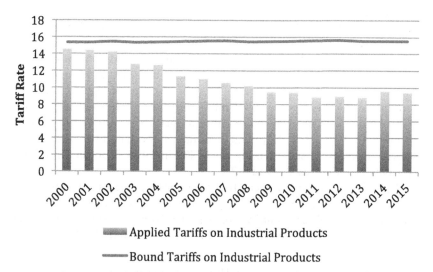

Figure 9.6 Tariff Rates in Jordan, 2000–15
Data source: World Integrated Trade Solution (WITS) 2016

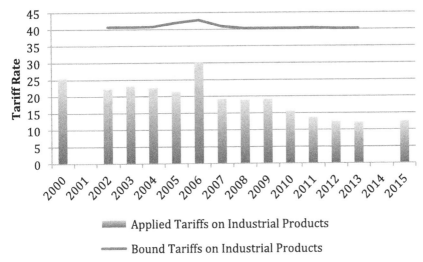

Figure 9.7 Tariff Rates in Tunisia, 2000–15
Data source: WITS 2016

Global Competitiveness Report[20] identified Tunisia as one of Africa's most competitive countries. In contrast, Jordan has not increased its exports as significantly, despite larger tariff reductions (and lower tariff levels) than Tunisia.[21] Figures 9.8 and 9.9 demonstrate how Tunisia's exports have been increasing steadily, while Jordan's remain more stagnant.

Despite differing levels of success in export growth post-trade liberalization, both Jordan and Tunisia were able to successfully replace the relatively large loss of trade tax revenues during this process. Tunisia's tax reforms have compensated for the revenue loss from trade, so that total government revenue levels are now reaching pre-liberalization levels. Jordan's tax reforms have resulted in a tax base that surpasses pre-liberalization revenue levels.

Both nations have implemented domestic tax reform to broaden their tax base and better rationalize their tax and tariff structure. In 1988, Jordan began to reform its taxes through the establishment of a consumption tax. The consumption tax base was further broadened in 1992, resulting in a strong increase in tax revenue.[22] Jordan's second major post-liberalization tax reforms began in 1994 with the introduction of the General Sales

---

[20] "Tunisia: 2008–2009 Davos WEF Global Competitiveness Report" 2008.
[21] World Bank 2016a.
[22] McDermott 1996.

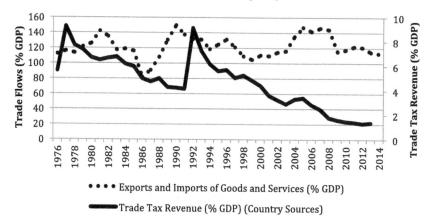

Figure 9.8 Trade and Trade Tax Revenue (Percent of GDP) in Jordan, 1976–2014

Data source: World Bank 2016a and Central Bank of Jordan

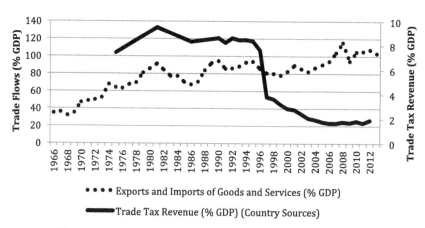

Figure 9.9 Trade and Trade Tax Revenue (Percent of GDP) in Tunisia, 1966–2013

Data source: World Bank 2016a, IMF 1995 for years 1975–92, and World Bank 2016a for years 1993–2012

Tax (GST), which evolved into a full-fledged VAT by 1999. Government officials also took steps to widen the tax base for the GST by extending it to retail sales and a broad range of services, as well as reducing instances of exemptions and zero-rating (other than for exports).[23]

[23] IMF 2004a.

Jordan's personal income tax (PIT) and corporate income tax (CIT) reforms to expand the base occurred throughout the late 1990s and early 2000s, through the exclusion of tax holidays and lowering of minimum rates. Income taxes were recently reformed in 2014 to increase the tax rates for individuals and corporations.[24] However, similar to the other case studies in this book, direct income taxes still comprise the lowest contribution to Jordan's tax base.[25]

Tax reforms in Tunisia first occurred in 1987 and 1988 with the adoption of the VAT, the introduction of a single PIT, and the simplification of the CIT. While the 1988 VAT reform essentially unified the previous three turnover taxes and excise tax, the VAT was further simplified and the coverage broadened throughout the 1990s. Reforms to the PIT and CIT in the 1990s in Tunisia reduced the brackets from 18 to 6 and 6 to 2, respectively.[26] Tariffs were also reduced and simplified during this time period. Tunisia's second major set of tax reforms occurred in 1997 and 1998 with increases and extensions of the VAT and income taxes. It was the second phase of tax reforms that resulted in enough revenue generation for Tunisia to compensate for the rapid decline in trade tax revenue.[27]

Figures 9.10 and 9.11 present the composition of tax revenue in Jordan and Tunisia between the 1970s and today. Jordan's GST revenue is a major contributing factor to the increases in government revenue (see Figure 9.10). Such GST revenue collection has been (more than) sufficient to replace the declines in trade tax revenue in Jordan.[28] Since the mid-1990s, Tunisia has seen large increases in GST revenue and the resulting recovery of government revenue lost from trade liberalization. In recent years, with the larger increases in income tax revenue, government revenues have seen a larger upward trend in Tunisia (see Figure 9.11).

Total government revenue trends pre- and post-liberalization are depicted in Figures 9.12 and 9.13. In essence, in Jordan, total government revenues increased after the first set of major reforms in the late 1980s, and then remained relatively stable after the implementation of GST in the early 1990s (see Figure 9.12). This is an impressive revenue recovery after the large reductions in Jordan's trade tax revenue. Total government revenue then increased in the early 2000s, with the final adoption of the VAT and subsequent widening of the base and increases in rates. Overall, Jordan's government revenues have recovered

[24] PricewaterhouseCoopers 2015a.
[25] USAID 2010.
[26] IMF 2000.
[27] Baliamoune-Lutz 2009.
[28] USAID 2014a.

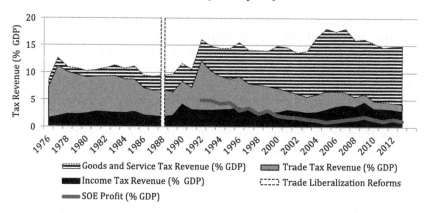

Figure 9.10 Tax Revenue (Percent of GDP) in Jordan, 1976–2013
Data source: Central Bank of Jordan and General Budget Department in Jordan Government. Government of Jordan. Ministry of Finance.

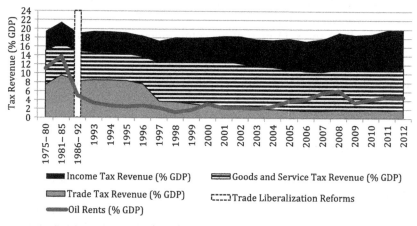

Figure 9.11 Tax Revenue (Percent of GDP) in Tunisia, 1975–2012
Data source: IMF 1995 for years 1975–92 and World Bank 2016a for years 1993–2012

from steep declines in both trade tax revenue and SOE profit. In Tunisia, the first reform period did not result in a rise in total government revenue – large drops in oil rents and trade taxes contributed to the overall revenue declines. However, subsequent reforms and increased direct taxation revenue have contributed to increasing government revenue in the mid-2000s in Tunisia (see Figure 9.13). Despite large losses of trade tax

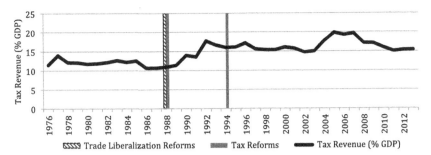

Figure 9.12 Total Tax Revenue (Percent of GDP) in Jordan, 1976–2013
Note: We employ total tax revenue instead of government revenue due
to data limitations.
Data source: Central Bank of Jordan

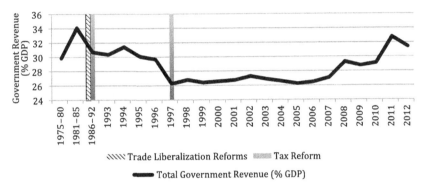

Figure 9.13 Total Government Revenue (Percent of GDP) in Tunisia,
1975–2012
Data source: World Bank 2016a and IMF 1995

revenue (compared to other developing countries), Tunisia's government
revenue is now reaching pre-liberalization levels because of large annual
increases between 2005 and 2012.

In sum, both Jordan and Tunisia adopted and implemented successful
tax reforms post-liberalization.[29] As the Head of the National Economy
Division at the Central Bank of Jordan explains, "we did very well
compared to our neighbors."[30] Many scholars and practitioners have

[29] In the 2000s, SOE revenue comprised less than 15 percent of total government revenue
in both countries (United Nations 2008).
[30] Alkhdour 2015.

highlighted both Jordan and Tunisia's ability to recover from declining trade tax revenue. According to one, "Jordan has succeeded in stabilizing its economy and entering into a process of liberalization,"[31] and another says, "Progress in trade liberalization ... saw a significant decrease in revenues from international trade taxes ... But in ... Tunisia, this did not translate into higher deficits."[32] Post-liberalization, reforms that helped improve the tax administration system contributed to Jordan and Tunisia's success in mobilizing domestic revenue alongside the loss of trade tax revenue.

Political Resistance to Taxes in Globalizing Environment

Unlike India and China, government confidence in Jordan and Tunisia was relatively high in the protectionist era, a critical prerequisite to successful domestic tax reforms and quasi-voluntary compliance. Against the backdrop of ongoing tax reforms, regime confidence was maintained by investments in universal public goods such as rural development, education, and food and fuel subsidies (see Figure 9.14). In Jordan, public goods provision appeased opposition groups and brought together different factions in support of the regime. The Kingdom was thus able to effectively maintain the loyalty of rich and poor members of ruling coalition members (East Jordanians) and coopt the opposition (Palestinian Jordanians). Tunisia's government has a long history of investing in broad-based social welfare programs to ensure the loyalty of the majority of their more homogenous population, while simultaneously de-legitimizing the primary opposition (Islamist political) groups' tactic of providing public goods – Islamic opposition groups could not compete with the Tunisian's government's effective pro-poor spending. Although trade liberalization and resulting changes in fiscal resources seriously shook government confidence in both nations, leaders in the two regimes were still able to maintain the social compact – albeit a lot more fragile and streamlined – and preserve stability, at least through the domestic tax reform phase.

To elaborate, in Jordan, the Hashemite regime has historically maintained stability by balancing two opposing groups: the Transjordanians, or East Jordanians, and the Palestinian Jordanians. Transjordanians, whose origins lie in the East Bank of the Jordan River, represent the regime's traditional power base. Pre-liberalization, the Jordanian government maintained their political support by providing

---

[31] Alissa 2007.
[32] Baliamoune-Lutz 2009.

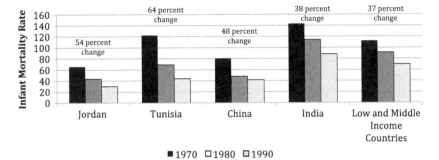

Figure 9.14 Pre-Liberalization Trends in Infant Mortality
Data source: World Bank 2016a

both the rich and the poor extensive social benefits, primarily public
employment (in civil and military)[33], social security and pensions, and
consumer price subsidies.[34] The Palestinian Jordanians, whose origins lie
in the West Bank of the Jordan River, have remained loyal to the ruling
coalition, despite being outsiders. They have benefitted from private
sector development and extensive subsidies on basic goods.[35] In this way,
the ruling coalitions managed to secure the confidence of both rich and
poor Palestinian Jordanians and East Jordanians pre-liberalization.[36]

Tunisia, in contrast, is more ethnically homogenous, allowing the
ruling coalition to maintain government confidence through an emphasis
on solidarity, or participatory programs that provided broad-based social
assistance. Both better-off and poor citizens actively benefitted from the
state welfare system, which included benefits such as job training and
employment assistance, access to water, and microcredit. Such programs
helped provide mass support for the regime. As the former President
Ben Ali explained, "Solidarity, in our view, is a social bond. It transcends
mere ethical and charitable values. It is indeed a mechanism to achieve
justice, equality and equal opportunities for all; as well as an efficient tool
to dispense with the aid-receiving mentality of our people, and stimulate
the sense of initiative and self-reliance."[37]

Before and in the beginning stages of liberalization, Tunisia
emphasized this solidarity strategy with the Regional Development
Program (Programme Regional de Developpement [PRD]) in 1989, the

---

[33] Their employment reached 90 percent of all employed in some areas. Those employed
in the public sector also enjoyed free healthcare (Baylouny 2010).
[34] Baylouny 2010; Peters and Moore 2009.
[35] Abu-Rish 2014.
[36] Baylouny 2008; Peters and Moore 2009; Ryan 2011.
[37] "National Solidarity System Bridges the Gap" 2010.

Integrated Rural Development Program (Programme de Developpement Rural Integre [PDRI]) in 1988, the Needy Family Program (Programme des Familles Necessiteuses) in 1986, and extensive education reforms in 1989.[38] As Sasoon (2016) argues, Tunisia was able to develop its institutional capacity despite the shortcomings of Ben Ali's regime. Labor unions, for example, had an important voice in political affairs, despite being coopted by the regime.[39]

IMF imposed structural adjustment policies (SAPs), followed by major domestic tax reforms, threatened government confidence, and posed new challenges to regime stability in liberalizing Jordan and Tunisia. A cornerstone of the SAPs was "accelerating the pace" of trade liberalization through tariff reform.[40] SAP reforms also included reducing subsidies, enforcing new property regulations, setting up free trade zones, and privatizing SOEs. Protests erupted in both Jordan and Tunisia in response to the IMF-mandated SAPs. Both rich and poor rioted against the removal of subsidies, greater exposure to international market competition, labor repression, and increases in the price of basic necessities. Tax reform followed shortly after, with great resistance from business and public sector elites.[41] It is nothing short of remarkable that tax reforms were relatively successful against the backdrop of growing inequality and unemployment, post-IMF restructuring. Liberal autocrats of both nations nonetheless managed to sustain government confidence – albeit precariously – by providing select incentives to their core supporters, alongside some critical universal social benefits.

In Jordan, Transjordanians protested subsidy cuts and public sector reductions, while the industrial elites (some Transjordanians and Palestinian Jordanians) protested the new tax structure. East Jordanians were particularly impacted by reforms that undermined public sector patronage, upon which they were particularly dependent.[42] For example, in 1989, the *New York Times* reported protesting in Jordan, with the demonstrators discussing how they are "angry with the government" because of declining subsidy support.[43] East Jordanian business elites also expressed opposition to the introduction of tax reforms such as the new GST, introduced in 1989–91. The Amman Chamber of Commerce and other business

---

[38] Tunisia's education reforms in the late 1980s provided free education for children up to age 16 and were associated with the recruitment of qualified teachers.
[39] Sasoon 2016: 243.
[40] International Monetary Fund Independent Evaluation Office 2005; Mohamadieh 2013.
[41] Wils 2004.
[42] Baylouny 2010; Itani 2013.
[43] Cowell 1989.

associations lamented the lack of consultation between the government and business during the tax reform process.[44]

Palestinian Jordanians fared better, in part because they had already developed a dependence on the private sector, and the reforms did not cost them as much. The Palestinian business elite worked in the construction, transportation, and manufacturing sectors.[45] They thus prospered in the private sector boom associated with increased oil prices and remittances from workers in Gulf States in the late 1970s and early 1980s.[46] With liberalization and privatization, along with the resulting close ties to the USA and EU, and the increase in capital-intensive projects, this Palestinian business elite thrived in banking and commerce.[47]

The Jordanian monarchy strategically addressed the declining confidence of their increasingly restive supporters in three ways. First, they began to consult with the East Jordanian business elite during the tax reform period and provided Palestinian merchant elites with a host of special exemptions and tax concessions.[48] Second, in direct violation of the IMF program, public employment and its associated benefits were not drastically cut;[49] privatization and reduction in subsidies were implemented only gradually after liberalization.[50] The Hashemite regime also used public employment (e.g., employment in the military), pensions, and higher compensation to maintain confidence and shelter regime supporters from the costs imposed by the VAT and the decline of food subsidies.[51] Third, they provided rents during reform by allowing East Jordanians privileged access to the purchase of public enterprises and land or the opportunity to serve as middlemen for foreign (Gulf) investors.[52]

Jordan also adopted specialized programs to target poor Jordanian Palestinians and East Bankers. The National Aid Fund (NAF), adopted in 1986, provided cash transfers and subsidized loans to the poor masses.[53] Nongovernmental workers also qualified for the Social Security Corporation social insurance, starting in 1981. Ultimately,

---

[44] IMF 2005.
[45] Wils 2004.
[46] Wils 2004.
[47] Lobell 2012.
[48] Wils 2004. For example, the first sales tax rate in Jordan was 7 percent, not the initially proposed 10 percent. When the GST was increased to 10 percent in 1995, exempt items expanded and corporate income taxes were reduced from 38–55 percent to 15–35 percent (Wils 2004).
[49] Peters and Moore 2009.
[50] Baylouny 2010.
[51] Baylouny 2008; Peters and Moore 2009.
[52] Abu-Rish 2014; Wils 2004.
[53] IMF 2004b.

as Rajeh Alkhdour, Head of the National Economy Division at the Central Bank of Jordan, explained, Jordan's "Education and health services [are the] best in the region ... [and this results in] confidence with government and private sector."[54] Broad-based welfare systems ensure continued support of and confidence in the government. The Hashemite monarchy skillfully maintained broader public confidence by bringing together multiple communities with calls for national unity: "From the perspective of many elites within the regime, the Hashemite strategy is not a matter of divide and rule, but a deft royal policy of pluralism and inclusion. This can be seen in the appointment of prime ministers and cabinets, in which Palestinians will be included; however, East Jordanian majorities will usually be maintained."[55]

As a result, confidence in government remained relatively high in Jordan during critical tax reform periods. According to the World Values Survey, Jordan's average survey response on confidence in government (scaled 1–4) was nearly one point higher than the developing country average (3.4 and 2.5, respectively). Figure 9.15 depicts additional data on government performance and trust in government in Jordan from the Arab Barometer. Respondents were asked whether government performance on education, healthcare, and employment was very bad, bad, good, or very good. Individuals were also surveyed on their level of trust in government: do not trust, limited extent, medium extent, and a great extent. As Figure 9.15 indicates, an overwhelming majority of respondents indicated that they had high confidence in the government and that the performance of the Jordanian government in addressing educational needs and improving basic health services was good or very good. Creating employment opportunities continues to be a challenge for the Jordanian government. A lower percentage of respondents indicated they were satisfied with government performance on employment compared to other indicators; nonetheless, the percentage of respondents happy with the government's performance on unemployment has increased since 2007. Such an increase corresponds to the declining unemployment trends in Jordan (detailed in Figure 9.18).

Tunisia likewise faced mass uprisings and strikes with liberalization, for similar reasons – the loss of state subsidies and resulting increase in the price of food and disruptions to the public sector.[56] Bread riots and public sector strikes occurred in the mid-1980s.[57] Thus, with

---

[54] Alkhdour 2015.
[55] Ryan 2011: 567.
[56] Dillman 1998; Willis 2014.
[57] Dillman 1998.

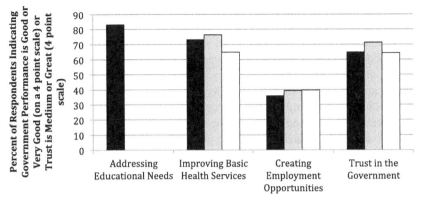

Figure 9.15 Evaluation of Government Performance in Jordan, 2007–13

Data source: Arab Barometer 2007–13

IMF-directed structural adjustment and liberalization in the late 1980s, Tunisia opted to take a gradual approach to reducing subsidies, supplementing them with targeted subsidy programs for the poor, in order to prevent continued protest and opposition.[58]

It is notable that these protests occurred in an environment of relatively successful government programs. Tunisia has had remarkably high human development – infant mortality declined from 135 in 1970 to 15 in 2010, primary education enrollment was almost universal at 99 percent in 2010, 96 percent of the population had access to water in 2010 (up from 81 percent in 1990), and poverty was halved between 2000 and 2010 (32 to 16 percent).[59] Tunisia also prioritized gender equality with inclusive marriage and divorce, voting, and election laws.[60] These factors have helped to maintain some level of government confidence that ensured tax reforms would not incur systemic tax revolts and political instability.[61]

Zine al-Abdine Ben Ali's government also formalized pro-poor social programs that marginalized and de-legitimized Islamic opposition organizations during the liberalization process.[62] In 1992, Ben Ali implemented the "Solidarity Network" (National Solidarity Fund (FNS)),

---

[58] Tuck and Lindert 1996.
[59] Baliamoune-Lutz 2009; World Bank 2014; World Bank 2016a.
[60] Baliamoune-Lutz 2009.
[61] Alm et al. 1993.
[62] Lust 2013; Zayani 2015.

Tunisian Solidarity Bank, and National Employment Fund) to cope with socioeconomic exclusion and declining government confidence as trade liberalization progressed. The FNS was a continuation of social policy designed to increase solidarity between citizens – the poor and nonpoor alike – and leadership.[63] It was financially supported by "voluntary" individual and corporate donations as well as the state.[64] In reality, however, the FNS was commonly seen as a "symbol of Ben Ali's personality cult"; all donations were made in the name of the President.[65]

Hibou best summarizes how the government balanced coercion with confidence:

> Modes of government, concrete measures and, in particular, practices of power did indeed often make repression painless, or even [an] invisible and insidious process, precisely because they also rested on the positive elements embodied in responses to popular demands. For instance, social policies enabled inequalities to be reduced, solidarities to be expressed, and social integration to be achieved – but at the same time they brought control, disciplining, punishment.[66]

Of course, coercion was also a factor in successful revenue mobilization in Tunisia. Although tax evasion occurs in all regime types, authoritarian states respond arbitrarily in their law enforcement, particularly when politically expedient. Such arbitrary, coercive practices are challenging to utilize in democracies, but often a convenient tool for punishing opposition movements in authoritarian countries, as we saw in China's Ai Weiwei case. Taxpayers outside the winning coalition thus face higher levels of risk when engaging in fraud or evasion.

In Tunisia, for example, tax legislation was sometimes purposefully ambiguous and inaccessible, so that it could be used as a tool for maintaining support from ruling coalitions. Hibou and Hulsey summarize this point: "[In Tunisia] Tax fraud enables central power to justify its arbitrary interventions in economic matters and allows civil servants in the tax administration to benefit from bonuses in proportion to recovered taxes."[67] At the same time, however, the loss of revenues from trade liberalization forced the government to increase tax control in Tunisia. Tunisian entrepreneurs who did not openly participate in providing solidarity funds, for example, would be punished by the regime with tax controls, bureaucratic delays, and limited access to

---

[63] Hibou 2011; Hibou and Hulsey 2006.
[64] Although technically voluntary, most donations are solicited under duress and state pressure (see Hibou and Hulsey 2006).
[65] Hibou and Hulsey 2006: 201.
[66] Hibou 2011: xvii.
[67] Hibou and Hulsey 2006: 191.

public markets. This tax system is particularly efficient mobilizing revenue in that, according to Hibou (2011): "what counts is, in this case, the perception of the tax system as an instrument of punishment *par excellence* ... When there is a tussle between the authorities in place and recognized political opponents, taxation is indubitably one of the first repressive measures to be mobilized."[68]

Coercive tax administrative practices and harsh tax evasion penalties are not as common in Jordan, especially in comparison to Tunisia and China. In Jordan, however, addendums to tax laws were implemented outside the parliament to favor elites that had stronger direct access to the cabinet.[69] For instance, tax-exempt items were demanded and then added to GST reforms in Jordan in the mid-1990s to selectively appease the private sector elites.[70] Additionally, Jordan has recently enacted more severe penalties for noncompliance. In the 2015 income tax reform, the monetary fine for evasion became equivalent to the amount evaded, instead of the former policy of a flat-rate (small) monetary fine.[71] In general, however, Jordan is less likely to apply arbitrary and harsh penalties for evasion, even to those outside the ruling coalition. Media reports, legal summaries, and an interview with the Head of the National Economy Division at the Central Bank of Jordan confirm the relatively limited tax penalties for evasion and fraud.[72] Jordan does not need harsh or arbitrary tax penalties because of its successful improvement in tax administration, with the support of the IMF and USAID.[73] Its tax administration is improving with improved computerization, and technology training for government employees.

Finally, in seeming contrast to India, corporate interests facing increased market competition appear to face an uphill battle fighting new tax policies aimed at increasing revenue. For instance, Jordan's manufacturing sector panicked when the government proposed increasing the sales and income tax rates without consulting them. The legislation aimed to generate more revenue by increasing tax rates on large firms, particularly banks, telecom operators, and mining companies. Chairman of the Jordan Exporters Association Omar Abu Wishah argued that higher taxes on industry would be "destructive for the sector and all successful businesses in the country" and lead to "unfair competition

---

[68] Hibou 2011: 146. All information in this paragraph is from Hibou (2011) and Hibou and Husley (2006).
[69] Wils 2004.
[70] Wils 2004.
[71] PricewaterhouseCoopers 2015a.
[72] Alkhdour 2016; Nsour 2014; PricewaterhouseCoopers 2015a.
[73] IMF 2004c; USAID 2014b.

with products manufactured in neighboring countries."[74] Interestingly, while Jordan has traditionally relied on the GST, which many argue puts more burden on low-income groups, it is now increasing corporate tax rates at a time when businesses are feeling greater pressures from international market competition. The income tax reform was implemented in 2015. There was ultimately no change in the tax rate for the industrial sector (though it significantly increased in other sectors). It is notable, however, that Jordan's corporate tax rates are either increasing or staying constant, while declining in most other countries; Jordan increased its GST by almost 10 percentage points during the 1990s and 2000s.

Result: Higher Government Revenues

Jordan and Tunisia have been touted by the IMF and World Bank as success stories, both in terms of trade liberalization efforts and tax reform.[75] In fact, Anne Krueger, Acting Managing Director and Chair of the IMF, stated that Jordan "should be commended for their continued commitment to prudent macroeconomic policies and far-reaching structural reforms, which has [sic] resulted in strong export growth, low inflation, higher investment, and surge in international reserves."[76] Despite similar levels of trade tax revenue loss, Jordan has been more successful than Tunisia in replacing lost trade taxes with even higher revenues. This is in large part because of its emphasis on administrative reform. In the 1990s and 2000s, Jordan streamlined GST legislation, simplified the administrative structure, and created a centralized, online taxpayer database.[77] These bureaucratic and technical reforms contributed greatly to Jordan's success in increasing domestic tax revenue.

Jordan and Tunisia have room to improve on their tax systems. Specifically, Tunisia has been advised to broaden the corporate income tax base[78] and reduce tax evasion.[79] Corporate income tax reform is critical, as only 1 percent of firms account for 80 percent of CIT revenue.[80] In line with the need to improve tax collection, Tunisia is actively continuing to reform its tax system. In 2014, for example, Tunisia reformed

---

[74] Obeidat 2013.
[75] Abed 1998; Lust 2013.
[76] IMF 2004a.
[77] IMF 2005; USAID 2010.
[78] Abed 1998; Achy 2011; OECD 2015.
[79] OECD 2015.
[80] OECD 2015.

corporate income taxes by simplifying the rates and implementing a new tax on dividends, thus broadening the base and limiting exemptions.

Jordan is still challenged to reduce tax evasion and increase direct tax revenue.[81] Expanding the base of income taxes is particularly pertinent: USAID (2010) indicates, "94 percent of the tax base [is] exempt from personal income taxation … [which costs Jordan] 6.1 percent of GDP." Jordan's most recent tax reform, implemented in 2015, does begin to address compliance and direct taxation concerns by raising the corporate and personal income tax rate and amending the penal system to more effectively address evasion.[82] The IMF (2014) indicates that this new law can contribute 0.7 percent of GDP in revenue.

It is arguable that the Jordanian government has a higher motivation to increase their revenues compared to Tunisia. Jordan consistently maintains a large fiscal deficit, one that is significantly larger than Tunisia's.[83] Pensions for civil servants and the military and government wages directly contribute to this deficit in Jordan (IMF 2004b). Tunisia may be increasing its tax revenue at a slower pace, but it is more successfully doing so in tandem with lowering its fiscal deficit (Harrigan and El-Said 2010; Pfeifer 1999).

So What?

Jordan and Tunisia maintained stable government revenues and government confidence throughout the initial liberalization and domestic tax reform period. However, the sustainability and stability of government confidence differed in the long run in these two regimes. Jordan has been using its government revenues to support cross-class coalitions and maintain the political status quo. East Jordanians, although disgruntled with the distributional impacts of the reforms, have been disproportionately benefitting from the increased revenues as members of the government's main support group. The opposition, the Jordanian Palestinians, have also benefitted from private sector development as well as access to tax reform dialogues in the government. Furthermore, revenues post-liberalization have enabled the Jordanian government to provide public goods and specialized poverty reduction programs for poor Palestinian and East Jordanians.

In contrast, despite stable government revenues, Ben Ali in Tunisia was ultimately unable to appease members of the broad coalition that

---

[81] Malkawi and Haloush 2008.
[82] PricewaterhouseCoopers 2015a.
[83] IMF 2014.

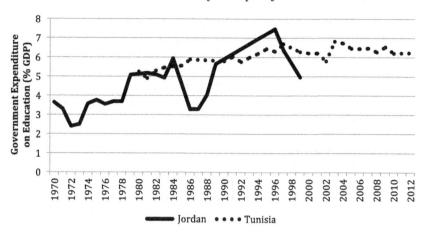

Figure 9.16 Government Expenditure on Education (Percent of GDP) in Jordan and Tunisia, 1970–2012
Data source: UNESCO Institute for Statistics (2014)

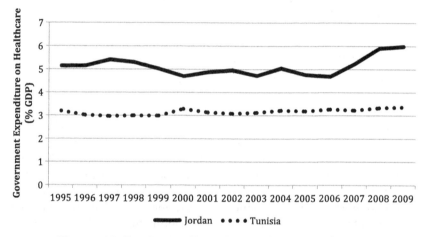

Figure 9.17 Government Expenditure on Health (Percent of GDP) in Jordan and Tunisia, 1995–2009
Data source: World Bank 2016a

united against him in the Arab Spring. Public goods provision in Tunisia was insufficient to maintain government confidence among the rich and poor – unemployment worsened, and support for Ben Ali plummeted in 2010 and 2011. Of course, factors such as increasing food prices and increasing corruption – particularly in response to the power and privileges granted to the powerful members of Ben Ali's family – contributed to government's overthrow.[84] Tunisia's ranking on the corruption perception index declined from 43rd in 2005 to 59th in 2010, out of a total of 178 countries monitored by Transparency International.[85] Jordan, on the other hand, was able to maintain cross-class support through its strategic and universal public goods programs and reduce its corruption perception index in recent years.[86]

The bottom line is that, despite economic crises in the late 1980s that hurt economic growth and increased poverty and inequality, Jordan and Tunisia have maintained commitments to strong human development outcomes throughout the 1990s. For example, alongside trade liberalization, both Jordan and Tunisia increased government spending on health and education (see Figures 9.16 and 9.17). While Jordan's government expenditure is increasing at a faster rate than Tunisia's, Jordan did see declining education spending after 1998, in line with the Kingdom's IMF-directed efforts to reduce budget deficits.

The Jordanian government has been committed to ensuring public access to basic health and education services for its citizens post-liberalization.[87] Jordan's health and education indicators, for example, compare favorably with those in other countries in the Middle East and North Africa, and other lower-middle-income countries in general. In the late 1990s, Jordan "replaced generalized and open-ended subsidies with a system of means-tested cash transfers administered through the National Aid Fund (NAF)."[88] This program was "more successful reaching the poor," and resulted in a decline in the percent of the population below the poverty line.[89]

Jordan does face challenges accessing and incorporating the poorest in its poverty reduction programs. The UNDP, for example, points to increases in the total number of households living under the absolute poverty line, despite select programs to help the poor.[90] Others highlight Jordan's need to expand the eligibility requirements of social welfare programs to ensure inclusion of the majority of the poor.[91] Yet, overall, Jordan has seen a declining poverty trend between 1985 and 2010.

---

[84] Chomiak 2011; Schraeder and Redissi 2011.
[85] Transparency International 2016.
[86] Jordan's corruption perception index data based on Transparency International 2016.
[87] See Shaban, Assaad, and Al-Qudsi (1995).
[88] IMF 2004b.
[89] IMF 2004b.
[90] UNDP 2013.
[91] Baliamoune-Lutz 2009; UNDP 2013.

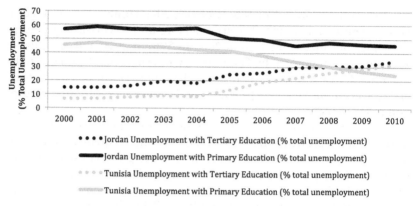

Figure 9.18 Unemployment in Jordan and Tunisia, 2000–10
Data source: World Bank 2016a

Tunisia has seemingly done better in the provision of broad-based public goods, at least during the period just after the liberalization process began. It has been praised for its rapid growth and poverty reduction, especially in comparison to the greater Middle Eastern and North African region.[92] Between 2000 and 2010, poverty (measured at $2 a day PPP) dropped from 12.8 percent to 4.3 percent.[93] Tunisia's achievements occurred in both gender equality and human development indicators such as fertility, literacy, and access to education.[94] Overall poverty declined in Tunisia between 1985 and 2010. This success in poverty reduction has resulted in a large middle class.[95]

Ultimately, the biggest challenge for both nations is rising and persistent unemployment. Large percentages of women and youth are unemployed in Jordan and Tunisia.[96] In recent years, however, the more educated have experienced lower levels of unemployment in Jordan; whereas the more educated maintain higher levels of unemployment in Tunisia (see Figure 9.18).

Despite Tunisia's strong human development outcomes post-shock, confidence in Ben Ali's government plummeted in 2010, the year of the Arab Spring. In addition to widespread resentment concerning corruption and unemployment, satisfaction with infrastructure and basic

[92] Baliamoune-Lutz 2009; World Bank 2014.
[93] World Bank 2014.
[94] Baliamoune-Lutz 2009.
[95] African Development Bank 2011.
[96] Barcucci and Mryyan 2014; Romagnoli and Mengoli 2013.

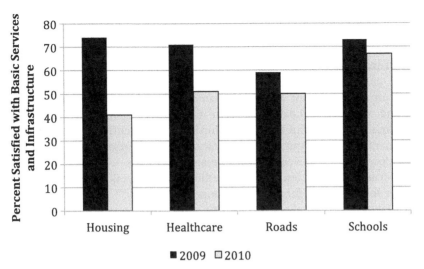

Figure 9.19 Satisfaction with Social Services and Infrastructure in Tunisia, 2009–10
Data source: Gallup Poll

goods fell, on average, by 24 percent from 2009 to 2010. In 2010, Gallup polls report that 41 percent of Tunisians were satisfied with the availability of affordable housing, a sharp decline from 2009, when 74 percent shared this view. Tunisians' satisfaction with other public infrastructure, such as transportation systems, also experienced a notable decline from 2009 (74 percent) to 2010 (55 percent). Tunisians were also less satisfied with the quality of the roads and highways in 2010 (50 percent) than in 2009 (59 percent) (see Figure 9.19).

Ultimately, the combination of economic grievances, discrimination,[97] and a broadly shared cynicism regarding Ben Ali's governing practices resulted in a broad coalition that demanded his exit.[98] In other words, both insiders and outsiders of the ruling coalition successfully united to overthrow Ben Ali. Although the National Solidarity Fund was successful at preventing and reducing poverty, inequality still increased,

---

[97] The big socioeconomic cleavages in Tunisia are between labor and industry and the urban and rural sectors. Labor's bargaining power became limited under structural adjustment, with privatization and increased repression (Dillman 1998; King 1998). Rural citizens similarly felt disadvantaged as regional disparities in income and employment persisted (Gana 2012; World Bank 2014).

[98] See Goldstone (2011).

and higher revenues did little to address the myriad of perceived government failings. Clearly, higher public revenue followed by social welfare investments is not a magic bullet for curing all societal ills, which include government misdoings.

In contrast, Jordan has been using revenues to disproportionately buy off rich and poor East Jordanians. This appears to have prevented strong cross-class coalitions from organizing against the regime.[99] Regime outsiders, the Palestinian Jordanians, benefitted less from government revenues, but continued to support the regime for economic reasons. Business-oriented Palestinian Jordanians who gained markedly from liberalization and the plethora of tax breaks did not want to upset the regime's embrace of economic openness.[100] Poorer subgroups experienced some – albeit insufficient – relief from government spending with new anti-poverty programs. For instance, the mid-1990s subsidy reform led to a targeted cash payment system by the National Aid Fund, which was a major source of welfare for the poor.[101] The Jordanian government also invested in improving government services such as education with its 2001 Plan for Social and Economic Transformation, and reducing poverty through social assistance with the 2002 Poverty Alleviation Strategy and 2007 Ministry of Social Development National Executive Program.[102]

The consequence of this commitment to high government spending in Jordan has been that higher revenues post-liberalization did not translate into lower deficits. Although the government successfully increased domestic taxes to replace trade taxes, it did not sustain its pledge to cut subsidies (directed at its primary support group) to reduce its large budget deficit. Jordan's fiscal deficit improved throughout the late 1990s and early 2000s because of: (1) a debt management strategy based on accessing lower cost loans and rescheduling and reducing existing debt; and (2) prudent fiscal expenditure and public enterprise policies.[103]

---

[99] While both rich and poor groups were disappointed with Jordan's poverty alleviation, recall that, historically, the regime has maintained a coalition of East Jordanians and Palestinian Jordanians that included both socioeconomic groups. They were not unitary in their demands, and the Jordanian state was a "unifying force bringing together multiple communities" (Ryan 2011: 568).

[100] Ryan 2013.

[101] IMF 2004b; Louzi 2007.

[102] IMF 2004b; UNDP 2013; USAID 2011.

[103] IMF 2004b.

Summary

The cases of Jordan and Tunisia confirm how liberal authoritarian countries have been successful in mobilizing domestic tax revenue post-liberalization by maintaining confidence in government among the both the rich and the poor. Following crises in the 1980s, Jordan and Tunisia liberalized their economies and faced both dramatic declines in trade tax revenues and protests against SAP reforms from regime supporters. To provide stability and loyalty during the tax reform period, Jordan and Tunisia engaged in national unity efforts founded in the delivery of broad-based public goods. Specialized poverty reduction programs and subsidies were targeted to the poor, and public employment opportunities and assistance programs benefitted the relatively well off. This political strategy helped ensure quasi-voluntary compliance with domestic tax reforms. Jordan and Tunisia have thus effectively reformed their goods and services taxes and continue to see improvements in income tax collection.

Yet a serious caution persists; revenue generation is not the panacea for development. Despite successful revenue generation post-liberalization, Jordan and Tunisia face critical challenges for regime stability and confidence in the future. Jordan's revenue mobilization has failed to keep pace with its spending, and the country faces growing deficits – current public debt is significant, at 90 percent of GDP.[104] More recently, the Syrian crisis and refugee influx further challenge both Jordan's fiscal health and regime stability.[105] For Tunisia, successful revenue reform coupled with Ben Ali's investment in solidarity programs could not outweigh the political repercussions of his corrupt governing tactics. Moving forward, fostering confidence in the new government, while simultaneously maintaining strong tax efforts, is imperative as the government strives to build its democracy.

---

[104] IMF 2014.
[105] UNDP 2013.

Conclusion

All good things must be paid for.[1]

Prime Minister Lee Hsien Loong, Singapore
2013 National Day Rally Speech

We started our analysis with our fictional Subodh's very real revenue problems in Andhra Pradesh which, it turns out, are typical of many governments in developing democracies, wanting to make real changes and facing a dearth of funds with which to accomplish them. The expansion of free trade and prosperity frequently go hand-in-hand. But that economic progress doesn't necessarily extend to the majority who are poor in developing world democracies. This is even more surprising in light of recent studies that reveal democracies have higher economic growth.[2] The assumption that government coffers will fill alongside trade openness and growth has, unfortunately, proven overly optimistic. Obvious benefits of expanded global markets include greater employment opportunities, improvements in government transparency, greater consumer satisfaction, and economic efficiency. However, revenue generation in a globalizing economy, particularly in democracies, has frequently been disappointing. The optimistic expectations underestimated the true extent of revenue loss with initial trade liberalization, and rested on two questionable assumptions: (1) firms and consumers would willingly pay higher taxes in the globalizing environment; and (2) developing countries had the tax administration bureaucracy and capacity to administer, monitor, and collect new domestic taxes that were to replace trade taxes.

This book argues that the culprit is *not* free trade. It is the political response to it. Recovering the money lost from tariffs requires a committed and persistent effort to broaden tax bases, improve administration, simplify rate structures, curb exemptions, and implement new taxes such as the VAT. Otherwise, trade liberalization can end up making

---

[1] Khim and Wright 2014.
[2] Acemoglu et al. 2016.

186

already fragile fiscal positions even worse and ultimately subvert its beneficial impacts. We find that this is precisely what happens, but only in a subset of developing countries: democracies.

Democracies are particularly susceptible to revenue shocks because of business and citizen resistance to new taxes. They have neither the confidence to share their earnings with the government nor sufficient incentive to comply with tax reforms. This is especially true for large, previously protected firms that oppose tax reform because they are struggling to compete in the global economy. The government is caught between balancing pressures from less productive firms for lower taxes with exporting firms' demands for low tariffs. A direct consequence has been declining corporate tax rates and slow revenue growth in democracies.

Authoritarian regimes, facing fewer political constraints, have been more effective in recovering revenue. Although they differ in how they foster citizen compliance to domestic tax reform – with some relying disproportionately on coercion for tax enforcement and implementation, and others engaging in quasi-voluntary compliance based on more broad-based social spending to ensure citizen satisfaction – their record on raising revenue is better than that of democracies.

Slow tax revenue growth has very real consequences for citizens of democracies. The problem is that, when faced with fiscal constraints, politicians in democracies tend to protect wealthier voters often at the expense of the poor. Elected officials appear to be compromising on poverty reduction programs post-liberalization. So, although improved economic growth has accompanied trade liberalization in most developing countries, revenue gains remain lackluster, and marginalized populations are likely to be the first ones denied opportunities to share in the benefits of trade as a consequence.

A World Bank official, with extensive experience assisting developing economies with tax reforms, aptly summarizes the political dilemma for democracies, such as Guatemala, undergoing tax reforms once the liberalization process is well under way:[3]

In democracies, the bottom line is there are interest groups involved, and they can be powerful. In democratic societies, these interest groups have a big voice

---

[3] David Gould's views are based on his experience supporting Guatemala with economic policy reforms (as the World Bank's Lead Economist Poverty Reduction Economic Management Group [2003–8], Lead Economist and Sector Leader for Central American Country Unit [2005–8], Visiting Researcher in Chile, Central Bank [1997], Federal Reserve US).

influencing tax reforms. In the case of Guatemala [for example], the business groups and their lobbying efforts have been able to thwart increasing tax rates. It's through a democratic process, but it's not always the process by which we get the optimal outcome ... *The major business group had the sense that the government was corrupt and giving them more money would increase corruption* [emphasis ours].[4]

Case Study Findings - Additional Lessons

Across our illustrative case examples of India, China, Jordan, and Tunisia, we saw the same initial pattern: a dependence on "easy to collect" taxes – including trade taxes – in the mid-to-late 1980s, followed by a drastic decline in such revenue upon liberalization. However, afterwards, in response to the drop in trade tax revenue, the patterns diverge. Despite citizen protest and political opposition to tax collection and reform, authoritarian countries, such as China, Jordan, and Tunisia, were able to recover from revenue shocks, successfully replacing and often surpassing the loss of trade tax revenues. Democratic India, on the other hand, has had far greater difficulties mobilizing revenue. Instead, as the government attempts to balance revenue needs with business demands in the globalizing environment, we see growing complexity and exemptions in tax codes that seriously hinder tax mobilization. Our cases show how different types of governments use different tools to accomplish their revenue goals. In particular, regimes differ in their effective use of coercion and their ability to secure quasi-voluntary compliance with domestic tax reforms in the new economic environment.

In India, the general public is clearly frustrated with government incompetencies; confidence remains low, and frequent protests over inadequate public goods, such as water access, healthcare, and infrastructure, are cases in point. Citizens' resistance to tax reform was predictable, given the inability of the Indian government to provide functioning, broad-based public goods. The very large population of tax evaders amongst India's fast-growing economic elites magnifies this resistance. Some estimates of India's growing "black economy" suggest that it is up to 40 percent of GDP.[5] As we saw in earlier examples, despite Prime Minister Modi's efforts to implement measures to curb tax evasion, India's wealthy are finding new ways around them. The recent demonetization effort in India, for example, has been considered to be "all pain and no gain."[6] The collection of black money was less than

---

[4] Gould 2016.
[5] Kumar 2002.
[6] White 2017.

expected, poor and informal workers suffered the most during this effort, and the wealthy continue to evade taxes.[7] Throughout India, growing market competition and increasing opportunities for tax evasion add to the political opposition to higher taxes.

Confidence in government is more difficult to gauge in authoritarian China, but select surveys suggest that poor welfare provision is one of the primary areas of dissatisfaction with officials. Government efforts to ameliorate the now deeply rooted inequality between urban and rural areas have ramped up but still it has seen minimal success thus far. China has balanced this inequality with coercive tactics to ensure tax collection, particularly at the local level. Additionally, China has become aggressive in implementing policies aimed at curtailing tax evasion, particularly on the part of firms.

In contrast, we found that governments in Jordan and Tunisia have generally maintained citizens' confidence – at least until the Arab Spring – through public goods spending that is more universally targeted and/or directed towards buying off the opposition. In Jordan, King Abdullah has been able to use social spending to keep diverse coalitions united and supportive of the regime's policies. Tunisia (like China) improved tax reforms by force – specifically by arbitrary enforcement of harsh punishments. Jordan was an exception among our authoritarian cases in terms of its more limited use of coercion to improve revenue mobilization. Regardless, despite having the relatively largest dependence on trade taxes amongst our case illustrations, Jordan and Tunisia were both effective in improving revenue generation over and above the tax levels in the pre-liberalization era in large part through quasi-voluntary compliance.

Our case examples provide additional lessons. First, in some developing countries, other "easy to collect" revenues in addition to trade taxes were important before liberalization – particularly SOE revenues, oil rents, and foreign aid. This is exemplified in the Chinese case, where 90 percent of government revenue was based in SOEs in the early 1980s. The critical point is that *all* such "easy to collect" revenues declined with trade liberalization, and countries were forced to address these shortfalls alongside the loss from trade tax reform.

Second, central and state tax dynamics matter and pose both challenges and opportunity for tax mobilization. In China and India, complicated and archaic federal tax structures inhibited tax collection for local and central governments; tax-on-tax concerns, for example, led to complexity and inefficiencies that often fueled business resistance. China has been more effective in reforming its tax structure with a central-local revenue-sharing plan. While still imperfect, it has successfully improved incentives

---

[7] Chakravorti 2017; White 2017.

for local governments to collect taxes that help balance central budgets. In democratic India, however, central-local arguments about reform are all too common. For example, states ardently resisted the single Goods and Services Tax (GST) Bill, and are currently demanding compensation for lost revenue as well as exemptions for numerous goods in the new GST negotiations. These calls for modifications to the new GST have led economists to claim that the new GST is "not a silver bullet" to greater growth or revenue mobilization.[8] It may well be that federalist tax reforms in authoritarian nations are easier to enact, since governments can coerce state and local sub-units into accepting their decisions.

Finally, our case studies underscore the need to exercise caution in assuming that improved revenue collection on its own is a cure for all development ills. Tunisia is a case in point. The birth of the Arab Spring occurred in this nation in large part because central government officials could not address the growing unemployment and inequality problems that accompanied trade liberalization. This unrest occurred despite high government spending on public goods and historically high public confidence. The lesson learned is that government revenue and spending in developing economies, though important, may be a necessary but not sufficient condition to address the negative distributional effects of globalization.

By the same token, successful tax reforms must necessarily be balanced with fiscal constraint. Jordan, in contrast to Tunisia, successfully avoided revolution, and scholars debate the reasons behind its exceptionalism.[9] One explanation is that the Jordanian government's continued spending on health and education, subsidies to rich and poor, and maintaining high levels of public employment, all helped to prevent the emergence of cross-class alliances against the regime. The consequence, however, has been high levels of debt, despite the increasing revenues. Today, with the crisis in Syria, Jordan's large and growing deficit is a grave worry. As this spending continues, Jordan's fiscal environment could be in jeopardy despite its revenue generation capabilities. In effect, Jordan traded in fiscal imprudence for political stability.

Our larger point is that democracy can pose revenue problems when countries with weak tax administration systems open up to the global economy. Figure C.1 underscores this point with examples of revenue growth in a sampling of non-oil rich developing countries that changed

---

[8] Awasthi 2016.
[9] See, for example, Beck and Huser (2015) and Yom and Gause (2012) for the competing explanations relating to Jordan's rent revenues, cultural and institutional structures of its monarchy, and coalition formations.

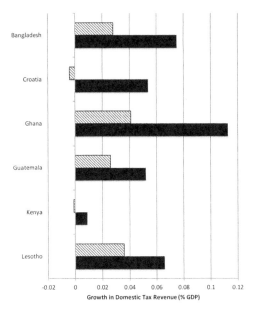

Figure C.1 Average Annual Changes in Domestic Tax Revenues in Select Countries that Experienced both Regime Types after Liberalizing
Note: Although Croatia began dismantling trade barriers in the early 1990s while it was nondemocratic, major progress towards trade liberalization (and reduction in trade taxes) began closer to 2000 when it was a democracy.
Data source: World Bank 2016a

regime type *after* embarking on liberalization.[10] It seems clear that growth in tax revenues in countries that were nondemocratic is higher than the growth rate when that *same country* is democratic. The countries in this figure are representative of different regions and income levels.

Democracies in Peril? The Broader Consequences

A widely noted 2004 United Nations survey of 19,000 Latin Americans in 18 countries rang alarm bells for proponents of democracy. A majority of respondents indicated a toxic impatience with

[10] We do not consider transitional and failed states here.

democracy; they preferred a dictator to an elected leader if their standard of living improved.[11] The root of their discontent, according to analysts, was the pervasive feeling that elected leaders had failed to improve the lives of the poor. In 2004, the brutal killing of a mayor in Peru, Fernando Cirilo Robles, during a council meeting, is a dramatic example. He failed to fulfill his promise to pave a highway and build a market for vendors.[12] An interview in the *New York Times* of a young man, whose father was accused of being involved with the lynching of Robles, highlights the lack of confidence in democracy in Peru: he said, "I believe in an authoritarian government, if it works …They do this in other countries and it works. Look at Cuba, that works. Look at Pinochet in Chile, that worked."[13]

The post-liberalization low-revenue trap may indeed place democracies in peril. History is replete with examples of democracies turning into dictatorships because of mass discontent (e.g., Argentina 1955 and 1976, Chile 1973, Pakistan 1977).[14] Amartya Sen (1999) more cautiously argues that the noneconomic benefits of democracy – civil liberties, human rights, and, in principle, political freedoms – make it unlikely that the poor would stage a wholesale revolt against the democratic system. Nonetheless, a danger lies in upsetting the delicate balance between a desire for civil liberties and widespread discontent with the (persistent) undersupply of public goods, which can directly impact the living standards of the poor.

Another unexpected implication is that it may well be that democracies will be the first to turn against liberalization, contrary to predictions in existing research.[15] According to recent polls, citizens of developing countries have far greater faith in the benefits of liberalization than their developed country counterparts.[16] But this could change if domestic taxes persistently remain low and public goods continue to decline. Democracies do not want to be in the difficult position of maintaining an ineffective domestic revenue generation system and forestalling the efficiency and prosperity gains of trade liberalization. Indeed, several democracies have begun resisting the adoption of deeper trade

[11] UNDP 2004.
[12] Forero 2004.
[13] Forero 2004.
[14] See also Fairfield (2014) and Przeworski et al. (2000).
[15] Milner and Kubota 2005.
[16] The PEW Research Center's Global Attitudes and Trends (PEW Research Center 2014) survey indicates that 87 percent of citizens in developing countries responded that trade is good, 66 percent that trade creates jobs, and 55 percent that trade raises wages. Among respondents in the advanced economies, 84 percent found trade to be good, 44 percent that trade creates jobs, and 25 percent that trade raises wages.

liberalization reforms for exactly this reason (for example, Argentina and India).[17] Many authoritarian leaders, on the other hand, are successfully increasing domestic revenues as openness advances. It is remarkable that, under conditions of openness, authoritarian leaders may be finding it easier to address the issue of tax reform and, in some cases, maintain a level of public goods provision that helps improve the lives of less well-off citizens.

What Can Democracies Do?

What measures might democracies take to avoid such doomsday scenarios? Findings from this book suggest policymakers might want to move on two fronts simultaneously: (1) implement measures to improve confidence in government; and (2) pursue more rigorous enforcement of existing tax policies. To do so, local politicians must overcome the free-rider problem and stop depending on other governing officials to enforce tax reform while they pursue white elephants for electoral gain. Although challenging in practice, this strategy is not unprecedented.

El Salvador is a good case in point. Domestic tax revenues have been low in El Salvador post-liberalization (10 percent of GDP compared to 12.5 percent in other Latin American countries in 2004). To address this, the government has prioritized two goals: increasing tax revenues; and expanding basic social services in rural and urban areas, "especially to vulnerable segments of the population."[18] On the revenue-expansion side, examples of tax reforms that have been implemented are a 10 percent VAT, a 5 percent stamp tax, and concerted efforts to reduce corporate and personal income tax evasion.

For social services, El Salvador's government committed to improving programs that benefit both the rich and the poor. Recently enacted programs include cash transfers to the elderly and the Comunidades Solidarias program, which supports the consumption of poor households and increasing children's access to basic health, nutrition, and education services. In addition, the government established a gender equity program that supports a consulting committee for monitoring gender equity progress in the public sector and a center with information on women's rights in each region of the country. In terms of infrastructure, the Ministry of Public Works, Transportation,

---

[17] Datt, Hoekman, and Malouche 2011.
[18] "El Salvador/World Bank: Expanding Social Programs to Assist 5,500 Elders and 20,000 Households in Poor Areas" 2011.

Housing, and Urban Development launched a highway development plan, anticipated to benefit 21,000 local people and 650 employees.[19] We surmise that it is no coincidence that El Salvador's tax reforms were subsequently successful; domestic tax revenue collection improved from 9.6 percent of GDP in 2002 to 13.1 percent in 2008, or a 36 percent increase in revenue growth. Domestic tax revenue growth in other middle-income democracies during the same time period paled in comparison (for example, 6 percent in Brazil, 5 percent in the Philippines, and *negative* 23 percent in Namibia).[20]

Mauritius is another example of a democracy that has been successful in generating domestic tax revenues. In 1994, Mauritius engaged in trade tax reforms to reduce its export and import taxes and saw a corresponding "sharp deterioration" in its public finances with a deficit of over 7 percent of GDP in 1996.[21] In 1998, with support from the IMF, Mauritius introduced a VAT and saw strong revenue performance after its implementation.[22] Mauritius increased social assistance and transfers in tandem with its tax reforms and poverty rates declined from 20 percent in 1997 to 8 percent in 2006.[23] Yet, the case of Mauritius also highlights that despite large gains in tax revenue, the loss in trade tax revenues has been larger.[24] Fiscal imbalances and debt challenges have plagued Mauritius throughout the 2000s.[25] Even tremendous tax reform success in democracies is not always enough.

Another strategy to consider for democratic policymakers who care about maintaining openness is viable, easy-to-collect taxes, such as excise taxes on certain luxury goods, select user fees, and taxes on multinational corporations. The latter promises to be an especially lucrative source of

---

[19] These programs are highlighted in the "El Salvador/World Bank: Expanding Social Programs to Assist 5,500 Elders and 20,000 Households in Poor Areas" (2011) World Bank Press Release and on the El Salvadorian Ministry of Public Works, Transportation, Housing, and Urban Development website: www.mop.gob.sv/index.php?option=com_content&view=article&id=787&Itemid=77.

[20] The Inter-American Development Bank (2015) discusses how despite some increases in tax-to-GDP ratios in Latin America, the region lags far behind the OECD tax average. The World Bank (2016a) depicts stagnant domestic tax revenue in Latin America in the past five years.

[21] Yao et al. 2005: 60–61.

[22] Yao et al. 2005.

[23] Prasad 2008. In fact, according to an African Development Bank report (2009), Mauritius increased its "spending on social programs oriented toward achieving the Millennium Development Goals … [and] beneficiaries will include … taxpayers."

[24] Data indicates that between 1990 and 2013 Mauritius gained 8.9 percent of GDP in domestic tax revenue in the face of a decline of 10.2 percent of GDP in trade taxes (Prichard et al. 2014).

[25] Yao et al. 2005.

finance for developing countries, but one that is becoming increasingly challenging to levy as countries vie for foreign investment.

It is incumbent upon democracies to win the public relations battle when attempting to raise taxes on foreign capital. They face fierce political challenges justifying any tax increase, let alone ones that impact wealthy elites and foreign investors. For example, the media, investors, opposition parties, and businesses alike have labeled India's retrospective income tax laws as "tax terrorism."[26] And since India, like most democracies, generally has fewer capital controls than most nondemocracies, it is common for foreign investments to be routed through countries like Mauritius and Singapore, which are tax exempt, thanks to bilateral tax treaties. Such are the complex pressures of globalization on revenue mobilization in countries with weak tax systems.[27]

The tax collection process needs to be improved not only for the sake of public goods and economic advancement, but also for democratic development. Improving tax compliance – especially by the elite – can help strengthen democracy.[28] As Boucoyannis (2015) argues, elites have the necessary political muscle to demand greater accountability and checks on the central government. But elites will only have motivation to declare "no taxation without representation" if and when they are "compelled to contribute to public revenues."[29]

Democracies should be able to implement some less politically controversial reforms, such as digitizing tax collections and administrations. South Korea, for example, has had tremendous success in revenue generation due to improvements in its tax bureaucracy in part because of cooperation with and assistance from the IMF, OECD, United States, and international tax consultants.[30] As one Korean Institute of Public Finance researcher commented, "As the nation's tax collection process is getting more efficient, the government finds more hidden tax bases, which would otherwise be excluded from total tax revenues."[31]

---

[26] The retrospective income tax law in India was a 2012 amendment to the Indian Income Tax of 1961 which "allows for retrospective taxation of a share transaction between two non-resident entities that results in indirect transfer of assets lying in India" (Ranjan 2016).
[27] See the following news articles: "Corporate Tax Schemes Hurt Developing Countries" 2014; Leung 2001; "Scrap Tax Incentives, Civil Society Urges Governments" 2011; Sheng 2009.
[28] See Bates and Lien (1985), Boucoyannis (2015), North and Weingast (1989), for examples.
[29] Boucoyannis 2015: 319.
[30] Choi 1997.
[31] Byung-joon 2003.

South Korea also has the advantage of being a high-income country and OECD member, although it ranks lowest in tax collection efforts out of 28 advanced nations.[32] And, of course, efforts at improving tax transparency can still be politically contentious, as our India example (Chapter 7) shows.

Ultimately, rich countries and international financial institutions involved in global crusades promoting open markets and democracy may want to take note of the repercussions when these go hand-in-hand. What our book contributes to this discussion is that many of these challenges are conditional upon regime type. Democracies have particular struggles with tax reforms post-liberalization, and deserve specialized attention.

Final Thoughts

For developing country democracies, free trade, in the end, may not necessarily translate into healthy government budgets and greater pro-poor redistribution spending. The unfortunate reality is that, when faced with globalization pressures, democracies are struggling to generate critical government revenue to support their development needs, creating even greater challenges for the provision of public goods. This, in turn, puts more strain on governments' ability to make the necessary tax reforms to solve the problem. And now, raising tariffs is politically and economically difficult; governments depend on the support – and broader macroeconomic impacts – of large, productive firms who benefit from low tariffs.[33]

Democracies are essentially caught in a low confidence–low tax equilibrium that may have serious societal implications post-liberalization. Inadequate provision of public goods will only get worse with unsuccessful tax reforms, widespread cheating, and preferential treatment for elites. Confidence in government will likely fall, generating yet more resistance to taxation. Can these countries escape from this cycle of disappointments? The vicious circle of low citizen faith in government, undersupply of public goods, and revenue shortfalls could prove unsustainable in a democratic system. In this scenario, the benefits of higher economic growth in democracies that is predicted by Acemoglu et al.

---

[32] Kyong-ae 2013. We included South Korea in our sample because it was a non-OECD country for several of the years covered in our dataset.

[33] Reverse liberalization is increasingly uncommon amongst most developing economies, even though it sometimes does occur. Countries today are far more interdependent through supply chains, imported inputs, and services. Additionally, successive GATT/WTO agreements have provided much greater legal stability of trading relations (Gamberoni and Newfarmer 2009).

(2016) are likely bypassing a large, underprivileged population, and stirring angst. Put bluntly, if the poor cannot compete against the political muscle of concentrated elite interests over sustained periods, mass unrest could result.

Citizens of developing world democracies are hardly alone in their desire to avoid taxes. However, governments in these countries find themselves in a particular conundrum because of political constraints combined with the sudden loss of revenue from liberalization. This shock placed them in a fragile fiscal position and their inability to recover has possibly made it worse. Democracies would do well to adopt fiscally responsible social programs and administrative reforms in conjunction with tax reforms. Prioritizing services that benefit the majority of the population rather than the wealthiest would help improve governance in a variety of ways. Only then will the broader public be willing to be a part of the process, and arrive at the quasi-voluntary compliance that exists more readily in rich countries – and remains so pivotal to revenue mobilization and continuing development in the global economy. The ideal and promise of a democracy is a government of, by, and for the people. Democracies in developing countries should start living up to that ideal, or the promise could prove all too fleeting.

Appendices

APPENDIX A

A.1 Determinants of Goods and Income Tax Revenue (Percent of GDP): Baseline Model

DV	(1)	(2)	(3)	(4)
	Goods Tax Revenue (% GDP)	Income Tax Revenue (% GDP)	Goods Tax Revenue (% GDP)	Income Tax Revenue (% GDP)
Trade Tax Revenue (% GDP) $_{t-1}$	−0.189*** (0.0486)	−0.0253 (0.0435)	−0.147*** (0.0431)	−0.0606 (0.0429)
Democracy $_{t-1}$	−0.258 (0.206)	−0.125 (0.191)		
Trade Tax Revenue (% GDP)ˈDemocracy $_{t-1}$	0.249*** (0.0722)	0.102 (0.0713)		
Polity $_{t-1}$			−0.0392* (0.0223)	−0.0636*** (0.0242)
Trade Tax Revenue (% GDP)ˈPolity $_{t-1}$			0.0320*** (0.00814)	0.0297*** (0.00948)
GDP Per Capita (Logged) $_{t-1}$	0.162 (0.163)	0.866*** (0.207)	0.187 (0.163)	0.914*** (0.211)
Fuel Exports $_{t-1}$	0.00109 (0.00621)	0.0293** (0.0117)	0.000103 (0.00600)	0.0308*** (0.0118)
Capital Account Openness $_{t-1}$	0.0322 (0.0709)	−0.125 (0.0857)	0.00260 (0.0739)	−0.126 (0.0868)
Observations	1,045	1,066	1,045	1,066
R-squared	0.928	0.902	0.932	0.903
Number of Countries	104	105	104	105

*** p<0.01, ** p<0.05, * p<0.1

Standard errors in parentheses

A.2 *Determinants of Goods and Income Tax Revenue (Percent of GDP): Full Model*[a]

DV	(1)	(2)	(3)	(4)	(5)	(6)
	Goods Tax Revenue (% GDP)	Income Tax Revenue (% GDP)	Goods Tax Revenue (% GDP)	Income Tax Revenue (% GDP)	Goods Tax Revenue (% GDP)	Income Tax Revenue (% GDP)
Trade Tax Revenue (% GDP) $_{t-1}$	-0.109 (0.0849)	0.0882 (0.0641)				
Polity $_{t-1}$	-0.0279 (0.0229)	-0.127*** (0.0397)				
Trade Tax Revenue (% GDP)* Polity $_{t-1}$	0.0447*** (0.0119)	0.0307*** (0.0101)				
Trade Tax Shock			-0.166 (0.388)	0.890*** (0.331)		
Polity			9.50e-05 (0.0337)	0.0197 (0.0298)	0.0437 (0.0368)	0.0132 (0.0226)
Trade Tax Shock* Polity			0.0398 (0.0457)	0.0161 (0.0208)		
Δ Trade Tax Revenue (% GDP)					-0.0110* (0.00638)	-0.000596 (0.00417)
Δ Trade Tax Revenue (% GDP)*Polity					0.00136 (0.00124)	0.00118 (0.000956)
GDP Per Capita (Logged) $_{t-1}$	0.328 (0.312)	1.346*** (0.412)	-0.717* (0.388)	0.0487 (0.368)	-0.306 (0.503)	1.311** (0.601)
Debt (% GDP) $_{t-1}$	-0.0102**	-0.0134**	-0.00811*	-0.00959*	-0.0179***	-0.0164***

	(1)	(2)	(3)	(4)	(5)	(6)
	(0.00471)	(0.00578)	(0.00436)	(0.00558)	(0.00530)	(0.00602)
Capital Account Openness $_{t-1}$	0.328***	−0.180*	0.227**	−0.128	−0.412**	−0.422*
	(0.105)	(0.105)	(0.0956)	(0.0945)	(0.187)	(0.235)
Population (Logged) $_{t-1}$	−0.400	2.564	4.447***	4.022***	−0.794	−3.311
	(1.472)	(1.630)	(1.604)	(1.168)	(2.294)	(2.310)
GDP Growth $_{t-1}$	0.00247	−0.0149	0.0234*	−0.00332	−0.0118	−0.0162
	(0.0136)	(0.0130)	(0.0133)	(0.0135)	(0.0216)	(0.0186)
Aid (% GDP) $_{t-1}$	0.00521	−0.0613***	0.0271*	−0.0184*	0.0151	−0.0444**
	(0.0234)	(0.0171)	(0.0151)	(0.0106)	(0.0239)	(0.0199)
Fuel Exports $_{t-1}$	0.00821	0.0595***	0.00622	0.0500***	−0.00224	0.0250
	(0.00815)	(0.0130)	(0.00934)	(0.0149)	(0.0122)	(0.0178)
IMF Credits (% GDP) $_{t-1}$	−0.0276	0.00656	0.0498	−0.0101	−0.226***	0.00358
	(0.0388)	(0.0262)	(0.0483)	(0.0491)	(0.0640)	(0.0449)
Observations	338	337	204	204	203	202
R-squared	0.953	0.960	0.938	0.980	0.963	0.973
Number of Countries	45	45	21	21	33	33

[a] We attribute the statistically insignificant interaction in columns 3–6 to the loss of observations when employing the shock and change in trade tax revenue variables. Baseline models exhibit statistically significant conditional coefficients.

*** $p<0.01$, ** $p<0.05$, * $p<0.1$

Standard errors in parentheses

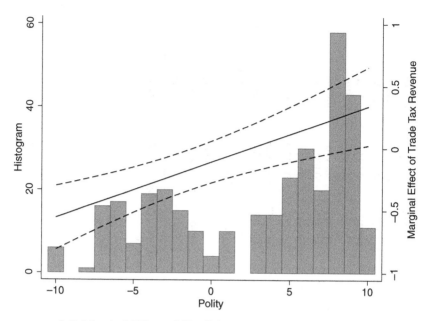

A.3 Marginal Effect of (Declining) Trade Tax Revenue on Goods Tax
Revenue Conditional on Polity

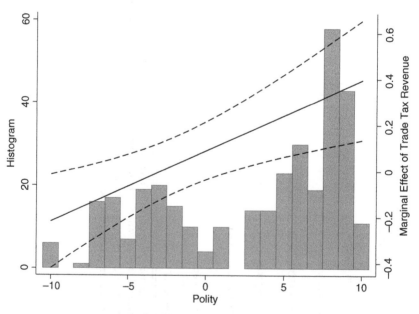

A.4 Marginal Effect of (Declining) Trade Tax Revenue on Income Tax
Revenue Conditional on Polity

A.5 *Determinants of Percent Change in Goods and Income Tax Revenue (Percent of GDP)*

DV	(1)	(2)
	%Δ Income Tax Revenue (% GDP)	%Δ Goods Tax Revenue (% GDP)
%Δ Trade Tax Revenue (% GDP) $_{t-1}$	−0.0187 (0.0405)	−0.0440** (0.0224)
Polity $_{t-1}$	0.104 (0.488)	0.793* (0.415)
%Δ Trade Tax Revenue (% GDP)*Polity $_{t-1}$	0.00426 (0.00642)	0.00391* (0.00218)
GDP Per Capita (Logged) $_{t-1}$	−2.125 (8.613)	−7.609** (3.267)
Fuel Exports $_{t-1}$	−0.373 (0.308)	0.407** (0.175)
Capital Account Openness $_{t-1}$	−0.0947 (2.830)	−3.910*** (1.407)
Debt (% GDP) $_{t-1}$	−0.0835 (0.151)	−0.109 (0.0797)
Population (Logged) $_{t-1}$	−58.51 (37.30)	18.14 (16.32)
GDP Growth $_{t-1}$	0.281 (0.483)	0.414** (0.193)
Aid (% GDP) $_{t-1}$	−0.287 (0.462)	1.145*** (0.335)
IMF Credits (% GDP) $_{t-1}$	−0.953 (1.030)	−0.125 (0.467)
Observations	308	310
R-squared	0.236	0.384
Number of Countries	43	43

*** $p<0.01$, ** $p<0.05$, * $p<0.1$
Standard errors in parentheses

A.6 *Determinants of Tax Revenue (Per Capita): Employing Trade Tax Revenue Per Capita*

DV	(1)	(2)	(3)
	Domestic Tax Revenue (Per Capita)	Goods Tax Revenue (Per Capita)	Income Tax Revenue (Per Capita)
Trade Tax Revenue (Per Capita)$_{t-1}$	**7.096***	**3.952***	**3.394***
	(1.258)	**(0.760)**	**(0.735)**
Polity $_{t-1}$	**1.491e+06***	**674,633**	**657,643**
	(499,949)	**(278,896)**	**(299,828)**
Trade Tax Revenue (Per Capita)* Polity $_{t-1}$	**0.726***	**0.320***	**0.463***
	(0.184)	**(0.108)**	**(0.104)**
GDP Per Capita (Logged) $_{t-1}$	9.620e+06	2.576e+06	5.624e+06*
	(7.350e+06)	(5.232e+06)	(2.995e+06)
Debt (% GDP) $_{t-1}$	194,533*	88,383	81,614
	(100,296)	(61,381)	(50,349)
Capital Account Openness $_{t-1}$	−1.011e+06	180,228	−1.347e+06*
	(1.928e+06)	(1.753e+06)	(800,080)
Population (Logged) $_{t-1}$	9.442e+06	−959,948	1.070e+07*
	(1.300e+07)	(1.227e+07)	(5.728e+06)
GDP Growth $_{t-1}$	−105,897	−33,541	−61,092
	(157,067)	(122,463)	(72,635)
Aid (% GDP) $_{t-1}$	−123,628	−16,132	−60,744
	(157,041)	(109,367)	(93,867)
Fuel Exports $_{t-1}$	−258,494	−192,321	−53,193
	(200,423)	(176,268)	(76,362)
IMF Credits (% GDP) $_{t-1}$	604,328	367,497	206,270
	(591,939)	(498,812)	(183,702)
Observations	338	338	337
R-squared	0.884	0.857	0.928
Number of Countries	45	45	45

*** $p<0.01$, ** $p<0.05$, * $p<0.1$
Standard errors in parentheses

A.7 *Determinants of Tax Revenue (Percent of GDP): Sample of Longstanding Democracies and Nondemocracies*

DV	(1)	(2)	(3)
	Domestic Tax Revenue (% GDP)	Goods Tax Revenue (% GDP)	Income Tax Revenue (% GDP)
Trade Tax Revenue (% GDP) $_{t-1}$	**0.00268**	**−0.0474**	**0.129***
	(0.123)	**(0.0677)**	**(0.0682)**
Polity $_{t-1}$	**−0.125**	**−0.0803***	**−0.0866**
	(0.0808)	**(0.0471)**	**(0.0550)**
Trade Tax Revenue (% GDP)*Polity $_{t-1}$	**0.130***	**0.0828***	**0.0353***
	(0.0203)	**(0.0111)**	**(0.0128)**
GDP Per Capita (Logged) $_{t-1}$	0.676	−0.283	1.514***
	(0.541)	(0.368)	(0.357)
Debt (% GDP) $_{t-1}$	0.00716	−0.0105	0.00278
	(0.0111)	(0.00646)	(0.00664)
Capital Account Openness $_{t-1}$	−0.155	0.0215	−0.414***
	(0.296)	(0.164)	(0.141)
Population (Logged) $_{t-1}$	7.116***	3.244**	3.497**
	(2.012)	(1.482)	(1.482)
GDP Growth $_{t-1}$	0.0671**	0.0470***	0.00169
	(0.0265)	(0.0143)	(0.0161)
Aid (% GDP) $_{t-1}$	0.0880*	0.0249	0.0420
	(0.0529)	(0.0256)	(0.0286)
Fuel Exports $_{t-1}$	0.0743***	0.00183	0.0556***
	(0.0153)	(0.00812)	(0.0135)
IMF Credits (% GDP) $_{t-1}$	0.138	0.0899	0.0243
	(0.0877)	(0.0613)	(0.0516)
Observations	170	170	170
R-squared	0.982	0.976	0.981
Number of Countries	22	22	22

*** $p<0.01$, ** $p<0.05$, * $p<0.1$
Standard errors in parentheses

A.8 *Determinants of Government Revenue and Nontax Revenue (Percent of GDP)*

DV	(1)	(2)
	Revenue (% GDP)	Nontax Revenue (% GDP)
Trade Tax Revenue (% GDP) $_{t-1}$	**0.695*****	**0.186****
	(0.146)	**(0.0764)**
Polity $_{t-1}$	**−0.0342**	**0.0935****
	(0.0570)	**(0.0379)**
Trade Tax Revenue (% GDP)* Polity $_{t-1}$	**0.0595*****	**0.00174**
	(0.0198)	**(0.0122)**
GDP Per Capita (Logged) $_{t-1}$	1.613**	0.142
	(0.658)	(0.358)
Debt (% GDP) $_{t-1}$	−0.0295***	−0.0157***
	(0.00860)	(0.00487)
Capital Account Openness $_{t-1}$	0.130	−0.0332
	(0.183)	(0.115)
Population (Logged) $_{t-1}$	−5.730***	−3.234**
	(2.043)	(1.589)
GDP Growth $_{t-1}$	−0.0117	−0.00357
	(0.0280)	(0.0177)
Aid (% GDP) $_{t-1}$	−0.106**	−0.0181
	(0.0428)	(0.0227)
Fuel Exports $_{t-1}$	0.0688***	−0.0329*
	(0.0181)	(0.0177)
IMF Credits (% GDP) $_{t-1}$	−0.0247	−0.0170
	(0.0744)	(0.0375)
Observations	338	338
R-squared	0.983	0.980
Number of Countries	45	45

*** $p<0.01$, ** $p<0.05$, * $p<0.1$
Standard errors in parentheses

A.9 *Determinants of Tax Revenue (Percent of GDP): Omitting Major Oil Producers*

DV	(1)	(2)	(3)
	Domestic Tax Revenue (% GDP)	Goods Tax Revenue (% GDP)	Income Tax Revenue (% GDP)
Trade Tax Revenue (% GDP) $_{t-1}$	**−0.0696**	**−0.113**	**0.0794**
	(0.113)	**(0.0866)**	**(0.0650)**
Polity $_{t-1}$	**−0.0944****	**−0.0263**	**−0.114*****
	(0.0426)	**(0.0233)**	**(0.0389)**
Trade Tax Revenue (% GDP)* Polity $_{t-1}$	**0.0636*****	**0.0458*****	**0.0292*****
	(0.0197)	**(0.0118)**	**(0.0104)**
GDP Per Capita (Logged) $_{t-1}$	1.372**	0.268	1.537***
	(0.694)	(0.328)	(0.507)
Debt (% GDP) $_{t-1}$	−0.0230***	−0.0106**	−0.0131**
	(0.00709)	(0.00475)	(0.00589)
Capital Account Openness $_{t-1}$	0.00627	0.315***	−0.132
	(0.174)	(0.109)	(0.105)
Population (Logged) $_{t-1}$	3.046	−0.229	2.154
	(2.617)	(1.538)	(1.805)
GDP Growth $_{t-1}$	0.00271	0.00119	−0.0171
	(0.0263)	(0.0143)	(0.0137)
Aid (% GDP) $_{t-1}$	−0.0585	0.00297	−0.0605***
	(0.0357)	(0.0233)	(0.0172)
Fuel Exports $_{t-1}$	0.0625***	0.00842	0.0524***
	(0.0239)	(0.0139)	(0.0161)
IMF Credits (% GDP) $_{t-1}$	0.00945	−0.0280	0.0224
	(0.0643)	(0.0389)	(0.0273)
Observations	321	321	320
R-squared	0.957	0.952	0.953
Number of Countries	42	42	42

*** $p<0.01$, ** $p<0.05$, * $p<0.1$
Standard errors in parentheses

A.10 *Determinants of Tax Revenue (Percent of GDP): Omitting Transitional States*

DV	(1)	(2)	(3)
	Domestic Tax Revenue (% GDP)	Goods Tax Revenue (% GDP)	Income Tax Revenue (% GDP)
Trade Tax Revenue (% GDP) $_{t-1}$	−0.114	−0.177***	0.0890
	(0.0953)	(0.0525)	(0.0644)
Polity $_{t-1}$	−0.132***	−0.0588**	−0.127***
	(0.0418)	(0.0264)	(0.0424)
Trade Tax Revenue (% GDP)* Polity $_{t-1}$	0.0835***	0.0598***	0.0419***
	(0.0177)	(0.0111)	(0.0148)
GDP Per Capita (Logged) $_{t-1}$	0.252	−0.659**	1.051***
	(0.376)	(0.268)	(0.364)
Debt (% GDP) $_{t-1}$	−0.0125**	−0.00102	−0.0111**
	(0.00593)	(0.00354)	(0.00534)
Capital Account Openness $_{t-1}$	0.0307	0.187**	−0.132
	(0.124)	(0.0791)	(0.0985)
Population (Logged) $_{t-1}$	7.131***	3.125**	3.731***
	(1.942)	(1.253)	(1.321)
GDP Growth $_{t-1}$	0.0321	0.0357***	−0.0170
	(0.0206)	(0.0120)	(0.0137)
Aid (% GDP) $_{t-1}$	−0.0358	0.00465	−0.0595***
	(0.0257)	(0.0146)	(0.0179)
Fuel Exports $_{t-1}$	0.0627***	0.00462	0.0574***
	(0.0139)	(0.00845)	(0.0137)
IMF Credits (% GDP) $_{t-1}$	0.129*	0.100**	−0.00605
	(0.0710)	(0.0423)	(0.0590)
Observations	282	282	282
R-squared	0.982	0.961	0.971
Number of Countries	36	36	36

*** $p<0.01$, ** $p<0.05$, * $p<0.1$
Standard errors in parentheses

A.11 *Determinants of Tax Revenue (Percent of GDP): Error Correction Model*

DV	(1)	(2)	(3)
	Δ Domestic Tax Revenue (% GDP)	Δ Goods Tax Revenue (% GDP)	Δ Income Tax Revenue (% GDP)
Trade Tax Revenue (% GDP) $_{t-1}$	**0.196**	**−0.0523**	**0.178****
	(0.156)	**(0.107)**	**(0.0709)**
Polity $_{t-1}$	**−0.0872***	**−0.0366**	**−0.123*****
	(0.0507)	**(0.0261)**	**(0.0437)**
Trade Tax Revenue (% GDP)* **Polity** $_{t-1}$	**0.122*****	**0.0724*****	**0.0378*****
	(0.0231)	**(0.0140)**	**(0.0133)**
GDP Per Capita (Logged) $_{t-1}$	1.236**	0.336	0.895***
	(0.571)	(0.355)	(0.343)
Debt (% GDP) $_{t-1}$	−0.0118	−0.00488	−0.00222
	(0.0121)	(0.00751)	(0.00896)
Capital Account Openness $_{t-1}$	0.0384	0.347**	−0.0654
	(0.300)	(0.155)	(0.172)
Population (Logged) $_{t-1}$	2.032	−1.418	4.087**
	(2.842)	(1.721)	(1.682)
GDP Growth $_{t-1}$	0.0289	−0.0140	−0.00936
	(0.0466)	(0.0277)	(0.0280)
Aid (% GDP) $_{t-1}$	0.00798	0.00856	0.0225
	(0.0524)	(0.0254)	(0.0247)
Fuel Exports $_{t-1}$	0.104***	0.00783	0.0827***
	(0.0205)	(0.0124)	(0.0122)
IMF Credits (% GDP) $_{t-1}$	−0.108	−0.143***	−0.0262
	(0.109)	(0.0529)	(0.0521)
Δ Trade Tax Revenue (% GDP)	0.209	−0.0627	0.122
	(0.178)	(0.107)	(0.0789)
Δ Polity	−0.0311	−0.0297	−0.0194
	(0.0476)	(0.0247)	(0.0378)
Δ Trade Tax Revenue (% GDP)*Polity	0.0527*	0.0292**	0.0187
	(0.0294)	(0.0142)	(0.0159)
Δ GDP Per Capita (Logged)	2.155**	1.090*	0.874
	(0.928)	(0.638)	(0.903)
Δ Debt (% GDP)	0.00250	0.000368	0.00586
	(0.0110)	(0.00792)	(0.00925)
Δ Capital Account Openness	−0.0787	0.0886	0.0456
	(0.255)	(0.146)	(0.162)

(continued)

A.11 *(Cont.)*

DV	(1)	(2)	(3)
	Δ Domestic Tax Revenue (% GDP)	Δ Goods Tax Revenue (% GDP)	Δ Income Tax Revenue (% GDP)
Δ Population (Logged)	−4.930	−12.28	19.57**
	(14.92)	(7.563)	(7.678)
Δ GDP Growth	0.00282	−0.00564	−0.0112
	(0.0344)	(0.0222)	(0.0213)
Δ Aid (% GDP)	0.0617	−0.00225	0.0623*
	(0.0613)	(0.0367)	(0.0338)
Δ Fuel Exports	0.0515**	−0.0117	0.0550***
	(0.0251)	(0.0108)	(0.0161)
Δ IMF Credits (% GDP)	0.0100	−0.0361	−0.0104
	(0.0967)	(0.0527)	(0.0507)
Observations	299	299	298
R-squared	0.968	0.960	0.959
Number of Countries	38	38	38

*** $p<0.01$, ** $p<0.05$, * $p<0.1$
Standard errors in parentheses

A.12 *Determinants of Tax Revenue (Percent of GDP): Controlling for Bureaucratic Quality*

DV	(1) Domestic Tax Revenue (% GDP)	(2) Goods Tax Revenue (% GDP)	(3) Income Tax Revenue (% GDP)	(4) Domestic Tax Revenue (% GDP)	(5) Goods Tax Revenue (% GDP)	(6) Income Tax Revenue (% GDP)
Trade Tax Revenue (% GDP) $_{t-1}$	−0.0623 (0.106)	−0.182*** (0.0660)	0.127** (0.0509)	−0.410 (0.294)	−0.271 (0.172)	0.0452 (0.115)
Polity $_{t-1}$	−0.232*** (0.0471)	−0.0400* (0.0236)	−0.219*** (0.0516)			
Trade Tax Revenue (% GDP)* Polity $_{t-1}$	0.102*** (0.0187)	0.0591*** (0.0108)	0.0411*** (0.0123)			
Bureaucratic Quality $_{t-1}$	0.349 (0.244)	−0.0462 (0.134)	0.378** (0.187)	−0.624 (0.469)	−0.286 (0.331)	−0.0817 (0.316)
Trade Tax Revenue (% GDP)* Bureaucratic Quality $_{t-1}$				0.206 (0.139)	0.0589 (0.0856)	−0.00620 (0.0655)
GDP Per Capita (Logged) $_{t-1}$	0.589 (0.646)	−0.260 (0.266)	0.888** (0.372)	0.0427 (0.683)	−0.753* (0.395)	0.485 (0.384)
Debt (% GDP) $_{t-1}$	−0.0139* (0.00744)	−0.00417 (0.00485)	−0.0109* (0.00634)	−0.0122* (0.00654)	−0.00227 (0.00451)	−0.0111** (0.00558)
Capital Account Openness $_{t-1}$	0.154 (0.163)	0.337*** (0.0953)	−0.136 (0.124)	0.0472 (0.161)	0.211** (0.0925)	−0.0582 (0.0950)
Population (Logged) $_{t-1}$	5.910*** (2.207)	1.731 (1.205)	3.269** (1.417)	8.747*** (1.880)	4.729*** (1.658)	4.113*** (1.252)

(*continued*)

A.12 (Cont.)

DV	(1) Domestic Tax Revenue (% GDP)	(2) Goods Tax Revenue (% GDP)	(3) Income Tax Revenue (% GDP)	(4) Domestic Tax Revenue (% GDP)	(5) Goods Tax Revenue (% GDP)	(6) Income Tax Revenue (% GDP)
GDP Growth $_{t-1}$	0.00356	0.0105	-0.0183	0.0225	0.0230	-0.000746
	(0.0268)	(0.0157)	(0.0123)	(0.0238)	(0.0155)	(0.0118)
Aid (% GDP) $_{t-1}$	-0.0639	0.00236	-0.0497**	0.00837	0.0335	-0.0194
	(0.0401)	(0.0267)	(0.0228)	(0.0371)	(0.0261)	(0.0174)
Fuel Exports $_{t-1}$	0.0854***	0.0171**	0.0783***	0.0742***	0.0138	0.0623***
	(0.0167)	(0.00863)	(0.0128)	(0.0164)	(0.00933)	(0.0119)
IMF Credits (% GDP) $_{t-1}$	0.00197	0.00570	-0.000810	-0.0418	-0.0381	0.0232
	(0.0695)	(0.0446)	(0.0273)	(0.0827)	(0.0510)	(0.0409)
Observations	264	264	264	294	294	294
R-squared	0.975	0.973	0.970	0.977	0.953	0.971
Number of Countries	36	36	36	37	37	37

*** p<0.01, ** p<0.05, * p<0.1
Standard errors in parentheses

A.13 *Determinants of Tax Revenue (Percent of GDP): Selection into Trade Liberalization*

DV	(1) Domestic Tax Revenue (% GDP)	(2) Goods Tax Revenue (% GDP)	(3) Income Tax Revenue (% GDP)	(4) Domestic Tax Revenue (% GDP)	(5) Goods Tax Revenue (% GDP)	(6) Income Tax Revenue (% GDP)
Trade Tax Revenue (% GDP) $_{t-1}$	**0.491**	**0.125**	**0.409****	**0.450****	**0.0850**	**0.422*****
	(0.448)	**(0.203)**	**(0.207)**	**(0.210)**	**(0.116)**	**(0.126)**
Polity $_{t-1}$	**−0.291**	**−0.0721**	**−0.284*****	**−0.303*****	**−0.0697**	**−0.303*****
	(0.213)	**(0.0966)**	**(0.0984)**	**(0.0978)**	**(0.0516)**	**(0.0593)**
Trade Tax Revenue (% GDP)*Polity $_{t-1}$	**0.110***	**0.0843*****	**0.0468**	**0.105*****	**0.0817*****	**0.0472****
	(0.0658)	**(0.0299)**	**(0.0305)**	**(0.0311)**	**(0.0176)**	**(0.0185)**
GDP Per Capita (Logged) $_{t-1}$	2.163	0.575	1.725	4.625***	1.378***	3.137***
	(2.468)	(1.119)	(1.145)	(0.938)	(0.506)	(0.564)
Debt (% GDP) $_{t-1}$	−0.0268	−0.000702	−0.0287**	−0.0219	0.00219	−0.0274***
	(0.0305)	(0.0138)	(0.0141)	(0.0138)	(0.00768)	(0.00824)
Capital Account Openness $_{t-1}$	−0.288	0.344	−0.534*	−0.136	0.414**	−0.475**
	(0.671)	(0.304)	(0.310)	(0.304)	(0.169)	(0.182)
Population (Logged) $_{t-1}$	−1.659	−3.126	1.972	−3.351	−3.173	0.593
	(8.306)	(3.767)	(3.835)	(3.839)	(2.121)	(2.301)
GDP Growth $_{t-1}$	−0.0720	−0.0352	−0.0543	−0.0646	−0.0421	−0.0414
	(0.129)	(0.0585)	(0.0596)	(0.0610)	(0.0342)	(0.0364)
Aid (% GDP) $_{t-1}$	0.178	0.121	0.00748	0.149	0.0687	0.0106
	(0.309)	(0.140)	(0.142)	(0.166)	(0.0940)	(0.0988)

(continued)

213

A.13 (Cont.)

DV	(1) Domestic Tax Revenue (% GDP)	(2) Goods Tax Revenue (% GDP)	(3) Income Tax Revenue (% GDP)	(4) Domestic Tax Revenue (% GDP)	(5) Goods Tax Revenue (% GDP)	(6) Income Tax Revenue (% GDP)
Fuel Exports $_{t-1}$	−0.00566 (0.111)	−0.0605 (0.0503)	0.0353 (0.0512)	−0.0242 (0.0483)	−0.0746*** (0.0263)	0.0312 (0.0291)
IMF Credits (% GDP) $_{t-1}$	−0.00599 (0.217)	−0.141 (0.0984)	0.142 (0.100)	−0.00554 (0.105)	−0.168*** (0.0597)	0.171*** (0.0625)
Selection Equation (DV= Trade Tax)						
WTO	0.199* (0.118)	0.199* (0.118)	0.196* (0.118)			
NSPTAs				0.506*** (0.159)	0.506*** (0.159)	0.510*** (0.159)
IMF Credits (% GDP)	−0.00452 (0.00968)	−0.00452 (0.00968)	−0.00495 (0.00977)	−0.0106 (0.0111)	−0.0106 (0.0111)	−0.0112 (0.0112)
Democracy	−0.00618 (0.00938)	−0.00618 (0.00938)	−0.00645 (0.00938)	−0.00675 (0.0102)	−0.00675 (0.0102)	−0.00721 (0.0102)
GDP Per Capita (Logged)	0.227*** (0.0542)	0.227*** (0.0542)	0.227*** (0.0543)	0.212*** (0.0600)	0.212*** (0.0600)	0.211*** (0.0601)
Observations	788	788	787	684	684	683

*** p<0.01, ** p<0.05, * p<0.1
Standard errors in parentheses

A.14 *Determinants of Tax Revenue (Percent of GDP): Selection into Democracy*

DV	(1)	(2)	(3)
	Domestic Tax Revenue (% GDP)	Goods Tax Revenue (% GDP)	Income Tax Revenue (% GDP)
Trade Tax Revenue (% GDP) $_{t-1}$	−4.306**	−0.0315	−4.241***
	(1.986)	(1.231)	(1.233)
Polity $_{t-1}$	−1.651***	−0.468**	−0.813***
	(0.363)	(0.224)	(0.237)
Trade Tax Revenue (% GDP)* Polity $_{t-1}$	0.564**	0.0679	0.499***
	(0.235)	(0.146)	(0.144)
GDP Per Capita (Logged) $_{t-1}$	5.058***	1.243**	2.765***
	(0.829)	(0.511)	(0.561)
Debt (% GDP) $_{t-1}$	−0.0107	−0.00197	−0.0117
	(0.0111)	(0.00683)	(0.00730)
Capital Account Openness $_{t-1}$	−0.0471	−0.113	0.247
	(0.312)	(0.193)	(0.205)
Population (Logged) $_{t-1}$	−6.424	−5.729**	0.436
	(4.054)	(2.500)	(2.689)
GDP Growth $_{t-1}$	0.00743	−0.0332	0.0271
	(0.0366)	(0.0226)	(0.0244)
Aid (% GDP) $_{t-1}$	−0.0619	0.168***	−0.137***
	(0.0558)	(0.0347)	(0.0333)
Fuel Exports $_{t-1}$	−0.00231	−0.0532**	0.0697**
	(0.0425)	(0.0260)	(0.0309)
IMF Credits (% GDP) $_{t-1}$	0.0975	−0.201***	0.255***
	(0.0783)	(0.0483)	(0.0514)
Selection Equation (DV= Democracy)			
GDP Per Capita (Logged) $_{t-2}$	0.0640*	0.0640*	0.0648*
	(0.0337)	(0.0337)	(0.0337)
Regional Democracy $_{t-2}$	0.141***	0.141***	0.141***
	(0.0117)	(0.0117)	(0.0117)
Observations	3,329	3,329	3,328

*** p<0.01, ** p<0.05, * p<0.1
Standard errors in parentheses

APPENDIX B

B.1 *International Centre for Tax and Development (ICTD) Data Descriptions*

Variable	Mean	St. Dev.	Min	Max	Definition
Domestic Tax Revenue (% GDP) (ICTD)	10.69	6.50	2.8e−6	41.36	Total Tax Revenue excluding social contributions and natural resource revenue MINUS Total Taxes on International Trade
Goods Tax Revenue (% GDP) (ICTD)	6.32	4.51	0	35.90	Total Indirect Taxes excluding resource revenues, calculated as the sum of Taxes on Goods and Services and Other Taxes
Income Tax Revenue (% GDP) (ICTD)	4.61	3.10	0	17.39	Total Direct Taxes excluding social contributions and resource revenue, calculated as the sum of Taxes on Income Profits and Capital Gains, Taxes on Payroll and Workforce and Property Tax
Trade Tax Revenue (% GDP)	3.62	3.97	−0.03	42.12	Total Taxes on International Trade

Source: Prichard et al. 2014

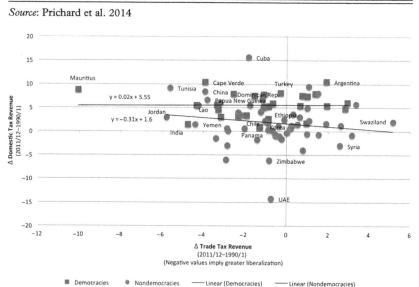

B.2 Revenue Shock and Domestic Tax Revenue by Regime Type, ICTD Imputed Data

Note: We omit Eastern European Countries from the sample because of their unique liberalization process as discussed in Chapter 2.

B.3 ICTD Model Description

We use the ICTD data for the value added in utilizing a longer time trend and increasing observations, while keeping its limitations in mind. Overall the pattern is consistent with World Development Indicators (WDI) data models. Assessing the marginal effects of declining trade taxes conditional on different values of polity, the primary difference is that trade taxes have no statistically significant impact on domestic taxes in democracies. This is still consistent with our hypothesis; domestic tax revenue generation fails to increase in response to trade liberalization. The models below also suggest that democracies are finding it harder to increase their income taxes – relative to their goods taxes– as trade taxes decline.

B.4 *Determinants of Tax Revenue (Percent of GDP): All Developing Countries, ICTD Data*

DV	(1)	(2)	(3)	(4)	(5)	(6)
	Domestic Tax Revenue (% GDP)	Income Tax Revenue (% GDP)	Goods Tax Revenue (% GDP)	Domestic Tax Revenue Growth	Income Tax Revenue Growth	Goods Tax Revenue Growth
Trade Tax Revenue (% GDP) $_{t-1}$	−0.136*	−0.0161	−0.0721	0.446	0.659	0.575
	(0.0821)	(0.0600)	(0.0815)	(0.450)	(0.728)	(1.632)
Polity $_{t-1}$	0.0532	−0.00259	0.0907***	0.322	−0.0661	1.290**
	(0.0450)	(0.0213)	(0.0325)	(0.222)	(0.342)	(0.618)
Trade Tax Revenue (% GDP)* Polity $_{t-1}$	0.0179*	−0.00158	0.00531	0.144**	0.221**	0.0495
	(0.0105)	(0.00808)	(0.00889)	(0.0631)	(0.0934)	(0.147)
GDP Per Capita (Logged) $_{t-1}$	1.279***	0.634*	0.551	−1.926	0.366	−6.934
	(0.466)	(0.325)	(0.372)	(2.387)	(3.794)	(5.598)
Debt (% GDP) $_{t-1}$	−0.00621	−0.000361	−0.0123*	−0.00678	0.0284	−0.266
	(0.00961)	(0.00517)	(0.00722)	(0.0478)	(0.0857)	(0.163)
Capital Account Openness $_{t-1}$	−0.172	−0.271***	0.165	−0.910	1.977	−2.233
	(0.171)	(0.0861)	(0.135)	(0.926)	(1.495)	(2.932)
Population (Logged) $_{t-1}$	3.516*	2.705**	−0.669	11.81	−24.95*	14.36
	(1.810)	(1.143)	(1.221)	(9.157)	(14.56)	(27.08)
GDP Growth $_{t-1}$	0.00620	0.00207	0.00128	0.203	0.815***	0.625*
	(0.0213)	(0.0119)	(0.0150)	(0.154)	(0.210)	(0.374)
Aid (% GDP) $_{t-1}$	−0.000965	0.00580	−0.0632	0.161	−0.492	1.415
	(0.0533)	(0.0260)	(0.0432)	(0.312)	(0.422)	(1.115)
Fuel Exports $_{t-1}$	0.00971	0.00102	0.00343	0.0270	−0.0664	−0.0143
	(0.0156)	(0.0112)	(0.00694)	(0.119)	(0.144)	(0.169)
IMF Credits (% GDP) $_{t-1}$	0.0291	−0.00760	0.0182	0.231	0.465	0.705
	(0.0465)	(0.0268)	(0.0391)	(0.236)	(0.490)	(0.865)

Observations	267	266	269	266	264	264
R-squared	0.985	0.981	0.976	0.338	0.322	0.355
Number of Countries	38	38	37	38	38	37

*** p<0.01, ** p<0.05, * p<0.1
Standard errors in parentheses

B.5 *Determinants of Tax Revenue (Percent of GDP): Sample of Longstanding Democracies and Nondemocracies, ICTD Data*

DV	(1) Domestic Tax Revenue (% GDP)	(2) Income Tax Revenue (% GDP)	(3) Goods Tax Revenue (% GDP)	(4) Domestic Tax Revenue (% GDP)	(5) Income Tax Revenue (% GDP)	(6) Goods Tax Revenue (% GDP)
Trade Tax Revenue (% GDP) $_{t-1}$	**0.0183**	**0.143***	**−0.133**	**−0.158**	**0.143**	**−0.214**
	(0.176)	(0.0805)	(0.174)	(0.187)	(0.0999)	(0.184)
Polity $_{t-1}$	−0.0609	−0.0724	−0.0105			
	(0.0966)	(0.0599)	(0.0682)			
Trade Tax Revenue (% GDP)* Polity $_{t-1}$	0.0718**	0.0183	0.0558**			
	(0.0297)	(0.0176)	(0.0263)			
Democracy Dummy $_{t-1}$ **(1 = Dem; 0 = LibAuth or ConservAuth)**				−152.2***	−121.5***	−23.74
				(49.34)	(30.28)	(24.00)
Trade Tax Revenue (% GDP)*Democracy Dummy $_{t-1}$ **(1 = Dem; 0 = LibAuth or ConservAuth)**				0.897***	0.124	0.737***
				(0.330)	(0.193)	(0.208)
GDP Per Capita (Logged) $_{t-1}$	0.646	1.306***	−0.499	0.230	1.338***	−0.645

(continued)

B.5 (*Cont.*)

DV	(1) Domestic Tax Revenue (% GDP)	(2) Income Tax Revenue (% GDP)	(3) Goods Tax Revenue (% GDP)	(4) Domestic Tax Revenue (% GDP)	(5) Income Tax Revenue (% GDP)	(6) Goods Tax Revenue (% GDP)
	(0.893)	(0.404)	(0.556)	(0.874)	(0.454)	(0.477)
Debt (% GDP) $_{t-1}$	0.00707	0.0126**	-0.00121	0.0162	0.00827	0.00352
	(0.0133)	(0.00566)	(0.00954)	(0.0134)	(0.00637)	(0.00982)
Capital Account Openness $_{t-1}$	-0.273	-0.461***	0.199	-0.305	-0.503***	0.131
	(0.320)	(0.148)	(0.268)	(0.306)	(0.150)	(0.254)
Population (Logged) $_{t-1}$	6.497**	5.090***	1.941	7.689***	5.571***	2.930
	(3.070)	(1.551)	(2.350)	(2.436)	(1.481)	(1.792)
GDP Growth $_{t-1}$	0.0182	-0.0281**	0.0332*	0.000243	-0.0286**	0.0211
	(0.0274)	(0.0132)	(0.0192)	(0.0264)	(0.0138)	(0.0187)
Aid (% GDP) $_{t-1}$	0.00887	0.0620**	-0.0467	-0.0402	0.0647**	-0.0757
	(0.0688)	(0.0281)	(0.0547)	(0.0666)	(0.0280)	(0.0560)
Fuel Exports $_{t-1}$	0.00118	0.000252	-0.00122	-0.00728	-0.00232	-0.00486
	(0.0185)	(0.0130)	(0.00813)	(0.0227)	(0.0134)	(0.0112)
IMF Credits (% GDP) $_{t-1}$	0.186**	0.0429	0.129*	0.130*	0.0471	0.105*
	(0.0850)	(0.0371)	(0.0710)	(0.0753)	(0.0414)	(0.0627)
Observations	136	136	137	136	136	137
R-squared	0.987	0.994	0.980	0.988	0.994	0.977
Number of Countries	21	21	20	21	21	20

*** p<0.01, ** p<0.05, * p<0.1
Standard errors in parentheses

APPENDIX C

C.1 *Data Descriptions*

Variable	Source	Definition
Aid (% GDP)	World Bank 2016a	Net official development assistance is disbursement flows (net of repayment of principal) that meet the Development Assistance Committee (DAC) definition of official development assistance (ODA) and are made to countries and territories on the DAC list of aid recipients. Net official aid refers to aid flows (net of repayments) from official donors to countries and territories in part II of the DAC list of recipients.
Bureaucratic Quality	ICRG 2012	Institutional strength and quality of bureaucracy. Coded 1 (low quality) through 4 (high quality).
Capital Account Openness	Chinn and Ito 2015	KAOPEN is based on the binary dummy variables that codify the tabulation of restrictions on cross-border financial transactions reported in the IMF's Annual Report on Exchange Arrangements and Exchange Restrictions (AREAER).
Debt	World Bank 2016a	Debt is the entire stock of direct government fixed-term contractual obligations to others outstanding on a particular date. It includes domestic and foreign liabilities such as currency and money deposits, securities other than shares, and loans. It is the gross amount of government liabilities reduced by the amount of equity and financial derivatives held by the government.
Democracy (Boix et al.)	Boix, Miller, and Rosato 2012	Dichotomous Democracy Measure (1 Democracy, 0 Not Democracy).
Democracy (Freedom House)	FH 2016	Sum of political rights. Data is rescaled so 0 is lowest level of freedom and 7 is highest level of freedom.

(continued)

C.1 (*Cont.*)

Variable	Source	Definition
Democracy Dummy (Polity)	Marshall and Gurr 2016	Polity scores converted to dichotomous regime categories: nondemocracies (−10 to 5) and democracies (+6 to +10). Coded as 1: democracy and 0: nondemocracy.
Domestic Tax Revenue	World Bank 2016a	Tax Revenue minus Taxes on International Trade
Fuel Exports	World Bank 2016a	Fuels comprise SITC section 3 (mineral fuels). As a percent of merchandise exports.
GDP Growth	World Bank 2016a	Annual percentage growth rate of GDP at market prices based on constant local currency. Aggregates are based on constant 2000 US dollars.
Goods Tax Revenue	World Bank 2016a	Taxes on goods and services include general sales and turnover or value-added taxes, selective excises on goods, selective taxes on services, taxes on the use of goods or property, taxes on extraction and production of minerals, and profits of fiscal monopolies.
Gross Domestic Product Per Capita	World Bank 2016a	GDP per capita is gross domestic product divided by midyear population. GDP is the sum of gross value added by all resident producers in the economy plus any product taxes and minus any subsidies not included in the value of the products.
IMF Credits	World Bank 2016a	Use of IMF credit denotes members' drawings on the IMF other than those drawn against the country's reserve tranche position. Use of IMF credit includes purchases and drawings under the Extended Credit Facility, Standby Credit Facility, Rapid Credit Facility, Standby Arrangements, Flexible Credit Line, and the Extended Fund Facility.

C.1 (*Cont.*)

Variable	Source	Definition
Income Tax Revenue	World Bank 2016a	Taxes on income, profits, and capital gains are levied on the actual or presumptive net income of individuals, on the profits of corporations and enterprises, and on capital gains, whether realized or not, on land, securities, and other assets. Intragovernmental payments are eliminated in consolidation.
NSPTAs (North-South Preferential Trade Agreements)	Dür, Baccini, and Elsig 2014	Binary variable equal to one when a country has signed an NSPTA in that year.
Polity	Marshall and Gurr 2016	Democracy is conceived as three essential, interdependent elements. One is the presence of institutions and procedures through which citizens can express effective preferences about alternative policies and leaders. Second is the existence of institutionalized constraints on the exercise of power by the executive. Third is the guarantee of civil liberties to all citizens in their daily lives and in acts of political participation. Other aspects of plural democracy, such as the rule of law, systems of checks and balances, freedom of the press, and so on are means to, or specific manifestations of, these general principles.
Population	World Bank 2016a	Total population is based on the de facto definition of population, which counts all residents regardless of legal status or citizenship – except for refugees not permanently settled in the country of asylum, who are generally considered part of the population of their country of origin.
Revenue	World Bank 2016a	Revenue is cash receipts from taxes, social contributions, and other revenues such as fines, fees, rent, and income from property or sales. Grants are also considered as revenue but are excluded here.

(*continued*)

C.1 (*Cont.*)

Variable	Source	Definition
Tax Revenue	World Bank 2016a	Tax revenue refers to compulsory transfers to the central government for public purposes. Certain compulsory transfers such as fines, penalties, and most social security contributions are excluded. Refunds and corrections of erroneously collected tax revenue are treated as negative revenue.
Trade Tax Revenue	World Bank 2016a	Taxes on international trade include import duties, export duties, profits of export or import monopolies, exchange profits, and exchange taxes.
WTO	WTO 2017	Binary variable equal to one when a country is a member of the World Trade Organization

C.2 *Summary Statistics*

Variable	Mean	SD	Min	Max
Aid (% GDP)	8.52	13.19	−2.39	241.71
Bureaucratic Quality	1.63	1.05	0	4
Capital Account Openness	−0.06	1.47	−1.89	2.39
Debt (% GDP)	55.16	41.16	0.21	289.84
Democracy (Boix et al.)	0.37	0.48	0	1
Democracy (Freedom House)	3.87	2.11	1	7
Democracy Dummy (Polity)	0.33	0.47	0	1
Domestic Tax Revenue (% GDP)	12.49	7.19	0.018	65.58
Domestic Tax Revenue (Logged)	23.74	3.75	0.04	34.07
Domestic Tax Revenue Growth	0.02	0.17	−0.82	2.02
Fuel Exports (% Merchandise Exports)	16.95	28.19	0	99.79
GDP Growth	3.87	7.20	−64.05	149.97
GDP Per Capita (Logged)	7.73	1.50	4.17	12.17
Goods Tax Revenue (% GDP)	7.19	5.23	0.01	40.41
Goods Tax Revenue (Logged)	23.12	3.73	1.27	33.23
Goods Tax Revenue Growth	4.01	30.30	−84.57	598.86
IMF Credits (% GDP)	3.63	11.16	0	249.38
Income Tax Revenue (% GDP)	5.08	4.01	0.01	29.53
Income Tax Revenue (Logged)	22.80	3.70	1.95	33.42
Income Tax Revenue Growth	4.50	32.11	−86.90	580.57
NSPTAs	0.08	0.28	0	1
Polity	1.88	6.53	−10	10

C.2 (*Cont.*)

Variable	Mean	SD	Min	Max
Population (Logged)	14.90	2.38	9.10	21.03
Revenue (% GDP)	23.46	12.47	0.02	98.69
Revenue (Logged)	24.46	3.56	0.82	34.58
Trade Tax Revenue (% GDP)	3.31	4.13	0.00	41.53
Trade Tax Revenue (% Revenue)	16.04	15.37	0.00	75.17
WTO	0.29	0.45	0	1

C.3 *Country List*

Albania	Gambia, The	Pakistan
Algeria	Georgia	Panama
Argentina	Ghana	Papua New Guinea
Armenia	Guatemala	Paraguay
Azerbaijan	Guinea	Peru
Bahrain	Honduras	Philippines
Bangladesh	Hungary	Poland
Belarus	India	Qatar
Benin	Indonesia	Romania
Bhutan	Iran, Islamic Rep.	Russian Federation
Bolivia	Jamaica	Rwanda
Botswana	Jordan	Senegal
Brazil	Kazakhstan	Serbia
Bulgaria	Kenya	Singapore
Burkina Faso	Korea, Rep.	Slovak Republic
Burundi	Kuwait	Slovenia
Cape Verde	Kyrgyz Republic	South Africa
Cambodia	Latvia	Sri Lanka
Cameroon	Lebanon	Suriname
Central African Republic	Lesotho	Syrian Arab Republic
Chile	Lithuania	Tajikistan
China	Macedonia, FYR	Tanzania
Colombia	Madagascar	Thailand
Congo, Rep.	Malaysia	Togo
Costa Rica	Mali	Trinidad and Tobago
Cote d'Ivoire	Mauritius	Tunisia
Croatia	Mexico	Turkey
Cyprus	Moldova	Uganda
Czech Republic	Mongolia	Ukraine
Dominican Republic	Morocco	Uruguay
Ecuador	Mozambique	Venezuela, RB
Egypt, Arab Rep.	Namibia	Yemen, Rep.
El Salvador	Nepal	Zambia
Estonia	Nicaragua	Zimbabwe
Ethiopia	Niger	
Fiji	Oman	

C.4 *Constant Regime (1990–2012) Country List*

Democracies		Nondemocracies	
Argentina	Korea, Rep.	Algeria	Kuwait
Bolivia	Latvia	Azerbaijan	Morocco
Botswana	Lithuania	Bahrain	Mozambique
Brazil	Macedonia	Bhutan	Oman
Bulgaria	Mauritius	Burkina Faso	Papua New Guinea
Chile	Namibia	Cambodia	Qatar
Colombia	Nicaragua	Cameroon	Rwanda
Costa Rica	Panama	Central African Republic	Singapore
Cyprus	Philippines	China	Suriname
Czech Republic	Slovak Republic	Congo, Rep.	Syria
El Salvador	Slovenia	Cote d'Ivoire	Tajikistan
Estonia	Trinidad and	Egypt	Tanzania
Honduras	Tobago	Ethiopia	Togo
Hungary	Turkey	Guinea	Tunisia
India	Ukraine	Iran	Uganda
Jamaica	Uruguay	Jordan	Yemen
		Kazakhstan	Zimbabwe

APPENDIX D

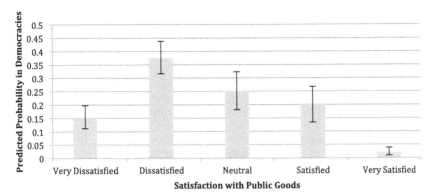

D.1 Predicted Probabilities of Satisfaction with Public Goods for Respondents in Democracies (MTurk)

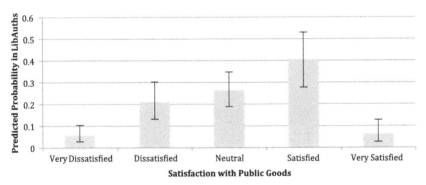

D.2 Predicted Probabilities of Satisfaction with Public Goods for Respondents in Liberal Authoritarian Countries (MTurk)

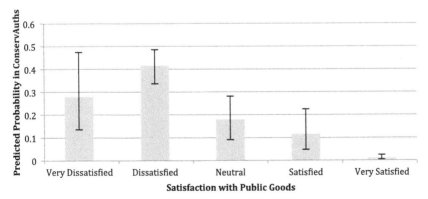

D.3 Predicted Probabilities of Satisfaction with Public Goods for Respondents in Conservative Authoritarian Countries (MTurk)

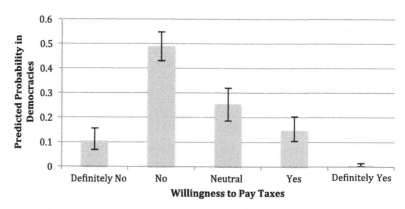

D.4 Predicted Probabilities of Willingness to Pay Taxes for Respondents
in Democracies (MTurk)

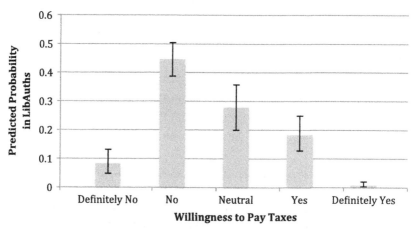

D.5 Predicted Probabilities of Willingness to Pay Taxes for Respondents
in Liberal Authoritarian Countries (MTurk)

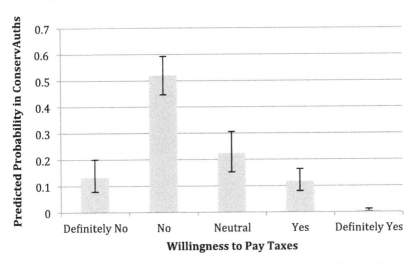

D.6 Predicted Probabilities of Willingness to Pay Taxes for Respondents in Conservative Authoritarian Countries (MTurk)

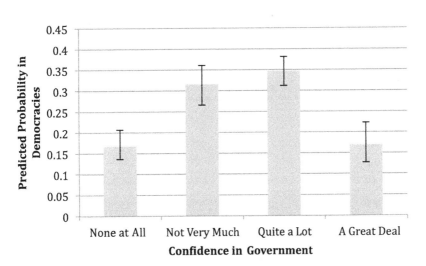

D.7 Predicted Probabilities of Confidence in Government for Respondents in Democracies (World Values Survey)

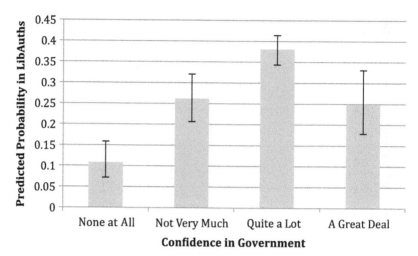

D.8 Predicted Probabilities of Confidence in Government for Respondents in Liberal Authoritarian Countries (World Values Survey)

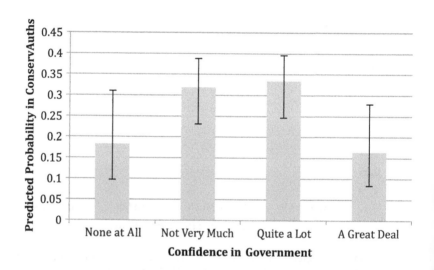

D.9 Predicted Probabilities of Confidence in Government for Respondents in Conservative Authoritarian Countries (World Values Survey)

D.10 *Multi-Level Ordered Logit Estimations of S1 (MTurk and World Values Survey)*

DV	(1)	(2)	(3)	(4)	(5)
	Satisfaction Public Goods	Satisfaction Public Goods	Willingness Pay Taxes	Willingness Pay Taxes	Confidence in Govt
Strategy	S1	S1	S1	S1	S1
LibAuth	*1.193*** *(0.322)*		*0.284** *(0.160)*		
Democracy		*−1.125*** *(0.318)*		*−0.263** *(0.157)*	*−0.671*** *(0.0477)*
ConservAuth		*−1.879*** *(0.507)*		*−0.525*** *(0.221)*	*0.0178* *(0.0612)*
Income	−0.464* (0.263)	−0.383 (0.283)	0.886** (0.363)	0.905** (0.364)	−0.0404** (0.0198)
Age	−0.0945 (0.186)	−0.116 (0.184)	−0.567*** (0.153)	−0.568*** (0.155)	0.00682*** (0.00162)
Male	−0.00983 (0.299)	0.0756 (0.318)	0.131 (0.238)	0.161 (0.241)	−0.0531 (0.0368)
Elite Status	0.324 (0.238)	0.348 (0.240)	0.147 (0.261)	0.156 (0.265)	−0.193*** (0.0566)
Unemployment	−0.0238 (0.0239)	−0.0371 (0.0268)	−0.00431 (0.00885)	−0.00889 (0.00902)	−0.0151*** (0.00421)
GDP Per Capita (Logged)	0.927*** (0.196)	0.904*** (0.170)	0.102 (0.0987)	0.0926 (0.0921)	−0.278*** (0.0305)
Govt Effectiveness	0.377 (0.235)	0.365 (0.234)	0.645** (0.264)	0.645** (0.265)	−0.160*** (0.0338)
Illicit Economy	−0.00342 (0.0124)	0.000134 (0.0125)	−0.00518 (0.00863)	−0.00447 (0.00868)	−0.0365*** (0.00250)
Cheat Norm			2.076*** (0.185)	2.068*** (0.189)	
AIC	762.01	761.51	654.56	656.26	141571.1
BIC	826.92	830.02	723.07	728.38	141732.4
Observations	272	272	272	272	57,403

*** $p<0.01$, ** $p<0.05$, * $p<0.1$
Standard errors in parentheses

APPENDIX E

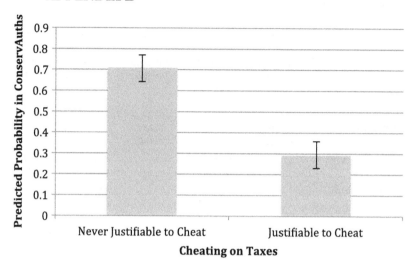

E.1 Predicted Probabilities of Cheating on Taxes for Respondents in Conservative Authoritarian Countries (World Values Survey)

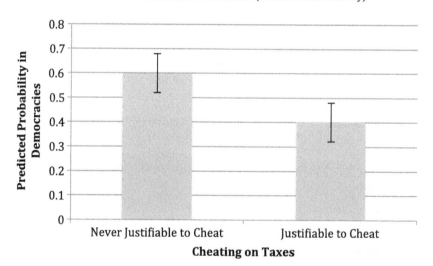

E.2 Predicted Probabilities of Cheating on Taxes for Respondents in Democracies (World Values Survey)

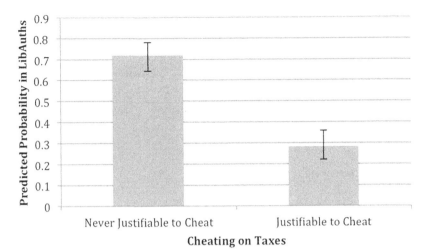

E.3 Predicted Probabilities of Cheating on Taxes for Respondents in Liberal Authoritarian Countries (World Values Survey)

E.4 *Multi-Level Logit Estimations of S2 (World Values Survey)*

DV	(1)
	Cheating on Taxes
Strategy	S2
LibAuth	**−1.241***
	(0.186)
ConservAuth	**−1.536***
	(0.318)
Income	−0.0348★★
	(0.0166)
Age	−0.00897***
	(0.00146)
Male	0.100***
	(0.0377)
Elite Status	−0.0247
	(0.0478)
Unemployment	−0.248***
	(0.0669)
GDP Per Capita (Logged)	0.243***
	(0.0428)

(continued)

E.4 (*Cont.*)

DV	(1)
	Cheating on Taxes
Strategy	S2
Govt Effectiveness	−0.0814
	(0.0760)
Illicit Economy	−0.0487***
	(0.0183)
Cheat Norm	1.308***
	(0.281)
AIC	74650.77
BIC	74813.55
Observations	62,538

*** p<0.01, ** p<0.05, * p<0.1
Standard errors in parentheses

APPENDIX F

F.1 *Ordered Logit Estimations of S1 among Elites (World Values Survey)*

DV	(1)	(2)	(3)	(4)	(5)	(6)
	Confidence in Govt	Confidence in Govt	Confidence in Govt	Confidence in Govt	Confidence in Govt	Confidence in Govt
Strategy:	S1	S1	S1	S1	S1	S1
Democracy	−0.852*** (0.229)		−0.773*** (0.235)		−1.133*** (0.424)	
LibAuth		0.712*** (0.250)		0.758*** (0.251)		1.097** (0.440)
ConservAuth	−0.286 (0.392)		−0.403 (0.497)		−0.682 (0.511)	
Trade Tax Revenue (% GDP)			0.116* (0.0597)	0.0991* (0.0573)	−0.0234 (0.222)	0.122** (0.0588)
*LibAuth*Trade Tax Revenue (% GDP)*						−0.159 (0.242)
*ConservAuth*Trade Tax Revenue% GDP*					0.108 (0.310)	
*Democracy*Trade Tax Revenue (% GDP)*					0.169 (0.226)	
Income	−0.0220 (0.0248)	−0.0190 (0.0247)	−0.0159 (0.0347)	−0.0154 (0.0342)	−0.0174 (0.0338)	−0.0163 (0.0337)
Age	0.00546* (0.00290)	0.00581* (0.00297)	0.00162 (0.00349)	0.00192 (0.00346)	0.00152 (0.00349)	0.00192 (0.00348)

(continued)

235

F.1 (*Cont.*)

DV	(1)	(2)	(3)	(4)	(5)	(6)
	Confidence in Govt	Confidence in Govt	Confidence in Govt	Confidence in Govt	Confidence in Govt	Confidence in Govt
Strategy:	S1	S1	S1	S1	S1	S1
Male	-0.0237	-0.0141	0.0467	0.0469	0.0608	0.0543
	(0.0569)	(0.0568)	(0.0733)	(0.0741)	(0.0653)	(0.0747)
Unemployment	-0.0329*	-0.0378**	-0.0157	-0.0226	-0.0151	-0.0219
	(0.0180)	(0.0187)	(0.0217)	(0.0198)	(0.0204)	(0.0190)
GDP Per Capita (Logged)	-0.139	-0.222*	-0.135	-0.145	-0.171	-0.177
	(0.121)	(0.131)	(0.118)	(0.129)	(0.111)	(0.126)
Govt Effectiveness	-0.243	-0.254	-0.0311	-0.0756	0.0135	-0.0502
	(0.154)	(0.158)	(0.199)	(0.182)	(0.193)	(0.182)
Illicit Economy	-0.0351***	-0.0371***	-0.0325***	-0.0331***	-0.0343***	-0.0357***
	(0.0127)	(0.0114)	(0.0110)	(0.00936)	(0.0116)	(0.00922)
Region Dummies	Yes	Yes	Yes	Yes	Yes	Yes
Pseudo R-squared	0.040	0.038	0.028	0.028	0.028	0.029
Observations	11,176	11,366	7,701	7,891	7,701	7,891
Number of Countries	43	44	33	34	33	34

*** p<0.01, ** p<0.05, * p<0.1
Standard errors in parentheses

236

F.2 Logit Estimations of S2 among Elites (World Values Survey)

DV	(1)	(2)	(3)	(4)	(5)	(6)
	Cheating on Taxes	Cheating on Taxes	Cheating on Taxes	Cheating on Taxes	Cheating on Taxes	Cheating on Taxes
Strategy:	S2	S2	S2	S2	S2	S2
Democracy		0.582** (0.234)		0.157 (0.154)		0.437** (0.206)
LibAuth	−0.580** (0.262)		−0.0680 (0.179)		−0.625*** (0.228)	
ConservAuth	−0.666** (0.283)		−0.357 (0.350)		−0.105 (0.241)	
Trade Tax Revenue (% GDP)			−0.153*** (0.0431)	−0.142*** (0.0485)	−0.211*** (0.0429)	0.0295 (0.115)
LibAuth Trade Tax Revenue (% GDP)*					0.390*** (0.141)	
ConservAuth Trade Tax Revenue (% GDP)*					−0.0418 (0.122)	
Democracy Trade Tax Revenue (% GDP)*						−0.234** (0.118)
Income	−0.0378 (0.0353)	−0.0418 (0.0353)	0.0320* (0.0163)	0.0278 (0.0172)	0.0294* (0.0163)	0.0297* (0.0172)
Age	−0.0143*** (0.00261)	−0.0143*** (0.00265)	−0.0105*** (0.00214)	−0.0106*** (0.00214)	−0.0110*** (0.00219)	−0.0104*** (0.00216)

(*continued*)

F.2 (*Cont.*)

DV	(1)	(2)	(3)	(4)	(5)	(6)
	Cheating on Taxes	Cheating on Taxes	Cheating on Taxes	Cheating on Taxes	Cheating on Taxes	Cheating on Taxes
Strategy:	S2	S2	S2	S2	S2	S2
Male	0.240***	0.235***	0.111	0.112	0.121*	0.100
	(0.0697)	(0.0690)	(0.0723)	(0.0705)	(0.0656)	(0.0711)
Unemployment	-0.0462**	-0.0442**	-0.0317*	-0.0279**	-0.0374***	-0.0302**
	(0.0190)	(0.0181)	(0.0164)	(0.0128)	(0.0135)	(0.0130)
GDP Per Capita (Logged)	0.147	0.157	0.129	0.130	0.280***	0.239***
	(0.102)	(0.103)	(0.0943)	(0.103)	(0.0916)	(0.0920)
Govt Effectiveness	-0.117	-0.112	-0.149	-0.136	-0.227*	-0.288**
	(0.164)	(0.161)	(0.135)	(0.131)	(0.124)	(0.123)
Illicit Economy	0.0116	0.0138**	0.0267***	0.0238***	0.0285***	0.0213***
	(0.00858)	(0.00701)	(0.00730)	(0.00632)	(0.00827)	(0.00622)
Cheat Norm	0.609***	0.604***	0.893***	0.917***	1.100***	1.050***
	(0.179)	(0.182)	(0.152)	(0.154)	(0.133)	(0.140)
Region Dummies	Yes	Yes	Yes	Yes	Yes	Yes
Pseudo R-squared	0.076	0.074	0.085	0.082	0.090	0.084
Observations	12,286	12,476	8,737	8,927	8,737	8,927
Number of Countries	44	45	35	36	35	36

*** $p<0.01$, ** $p<0.05$, * $p<0.1$
Standard errors in parentheses

F.3 *Multi-Level Logit and Ordered Logit Estimations of S1 and S2 in Elite Sample (World Values Survey)*

DV	(1)	(2)	(3)	(4)	(5)
	Confidence in Govt	Confidence in Govt	Cheating on Taxes	Cheating on Taxes	Cheating on Taxes
Strategy:	S1	S1	S2	S2	S2
Democracy	*-0.928**** *(0.0407)*	*-1.713**** *(0.110)*			*0.563**** *(0.0599)*
LibAuth			*-0.0131* *(0.0864)*	*-0.892**** *(0.184)*	
ConservAuth	*-0.698**** *(0.0565)*	*-1.783**** *(0.120)*	*-0.210**** *(0.0715)*	*-0.141** *(0.0854)*	
Trade Tax Revenue (% GDP)	*0.219**** *(0.0134)*	*-0.212**** *(0.0370)*	*-0.166**** *(0.0260)*	*-0.214**** *(0.0354)*	*0.124**** *(0.0358)*
LibAuth* Trade Tax Revenue (% GDP)				*0.491**** *(0.117)*	
ConservAuth* Trade Tax Revenue (% GDP)		*0.651**** *(0.0541)*		*0.00513* *(0.113)*	
Democracy* Trade Tax Revenue (% GDP)		*0.507**** *(0.0421)*			
Income	-0.0157 (0.0309)	-0.0151 (0.0299)	0.0233 (0.0156)	0.0241 (0.0150)	0.0148 (0.0165)
Age	0.00295 (0.00361)	0.00301 (0.00371)	-0.0119*** (0.00234)	-0.0121*** (0.00236)	-0.0116*** (0.00226)

(continued)

239

F.3 (Cont.)

DV	(1)	(2)	(3)	(4)	(5)
	Confidence in Govt	Confidence in Govt	Cheating on Taxes	Cheating on Taxes	Cheating on Taxes
Strategy:	S1	S1	S2	S2	S2
Male	-0.0291	-0.0361	0.169**	0.167**	0.157**
	(0.0440)	(0.0426)	(0.0676)	(0.0700)	(0.0672)
Unemployment	-0.0172***	-0.0544***	-0.0522***	-0.0551***	-0.0376***
	(0.00321)	(0.00448)	(0.00388)	(0.00735)	(0.00409)
GDP Per Capita (Logged)	-0.114***	0.0262	0.289***	0.288***	0.361***
	(0.0338)	(0.0300)	(0.0510)	(0.0877)	(0.0493)
Govt Effectiveness	-0.184***	-0.0244	-0.0422	-0.202	-0.354***
	(0.0508)	(0.0390)	(0.0720)	(0.125)	(0.0688)
Illicit Economy	-0.0360***	-0.0559***	0.0436***	0.0275***	0.0159***
	(0.00239)	(0.00298)	(0.00740)	(0.00626)	(0.00226)
Cheat Norm			0.786***	1.044***	1.081***
			(0.0368)	(0.136)	(0.0583)
AIC	19,284.75	19,247.67	10,971.15	10,962.12	11,227.78
BIC	19,409.84	19,386.65	11,098.51	11,103.63	11,355.52
Observations	7,701	7,701	8,737	8,737	8,927

Standard errors in parentheses
*** p<0.01, ** p<0.05, * p<0.1

APPENDIX G

G.1 MTurk Survey Data Descriptions

Variable	Source	Definition	Min	Max	Mean	SD
Africa	World Bank 2015a	African regional dummy	0	1	0.1	0.3
Conservative Authoritarian Dummy	Geddes, Wright, and Frantz 2012; Marshall and Gurr 2016	Polity less than 6 and Polcomp less than 3 and personalist regimes.	0	1	0.2	0.4
Democracy Dummy	Marshall and Gurr 2016	Polity greater than 5, not personalist regimes.	0	1	0.7	0.5
Employment	MTurk	What is your employment status? 1: Full time; 2: Part time; 3: Self-employed; 4: Not currently employed; 5: Student	1	5	2.1	1.5
GDP Per Capita (Logged)	World Bank 2015a	GDP per capita is gross domestic product divided by midyear population. GDP is the sum of gross value added by all resident producers in the economy plus any product taxes and minus any subsidies not included in the value of the products.	6.4	11.5	8.5	1.0
Gender	MTurk	What is your gender? 1: Male; 2: Female	1	2	1.2	0.4
Government Effectiveness	MTurk	How much of this tax money do you think the government would use for improving your city and/or country? 1: None of it; 2: A small portion of it; 3: Most of it; 4: All of it	1	4	2.3	0.7
Income	MTurk	In what income group does your household fall into? 1: Low; 2: Medium; 3: High	1	3	1.9	0.4

(continued)

241

G.1 (*Cont.*)

Variable	Source	Definition	Min	Max	Mean	SD
Liberal Authoritarian Dummy	Geddes et al. 2012; Marshall and Gurr 2016	Polity less than 6, not personalist, and Polcomp score of 3 or greater	0	1	0.1	0.3
Public Goods	MTurk	How satisfied or dissatisfied are you with the (quality of government primary schools, quality of government hospitals, supply of clean water, quality of roads) in your country? 1: Very dissatisfied; 2: Dissatisfied; 3: Neutral; 4: Satisfied; 5: Very satisfied	1	5	2.6	1.2
Willingness to Pay More Taxes	MTurk	If the government needs more revenue, would you be willing to pay higher taxes? 1: Definitely no; 2: No; 3: Neutral; 4: Yes; 5: Definitely yes	1	5	2.5	1.1

G.2 *MTurk Country List*

Democracies	Liberal Authoritarian	Conservative Authoritarian	
Argentina	Macedonia	Algeria	Egypt
Bolivia	Mauritius	Bangladesh	Kazakhstan
Brazil	Mexico	Ecuador	Oman
Bulgaria	Moldova	Ethiopia	Qatar
Chile	Pakistan	Ivory Coast	Russia
Colombia	Philippines	Jordan	Saudi Arabia
Costa Rica	Poland	Malaysia	United Arab Emirates
Croatia	Romania	Morocco	
Dominican	Serbia	Nigeria	
Republic	Slovak Republic	Singapore	
Estonia	Slovenia	Sri Lanka	
Georgia	South Africa	Thailand	
Ghana	Trinidad	Ukraine	
Hungary	and Tobago		
India	Tunisia		
Indonesia	Turkey		
Jamaica	Uruguay		
Kenya	Zambia		
Latvia			
Lithuania			

G.3 *World Values Survey Data Descriptions*

Variable	Source	Definition	Mean	St.Dev	Min	Max
Age	WVS 2015	Question: Age	39.53	15.64	15	99
Bureaucratic Quality	ICRG 2012	Institutional strength and quality of bureaucracy. Coded 1 (low quality) through 4 (high quality).	2.01	0.82	0	4
Cheating on Taxes	WVS 2015	Question: Please tell me for each of the following statements whether you think it can always be justified, never be justified, or something in between, using this card. Cheating on taxes if you have a chance Response Range: 1 'Never Justifiable' through 10 'Always Justifiable'. We coded this variable as 1: Never Justifiable and 0: otherwise.	0.42	0.49	0	1
Cheating on Taxes Mean	WVS 2015	The average cheating on taxes score in each country.	2.18	0.58	1.06	3.85
Conservative Authoritarian Dummy	Marshall and Gurr 2016	Polity less than 6 and polcomp less than 3 and personalist regimes.	0.23	0.42	0	1
Control of Corruption	World Bank 2015b	Control of corruption captures perceptions of the extent to which public power is exercised for private gain, including both petty and grand forms of corruption, as well as "capture" of the state by elites and private interests.	0.10	1.03	-1.47	2.40
Democracy Dummy	Marshall and Gurr 2016	Polity greater than 5, not personalist regimes.	0.53	0.50	0	1
Fuel Exports	World Bank 2015a	Fuel (SITC section 3) exports as a percent of merchandise exports.	25.67	32.86	0	99.64
GDP Per Capita (Logged)	World Bank 2015a	GDP per capita is gross domestic product divided by midyear population. GDP is the sum of gross value added by all resident producers in the economy plus any product taxes and minus any subsidies not included in the value of the products. Current US dollars logged.	8.40	1.47	5.09	11.09
GDP Growth	World Bank 2015a	Annual percentage growth rate of GDP at market prices based on constant local currency. Aggregates are based on constant 2000 US dollars.	3.77	8.29	-14.8	54.16

Variable	Source	Question / Description	Mean	SD	Min	Max
Government Confidence	WVS 2015	Question: I am going to name a number of organizations. For each one, could you tell me how much confidence you have in them: is it a great deal of confidence, quite a lot of confidence, not very much confidence, or none at all? The government. Response Range: 1 "A great deal" through 4 "None at all." Recoded here so 1 "None at all" through 4 "A great deal"	2.49	0.98	1	4
Income	WVS 2015	Question: Scale of Income. Response Range: 1 "Lower step" through 10 "Tenth step"	4.65	2.19	1	10
Liberal Authoritarian Dummy	Marshall and Gurr 2016	Polity less than 6, not personalist, with polcomp score of 3 or greater.	0.24	0.43	0	1
Male	WVS 2015	Question: Sex. Response Range: 1 "Male" or 2 "Female" Recoded here as 1 Male 0 Female	0.49	0.50	0	1
Primary Education Spending	UNESCO Institute for Statistics 2014	Expenditure on primary education as a percentage of the total general government expenditure on education.	36.07	10.99	13.77	71.18
Profession	WVS 2015	In which profession/occupation do you or did you work? Coded as equal to 1 if employer or manager of establishment or nonmanual office worker. 0 if otherwise.	0.24	0.43	0	1
Under 5 Child Mortality	World Bank 2015a	The previous three-year average of under-5 child mortality.	37.19	40.26	2.83	196.8
Shadow Economy	Schneider 2005	The shadow economy includes all market-based legal production of goods and services that are deliberately concealed from public authorities for the following reasons: (1) to avoid payment of income, value-added or other taxes; (2) to avoid payment of social security contributions; (3) to avoid having to meet certain legal labor market standards, such as minimum wages, maximum working hours, safety standards, etc.; and (4) to avoid complying with certain administrative procedures, such as completing statistical questionnaires or other administrative forms.	32.31	12.33	0	65.1
Unemployment	World Bank 2015a	Unemployment refers to the share of the labor force that is without work but available for and seeking employment.	9.38	6.31	0.4	32.2

G.4 *World Values Survey Country List*

Democracies	Liberal Authoritarian	Conservative Authoritarian	
Argentina	Moldova	Albania	Armenia
Bangladesh	Pakistan	Algeria	Azerbaijan
Brazil	Peru	Ecuador	Bahrain
Bulgaria	Philippines	Egypt	Belarus
Chile	Poland	Ethiopia	Burkina Faso
Colombia	Romania	Iran	China
Cyprus	Slovenia	Iraq	Egypt
Estonia	South Africa	Jordan	Iraq
Georgia	South Korea	Malaysia	Kazakhstan
Ghana	Switzerland	Morocco	Kuwait
Guatemala	Taiwan	Nigeria	Kyrgyzstan
Hungary	Thailand	Rwanda	Libya
India	Trinidad and Tobago	Singapore	Pakistan
Indonesia	Turkey	Tanzania	Peru
Lebanon	Ukraine	Thailand	Qatar
Macedonia	Uruguay	Tunisia	Russia
Malaysia	Venezuela	Yemen	Rwanda
Mali		Zambia	Saudi Arabia
Mexico		Zimbabwe	Uganda
			Uzbekistan
			Vietnam

APPENDIX H

Just as in Chapter 3's revenue models, we control for: GDP per capita, GDP growth, fuel exports (percent of merchandise exports), and population (logged). See Chapter 3 appendix for details on the variable definitions, sources, and descriptive statistics. High growth should "mitigate demands by capital that it be liberated from onerous tax burdens" (Wibbels and Arce 2003: 124). Richer countries should be more attractive to capital and therefore less susceptible to downward tax rate pressures by corporations (Wibbels and Arce 2003). We control for oil wealth with fuel exports as natural resource-rich countries have a different tax structure due to their nontax revenue (Kenny and Winer 2006). As Genschel et al. (2016) indicate, country size is a strong predictor of CTR as it reflects the size of the country's labor endowments.

Then, we add additional global market integration and domestic fiscal and investment profile controls from Wibbels and Arce (2003) and Genschel et al. (2016). Building on Wibbels and Arce (2003), we include foreign direct investment inflows to capture the role of long-term investments on national taxation policy. Following Genschel et al. (2016), we include government spending (percent of GDP), agricultural employment (percent of total employment), and regime durability. Government spending captures both the expenditure requirements of the government as well as revenue buoyancy. The extent of agricultural employment controls for the taxability of the economy; high levels of agricultural employment should be associated with higher CTRs. The institutional control of regime durability addresses the political incentives and capabilities to implement CTR policy.

H.1 *Determinants of Corporate Tax Rates*

DV	(1)	(2)
	CTR	CTR
Trade Tax Revenue (% GDP)$_{t-1}$	−0.375	−0.318
	(0.585)	(0.489)
Democracy Dummy $_{t-1}$ (1 = Dem; 0 = LibAuth or ConservAuth)	−2.286**	
	(1.017)	
Trade Tax Revenue (% GDP) * **Democracy Dummy** $_{t-1}$ (1 = Dem; 0 = LibAuth or ConservAuth)	0.955++	
	(0.603)	
Polity $_{t-1}$		−0.285***
		(0.103)
Trade Tax Revenue (% GDP) * **Polity** $_{t-1}$		0.139**
		(0.0662)
Capital Account Openness $_{t-1}$	−0.233	−0.330
	(0.268)	(0.248)
Investment Profile $_{t-1}$	−0.265**	−0.273***
	(0.108)	(0.102)
Portfolio Flows (% GDP) $_{t-1}$	0.0113	0.00941
	(0.0388)	(0.0390)
IMF Credits (% GDP) $_{t-1}$	−0.0969	−0.0791
	(0.147)	(0.141)
GDP Growth $_{t-1}$	0.0474	0.0453
	(0.0387)	(0.0382)
GDP Per Capita (Logged) $_{t-1}$	−3.127***	−2.878***
	(0.758)	(0.726)
Population (Logged) $_{t-1}$	12.04*	11.58*
	(6.261)	(6.164)
Govt Spending (% GDP) $_{t-1}$	0.147	0.204**
	(0.110)	(0.0996)
FDI Inflows (% GDP) $_{t-1}$	−0.0781**	−0.0702**
	(0.0358)	(0.0350)
Regime Durable $_{t-1}$	0.0119	0.0177
	(0.0251)	(0.0238)
Agr. Employ $_{t-1}$	0.0270	0.0247
	(0.0589)	(0.0583)
Fuel Exports $_{t-1}$	−0.00759	−0.0133
	(0.0245)	(0.0232)
Observations	208	208
R-squared	0.980	0.984
Number of Countries	34	34

*** p<0.01, ** p<0.05, * p<0.1
++ Conditional coefficients are statistically significant for democracies
Standard errors in parentheses

DV	(1)	(2)	(3)	(4)
	ΔCTR	ΔCTR	ΔCTR	ΔCTR
Corporate Tax Rate $_{t-1}$	−0.541***	−0.552***	−0.754***	−0.753***
	(0.0846)	(0.0836)	(0.0976)	(0.100)
Trade Tax Revenue (% GDP)$_{t-1}$	−0.358	−0.303	−0.515	−0.557
	(0.327)	(0.306)	(0.455)	(0.578)
Democracy Dummy $_{t-1}$ (1 = Dem; 0 = LibAuth or ConservAuth)	−1.701**			−2.374**
	(0.779)			(1.031)
Trade Tax Revenue (% GDP)* Democracy Dummy $_{t-1}$ (1 = Dem; 0 = LibAuth or ConservAuth)	0.977***			1.125*
	(0.359)			(0.640)
Polity $_{t-1}$		−0.207**	−0.264**	
		(0.0907)	(0.104)	
Trade Tax Revenue (% GDP)* Polity $_{t-1}$		0.123***	0.154**	
		(0.0454)	(0.0641)	
Capital Account Openness $_{t-1}$	−0.261	−0.303	−0.215	−0.118
	(0.266)	(0.264)	(0.273)	(0.281)
Investment Profile $_{t-1}$	−0.175*	−0.165	−0.253**	−0.255**
	(0.0955)	(0.106)	(0.111)	(0.109)
Portfolio Flows (% GDP) $_{t-1}$	0.0210	0.0110	0.000973	0.00469
	(0.0377)	(0.0372)	(0.0454)	(0.0445)
IMF Credits (% GDP) $_{t-1}$	0.0591	0.0510	−0.0507	−0.0759
	(0.0506)	(0.0557)	(0.136)	(0.139)
GDP Growth $_{t-1}$			0.0306	0.0236
			(0.0378)	(0.0383)
GDP Per Capita (Logged) $_{t-1}$			−1.853**	−2.091***
			(0.733)	(0.759)
Population (Logged) $_{t-1}$			6.418	7.749
			(6.267)	(6.093)
Govt Spending (% GDP) $_{t-1}$			0.186*	0.153
			(0.0976)	(0.0975)
FDI Inflows (% GDP) $_{t-1}$			−0.0558	−0.0586*
			(0.0355)	(0.0342)
Regime Durable $_{t-1}$			0.00973	−0.00236
			(0.0220)	(0.0234)
Agr. Employ $_{t-1}$			0.0419	0.0400
			(0.0522)	(0.0506)
Fuel Exports $_{t-1}$			−0.0137	−0.0132
			(0.0172)	(0.0189)
Observations	262	262	198	198
R-squared	0.405	0.413	0.534	0.523
Number of Countries	36	36	33	33

*** p<0.01, ** p<0.05, * p<0.1
Standard errors in parentheses

APPENDIX I

I.1 *Determinants of Tax Inspections by Regime Type among All Domestic Firms*

DV	(1)	(2)
	Tax Inspect.	Tax Inspect.
LibAuth	0.374**	0.0786
	(0.148)	(0.300)
ConservAuth	0.849***	0.870***
	(0.179)	(0.327)
Exports (% Sales)		−0.000128
		(0.00149)
GDP Per Capita (Logged)		−0.261**
		(0.116)
Bureaucratic Quality		−0.0193
		(0.162)
Sales (Logged)		−0.00663
		(0.0349)
Employment (Logged)		0.273***
		(0.0529)
Region Controls	Yes	Yes
Year Dummies	Yes	Yes
Observations	93,541	42,675

*** $p<0.01$, ** $p<0.05$, * $p<0.1$
Standard errors in parentheses

I.2 *Determinants of Tax Inspections for Less Productive Firms*

DV	(1)	(2)
	Tax Inspect.	Tax Inspect.
Sample	Large Firms	Less Productive Firms
Democracy Dummy	−0.116	−0.486*
(1 = Dem; 0 = LibAuth or ConservAuth)	(0.268)	(0.262)
Exports (% Sales)	−0.00301	
	(0.00204)	
Exports (% Sales)'Democracy Dummy	0.00726***	
(1 = Dem; 0 = LibAuth or ConservAuth)	(0.00236)	
GDP Per Capita (Logged)	−0.159	−0.265**
	(0.115)	(0.126)
Bureaucratic Quality	−0.0443	−0.0576
	(0.170)	(0.166)
Sales (Logged)	0.0234	0.00465
	(0.0315)	(0.0369)
Employment (Logged)		0.265***
		(0.0589)
Region Control	Yes	Yes
Year Dummies	Yes	Yes
Observations	8,524	38,477

*** p<0.01, ** p<0.05, * p<0.1

Standard errors in parentheses

I.3 Determinants of Tax Inspections for Less Productive Firms

DV	(1)
	Tax Inspect.
Sample	Less Productive Firms
LibAuth	**0.124**
	(0.292)
ConservAuth	**0.876*****
	(0.332)
GDP Per Capita (Logged)	−0.279**
	(0.117)
Bureaucratic Quality	−0.02
	(0.163)
Sales (Logged)	−0.003
	(0.035)
Employment (Logged)	0.274***
	(0.056)
Region Controls	Yes
Year Dummies	Yes
Observations	37,707

*** $p<0.01$, ** $p<0.05$, * $p<0.1$
Standard errors in parentheses

I.4 Determinants of Tax Inspections for Large Firms

DV	(1)
	Tax Inspect.
Sample	Large Firms
Polity	**0.00313**
	(0.0224)
Exports (% Sales)	**0.000247**
	(0.00134)
Polity*Exports (% Sales)	**0.000378****
	(0.000161)
GDP Per Capita (Logged)	−0.176
	(0.132)
Bureaucratic Quality	−0.0587
	(0.165)
Sales (Logged)	0.0259
	(0.0315)
Region Control	Yes
Year Dummies	Yes
Observations	8,524

*** $p<0.01$, ** $p<0.05$, * $p<0.1$
Standard errors in parentheses

I.5 *ES Data Description*

Variable	Source	Definition	Min	Max	Mean	SD
Bureaucratic Quality	ICRG 2012	Institutional strength and quality of bureaucracy. Coded 1 (low quality) through 4 (high quality).	0	4	1.88	0.79
Conservative Authoritarian	Geddes et al. 2012; Marshall and Gurr 2016	Polity less than 6 and Polcomp less than 3 and personalist regimes.	0	1	0.17	0.38
Democracy Dummy	Marshall and Gurr 2016	Polity scores converted to dichotomous regime categories: nondemocracies (−10 to 5) and democracies (+6 to +10). No personalist regimes. Coded as 1: democracy and 0: nondemocracy.	0	1	0.59	0.49
Employment (Logged)	ES 2016	Sum of number of full-time temporary and permanent employees (logged) of last fiscal year	0	11.07	3.28	1.32
Exports (% Sales)	ES 2016	Sales exported directly as percentage of total sales.	0	100	5.71	19.28
GDP Per Capita (Logged)	ES 2016	GDP per capita is gross domestic product divided by midyear population. GDP is the sum of gross value added by all resident producers in the economy plus any product taxes and minus any subsidies not included in the value of the products.	4.05	12.17	7.95	1.12
Liberal Authoritarian	Geddes et al. 2012; Marshall and Gurr 2016	Polity less than 6, not personalist, with Polcomp score of 3 or greater.	0	1	0.24	0.43
Polity	Marshall and Gurr 2016	Democracy is conceived as three essential, interdependent elements. One is the presence of institutions and procedures through which citizens can express effective preferences about alternative policies and leaders. Second is the existence of institutionalized constraints on the exercise of power by the executive. Third is the guarantee of civil liberties to all citizens in their daily lives and in acts of political participation.	−10	10		
Sales (Logged)	ES 2016	Total annual sales (logged) of last fiscal year	0	35.53	16.71	3.07
Tax Inspections	ES 2016	Over the last year, was this establishment visited or inspected by tax officials? Response coded: 1 if yes, 0 if no.	0	1	0.59	0.49

I.6 *ES Country List*

Democracies	Liberal Authoritarian	Conservative Authoritarian	
Albania	Latvia	Angola	Armenia
Argentina	Liberia	Bangladesh	Azerbaijan
Bolivia	Lithuania	Ecuador	Belarus
Botswana	Malawi	Ethiopia	Burkina Faso
Brazil	Mali	Gabon	Cameroon
Bulgaria	Mexico	Iraq	Congo, Dem Rep.
Chile	Moldova	Madagascar	Congo, Rep.
Colombia	Mongolia	Mozambique	Cote d'Ivoire
Costa Rica	Namibia	Niger	Gambia
Croatia	Nicaragua	Nigeria	Guinea
Czech Republic	Panama	Pakistan	Kazakhstan
Dominican Republic	Paraguay	Sri Lanka	Russia
Ecuador	Peru	Suriname	Togo
El Salvador	Philippines	Tanzania	Uganda
Estonia	Poland	Zambia	Venezuela
Ghana	Romania	Zimbabwe	Vietnam
Guatemala	Senegal		Yemen
Guinea-Bissau	Serbia		
Guyana	Sierra Leone		
Honduras	Slovak		
Hungary	Republic		
Indonesia	South Africa		
Jamaica	Trinidad		
Kenya	and Tobago		
	Turkey		
	Ukraine		
	Uruguay		

APPENDIX J

J.1 *Difference in Domestic Tax Revenues Pre- and Post-WTO for ISI and Non-ISI Legacy Democracies*

	Pre-WTO Domestic Tax Revenue	Post-WTO Domestic Tax Revenue	Diff-in-Diff
Difference (Treated-Control)	3.118***	−1.702***	−4.820***
SE	(0.689)	(0.480)	(0.840)

J.2 *Difference in Income Tax Revenues Pre- and Post-WTO for ISI and Non-ISI Legacy Democracies*

	Pre-WTO Income Tax Revenue	Post-WTO Income Tax Revenue	Diff-in-Diff
Difference (Treated-Control)	−0.512	−1.864***	−1.352*
SE	(0.622)	(0.348)	(0.713)

APPENDIX K

K.1 *Summary Statistics*

	Source	Mean	St. Dev	Min	Max
Social Benefits for Poor					
Primary and Secondary Education Spending (% Government Spending on Education)	WB 2016a	71.0	10.4	0	100
Infant Mortality Rate (per 1,000)	WB 2016a	41.2	33.4	2.1	171.2
Poverty Headcount (% Population) (National Poverty Line)	WB 2016a	29.6	16.7	0.6	76.8
Female Literacy (% Population)	WB 2016a	75.7	24.7	4.6	100
Gini Index	WB 2016a	41.2	10.4	16.2	99.9
Poverty Gap (% Population)	WB 2016a	13.5	13.0	0.4	55.4
Social Benefits for Nonpoor					
Social Security Spending (% GDP)	IMF 2016a	0.7	1.8	−0.1	18.6
Public Sector Employee Compensation (% GDP)	IMF 2016a	7.2	7.4	0.6	182.6
Infrastructure					
Railroad Passengers (Logged)	WB 2016a	7.2	2.5	−2.7	14.0
Air Transport Freight (Logged)	WB 2016a	2.9	2.7	−7.8	9.8
Internet Users (Per 100 People)	WB 2016a	15.5	21.5	0	96.8
Water Access (% Population)	WB 2016a	82.2	18.5	13.2	100
Sanitation Access (% Population)	WB 2016a	65.4	30.5	2.1	171.2
Military Goods					
Armed Forces Personnel (% Labor Force)	WB 2016a	1.8	2.2	0	35.9
Military Spending (% Government Spending)	WB 2016a	13.0	27.1	0.4	695.8

K.2 *Determinants of Social Benefits for Poor: Poverty and Infant Mortality Indicators*

DV	(1)	(2)	(3)	(4)	(5)	(6)
	Poverty Headcount				Infant Mortality	
Trade Tax Revenue (% GDP) $_{t-1}$	0.203 (0.362)	−0.230 (0.246)	1.576 (1.113)	0.0852 (0.189)	0.169 (0.244)	−0.282 (0.198)
Democracy $_{t-1}$	7.821*** (1.389)			−0.392 (0.610)		
Trade Tax Revenue (%GDP)* Democracy $_{t-1}$	−2.636** (1.142)			−0.0840 (0.301)		
LibAuth $_{t-1}$		−8.622*** (1.283)			0.163 (0.774)	
Trade Tax Revenue (% GDP)* LibAuth $_{t-1}$		4.262*** (0.788)			−0.548 (0.388)	
ConservAuth $_{t-1}$			−0.996 (2.128)			1.768 (1.202)
Trade Tax Revenue (% GDP)* ConservAuth $_{t-1}$			−1.920 (1.211)			1.057*** (0.398)
GDP Per Capita (Logged) $_{t-1}$	−7.697*** (1.254)	−7.157*** (1.187)	−5.558*** (1.412)	−8.608*** (1.011)	−8.398*** (0.996)	−8.397*** (1.022)
Fuel Exports $_{t-1}$	−0.216*** (0.0453)	−0.214*** (0.0511)	−0.200*** (0.0584)	−0.0120 (0.0224)	−0.0148 (0.0233)	−0.0116 (0.0253)
Population (Logged) $_{t-1}$	−5.705 (5.149)	−4.070 (5.984)	−8.211 (8.056)	−42.08*** (5.119)	−44.22*** (4.938)	−44.59*** (5.435)

(continued)

257

K.2 (*Cont.*)

DV	(1)	(2)	(3)	(4)	(5)	(6)
	Poverty Headcount			Infant Mortality		
GDP Growth $_{t-1}$	0.113**	0.0245	0.112**	0.0781**	0.0868***	0.0730**
	(0.0484)	(0.0491)	(0.0541)	(0.0311)	(0.0319)	(0.0345)
Capital Account Openness $_{t-1}$	−0.976**	−1.455***	−1.106**	0.693***	0.752***	0.404
	(0.469)	(0.501)	(0.482)	(0.239)	(0.252)	(0.270)
Aid (% GDP) $_{t-1}$	0.134	−0.176	0.178	0.155***	0.0894*	0.130***
	(0.218)	(0.213)	(0.240)	(0.0466)	(0.0496)	(0.0416)
IMF Credits (% GDP) $_{t-1}$	−0.541***	−0.453***	−0.435**	−0.227***	−0.180**	−0.194***
	(0.163)	(0.139)	(0.179)	(0.0681)	(0.0714)	(0.0645)
Debt (% GDP) $_{t-1}$	0.113***	0.115***	0.147***	0.0244	0.0280*	0.0284*
	(0.0304)	(0.0278)	(0.0353)	(0.0155)	(0.0163)	(0.0171)
Trade (% GDP) $_{t-1}$	0.0385*	0.0430**	−0.00568	−0.0803***	−0.0849***	−0.0766***
	(0.0210)	(0.0188)	(0.0195)	(0.0168)	(0.0170)	(0.0174)
Observations	113	113	113	364	364	361
R-squared	0.979	0.979	0.979	0.993	0.994	0.991
Number of Countries	27	27	27	45	45	44

Standard errors in parentheses
*** p<0.01, ** p<0.05, * p<0.1

K.3 *Determinants of Social Benefits for the Poor: Inequality Baseline Models*

DV	(1)	(2)	(3)	(4)	(5)	(6)
	Gini: Base Model			Gini: Medium Model		
Trade Tax Revenue (% GDP) t-1	0.443***	0.0196	0.353*	0.476***	0.0129	0.349*
	(0.158)	(0.143)	(0.182)	(0.165)	(0.148)	(0.188)
Democracy t-1	2.295***			2.520***		
	(0.671)			(0.691)		
Trade Tax Revenue (%GDP)* Democracy t-1	−0.524**			−0.585**		
	(0.243)			(0.251)		
LibAuth t-1		−2.695***			−2.936***	
		(0.792)			(0.788)	
Trade Tax Revenue (% GDP)* LibAuth t-1		0.792***			0.840***	
		(0.254)			(0.254)	
ConservAuth t-1			0.480			0.438
			(0.856)			(0.891)
Trade Tax Revenue (% GDP)* ConservAuth t-1			−0.260			−0.244
			(0.172)			(0.177)
GDP Per Capita (Logged) t-1	−0.991***	−0.683**	−0.677*	−1.207***	−0.880***	−0.854**
	(0.334)	(0.321)	(0.347)	(0.358)	(0.337)	(0.366)
Fuel Exports t-1	−0.00248	−0.00372	−0.0107	0.00269	0.00411	−0.00557
	(0.0245)	(0.0242)	(0.0254)	(0.0253)	(0.0253)	(0.0263)
GDP Growth t-1				0.0191	0.0108	0.0130
				(0.0230)	(0.0234)	(0.0234)
Trade (% GDP) t-1				0.00676	0.00987	0.00694
				(0.0102)	(0.00966)	(0.00974)
Observations	477	477	472	473	473	468
R-squared	0.988	0.989	0.988	0.988	0.989	0.988
Number of Countries	84	84	82	83	83	81

Standard errors in parentheses
*** p<0.01, ** p<0.05, * p<0.1

K.4 *Determinants of Social Benefits for Poor: Poverty and Inequality Indicators*

DV	(1)	(2)	(3)	(4)	(5)	(6)
	Poverty Gap			Gini		
Trade Tax Revenue (% GDP) $_{t-1}$	1.523*** (0.447)	-0.601 (0.642)	1.058** (0.495)	0.399** (0.163)	-0.150 (0.187)	0.694*** (0.223)
Democracy $_{t-1}$	5.105*** (1.225)			3.332*** (0.835)		
Trade Tax Revenue (%GDP)* Democracy $_{t-1}$	-1.473** (0.648)			-0.831 (0.510)		
LibAuth $_{t-1}$		-4.578*** (1.216)			-2.547*** (0.517)	
Trade Tax Revenue (% GDP)* LibAuth $_{t-1}$		2.241*** (0.715)			1.252*** (0.272)	
ConservAuth $_{t-1}$			20.63*** (4.700)			-1.664* (0.970)
Trade Tax Revenue (% GDP)* ConservAuth $_{t-1}$			-14.76*** (2.802)			-1.054*** (0.229)
GDP Per Capita (Logged) $_{t-1}$	-4.592*** (0.950)	-4.665*** (0.977)	-3.367*** (0.761)	-0.779 (0.483)	-0.268 (0.471)	-0.263 (0.589)
Fuel Exports $_{t-1}$	-0.0811** (0.0387)	-0.0666* (0.0350)	-0.0127 (0.0216)	0.000675 (0.0294)	-0.0217 (0.0242)	-0.0118 (0.0269)
Population (Logged) $_{t-1}$	16.36*** (5.624)	17.14*** (6.212)	10.34* (6.013)	3.537 (3.367)	6.189* (3.476)	2.835 (3.511)
GDP Growth $_{t-1}$	0.0447 (0.0426)	0.0287 (0.0424)	0.0524 (0.0439)	0.0939*** (0.0357)	0.0646* (0.0348)	0.114*** (0.0396)

Capital Account Openness $_{t-1}$	-1.494***	-1.017**	-0.725	-1.020***	-1.141***	-0.712***
	(0.472)	(0.489)	(0.563)	(0.243)	(0.220)	(0.190)
Aid (% GDP) $_{t-1}$	0.384***	0.167	0.136	-0.0788	-0.0721*	-0.102**
	(0.148)	(0.142)	(0.174)	(0.0651)	(0.0416)	(0.0385)
IMF Credits (% GDP) $_{t-1}$	-0.518***	-0.449***	-0.319**	-0.199***	-0.227***	-0.261***
	(0.121)	(0.130)	(0.128)	(0.0702)	(0.0659)	(0.0704)
Debt (% GDP) $_{t-1}$	0.0509***	0.0606***	0.0490**	0.0807***	0.0742***	0.104***
	(0.0178)	(0.0192)	(0.0232)	(0.0225)	(0.0202)	(0.0209)
Trade (% GDP) $_{t-1}$	0.0142	0.0122	-0.0133	0.00199	-0.00196	-0.00870
	(0.0172)	(0.0167)	(0.0125)	(0.0135)	(0.0117)	(0.0145)
Observations	59	59	59	141	141	141
R-squared	0.987	0.987	0.990	0.992	0.993	0.991
Number of Countries	18	18	18	31	31	31

*** p<0.01, ** p<0.05, * p<0.1
Standard errors in parentheses

K.5 *Determinants of Social Benefits for Poor: Education and Literacy Indicators*

DV	(1)	(2)	(3)	(4)	(5)	(6)
	Primary and Secondary Education Spending			Female Literacy Rate		
Trade Tax Revenue (% GDP) $_{t-1}$	-2.471 (1.836)	1.264 (2.332)	-1.205 (1.559)	-3.219*** (0.696)	-1.472 (1.009)	-1.672*** (0.281)
Democracy $_{t-1}$	-5.014 (3.902)			-8.247*** (2.410)		
Trade Tax Revenue (%GDP)* Democracy $_{t-1}$	4.824* (2.769)			4.280*** (1.381)		
LibAuth $_{t-1}$		4.178 (3.414)			0.688 (1.230)	
Trade Tax Revenue (% GDP)* LibAuth $_{t-1}$		-3.520 (2.759)			-1.494* (0.892)	
ConservAuth $_{t-1}$			25.86*** (7.633)			3.858** (1.869)
Trade Tax Revenue (% GDP)* ConservAuth $_{t-1}$			-23.63*** (7.377)			3.009** (1.342)
GDP Per Capita (Logged) $_{t-1}$	-12.52*** (3.029)	-12.38*** (3.294)	-9.455*** (3.077)	5.312*** (1.236)	2.863* (1.646)	2.924** (1.257)
Fuel Exports $_{t-1}$	0.0570 (0.0903)	0.0609 (0.0914)	0.0491 (0.0794)	-0.294*** (0.0593)	-0.128 (0.0923)	-0.165*** (0.0424)
Population (Logged) $_{t-1}$	14.72 (19.47)	10.68 (20.72)	-11.41 (20.93)	26.83** (10.78)	31.42*** (8.569)	26.30*** (7.798)
GDP Growth $_{t-1}$	-0.131 (0.0966)	-0.127 (0.106)	-0.144 (0.120)	-0.00359 (0.0799)	-0.0427 (0.0849)	0.0212 (0.0579)

Capital Account Openness $_{t-1}$	0.292	0.409	0.121	-2.049***	-1.992**	-1.098*
	(0.976)	(1.001)	(0.959)	(0.569)	(0.792)	(0.619)
Aid (% GDP) $_{t-1}$	0.554	0.376	1.418*	1.507***	1.517***	0.509*
	(0.599)	(0.685)	(0.853)	(0.385)	(0.390)	(0.269)
IMF Credits (% GDP) $_{t-1}$	-0.595	-0.551	-1.111*	-0.0571	-0.132	0.160
	(0.501)	(0.573)	(0.653)	(0.149)	(0.193)	(0.123)
Debt (% GDP) $_{t-1}$	-0.0667	-0.0680	-0.0234	0.111***	0.0780***	0.0341*
	(0.0554)	(0.0531)	(0.0570)	(0.0285)	(0.0301)	(0.0194)
Trade (% GDP) $_{t-1}$	-0.0778	-0.0794	-0.0497	0.209***	0.157***	0.113***
	(0.0506)	(0.0521)	(0.0359)	(0.0338)	(0.0310)	(0.0215)
Observations	116	116	116	76	76	76
R-squared	0.995	0.995	0.995	1.000	0.999	1.000
Number of Countries	28	28	28	31	31	31

*** $p<0.01$, ** $p<0.05$, * $p<0.1$
Standard errors in parentheses

K.6 *Determinants of Social Benefits to Nonpoor: Social Security and Public Employment Indicators*

DV	(1)	(2)	(3)	(4)	(5)	(6)
	Social Security			Public Employees		
Trade Tax Revenue (% GDP) $_{t-1}$	−0.0684 (0.0621)	−0.184** (0.0857)	−0.595** (0.232)	0.142 (0.136)	−0.0876 (0.0739)	0.139 (0.131)
Democracy $_{t-1}$	3.549*** (0.673)			0.636** (0.276)		
Trade Tax Revenue (%GDP)* Democracy $_{t-1}$	−1.546*** (0.303)			−0.252 (0.153)		
LibAuth $_{t-1}$		−0.456 (0.380)			−0.565* (0.339)	
Trade Tax Revenue (% GDP)* LibAuth $_{t-1}$		0.250 (0.211)			0.334* (0.177)	
ConservAuth $_{t-1}$			−2.489*** (0.725)			−0.162 (0.363)
Trade Tax Revenue (% GDP)* ConservAuth $_{t-1}$			0.521** (0.234)			−0.301* (0.157)
GDP Per Capita (Logged) $_{t-1}$	0.839*** (0.217)	1.098*** (0.324)	0.843*** (0.261)	0.512 (0.425)	0.709 (0.448)	0.643 (0.449)
Fuel Exports $_{t-1}$	−0.0135 (0.00929)	−0.0202 (0.0130)	−0.0155 (0.0101)	0.0289 (0.0191)	0.0280 (0.0187)	0.0295 (0.0187)
Population (Logged) $_{t-1}$	−4.019*** (1.041)	−4.148*** (1.434)	−4.906*** (1.565)	−5.497** (2.526)	−5.409** (2.388)	−6.515** (2.670)
GDP Growth $_{t-1}$	−0.00956 (0.00978)	−0.0273* (0.0142)	−0.0117 (0.0108)	−0.00914 (0.0166)	−0.0155 (0.0158)	−0.00652 (0.0162)

Capital Account Openness $_{t-1}$	0.0507 (0.196)	0.0208 (0.251)	0.106 (0.189)	-0.00365 (0.137)	0.00226 (0.136)	0.0320 (0.148)
Aid (% GDP) $_{t-1}$	-0.0829** (0.0395)	-0.0652 (0.0532)	-0.0567 (0.0547)	-0.00585 (0.0541)	-0.0140 (0.0561)	-0.0134 (0.0534)
IMF Credits (% GDP) $_{t-1}$	-0.0606** (0.0255)	-0.0816** (0.0378)	-0.0679** (0.0300)	-0.00164 (0.0365)	0.00379 (0.0369)	-0.00359 (0.0366)
Debt (% GDP) $_{t-1}$	-0.00163 (0.00469)	-0.00140 (0.00584)	0.000349 (0.00586)	-0.00177 (0.00463)	-0.00127 (0.00479)	-0.00228 (0.00480)
Trade (% GDP) $_{t-1}$	0.00285 (0.00374)	0.00638 (0.00445)	0.00200 (0.00400)	0.00619 (0.00745)	0.00799 (0.00774)	0.00531 (0.00847)
Observations	187	187	186	293	293	291
R-squared	0.835	0.725	0.761	0.948	0.947	0.954
Number of Countries	29	29	29	37	37	36

*** p<0.01, ** p<0.05, * p<0.1

Standard errors in parentheses

K.7 *Determinants of Military Spending and Armed Forces Personnel*

DV	(1)	(2)	(3)	(4)	(5)	(6)
	Military Spending			Armed Forces Personnel		
Trade Tax Revenue (% GDP) t-1	-0.216 (0.186)	-0.504 (0.309)	0.0961 (0.203)	0.0698 (0.0456)	-0.0234 (0.0283)	0.0309 (0.0477)
Democracy t-1	0.213 (0.959)			0.283*** (0.109)		
Trade Tax Revenue (%GDP)* Democracy t-1	0.128 (0.453)			-0.128** (0.0509)		
LibAuth t-1		-0.695 (0.652)			-0.313** (0.134)	
Trade Tax Revenue (% GDP)* LibAuth t-1		0.511* (0.305)			0.138** (0.0679)	
ConservAuth t-1			0.199 (2.095)			-0.0371 (0.102)
Trade Tax Revenue (% GDP)* ConservAuth t-1			-0.951** (0.426)			-0.00259 (0.0585)
GDP Per Capita (Logged) t-1	1.374 (1.017)	1.714 (1.110)	1.747 (1.121)	0.318*** (0.111)	0.349*** (0.107)	0.343*** (0.118)
Fuel Exports t-1	-0.0313 (0.0252)	-0.0317 (0.0256)	-0.0301 (0.0257)	0.00294 (0.00287)	0.00178 (0.00238)	0.00199 (0.00258)
Population (Logged) t-1	-32.33*** (6.727)	-31.50*** (6.038)	-30.07*** (6.288)	-2.860*** (0.778)	-2.599*** (0.677)	-2.637*** (0.740)
GDP Growth t-1	-0.0224 (0.0363)	-0.0372 (0.0367)	-0.0329 (0.0350)	-0.00435 (0.00480)	-0.00569 (0.00472)	-0.00342 (0.00482)

	(1)	(2)	(3)	(4)	(5)	(6)
Capital Account Openness $_{t-1}$	0.347	0.330	0.410	-0.0633	-0.0828	-0.0649
	(0.380)	(0.374)	(0.446)	(0.0563)	(0.0537)	(0.0508)
Aid (% GDP) $_{t-1}$	-0.0610	-0.0632	-0.0425	0.00116	-0.00129	-0.00476
	(0.112)	(0.110)	(0.109)	(0.0101)	(0.00984)	(0.0103)
IMF Credits (% GDP) $_{t-1}$	-0.124	-0.130	-0.154	0.0230**	0.0226**	0.0259**
	(0.0950)	(0.0966)	(0.0939)	(0.0109)	(0.0108)	(0.0101)
Debt (% GDP) $_{t-1}$	-0.0286***	-0.0295***	-0.0284**	0.00252*	0.00273*	0.00289*
	(0.0110)	(0.0110)	(0.0120)	(0.00133)	(0.00141)	(0.00149)
Trade (% GDP) $_{t-1}$	0.0208	0.0230	0.0216	0.000833	0.00162	0.000705
	(0.0136)	(0.0141)	(0.0139)	(0.00286)	(0.00302)	(0.00243)
Observations	308	308	306	357	357	354
R-squared	0.890	0.891	0.895	0.929	0.933	0.928
Number of Countries	43	43	42	45	45	44

*** $p<0.01$, ** $p<0.05$, * $p<0.1$
Standard errors in parentheses

K.8 *Determinants of Infrastructure: Railways and Airways*

DV	(1)	(2)	(3)	(4)	(5)	(6)
	Railways (Logged)			Airways (Logged)		
Trade Tax Revenue (% GDP) $_{t-1}$	-0.0724*** (0.0158)	-0.00820 (0.0253)	-0.0540*** (0.0158)	-0.0274 (0.0384)	0.0573 (0.0460)	-0.0129 (0.0352)
Democracy $_{t-1}$	-0.272* (0.144)			-0.250** (0.0996)		
Trade Tax Revenue (%GDP)* Democracy $_{t-1}$	0.114*** (0.0351)			0.126** (0.0542)		
LibAuth $_{t-1}$		0.346** (0.149)			0.0102 (0.155)	
Trade Tax Revenue (% GDP)* LibAuth $_{t-1}$		-0.104*** (0.0334)			-0.117** (0.0478)	
ConservAuth $_{t-1}$			-0.282* (0.154)			0.299 (0.241)
Trade Tax Revenue (% GDP)* ConservAuth $_{t-1}$			-0.0130 (0.0273)			0.0519 (0.0970)
GDP Per Capita (Logged) $_{t-1}$	0.319*** (0.109)	0.292*** (0.110)	0.250*** (0.0945)	-0.139 (0.147)	-0.146 (0.160)	-0.0746 (0.161)
Fuel Exports $_{t-1}$	0.0148* (0.00789)	0.0152* (0.00803)	0.0160* (0.00878)	-1.55e-05 (0.00437)	-0.000400 (0.00428)	-0.00228 (0.00450)
Population (Logged) $_{t-1}$	-0.0274 (0.523)	-0.241 (0.501)	-0.616 (0.511)	-0.323 (0.999)	-0.558 (1.004)	-0.621 (1.039)
GDP Growth $_{t-1}$	0.00375 (0.00376)	0.00398 (0.00379)	0.00637 (0.00397)	0.0156*** (0.00529)	0.0177*** (0.00533)	0.0144*** (0.00537)

Capital Account Openness $_{t-1}$	-0.152^{***}	-0.153^{***}	-0.141^{***}	0.0323	0.0316	0.00100
	(0.0437)	(0.0408)	(0.0440)	(0.0514)	(0.0538)	(0.0620)
Aid (% GDP) $_{t-1}$	-0.0118^{**}	-0.00423	-0.00373	0.0315^{**}	0.0287^{*}	0.0241
	(0.00589)	(0.00573)	(0.00431)	(0.0153)	(0.0153)	(0.0156)
IMF Credits (% GDP) $_{t-1}$	0.0207^{**}	0.0171^{*}	0.0170^{**}	-0.0322^{**}	-0.0264	-0.0233
	(0.00930)	(0.00988)	(0.00842)	(0.0157)	(0.0163)	(0.0161)
Debt (% GDP) $_{t-1}$	0.00325^{*}	0.00265	0.00273	$-2.74\text{e}{-05}$	0.000125	0.000104
	(0.00171)	(0.00182)	(0.00191)	(0.00238)	(0.00239)	(0.00261)
Trade (% GDP) $_{t-1}$	0.00268	0.00189	0.00352^{*}	-0.000116	-0.000275	-0.000316
	(0.00192)	(0.00198)	(0.00195)	(0.00216)	(0.00227)	(0.00229)
Observations	214	214	212	341	341	339
R-squared	0.996	0.996	0.997	0.980	0.976	0.974
Number of Countries	29	29	29	42	42	42

*** p<0.01, ** p<0.05, * p<0.1
Standard errors in parentheses

K.9 *Determinants of Infrastructure: Access to Water and Sanitation*

DV	(1)	(2)	(3)	(4)	(5)	(6)
	Access to Sanitation			Access to Water		
Trade Tax Revenue (% GDP) $_{t-1}$	−0.108	0.0628	0.0199	−0.111	0.104	0.523**
	(0.130)	(0.129)	(0.110)	(0.0791)	(0.124)	(0.229)
Democracy $_{t-1}$	0.213			0.293		
	(0.447)			(0.261)		
Trade Tax Revenue (%GDP)* Democracy $_{t-1}$	0.249			0.0958		
	(0.221)			(0.109)		
LibAuth $_{t-1}$		−0.319			1.678***	
		(0.447)			(0.620)	
Trade Tax Revenue (% GDP)* LibAuth $_{t-1}$		−0.195			−0.113	
		(0.224)			(0.218)	
ConservAuth $_{t-1}$			−0.142			−3.233**
			(0.617)			(1.605)
Trade Tax Revenue (% GDP)* ConservAuth $_{t-1}$			−0.0771			−0.828*
			(0.167)			(0.503)
GDP Per Capita (Logged) $_{t-1}$	3.978***	4.004***	4.071***	4.607***	8.313***	6.687***
	(0.549)	(0.556)	(0.558)	(0.403)	(0.845)	(0.901)
Fuel Exports $_{t-1}$	−0.0282	−0.0311*	−0.0309*	−0.0480***	0.0162	−0.0455
	(0.0174)	(0.0176)	(0.0174)	(0.0155)	(0.0348)	(0.0719)
Population (Logged) $_{t-1}$	24.63***	25.36***	24.45***	18.27***	−0.0388	−0.627
	(2.093)	(2.215)	(2.133)	(1.333)	(0.591)	(0.701)
GDP Growth $_{t-1}$	−0.0278*	−0.0277*	−0.0304*	−0.0313**	−0.0996***	−0.0900***
	(0.0160)	(0.0158)	(0.0174)	(0.0132)	(0.0256)	(0.0339)

	(1)	(2)	(3)	(4)	(5)	(6)
Capital Account Openness $_{t-1}$	-0.506***	-0.564***	-0.566***	-0.313***	0.152	0.339
	(0.169)	(0.168)	(0.171)	(0.102)	(0.277)	(0.540)
Aid (% GDP) $_{t-1}$	-0.0358	-0.0291	-0.0118	-0.0495**	0.00846	-0.131
	(0.0335)	(0.0329)	(0.0271)	(0.0216)	(0.0554)	(0.0828)
IMF Credits (% GDP) $_{t-1}$	0.159***	0.163***	0.149***	0.111***	-0.105	-0.274**
	(0.0497)	(0.0508)	(0.0526)	(0.0283)	(0.0777)	(0.133)
Debt (% GDP) $_{t-1}$	-0.000934	-0.00162	0.000312	0.0125***	0.0312***	0.00140
	(0.00649)	(0.00657)	(0.00678)	(0.00386)	(0.0106)	(0.0207)
Trade (% GDP) $_{t-1}$	0.0120	0.0117	0.00998	0.0203***	-0.00789	0.0235
	(0.00732)	(0.00769)	(0.00695)	(0.00651)	(0.0243)	(0.0184)
Observations	364	364	361	364	364	361
R-squared	0.999	0.999	0.999	0.999	0.996	0.988
Number of Countries	45	45	44	45	45	44

*** $p<0.01$, ** $p<0.05$, * $p<0.1$
Standard errors in parentheses

K.10 *Determinants of Infrastructure: Internet Users*

DV	(1)	(2)	(3)
	Internet Users		
Trade Tax Revenue (% GDP) $_{t-1}$	−1.169***	−0.842***	−1.280***
	(0.297)	(0.301)	(0.419)
Democracy $_{t-1}$	−1.165		
	(0.884)		
Trade Tax Revenue (%GDP)* Democracy $_{t-1}$	0.309		
	(0.351)		
LibAuth $_{t-1}$		0.957	
		(0.945)	
Trade Tax Revenue (% GDP)* LibAuth $_{t-1}$		−0.947**	
		(0.439)	
ConservAuth $_{t-1}$			1.307
			(1.191)
Trade Tax Revenue (% GDP)* ConservAuth $_{t-1}$			0.783
			(0.503)
GDP Per Capita (Logged) $_{t-1}$	16.91***	16.03***	16.12***
	(1.943)	(1.968)	(1.924)
Fuel Exports $_{t-1}$	0.164***	0.170***	0.157***
	(0.0495)	(0.0502)	(0.0484)
Population (Logged) $_{t-1}$	−11.50*	−10.56	−6.177
	(6.920)	(6.758)	(7.101)
GDP Growth $_{t-1}$	−0.405***	−0.385***	−0.405***
	(0.0605)	(0.0603)	(0.0651)
Capital Account Openness $_{t-1}$	0.279	0.398	−0.000510
	(0.402)	(0.368)	(0.356)
Aid (% GDP) $_{t-1}$	0.161*	0.141*	0.189**
	(0.0829)	(0.0816)	(0.0807)
IMF Credits (% GDP) $_{t-1}$	0.319**	0.321**	0.309**
	(0.150)	(0.153)	(0.153)
Debt (% GDP) $_{t-1}$	−0.0227	−0.0279	−0.0217
	(0.0264)	(0.0262)	(0.0239)
Trade (% GDP) $_{t-1}$	0.0840***	0.0820***	0.0806***
	(0.0262)	(0.0274)	(0.0245)
Observations	322	322	319
R-squared	0.951	0.952	0.950
Number of Countries	44	44	43

*** $p<0.01$, ** $p<0.05$, * $p<0.1$
Standard errors in parentheses

APPENDIX L

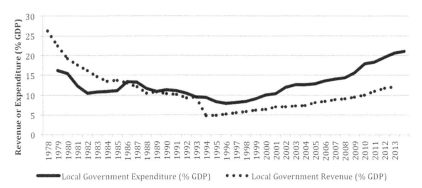

L.1 Local Government Revenue and Expenditure (Percent of GDP) in China, 1978–2012

L.2 *Annual Growth Rate of Expenditures in China*

Years	Expenditure Item	Average Annual Growth Rate
1990–2006	Subsidies Expenditure (% GDP)	−0.048318314
1990–2006	Capital Construction Expenditure (% GDP)	−0.00947168
1990–2006	Rural Production Expenditure (% GDP)	−0.006047796
1990–2006	National Defense Expenditure (% GDP)	−0.005499801
1990–2006	Culture, Education, Science, and Public Health Expenditure (% GDP)	0.003994351
1990–2006	Science and Technology Expenditure (% GDP)	0.008126387
1990–2006	Industry, Transport, and Commerce Expenditure (% GDP)	0.009243844
1990–2006	Administrative Expenses Expenditure (% GDP)	0.032233754
1990–2006	Social Security Expenditure (% GDP)	0.16389533
2007–13	General Public Services Expenditure (% GDP)	−0.043142715
2007–13	Foreign Affairs Expenditure (% GDP)	−0.041860991
2007–13	National Defense Expenditure (% GDP)	−0.00290576
2007–13	Public Security Expenditure (% GDP)	0.00776773
2007–13	Social Safety Net and Employment Effort Expenditure (% GDP)	0.037011247
2007–13	Science and Technology Expenditure (% GDP)	0.050884471
2007–13	Education Expenditure (% GDP)	0.065491032
2007–13	Urban and Rural Expenditure (% GDP)	0.083241438
2007–13	Environment Expenditure (% GDP)	0.088593246
2007–13	Agriculture, Forestry and Water Conservancy Expenditure (% GDP)	0.112010601
2007–13	Health Expenditure (% GDP)	0.122365524
2007–13	Transportation Expenditure (% GDP)	0.176377955

References

"A Rum Do." *The Economist*. November 24, 2012. Accessed March 21, 2017 at: www.economist.com/news/americas/21567090-new-president-faces-tax-revolt-rum-do.

Abbas, S. M. Ali and Alexander Klemm. (2012). "A Partial Race to the Bottom. Corporate Tax Developments in Emerging and Developing Economies." IMF Working Paper WP/12/28. Accessed March 21, 2017 at: www.imf.org/external/pubs/cat/longres.aspx?sk=25675.0.

Abed, George T. (1998). "Trade Liberalization and Tax Reform in the Southern Mediterranean Region." IMF Working Paper WP/98/49. Accessed March 21, 2017 at: www.imf.org/external/pubs/ft/wp/wp9849.pdf .

Abed, George T., Sanjeev Gupta, Liam Ebrill, Anthony Pellechio, Jerald Schiff, Benedict Clements, Ronald McMorran, and Marijn Verhoeven. (1998). "Fiscal Reform in Low-Income Countries." IMF Working Paper 160. Accessed March 21, 2017 at: www.imf.org/external/pubs/cat/longres.aspx?sk=2609.0.

Abidoye, Babatunde O., Peter F. Orazem, and Milan Vodopivec. (2014). "Mandatory Costs by Firm Size Thresholds: Firm Location, Growth and Death in Sri Lanka." *IZA Journal of Labor and Development*. 3: 36.

Abramovsky, Laura, Alexander Klemm, and David Phillips. (2014). "Corporate Tax in Developing Countries: Current Trends and Design Issues." *Fiscal Studies*. 35(4): 559–588.

Abu-Rish, Ziad. (2014). "Protests, Regime Stability, and State Formation in Jordan," in Mehran Kamrava (ed.), *Beyond the Arab Spring: The Evolving Ruling Bargain in the Middle East*. Oxford: Oxford University Press, pp. 277–312.

Acemoglu, Daron and James A. Robinson. (2006). "Persistence of Power, Elites, and Institutions." NBER Working Paper 12108. Accessed March 21, 2017 at: www.nber.org/papers/w12108.

Acemoglu, Daron, James Robinson, and Thierry Verdier. (2004). "Kleptocracy and Divide-and-Rule: A Model of Personal Rule." *Journal of the European Economic Association*. 2(2–3): 162–192.

Acemoglu, Daron, Suresh Naidu, Pascual Restrepo, and James A. Robinson. (2014). "Democracy, Redistribution, and Inequality." *Handbook of Income Distribution*. 2: 1885–1966.

(2016). "Democracy Does Cause Growth." NBER Working Paper 20004. Accessed February 16, 2018 at: www.nber.org/papers/w20004.

Acharya, S. (2005). "Thirty Years of Tax Reform in India." *Economic and Political Weekly.* 20(4): 2061–2070.

Achy, Lahcen. (2010). "Morocco's Experience with Poverty Reduction." *Carnegie Papers.* 25(December): 1–22. Accessed February 20, 2017 at: http://carnegieendowment.org/files/morocco_poverty1.pdf.

(2011). "Tunisia's Economic Challenges," in *The Carnegie Papers.* Washington, DC: Carnegie Endowment for International Peace. Accessed March 21, 2017 at: http://carnegieendowment.org/files/tunisia_economy.pdf.

Adam, Antonis. (2009). "Fiscal Reliance on Tariff Revenues: In Search of a Political Economy Explanation?" *Review of Development Economics.* 13(4): 610–625.

Adsera, Alicia and Carles Boix. (2002). "Trade, Democracy, and the Size of the Public Sector: The Political Underpinnings of Openness." *International Organization.* 56(2): 229–262.

African Development Bank. (2009). "Competitiveness and Public Sector Efficiency: Mauritius Appraisal Report." Accessed July 14, 2017 at: www.afdb.org/fileadmin/uploads/afdb/Documents/Project-and-Operations/Mauritius_-_The_Competitiveness_and_Public_Sector_Efficiency_Programme__CPSE__-_Appraisal_Report.pdf.

(2011). "The Middle of the Pyramid: Dynamics of the Middle Class in Africa." Market Brief. Accessed March 21, 2017 at: www.afdb.org/fileadmin/uploads/afdb/Documents/Publications/The%20Middle%20of%20the%20Pyramid_The%20Middle%20of%20the%20Pyramid.pdf.

African Trade Policy Centre. (2004). "Fiscal Implications of Trade Liberalization on African Countries." Accessed March 21, 2017 at: http://repository.uneca.org/handle/10855/5551.

Agenor, Pierre-Richard. (2002). "Does Globalization Hurt the Poor?" *International Economics and Economic Policy.* 1: 21–51.

Aidt, Toke and Peter Jensen. (2009). "Tax Structure, Size of Government, and the Extension of the Voting Franchise in Western Europe, 1860–1938." *International Tax Public Finance.* 16: 362–394.

Aizenman, Joshua and Yothin Jinjarak. (2009). "Globalization and Developing Countries: A Shrinking Tax Base?" *Journal of Development Studies.* 45(5): 653–671.

Albertus, Michael and Victor Menaldo. (2014). "Gaming Democracy: Elite Dominance during Transition and the Prospects for Redistribution." *British Journal of Political Science.* 44: 575–603.

Alfaro, Laura, Areendam Chanda, Sebnem Kalemli-Ozcan, and Selin Sayek. (2004). "FDI and Economic Growth: The Role of Local Financial Markets." *Journal of International Economics.* 64(1): 89–112.

Alissa, Sufyan. (2007). "Rethinking Economic Reform in Jordan," in *The Carnegie Papers.* Washington, DC: Carnegie Endowment for International Peace. Accessed March 21, 2017 at: http://carnegie-mec.org/2007/07/31/rethinking-economic-reform-in-jordan-confronting-socioeconomic-realities-pub-19465.

Alkhdour, Rajeh A. Interview with author. August 24, 2015.

Interview with author. February 4, 2016.

Allam, A. Sarvar. (2016). "GST and the States: Sharing Tax Administration." *Economic and Political Weekly.* 51(31). Accessed March 21, 2017 at:

www.epw.in/journal/2016/31/web-exclusives/gst-and-states-sharing-tax-administration.html.

Alm, James, Betty R. Jackson, and Michael McKee. (1993). "Fiscal Exchange, Collective Decision Institutions, and Tax Compliance." *Journal of Economic Behavior and Organization*. 22(3): 285–303.

Amann, Edmund. (2000). *Economic Liberalization and Industrial Performance in Brazil*. Oxford: Oxford University Press.

Amiti, Mary and Donald R. Davis. (2011). "Trade, Firms, and Wages: Theory and Evidence." *The Review of Economic Studies*. 79(1): 1–36.

"Andhra Government Expenditure on Healthcare Very Poor: Ex-Chief Secretary." *The New Indian Express*. January 22, 2017. Accessed February 22, 2017 at: www.newindianexpress.com/states/andhra-pradesh/2017/jan/22/andhra-government-expenditure-on-healthcare-very-poor-ex-chief-secretary-1562321.html.

"Andhra Pradesh Has Less Than 10% Sewerage Treatment Capacity." *Times of India*. July 28, 2016. Accessed February 22, 2017 at: http://timesofindia.indiatimes.com/city/visakhapatnam/Andhra-Pradesh-has-less-than-10-sewerage-treatment-capacity/articleshow/53429941.cms.

Angelopoulos, Konstantinos, George Economides, and Pantelis Kammas. (2007). "Tax-Spending Policies and Economic Growth." *European Journal of Political Economy*. 23: 885–902.

Appel, Hilary. (2006). "International Imperatives and Tax Reform: Lessons from Postcommunist Europe." *Comparative Politics*. 39(1): 43–62.

Armijo, Leslie Elliott. (1997). "Democratic Integrity and Financial Molasses: The Business Environment in India," in Richard D. Bingham and Edward W. Hill (eds.), *Global Perspective on Economic Development*. New Brunswick: Center for Urban Policy Research, pp. 200–239.

Arnold, J. (2012). "Improving the Tax System in Indonesia." OECD Economics Department Working Papers 998.

Arsenault, Steven J. (2013). "A Tale of Two Taxes: A Comparative Examination of the Individual Income Tax in the United States and the People's Republic of China." *Richmond Journal of Global Law and Business*. 12: 453–475.

Ashar, Sandeep A. "Maharashtra's Latest Tax Amnesty: An 'All-Carrot' Policy for Traders." *The Indian Express*. March 20, 2016. Accessed February 13, 2017 at: http://indianexpress.com/article/cities/mumbai/maharashtras-latest-tax-amnesty-an-all-carrot-policy-for-traders/.

Asian Development Bank. (July 2004). *Technical Assistance Performance Audit Report on Fiscal Management and Tax Administration in India*, Operations Evaluation Department. ADB Publication Services. Accessed April, 18 2018 at: www.adb.org/sites/default/files/evaluation-document/35498/files/tpar-ind-2004-05.pdf.

(September 2007). *Special Evaluation Study on ADB Support to Public Resource Management in India*. Operations Evaluation Department. ADB Publication Services. Accessed April 18, 2018 at: www.scribd.com/document/88673702/ADB-s-Support-to-Public-Resource-Management-in-India.

(September 2009). *Technical Assistance Completion Report*, India Resident Mission. ADB Publication Services. Accessed April 18, 2018 at: www.adb.org/sites/default/files/project-document/64323/37098-ind-tcr.pdf.

Auriol, Emmanuelle and Michael Warlters. (2005). "Taxation Base in Developing Countries." *Journal of Public Economics*. 89: 625–646.

"Authorities Get a Wake Up Call on the State of Roads." *Times of India*. March 26, 2012. Accessed August 7, 2015 at: http://timesofindia.indiatimes.com/city/mangaluru/Authorities-get-a-wake-up-call-on-the-state-of-roads/articleshow/12409370.cms.

Avelino, George, David S. Brown, and Wendy Hunter. (2005). "The Effects of Capital Mobility, Trade Openness, and Democracy on Social Spending in Latin America, 1980–1999." *American Journal of Political Science*. 49(3): 625–641.

Avi-Yonah, Reuven and Yoram Margalioth. (2007/8). "Taxation in Developing Countries: Some Recent Support and Challenges to the Conventional View." *Virginia Tax Review*. 27(1): 1–21.

Aw, Bee Yan, Mark J. Roberts, and Daniel Yi Xu. (2011). "R&D Investment, Exporting, and Productivity Dynamics." *The American Economic Review*. 101(4): 1312–1344.

Awasthi, Rajul. "Far from Silver Bullet, GST Will Likely Have Negative Impact on Growth." *The Wire*. July 25, 2016. Accessed February 15, 2018 at: http://thewire.in/53664/far-silver-bullet-gst-will-likely-negative-impact-growth/.

Ayyagari, Meghana, Asli Demirguc-Kunt, and Vojislav Maksimovic. (2015). "Are Large Firms Born or Made? Evidence from Developing Countries." World Bank Policy Research Working Paper 7406. Accessed March 27, 2017 at: https://openknowledge.worldbank.org/bitstream/handle/10986/22671/Are0large0firm0developing0countries.pdf?sequence=1&isAllowed=y.

Baer, Werner and Antonio Fialho Galvao. (2008). "Tax Burden, Government Expenditures and Income Distribution in Brazil." *The Quarterly Review of Economics and Finance*. 48: 345–358.

Bagchi, A. (2002). "Vision of the Kelkar Papers: A Critique." *Economic and Political Weekly*. 37(51): 5125–5134.

Bahl, Roy W. and Richard Bird. (2008). "Subnational Taxes in Developing Countries: The Way Forward." *Public Budgeting and Finance*. (Winter): 1–25.

Bajona, Claustre and Tianshu Chu. (2010). "Reforming State Owned Enterprises in China: Effects of WTO Accession." *Review of Economic Dynamics*. 13: 800–823.

Baldwin, Richard E. and Frederic Robert-Nicoud. (2007). "Entry and Asymmetric Lobbying: Why Governments Pick Losers." *Journal of the European Economic Association*. 5(5): 1064–1093.

Baliamoune-Lutz, Mina. (2009). "Tunisia's Development Experience: A Success Story?" UNU-WIDER Working Paper 2009.32. Accessed March 21, 2017 at: www.wider.unu.edu/publication/tunisias-development-experience.

"Bandh Against VAT Planned." *The Hindu*. March 26, 2005. Accessed March 16, 2017 at: www.thehindu.com/2005/03/26/stories/2005032612301100.htm.

Banerjee, A. and T. Piketty. (2005). "Top Indian Incomes, 1922–2000." *The World Bank Economic Review*. 19(1): 1–20.

Banerjee, Chandrajit. "GST: A High Standard Rate Would Impact Prices and Hamper Acceptance." *The Hindu*. August 28, 2016. Accessed February 13, 2017 at: www.thehindu.com/business/Economy/gst-a-high-standard-rate-would-impact-prices-and-hamper-acceptance/article9043068.ece.

Barbone, Luca, Arindam Das-Gupta, Luc De Wulf, and Anna Hansson. (1999). "Reforming Tax Systems: The World Bank Record in the 1990s." Tax Policy and Administration Thematic Group. The World Bank Policy Research Working Paper 2237. Accessed March 21, 2017 at: http://elibrary. worldbank.org/doi/abs/10.1596/1813-9450-2237.

Barcucci, Valentina and Nader Mryyan. (2014). "Labour Market Transitions of Young Women and Men in Jordan." International Labour Office. Work4Youth Public Series 14. Accessed March 21, 2017 at: www.ilo.org/wcmsp5/groups/ public/---dgreports/---dcomm/documents/publication/wcms_245876.pdf.

Barkey, Henri J. (1989). "State Autonomy and the Crisis of Import Substitution." *Comparative Political Studies*. 22(3): 291–314.

Barnes, Lucy. (2010). "Trade Policy, Fiscal Coalitions and the Structure of Taxation in Industrialized Countries, 1870–1918." Paper presented to the Annual Meetings of the APSA, Washington, DC, August 2010. Available at SSRN: http:// ssrn.com/abstract=1667966 or http://dx.doi.org/10.2139/ssrn.1667966.

Barone, Guglielmo and Sauro Mocetti. (2011). "Tax Morale and Public Spending Inefficiency." *International Tax Public Finance*. 18: 724–749.

Bartels, Larry M. (2008). *Unequal Democracy: The Political Economy of the New Gilded Age*. Princeton: Princeton University Press.

Bartelsman, Eric J. and Roel M. W. J. Beetsma. (2003). "Why Pay More? Corporate Tax Avoidance through Transfer Pricing in OECD Countries." *Journal of Public Economics*. 87: 2225–2252.

Basinger, Scott and Mark Hallerberg. (2004). "Remodeling the Competition for Capital: How Domestic Politics Erases the Race to the Bottom." *APSR*. 98(2): 261–276.

Bastiaens, Ida and Nita Rudra. (2016). "Trade Liberalization and the Challenges of Revenue Mobilization: Can International Financial Institutions Make a Difference?" *Review of International Political Economy*. 23(2): 261–289.

Basu, Kaushik. (2006). "Globalization, Poverty, and Inequality: What is the Relationship? What Can Be Done?" *World Development*. 34(8): 1361–1373.

Bates, Robert. (1981). *Markets and States in Tropical Africa*. California: University of California Press.

Bates, Robert H. and Da-Hsiang Donald Lien. (1985). "A Note on Taxation, Development, and Representative Government." *Politics and Society*. 14: 53–70.

Baunsgaard, Thomas and Michael Keen. (2010). "Tax Revenue and (or?) Trade Liberalization." *Journal of Public Economics*. 94: 563–577.

Baylouny, Anne Marie. (2008). "Militarizing Welfare: Neo-liberalism and Jordanian Policy." *Middle East Journal*. 62(2): 277–303.

(2010). *Privatizing Welfare in the Middle East*. Bloomington: Indiana University Press.

Beck, Martin and Simone Huser. (2015). "Jordan and the 'Arab Spring': No Challenge, No Change?" *Middle East Critique*. 24(1): 83–97.

"Beijing Targeting Tax Evasion by Multinationals." *South China Morning Post*. March 22, 2015. Lexis Nexis.

Benassy-Quere, Agnes, Lionel Fontagne, and Amina Lahreche-Revil. (2005). "How Does FDI React to Corporate Taxation?" *International Tax and Public Finance*. 12: 583–603.

Berens, Sarah and Armin von Schiller. (2016). "Taxing Higher Incomes: What Makes the High-Income Earners Consent to More Progressive Taxation in Latin America?" *Political Behavior*, November, 39(3): 703–729.

Berg, Andrew and Anne O. Krueger. (2003). "Trade, Growth, and Poverty: A Selective Survey." IMF Working Paper WP/03/30. Accessed March 21, 2017 at: www.imf.org/external/pubs/ft/wp/2003/wp0330.pdf.

Bergh, Andreas and Martin Karlsson. (2010). "Government Size and Growth: Accounting for Economic Freedom and Globalization." *Public Choice*. 142(1–2): 195–213.

Bergman, Marcelo. (2010). *Tax Evasion and the Rule of Law in Latin America: The Political Culture of Cheating and Compliance in Argentina and Chile*. University Park: Penn State Press.

Berinsky, Adam J., Gregory A. Huber, and Gabriel S. Lenz. (2012). "Evaluating Online Labor Markets for Experimental Research: Amazon.com's Mechanical Turk." *Political Analysis*. 20: 351–368.

Bernard, Andrew B., J. Bradford Jensen, and Peter K. Schott. (2006). "Transfer Pricing by U.S.-Based Multinational Firms." NBER Working Paper 12493. Accessed October 8, 2017 at: www.nber.org/papers/w12493.pdf.

Bernard, Andrew B., J. Bradford Jensen, Stephen J. Redding, and Peter K. Schott. (2007). "Firms in International Trade." *The Journal of Economic Perspectives*. 21(3): 105–130.

Bernstein, Thomas and Xiaobo Lu. (2000). "Taxation without Representation: Peasants, the Central and the Local States in Reform China." *The China Quarterly*. 163: 742–763.

(2003). *Taxation without Representation in Contemporary Rural China*. Cambridge: Cambridge University Press.

Bertrand, Marianne, Matilde Bombardini, and Francesco Trebbi. (2014). "Is It Whom You Know or What You Know? An Empirical Assessment of the Lobbying Process." *American Economic Review*. 104(12): 3885–3920.

Beshkar, Mostafa, Eric W. Bond, and Youngwoo Rho. (2015). "Tariff Binding and Overhang: Theory and Evidence." *Journal of International Economics*. 97: 1–13.

Besley, Timothy and Torsten Persson. (2011). *Pillars of Prosperity*. Princeton: Princeton University Press.

(2014). "Why Do Developing Countries Tax So Little?" *Journal of Economic Perspectives*. 28(4): 99–120.

Bhagwati, Jagdish and Arvind Panagariya. (2013). *Why Growth Matters*. New York: Public Affairs.

Bhagwati, J. N. (2004). *In Defense of Globalization*, Vol. 1. New York: Oxford University Press.

Bhalla, Surjit S. (2002). *Imagine There's No Country: Poverty, Inequality, and Growth in the Era of Globalization*. Washington, DC: Peterson Institute.

Bhalotra, S. (2007). "Spending to Save? State Health Expenditure and Infant Mortality in India." *Health Economics*. 16: 911–928.

Biglaiser, Glen and David S. Brown. (2005). "The Determinants of Economic Liberalization in Latin America." *Political Research Quarterly*. 58(4): 671–680.

Bilal, Sanoussi, Melissa Dalleau, and Dan Lui. (2012). "Trade Liberalization and Fiscal Adjustments." European Centre for Development Policy

Management Discussion Paper. Accessed March 16, 2017 at: http://ecdpm. org/wp-content/uploads/2013/11/DP-137-Trade-Liberalisation-Fiscal-Adjustments-EPAs-Africa-2012.pdf.

Bird, Richard M. (2010). "Subnational Taxation in Developing Countries: A Review of the Literature." World Bank Policy Research Working Paper 5450.

Bird, Richard and Pierre-Pascal Gendron. (2007). *The VAT in Developing and Transitional Countries.* Cambridge: Cambridge University Press.

Bittleston, John. "What other Measures, if any, Should Singapore's 2016 Budget also Have Included?" *The Business Times Singapore.* April 4, 2016. Accessed October 5, 2017 at Lexis Nexis Academic.

Blanc, Florentin. (2012). "Inspection Reforms: Why, How, and With What Results." OECD. Accessed October 10, 2017 at: www.oecd.org/regreform/ Inspection%20reforms%20-%20web%20-F.%20Blanc.pdf.

Bode, Maarten. (2006). "Taking Traditional Knowledge to the Market: The Commoditization of Indian Medicine." *Anthropology and Medicine.* 13(3): 225–236.

Bodea, Cristina and Adrienne LeBas. (2016). "The Origins of Voluntary Compliance: Attitudes toward Taxation in Urban Nigeria." *British Journal of Political Science.* 46(1): 215–238.

Bogetic, Zeljko and Fareed Hassan. (1993). "Determinants of Value-Added Tax Revenue." World Bank Working Paper 1203.

Boix, Carles. (2001). "Democracy, Development, and the Public Sector." *American Journal of Political Science.* 45(1): 1–17.

Boix, Carles, Michael K. Miller, and Sebastian Rosato. (2012). "A Complete Data Set of Political Regimes, 1800–2007." *Comparative Political Studies.* 46(12): 1523–1554.

Bonelli, Regis and Armando Castelar Pinheiro. (2008). "New Export Activities in Brazil: Comparative Advantage, Policy or Self-Discovery?" Inter-American Development Bank. Research Network Working Paper R-55. Accessed March 21, 2017 at: www.iadb.org/res/publications/pubfiles/ pubR-551.pdf.

Borzello, Anna. "Multi-Party, No-Party: Uganda's Choice." *BBC News.* June 29, 2000. Accessed February 20, 2017 at: http://news.bbc.co.uk/2/hi/africa/ 811226.stm.

Boucoyannis, Deborah. (2015). "No Taxation of Elites, No Representation: State Capacity and the Origins of Representation." *Politics and Society.* 43(3): 303–332.

Bounds, Andrew. "Guatemalans Join Forces to Fight Tax Rises." *Financial Times.* July 27, 2001. Lexis Nexis.

Brambor, Thomas, William Clark, and Matt Golder. (2006). "Understanding Interaction Models: Improving Empirical Analyses." *Political Analysis.* 14(1): 63–82.

Branstetter, Lee G. and Robert C. Feenstra. (2002). "Trade and Foreign Direct Investment in China: A Political Economy Approach." *Journal of International Economics.* 58: 335–358.

Brautigam, Deborak, Odd-Helge Fjeldstad, and Mick Moore. (2008). *Taxation and State-Building in Developing Countries: Capacity and Consent.* Cambridge: Cambridge University Press.

"Brazil: Protesters Angry with Poor Services and High Taxes Keep Up Pressure at Sao Paulo March." *Associated Press*. June 18, 2013. Accessed March 22, 2017 at: www.foxnews.com/world/2013/06/18/brazil-protesters-angry-with-poor-services-and-high-taxes-keep-up-pressure-at.html.

"Brazilians See Austerity Breaking Development." *New York Times*. December 18, 1982.

"Brazil to Extend Tax Breaks to All Manufacturers." *Reuters*. March 14, 2013. Accessed March 16, 2017 at: www.reuters.com/article/brazil-taxes-manufacturing-idUSL1N0C68HK20130314.

Broadman, Harry G. "China's 'New' Silk Road's Flawed One-Way Design Will Flop." *Forbes*, May 31, 2017. Accessed October 10, 2017 at: www.forbes.com/sites/harrybroadman/2017/05/31/china-new-silk-road-flawed-one-way-design-will-flop/#37c4e0a31853.

Bruno, Michael. (1992). "Stabilization and Reform in Eastern Europe: A Preliminary Evaluation." *International Monetary Fund Staff Papers*. 39(4): 741–777.

Bueno de Mesquita, Bruce and Alastair Smith. (2010). "Leader Survival, Revolutions, and the Nature of Government Finance." *American Journal of Political Science*. 54(4): 936–950.

Bueno de Mesquita, Bruce, Alastair Smith, Randolph Siverson, and James Morrow. (2005). *The Logic of Political Survival*. Cambridge, MA: MIT Press.

Burgess, Robin and Nicholas Stern. (1994). "Tax Reform in India," in K. Pattaswamaiah (ed.), *Economic Policy and Tax Reform in India*. New Delhi: Indus Publishing Company, pp. 43–123.

Burke, J. and M. Kumar. "India Corruption Protesters Dump Snakes in Busy Tax Office." *The Guardian*. November 30, 2011. Accessed August 6, 2015 at: www.theguardian.com/world/2011/nov/30/india-corruption-protest-snakes-tax-office.

Burnside, Craig, Martin Eichenbaum, and Jonas Fischer. (2004). "Fiscal Shocks and their Consequences." *Journal of Economic Theory*. 115(1): 89–117.

Busch, Marc L. and Krzysztof J. Pelc. (2014). "Law, Politics, and the True Cost of Protectionism: The Choice of Trade Remedies or Binding Overhang." *World Trade Review*. 13(1): 39–64.

Buxton, Julia. (2014). "Social Policy in Venezuela." United Nations Research Institute for Social Development Working Paper 2014–16. Accessed March 21, 2017 at: www.unrisd.org/80256B3C005BCCF9/(httpAuxPages)/1D4EF25E12C57738C1257D9E00562542/$file/Buxton.pdf.

Byung-joon, Koh. "Tax Revenues Grow Faster than GDP Since '90." *The Korea Herald*. October 22, 2003.

Cacho, Katlene O. "Tax Reforms 'Long Overdue'." *Sun Star*. August 31, 2016. Accessed August 9, 2017 at: www.sunstar.com.ph/cebu/business/2016/08/31/tax-reforms-long-overdue-494912.

Cai, Yongshun. (2008). "Local Governments and the Suppression of Popular Resistance in China." *The China Quarterly*. 193: 24–42.

Campos, Jose Edgardo and Hadi Salehi Esfahani. (1996). "Why and When Do Governments Initiate Public Enterprise Reform?" *The World Bank Economic Review*. 10(3): 451–485.

"Can India's Currency Ban Really Curb the Black Economy?" *BBC News*. November 10, 2016. Accessed October 12, 2017 at: www.bbc.com/news/world-asia-india-37933231.

Cardoso, Jose Luis and Pedro Lains. (2013). *Paying for the Liberal State*. Cambridge: Cambridge University Press.

Carnahan, Micahel. (2015). "Taxation Challenges in Developing Countries." *Asia and Pacific Policy Studies*. 2(1): 169–182.

Carstens, Agustín. (2005). "Making Regional Economic Integration Work." 20th Annual General Meeting and Conference of the Pakistan Society of Development Economists. Islamabad, Pakistan. January 12. Accessed March 16, 2017 at: www.imf.org/external/np/speeches/2005/011205.htm.

Carter, B. "Which Country Has the Highest Tax Rate?" *BBC News*. February 25, 2014. Accessed August 6, 2015 at: www.bbc.com/news/magazine-26327114.

Chakravorti, Bhaskar. "Early Lessons from India's Demonetization Experiment." *Harvard Business Review*. March 14, 2017. Accessed October 4, 2017 at https://hbr.org/2017/03/early-lessons-from-indias-demonetization-experiment.

Chan, John and James Conachy. (1999). "Rural Discontent Repressed in China." *International Committee of the Fourth International*. Accessed March 16, 2017 at: www.wsws.org/en/articles/1999/08/chin-a04.html.

Chandra, Siddharth and Nita Rudra. (2015). "Reassessing the Links between Regime Type and Economic Performance: Why Some Authoritarian Regimes Show Stable Growth and Others Do Not." *British Journal of Political Science*. 45(2): 253–285.

Chandran, Nyshka. "India Prime Minister Narenda Modi Hopes for Support for GST during Parliament Session." *CNBC*. August 1, 2016. Accessed February 13, 2017 at: www.cnbc.com/2016/08/01/india-prime-minister-narendra-modi-hopes-for-support-for-gst-during-parliament-session.html.

Chang, Gordon G. "Did China Just Launch World's Biggest Spending Plan?" *Forbes*. May 24, 2015. Accessed at: www.forbes.com/sites/gordonchang/2015/05/24/did-china-just-launch-worlds-biggest-spending-plan/.

Chaturvedi, Amit. "MNS Protest Against Toll Tax: Raj Thackeray to Meet Chief Minister Prithiviraj Chavan Today," *NDTV*, New Delhi. February 13, 2014. Accessed August 6, 2015 at: www.ndtv.com/convergence/ndtv/corporatepage/index.aspx.

Cheibub, Jose Antonio. (1998). "Political Regimes and the Extractive Capacity of Governments: Taxation in Democracies and Dictatorships." *World Politics*. 50(3): 349–376.

Cheibub, Jose Antonio, Jennifer Gandhi, and James Raymond Vreeland. (2009). "Democracy and Dictatorship Revisited." *Public Choice*. 143: 67–101.

Chen, An. (2008). "The 1994 Tax Reform and Its Impact on China's Rural Fiscal Structure." *Modern China*. 34(3): 303–343.

 (2015). *The Transformation of Governance in Rural China*. Cambridge: Cambridge University Press.

Chen, Tain-jy. (1987). "Comparing Technical Efficiency between Import-Substitution-Oriented and Export-Oriented Foreign Firms in a Developing Economy." *Journal of Development Economics*. 26(2): 277–289.

Chen, Tianhong and John A. Turner. (2014). "Extending Social Security Coverage to the Rural Sector in China." *International Social Security Review.* 67(1): 49–70.

Chen, Yuy and Ginger Zhe Jin. (2011). "Does Health Insurance Coverage Lead to Better Health and Educational Outcomes? Evidence from Rural China." *Journal of Health Economics.* 31(1): 1–14.

Chen, Zhiwu. "Building a Nation Demands More than Steel and Concrete; Why Does China Always Choose Infrastructure Spending to Boost Growth?" *The Globe and Mail.* November 26, 2008.

Cheung, Daniel K. C. (2012). "An Update on General Anti-Tax Avoidance Rules in China." *International Tax Journal.* (January–February): 35–45.

"China: 533 Officials Punished for Ties with Tax Agents." *Anadolu Agency.* October 3, 2015. Accessed February 15, 2017 at: http://aa.com.tr/en/world/china-533-officials-punished-for-ties-with-tax-agents/408710.

"China Plans to Get Tough on Corporate Tax Evasion." *Wall Street Journal.* May 18, 2016. Accessed August 9, 2017 at: www.wsj.com/articles/china-plans-to-get-tough-on-corporate-tax-evasion-1463566119.

"China Puts Railways and Houses at Heart of New Stimulus Measures." *The Guardian.* April 3, 2014. Accessed March 24, 2017 at: www.theguardian.com/world/2014/apr/03/china-railways-new-economic-stimulus-measures.

"China's Poor Rural Areas Said in Urgent Need of Teachers." *BBC Monitoring Asia Pacific.* December 15, 2008.

China Statistical Yearbook. (2016). National Bureau of Statistics of China. www.stats.gov.cn/english/statisticaldata/AnnualData/.

"Chinese Dissident's Firm Challenges Tax Evasion Allegations." *CNN.* July 15, 2011. Accessed May 1, 2017 at: www.cnn.com/2011/WORLD/asiapcf/07/14/china.weiwei.taxes/.

Chinn, Menzie and Hiro Ito. (2015). "The Chinn-Ito Index: A De Jure Measure of Financial Openness." Accessed March 16, 2017 at: http://web.pdx.edu/~ito/Chinn-Ito_website.htm.

Cho, SungChan and Philip Pilsoo Choi. (2014). "Introducing Property Tax in China as an Alternative Financing Source." *Land Use Policy.* 38: 580–586.

Choi, Kwang. (1997). "Tax Policy and Tax Reforms in Korea," in Wayne Thirsk (ed.), *Tax Reform in Developing Countries.* Washington, DC: World Bank.

Chomiak, Laryssa. (2011). "The Making of a Revolution in Tunisia." *Middle East Law and Governance.* 3: 68–83.

Choudhary, Amit and Dhananjay Mahapatra. "Not Just Fine, Evading Tax Could Soon Invite Jail Term." *Times of India.* January 21, 2015. Accessed March 24, 2017 at: http://timesofindia.indiatimes.com/india/Not-just-fine-evading-tax-could-soon-invite-jail-term/articleshow/45960425.cms.

Collier, Paul and David Dollar. (2002). "Globalization, Growth, and Poverty: Building an Inclusive World Economy." *World Bank Policy Research Report 23591.* Accessed March 21, 2017 at: http://documents.worldbank.org/curated/en/954071468778196576/Globalization-growth-and-poverty-building-an-inclusive-world-economy.

Central Bank of Jordan. Statistical Database. Accessed March 16, 2017 at: www.cbj.gov.jo.

CIRI. (2010). Human Rights Data Project. Accessed March 16, 2017 at: www .humanrightsdata.com.

Cnossen, S. (2013). "Preparing the Way for a Modern GST in India." *International Tax and Public Finance.* 20: 715–723.

"Cong Gherao Against 'Poor' Healthcare in Nabarangpur." *Times of India.* September 20, 2012. Accessed August 7, 2015 at: http://timesofindia. indiatimes.com/city/bhubaneswar/Cong-gherao-against-poor-healthcare-in-Nabarangpur/articleshow/16460867.cms?.

Conover, Teresa L. and Nancy B. Nichols. (2000). "A Further Examination of Income Shifting Through Transfer Pricing Considering Firm Size and/or Distress." *The International Journal of Accounting.* 35(2): 189–211.

Conrad, Courtenay. (2011). "Constrained Concessions: Beneficent Dictatorial Responses to the Domestic Political Opposition." *International Studies Quarterly.* 55(4): 1167–1187.

Cooper, Joel, Randall Fox, Jan Loeprick, and Komal Mohindra. (2016). "Transfer Pricing and Developing Economies." World Bank Group. Accessed March 16, 2017 at: https://openknowledge.worldbank.org/handle/ 10986/25095.

"Corporate Tax Schemes Hurt Developing Countries." *The New Nation (Bangladesh).* June 27, 2014. Lexis Nexis.

Cottarelli, Carlo. (2011). "Revenue Mobilization in Developing Countries." IMF Fiscal Affairs Department. Accessed March 16, 2017 at: www.imf.org/ external/np/pp/eng/2011/030811.pdf.

Cowell, Alan. "Jordan's Revolt is Against Austerity." *New York Times.* April 21, 1989. Accessed on November 3, 2015, at: www.nytimes.com/1989/04/21/ world/jordan-s-revolt-is-against-austerity.html.

"Cows Have Come to the Rescue of Cash-Strapped Indian States." *Sputnik News.* May 13, 2016. Accessed on December 8, 2016, at: https://sputniknews.com/ asia/201605131039574086-india-cow-tax/.

Crabtree, J. "Foreign Funds Brace for India's Alternative Tax Demand." *Financial Times India,* Mumbai. April 8, 2015. Accessed August 6, 2015 at: www.ft.com/ intl/cms/s/d82d6aaa-ddd5-11e4-9d29-00144feab7de,Authorised=false. html?_i_location=http%3A%2F%2Fwww.ft.com%2Fcms%2Fs%2F 0%2Fd82d6aaa-ddd5-11e4-9d29-00144feab7de.html%3Fsiteedition%3D intl&siteedition=intl&_i_referer=#axzz3gShDETt1.

Crivelli, Ernesto, Ruud De Mooij, and Michael Keen. (2015). "Base Erosion, Profit Shifting and Developing Countries." IMF Working Paper WP/15/ 118. Accessed March 21, 2017 at: www.imf.org/external/pubs/ft/wp/2015/ wp15118.pdf.

Cui, Wei. (2014). "China's Business-Tax-to-VAT Reform: An Interim Assessment." *British Tax Review.* 5: 617–641.

Dahlman, Carl J., Douglas Z. Zeng, and Shuilin Wang. (2007). *Enhancing China's Competitiveness through Lifelong Learning.* Washington, DC: World Bank.

Das-Gupta, A. (2012). "An Assessment of the Revenue Impact of State-Level VAT in India." *Economic & Political Weekly.* XLVII(10): 55–64.

Das-Gupta, A., S. Ghosh, and D. Mookherjee. (2004). "Tax Administration Reform and Taxpayer Compliance in India." *International Tax and Public Finance.* 11: 575–600.

Das-Gupta, A., R. Lahiri, and D. Mookherjee. (1995). "Income Tax Compliance in India: An Empirical Analysis." *World Development.* 23(12): 2051–2064.

Datt, Mohini, Bernard Hoekman, and Mariem Malouche. (2011). "Taking Stock of Trade Protectionism since 2008." World Bank Economic Premise. Accessed March 21, 2017 at: http://siteresources.worldbank.org/INTPREMNET/Resources/EP72.pdf.

De, S. (2012). "Fiscal Policy in India: Trends and Trajectory." *Ministry of Finance, Government of India, Working Papers.* January. Accessed March 21, 2017 at: www.finmin.nic.in/WorkingPaper/FPI_trends_Trajectory.pdf.

Dean, Adam. (2017). "Voicing Opposition: Labor Repression and Trade Liberalization in Developing Countries." American Political Science Association Annual Conference Presentation. San Francisco, California.

Dedhia, Kartik. "The Challenges of Implementing GST." *Forbes India.* February 26, 2016. Accessed February 13, 2017 at: http://forbesindia.com/article/budget-2016/the-challenges-of-implementing-gst/42491/1.

De Figueiredo, John M. and Brian Kelleher Richter. (2014). "Advancing the Empirical Research on Lobbying." *Annual Review of Political Science.* 17: 163–185.

De la O, Ana. (2014). "How Governmental Corruption Breeds Clientelism," in Jorge I. Domínguez, Kenneth F. Greene, Chappell H. Lawson, and Alejandro Moreno (eds.), *Mexico's Evolving Democracy: A Comparative Study of the 2012 Elections.* Baltimore: Johns Hopkins University Press, pp. 181–199.

Dell'Anno, Roberto. (2009). "Tax Evasion, Tax Morale and Policy Makers' Effectiveness." *The Journal of Socio-Economics.* 38: 988–997.

De Mello, Luiz R. (2000). "Fiscal Decentralization and Intergovernmental Fiscal Relations: A Cross-Country Analysis." *World Development.* 28(2): 365–380.

Demick, Barbara. "China Lawyer Who Fought Unfair Arrest is Arrested." *Los Angeles Times.* August 7, 2009. Accessed March 16, 2017 at: http://articles.latimes.com/2009/aug/07/world/fg-china-lawyer7.

Desai, Raj M., Anders Olofsgard, and Tarik M. Yousef. (2009). "The Logic of Authoritarian Bargains." *Economics and Politics.* 21(1): 93–125.

Devonshire-Ellis, Chris. "Understanding China's Double Tax Agreement." *China Briefing.* February 12, 2014. Accessed March 16, 2017 at: www.china-briefing.com/news/2014/02/12/understanding-chinas-double-tax-agreements.html.

Diaz-Cayeros, Alberto, Federico Estevez, and Beatriz Magaloni. (2016). *Strategies of Vote Buying: Democracy, Clientelism, and Poverty Relief in Mexico.* Cambridge: Cambridge University Press.

Dillman, Bradford. (1998). "The Political Economy of Structural Adjustment in Tunisia and Algeria." *The Journal of North African Studies.* 3(3): 1–24.

Dinh, Hinh T., Dimitris A. Mavridis, and Hoa B. Nguyen. (2010). "The Binding Constraint on Firms' Growth in Developing Countries." World Bank Policy Research Working Paper 5485. Accessed March 27, 2017 at: http://documents.worldbank.org/curated/en/966571468137388733/pdf/WPS5485.pdf.

Dollar, David. (2001). "Globalization, Inequality, and Poverty since 1980." *World Bank Research Observer.* 20(2): 145–176. Accessed March 21, 2017 at: http://elibrary.worldbank.org/doi/abs/10.1093/wbro/lki008?journalCode=wbro.

Dollar, David and Aart Kraay. (2002). "Growth Is Good for the Poor." *Journal of Economic Growth*. 7(3): 195–225.

(2004). "Trade, Growth, and Poverty." *The Economic Journal*. 114(493): F22–F49.

Donohoe, Miriam. "7 Face Execution for Chinese Tax Fraud." *The Irish Times*. March 3, 2001.

Dornbusch, Rudiger. (2005). "The Case for Trade Liberalization in Developing Countries." *The Journal of Economic Perspectives*. 6(1): 69–85.

Drazen, Allan and Marcela Eslava. (2010). "Electoral Manipulation via Voter-Friendly Spending: Theory and Evidence." *Journal of Development Economics*. 92: 39–52.

Drèze, Jean and Amartya Sen. (2013). *An Uncertain Glory: India and Its Contradictions*. Princeton: Princeton University Press.

Dür, Andreas. (2007). "EU Trade Policy as Protection for Exporters: The Agreements with Mexico and Chile." *Journal of Common Market Studies*. 45(4): 833–855.

Dür, Andreas, Leonardo Baccini, and Manfred Elsig. (2014). "The Design of International Trade Agreements: Introducing a New Database." *Review of International Organizations*. 9(3): 353–375.

Easter, Gerald M. (2002). "The Russian Tax Police." *Post-Soviet Affairs*. 18(4): 332–362.

"El Salvador/World Bank: Expanding Social Programs to Assist 5,500 Elders and 20,000 Households in Poor Areas." *World Bank Press Release*. June 2, 2011. Accessed March 22, 2017 at: www.worldbank.org/en/news/press-release/2011/06/02/el-salvadorworld-bank-expanding-social-programs-to-assist-5500-elders-and-20000-households-in-poor-areas.

Etchemendy, Sebastián. (2001). "Constructing Reform Coalitions: The Politics of Compensations in Argentina's Economic Liberalization." *Latin American Politics and Society*. 43 (3): 1–35.

European Parliament. (2014). "Bhutan and its Political Parties." Accessed February 20, 2017 at: www.europarl.europa.eu/RegData/etudes/ATAG/2014/542164/EPRS_ATA(2014)542164_REV1_EN.pdf.

European Union. (2003). "Overview of the Terms of China's Accession to WTO." Accessed August 9, 2017 at: http://trade.ec.europa.eu/doclib/docs/2003/october/tradoc_111955.pdf.

EY. (2015). "2015 Worldwide VAT, GST and Sales Tax Guide." Accessed March 16, 2017 at: www.ey.com/GL/en/Services/Tax/Worldwide-VAT-GST-Sales-Tax-Guide---Country-list.

"Fair, Free Elections Government's Top Political Priority – PM." *The Jordan Times*. October 12, 2012. Accessed March 22, 2017 at: http://vista.sahafi.jo/art.php?id=7fce7d619ad289b95a85937c6fca56070cd8a309.

Fairfield, Tasha. (2010). "Business Power and Tax Reform: Taxing Income and Profits in Chile and Argentina." *Latin American Politics and Society*. 52(2): 37.

(2014). "The Political Economy of Progressive Tax Reform in Chile." Woodrow Wilson Center. Accessed August 12, 2017 at: www.wilsoncenter.org/sites/default/files/Tax%20Reform%20in%20Chile.pdf.

(2015). *Private Wealth and Public Revenue*. Cambridge: Cambridge University Press.

Fallah, Samwar S. "Liberia's Public Officials Salary Cut: Who Will the Feel the Pinch?" *All Africa.* July 10, 2015. Accessed March 16, 2017 at: http://allafrica.com/stories/201507101614.html.

Farah, Ana Gabriela Verotti. "Tax Reduction for the Oil Industry in Brazil." *The Brazil Business.* August 28, 2013. Accessed March 16, 2017 at: http://thebrazilbusiness.com/article/tax-reduction-for-the-oil-industry-in-brazil.

Farrell, Colin and Matthew Mui. "China Escalating Anti-Tax Avoidance Efforts." *International Tax Review.* August 13, 2013. Accessed March 24, 2017 at: www.internationaltaxreview.com/Article/3242876/China-escalating-anti-tax-avoidance-efforts.html.

Finger, J. Michael and Julio J. Nogues. (2002). "The Unbalanced Uruguay Round Outcome: The New Areas in Future WTO Negotiations." *The World Economy.* 25(3): 321–340.

Fisman, Raymond and Shang-Jin Wei. (2004). "Tax Rates and Tax Evasion: Evidence from 'Missing Imports' in China." *Journal of Political Economy.* 112(2): 471–496.

Fjeldstad, Odd-Helge. (2001). "Taxation, Coercion and Donors: Local Government Tax Enforcement in Tanzania." *The Journal of Modern African Studies.* 39(2): 289–306.

Ford, Peter. "China to Cut Income Tax for 60 Million People." *The Christian Science Monitor.* August 31, 2011. Accessed March 16, 2017 at: www.csmonitor.com/World/Asia-Pacific/2011/0831/China-to-cut-income-tax-for-60-million-people.

"Foreign Firms under Microscope; Efforts to Tackle Evasion Focus on Representative Offices as Beijing Eager to Boost Revenues." *South China Morning Post (Hong Kong).* July 31, 2002. Lexis Nexis.

Forero, Juan. "Latin American Graft and Poverty Trying Patience with Democracy." *New York Times.* June 24, 2004. Accessed on February 5, 2016, at: www.nytimes.com/2004/06/24/world/latin-america-graft-and-poverty-trying-patience-with-democracy.html.

Freedom House. (2016). "Freedom in the World." Accessed March 16, 2017 at: www.freedomhouse.org/report-types/freedom-world.

Fu, Teng M. (2005). "Unequal Primary Education Opportunities in Rural and Urban China." *China Perspectives.* 60: 2–8.

Fuest, Clemens and Nadine Riedel. (2010). "Tax Evasion and Avoidance in Developing Countries: The Role of International Profit Shifting." Oxford University Centre for Business Taxation, Working Paper 10/12.

Gallagher, Kevin P. (2008). "Trading Away the Ladder? Trade Politics and Economic Development in the Americas." *New Political Economy.* 13(1): 37–59.

Gallagher, Mary Elizabeth. (2011). *Contagious Capitalism: Globalization and the Politics of Labor in China.* Princeton: Princeton University Press.

Gallup. "Tunisia: Analyzing the Dawn of the Arab Spring." Accessed March 16, 2017 at: www.gallup.com/poll/157049/tunisia-analyzing-dawn-arab-spring.aspx.

Gamberoni, Elisa and Richard Newfarmer. (2009). "Trade Protection: Incipient but Worrisome Trends," in Richard Baldwin and Simon Evenett (eds.), *The Collapse of Global Trade, Murky Protectionism, and the Crisis: Recommendations for the G20*. Voxeu.org publication. Accessed February 14, 2018 at: https:// voxeu.org/epubs/cepr-reports/collapse-global-trade-murky-protectionism- and-crisis-recommendations-g20.

Gana, Alia. (2012). "The Rural and Agricultural Roots of the Tunisian Revolution: When Food Security Matters." *International Journal of Sociology of Agriculture and Food*. 19(2): 201–213.

Gandhi, Jennifer. (2008). *Political Institutions under Dictatorship*. New York: Cambridge University Press.

Gandhi, Jennifer and Adam Przeworski. (2006). "Cooperation, Cooptation, and Rebellion under Dictatorships." *Economics and Politics*. 18(1): 1–26.

   (2007). "Authoritarian Institutions and the Survival of Autocrats." *Comparative Political Studies*. 40(11): 1279–1301.

Gangopadhyay, P. and S. Nath. (2001). "Bargaining, Coalitions and Local Expenditure." *Urban Studies*. 38(13): 2379–2391.

Garrett, Geoffrey and Deborah Mitchell. (2001). "Globalization, Government Spending, and Taxation in the OECD." *European Journal of Political Research*. 39(2): 145–177.

Gayathri, Amrutha. "Massive Protests In Brazil over Tax Burden Coupled with Poor Public Services." *International Business Times*. June 18, 2013. Accessed March 16, 2017 at: www.ibtimes.com/massive-protests-brazil-over-tax- burden-coupled-poor-public-services-1311063.

Geddes, Barbara. (2003). *Paradigms and Sand Castles*. Ann Arbor: University of Michigan Press.

Geddes, Barbara, Joseph Wright, and Erica Frantz. (2012). "New Data on Autocratic Breakdown and Regime Transition." *Perspectives on Politics*. 12(2): 313–331.

Gelb, Alan, Gary Jefferson, and Inderjit Singh. (1992). "Can Communist Economies Transform Incrementally? The Experience of China." *NBER*. 8: 87–149.

Genschel, Philipp, Hanna Lierse, and Laura Seelkopf. (2016). "Dictators Don't Compete: Autocracy, Democracy, and Tax Competition." *Review of International Political Economy*. 23(2): 290–315.

Gensler, Howard. (1995). "The 1994 Individual Income Tax Law of the People's Republic of China." *California Western International Law Journal*. 26(1): 115–138.

Ghani, E., W. R. Kerr, and A. Segura. (2015). "Informal Tradables and the Employment Growth of Indian Manufacturing." World Bank, *Working Paper Series 7206*. Accessed March 21, 2017 at: http:// documents.worldbank.org/curated/en/302991468184160972/ Informal-tradables-and-the-employment-growth-of-Indian-manufacturing.

Ghosh, Jayati. (2002). "Globalization, Export-Oriented Employment for Women and Social Policy: A Case Study of India." *Social Scientist*. 20(11/12): 17–60.

Ghosh, J. "India's Rural Employment Programme Is Dying a Death of Funding Cuts." *The Guardian*. February 5, 2015. Accessed August 6, 2015 at: www.theguardian.com/global-development/2015/feb/05/india- rural-employment-funding-cuts-mgnrega.

Ghosh, S. K. and R. Kumar. "Last Straw on the Fisc Back." *The Indian Express Archive, The Indian Express*. February 16, 2012. Accessed August 6, 2015 at: http:// archive.indianexpress.com/news/last-straw-on-the-fisc-back/912534/0.

Gill, Indermit S. and Martin Raiser. (2012). *Golden Growth: Restoring the Lustre of the European Economic Model.* World Bank Publications. Accessed March 21, 2017 at: http://elibrary.worldbank.org/doi/abs/10.1596/978-0-8213-8965-2.

Gill, Stephen R. and David Law. (1989). "Global Hegemony and the Structural Power of Capital." *International Studies Quarterly.* 33(4): 475–499.

Giriprakash, K. "India's Auto Sector Can Gain from Thai Turmoil." *The Hindu Business Line.* July 5, 2015. Accessed August 6, 2015 at: www.thehindubusinessline.com/economy/indias-auto-sector-can-gain-from-thai-turmoil/article7389336.ece.

Glaser, Mark A. and W. Barley Hildreth. (1999). "Service Delivery Satisfaction and Willingness to Pay Taxes: Citizen Recognition of Local Government Performance." *Public Productivity and Management Review.* 23(1): 48–67.

Global Integrity. (2004). "Flawed Democracies." Accessed February 14, 2017 at: www.globalintegrity.org/wp-content/uploads/2013/08/KeyFindings2004.pdf.

Goch, Mary Ajith and Susan Nyiel Panchol. "Government Presents SSP 9.3 Billion Budget to Parliament." *The Citizen.* March 20, 2012.

Goerke, Laszlo and Marco Runkel. (2011). "Tax Evasion and Competition." *Scottish Journal of Political Economy.* 58(5): 711–736.

Goetzmann, William N., Andrey D. Ukhov, and Ning Zhu. (2007). "China and the World Financial Markets 1870–1939: Modern Lessons from Historical Globalization." *The Economic History Review.* 60(2): 267–312.

Goh, Brenda. "Lovely Airport, Where are the Planes? China's White Elephants Emerge." *Reuters.* April 10, 2015. Accessed March 16, 2017 at: www.reuters.com/article/2015/04/09/china-infrastructure-idUSL5N0WD04B20150409.

Goldberg, Pinelopi Koujianou and Nina Pavcnik. (2007). "Distributional Effects of Globalization in Developing Countries." *Journal of Economic Literature.* 45(1): 39–82.

Goldstone, Jack A. (2011). "Cross-Class Coalitions and the Making of the Arab Revolts of 2011." *Swiss Political Science Review.* 17(4): 457–462.

Goodman, Peter S. "China's Wealthy Facing Income Tax Crackdown." *The Washington Post.* October 22, 2002.

Gould, David, World Bank. Interview with author. March 9, 2016, Washington, DC.

Government of India. (2004). *The Report of the Task Force on Implementation of the Fiscal Responsibility and Budget Management Act, 2003.* Ministry of Finance, Government of India. Accessed April 17, 2018 at: https://dea.gov.in/task-force-report-implementation-fiscal-responsibility-and-budget-management-act-2003.

(2015). "Report on the Revenue Neutral Rate and Structure of Rates for the Goods and Service Tax." Accessed on February 13, 2017 at: www.cbec.gov.in/resources//htdocs-cbec/gst/cea-rpt-rnr.pdf;jsessionid=2852913C8E0F544C99BF8CF6A8300959.

Government of Jordan. Ministry of Finance. Accessed March 16, 2017 at: www.mof.gov.jo/en-us/mainpage.aspx.

Government of Tunisia. Ministry of Finance. Accessed March 16, 2017 at: www.finances.gov.tn.

Gray, Clive S., R. P. Short, and Robert H. Floyd. (1984). *Public Enterprise in Mixed Economies: Some Macroeconomic Aspects.* Washington, DC: IMF.

Grossman, Gene M. and Elhanan Helpman. (1994). "Protection for Sale." *The American Economic Review.* 84(4): 833–850.

Groves, Theodore, Yongmiao Hong, John McMillan, and Barry Naughton. (1994). "Autonomy and Incentives in Chinese State Enterprises." *The Quarterly Journal of Economics.* 109(1): 183–209.

Gupta, Abhijit Sen. (2007). "Determinants of Tax Revenue Efforts in Developing Countries." IMF Working Paper WP/07/184.

Haggard, Stephan and Robert R. Kaufman. (1995). *The Political Economy of Democratic Transitions.* Princeton: Princeton University Press.

(2008). *Development, Democracy, and Welfare States.* Princeton: Princeton University Press.

Hallerberg, Mark and Carlos Scartascini. (2017). "Explaining Changes in Tax Burdens in Latin America: Do Politics Trump Economics?" *European Journal of Political Economy.* 48: 162–179.

Hao, Yan. "China Revises Individual Income Tax Law, Raises Exemption Threshold." *Xinhua.* June 30, 2011. Accessed March 16, 2017 at: http://news.xinhuanet.com/english2010/china/2011-06/30/c_13958711.htm.

Harjani, Ansuya. "Will Singapore's Tax Hike on Top Earners Deter Top Talent?" *CNBC.com.* February 23, 2015. Accessed March 22, 2017 at: www.cnbc.com/2015/02/23/singapores-tax-hike-on-top-earners-deter-top-talent.html.

Harrigan, Jane R. and Hamed El-Said. (2010). "The Economic Impact of IMF and World Bank Programs in the Middle East and North Africa: A Case Study of Jordan, Egypt, Morocco, and Tunisia, 1983–2004." *Review of Middle East Economics and Finance.* 6(2): 1–25.

Harris, Gardiner. "Rival Economists in Public Battle over Cure for India's Poverty." *New York Times.* August 21, 2013. Accessed March 9, 2017 at: www.nytimes.com/2013/08/22/world/asia/rival-economists-in-public-battle-over-cure-for-indias-poverty.html.

Harrison, Ann. (2006). *Globalization and Poverty.* Washington, DC: National Bureau of Economic Research.

Hart, Austin. (2010). "Death of the Partisan? Globalization and Taxation in South America, 1990–2006." *Comparative Political Studies.* 43: 304.

Hasan, Rana, Devashish Mitra, and Beyza P. Ural. (2006). "Trade Liberalization, Labor-Market Institutions and Poverty Reduction: Evidence from Indian States." *India Policy Forum.* 3: 71–122.

Hays, Jude C. (2003). "Globalization and Capital Taxation in Consensus and Majoritarian Democracies." *World Politics.* 56(1): 79–113.

"Heavy Riot Policy Presence in Minsk Following Crackdown." Radio Free Europe. March 26, 2017. Accessed July 3, 2017 at: www.rferl.org/a/belarus-opposition-parasite-tax-protest-nyaklyaeu/28389979.html.

Helpman, Elhanan, Marc Melitz, and Stephen R. Yeaple. (2004). "Export versus FDI with Heterogeneous Firms." *American Economic Review.* 94(1): 300–316.

"Herb Today, Gone Tomorrow Seems to Be the Name of the Game." *India Business Insight.* February 4, 2003.

Hibou, Beatrice. (2011). *Forces of Obedience.* Cambridge: Polity Press.

Hibou, Beatrice and John Hulsey. (2006). "Domination and Control in Tunisia: Economic Levers for the Exercise of Authoritarian Power." *Review of African Political Economy.* 33(108): 185–206.

"Himalaya, India's Booming Herbal Healthcare Company." *Channel NewsAsia.* March 31, 2013. Accessed March 22, 2017 at: www.channelnewsasia.com/news/lifestyle/himalaya-india-s-booming-herba/622524.html.

Hines, James R. (2004). "Do Tax Havens Flourish?" NBER Working Paper 10936.

Hinz, Richard, Robert Holzmann, David Tuesta, and Noriyuki Takayama. (2013). *Matching Contributions for Pensions: A Review of International Experience.* Washington, DC: World Bank.

Hoda, Anwarul. (2001). *Tariff Negotiations and Renegotiations under the GATT and the WTO.* Cambridge: Cambridge University Press.

Hofman, Bert and Shahid Yusuf. (1995). "Budget Policy in China," in Ehtisham Ahmad, Qiang Gao, and Tanzi Vito (eds.), *Reforming China's Public Finances.* Washington, DC: IMF.

Honaker, James, Gary King, and Matthew Blackwell. (2015). "Amelia II: A Program for Missing Data." Accessed March 16, 2017 at: https://cran.r-project.org/web/packages/Amelia/vignettes/amelia.pdf.

Huber, Evelyne and Fred Solt. (2004). "Successes and Failures of Neoliberalism." *Latin American Research Review.* 39(3): 150–164.

Ianchovichina, Elena and Will Martin. (2001). "Trade Liberalization in China's Accession to WTO." *Journal of Economic Integration.* 16(4): 421–445.

Imai, Hiroyuki. (2000). "The Labor Income Tax Equivalent of Price Scissors in Pre-Reform China." *Journal of Comparative Economics.* 28(3): 524–544.

IMF. (1989). "Annual Report," Washington, DC. Accessed February 2, 2018, at: www.imf.org/external/pubs/ft/ar/archive/pdf/ar1989.pdf.

(1995). *Tax Policy Handbook.* Pathasarathi Shome (ed.). Washington, DC: IMF.

(1998). "India: Selected Issues." IMF Staff Country Report 98/112.

(2000). "Tunisia: Recent Economic Developments." Prepared by Edward Gardner, Christine Sampic, Shahpassand Sheybani, and Jean Le Dem. IMF Staff Country Report 00/37.

(2002). *India: Selected Issues and Statistical Appendix.* IMF Country Report 02/193. Washington, DC: IMF.

(2004a). "IMF Executive Board Completes Second Review of Jordan's Stand-By Arrangement." Press Release 04/71. Accessed March 16, 2017 at: www.imf.org/external/np/sec/pr/2004/pr0471.htm.

(2004b). "Jordan: Selected Issues and Statistical Appendix." IMF Country Report 04/121. Washington, DC. Accessed March 21, 2017 at: www.imf.org/external/pubs/ft/scr/2004/cr04121.pdf.

(2004c). "Jordan: Third Review under the Stand-By Arrangement; and Press Release on the Executive Board Discussion." Washington, DC. Accessed March 21, 2017 at: www.imf.org/external/pubs/cat/longres.aspx?sk=17703.0.

(2005). "Evaluation Report IMF Support to Jordan, 1989–(2004)." Independent Evaluation Office. Accessed March 21, 2017 at: www.ieo-imf.org/ieo/pages/CompletedEvaluation116.aspx.

(2011a). "Government Finance Statistics." Accessed March 16, 2017 at: www.imf.org/external/pubs/ft/gfs/manual/aboutgfs.htm.

(2011b). "Tax Policy and Administration." Accessed at: www.imf.org/external/np/otm/2010/100110.pdf.

(2011c). "The Gambia: Poverty Reduction Strategy Paper." IMF Country Report 11/27. Accessed February 20, 2017 at: www.imf.org/external/pubs/ft/scr/2011/cr1127.pdf.

(2014). "Arab Countries in Transition: Economic Outlook and Key Challenges." Accessed March 16, 2017 at: www.imf.org/external/np/pp/eng/2014/100914.pdf.

(2015a). "Fiscal Policy and Long-term Growth." Accessed March 16, 2017 at: www.imf.org/external/np/pp/eng/2015/042015.pdf.

(2015b). *2015 Article IV Consultation – Staff Report; Press Release; And Statement by the Executive Direction for India; Country Report 15/61*, IMF Mission to India March 2015, IMF Publication Services, Washington, DC. Accessed March 21, 2017 at: www.imf.org/external/pubs/ft/scr/2015/cr1561.pdf.

(2016a). "India: 2016 Article IV Consultation." IMF Country Report 16/75. Accessed March 21, 2017 at: www.imf.org/external/pubs/ft/scr/2016/cr1675.pdf.

(2016b). "India: 2016 Article IV Consultation – Press Release, Staff Report; and Statement by the Executive Director for India." IMF Country Report 16/75.

"Income Tax Exemption Limit 2014–15 Increased." *Maligadu*. July 10, 2014. Accessed August 6, 2015 at: http://malligadu.com/income-tax-exemption-limit-2014–15/.

"Indian Business Owners Protest Against New Tax." *BBC News*. May 12, 2013. Accessed August 6, 2015 at: www.bbc.com/news/business-22499682.

"India's Corporate Tax Rates among Highest Globally: World Bank Report." *The Hindu*. November 26, 2013. Accessed August 6, 2015 at: www.thehindu.com/business/Economy/indias-corporate-tax-rates-among-highest-globally-world-bank-report/article5394196.ece.

"India Tax Evasion Amnesty Uncovers Hidden Billions." *BBC World News*. October 1, 2016. Accessed March 22, 2017 at: www.bbc.com/news/world-asia-india-37530290.

Inter-American Development Bank. (1998). *Economic and Social Progress in Latin America*. Washington, DC: Johns Hopkins University Press.

(2015). "Latin America and the Caribbean: Tax Revenues Remain Stable." Accessed July 14, 2017 at: www.iadb.org/en/news/news-releases/2015-03-10/revenue-statistics-in-latin-america-and-the-caribbean,11082.html.

International Country Risk Guide. (2012). International Country Risk Guide Methodology. Accessed March 16, 2017 at: www.prsgroup.com/wp-content/uploads/2012/11/icrgmethodology.pdf.

International Monetary Fund Independent Evaluation Office. (2005). "Evaluation Report: IMF Support to Jordan, 1989–2004." Accessed August 9, 2017 at: www.ieo-imf.org/ieo/files/completedevaluations/12062005report.pdf.

Itani, Faysal. (2013). "Stability through Change: Toward a New Political Economy in Jordan." Atlantic Council. December 19. Accessed February 14, 2018 at: www.atlanticcouncil.org/publications/issue-briefs/stability-through-change-toward-a-new-political-economy-in-jordan.

Jha, R. (2000). "Reducing Poverty and Inequality in India Has Liberalization Helped?" *World Institute for Development Economics Research*. Working Papers

204, November. Accessed March 21, 2017 at: www.wider.unu.edu/sites/default/files/wp204.pdf.

Jiang, Yong. (2009). "China's Water Scarcity." *Journal of Environmental Management.* 90: 3185–3196.

Jianrong, Yu. (2007). "Social Conflict in Rural China." *China Security.* 3(2): 2–17.

Jinglian, Wu and Ma Guochuan. (2016). *Whither China? Restarting the Reform Agenda.* Oxford: Oxford University Press.

Jingqiong, Wang. "Two Former Officials Executed." *China Daily.* July 20, 2011. Accessed March 22, 2017 at: http://usa.chinadaily.com.cn/epaper/2011-07/20/content_12943026.htm.

Job, Jenny, Andrew Stout, and Rachel Smith. (2007). "Culture Change in Three Taxation Administrations: From Command-and-Control to Responsive Regulation." *Law and Policy.* 29(1): 84–101.

John, Wilson. (2009). *Pakistan: The Struggle Within.* London: Pearson Education India.

Kalra, A. "India Slashes Health Budget, Already One of the World's Lowest." *Reuters,* New Delhi. December 23, 2014. Accessed August 6, 2015 at: http://in.reuters.com/article/2014/12/23/india-health-budget-idINKBN0K10Y020141223.

Kamara, Tom. "Selling Democracy as an Endangered Demon to the Poor." *New Democrat (Monrovia).* June 11, 2012.

Kannan, S. "Protests Against Corruption and Tax Evasion in India." *BBC News.* June 15, 2011. Accessed August 6, 2015 at: www.bbc.com/news/business-13773293.

Kanaan, Taher H. (2001). "State-Owned Enterprise in Jordan," in Merih Celasun (ed.), *State-Owned Enterprises in the Middle East and North Africa.* New York: Routledge, pp. 189–202.

Kaplan, Stephen B. (2013). *Globalization and Austerity Politics in Latin America.* Cambridge: Cambridge University Press.

Katsimi, Margarita and Thomas Moutos. (2010). "Inequality and the Relative Reliance on Tariffs." *Review of International Economics.* 18(1): 121–137.

Kaufman, Robert R. and Alex Segura-Ubiergo. (2001). "Globalization, Domestic Politics, and Social Spending in Latin America." *World Politics.* 53(4): 553–587.

Kaul, Vivek. "Middle Class Exit Is Quietly On." *Bangalore Mirror Bureau.* March 8, 2016. Accessed November 3, 2016. www.bangaloremirror.indiatimes.com/columns/views/Middle-class-exit-is-quietly-on/articleshow/51316561.cms.

Keefer, Philip. (2007). "Clientelism, Credibility, and the Policy Choices of Young Democracies." *American Journal of Political Science.* 51(4): 804–821.

(2015). "Database of Political Institutions: Changes and Variable Definitions." *The World Bank.* http://econ.worldbank.org/WBSITE/EXTERNAL/EXTDEC/EXTRESEARCH/0,,contentMDK:20649465~pagePK:6421482 5~piPK:64214943~theSitePK:469382,00.html.

Keefer, Philip and Stuti Khemani. (2005). "Democracy, Public Expenditure, and the Poor: Understanding Political Incentives for Providing Public Services." *World Bank Research Observer.* 20(1): 1–27.

Keen, Michael. (2013). "The Anatomy of the VAT." IMF Working Paper 13/111. Accessed March 16, 2017 at: www.imf.org/external/pubs/cat/longres.aspx?sk=40543.0.

Keen, Michael and Mario Mansour. (2010). "Revenue Mobilization in Sub-Saharan Africa: Challenges from Globalization II– Corporate Taxation." *Development Policy Review*. 28(5): 573–596.

Keen, Michael and Alejandro Simone. (2004). "Tax Policy in Developing Countries: Some Lessons from the 1990s, and Some Challenges Ahead," in Sanjeev Gupta, Benedict Clements, and Gabriela Inchauste (eds.), *Helping Countries Develop: The Role of the Fiscal Policy*. Washington, DC: IMF, pp. 302–352.

Kennedy, John James. (2007). "From the Tax-for-Fee Reform to the Abolition of Agricultural Taxes: The Impact on Township Governments in North-west China." *The China Quarterly*. 189: 43–59.

Kenny, Lawrence W. and Stanley L. Winer. (2006). "Tax Systems in the World: An Empirical Investigation into the Importance of Tax Bases, Administration Costs, Scale and Political Regime." *International Tax and Public Finance*. 13: 181–215.

Kenyon, Thomas. (2008). "Tax Evasion, Disclosure, and Participation in Financial Markets: Evidence from Brazilian Firms." *World Development*. 36(11): 2512–2525.

Khattry, Barsha. (2003). "Trade Liberalization and the Fiscal Squeeze: Implications for Public Investment." *Development and Change*. 34(3): 401–424.

Khattry, Barsha and J. Mohan Rao. (2002). "Fiscal Faux Pas? An Analysis of the Revenue Implications of Trade Liberalization." *World Development*. 30(8): 1431–1444.

Khim, Lim Gek and Grahame Wright. "Is a Tax Hike in Sight?" *The Straits Times*, January 18, 2014, www.straitstimes.com/singapore/is-a-tax-hike-in-sight.

"King: Fiscal Reform Must Protect Middle Class, Low-Income People." *Petra News Agency*. October 10, 2017. Accessed October 10, 2017 at: www.petra.gov.jo/Public_News/Nws_NewsDetails.aspx?lang=2&site_id=1&NewsID=321104&CatID=13.

King, Stephen. (1998). "Economic Reform and Tunisia's Hegemonic Party: The End of the Administrative Elite." *Arab Spring Quarterly*. 20(2): 59–87.

Kingstone, Peter. (1999). *Crafting Coalitions for Reform: Business Preferences, Political Institutions, and Neoliberalism in Brazil*. Princeton: Princeton University Press.

Kirkpatrick, David. "Saudi Arabia Arrests 11 Princes, Including Billionaire Alwaleed bin Talal." *New York Times*. November 4, 2017. Accessed March 9, 2018 at: https://www.nytimes.com/2017/11/04/world/middleeast/saudi-arabia-waleed-bin-talal.html?_r=0.

Kohli, Atul. (2006). "Politics of Economic Growth in India, 1980–2005." *Economic and Political Weekly*. (April) 41(14): 1361–1370.

(2012). "State and Redistributive Development in India," in Rayaprolu Nagaraj (ed.), *Growth, Inequality, and Social Development in India*. New York: Palgrave Macmillan, pp. 194–226.

Kosack, Stephen and Jennifer Tobin. (2006). "Funding Self-Sustaining Development: The Role of Aid, FDI and Government in Economic Success." *International Organization*. 60: 205–243.

KPMG. (2012). "India Tax Profile." Accessed March 16, 2017 at: www.kpmg.com/Global/en/services/Tax/regional-tax-centers/asia-pacific-tax-centre/Documents/CountryProfiles/India.pdf.

(2014). "People's Republic of China Tax Profile." Accessed March 16, 2017 at: www.kpmg.com/Global/en/services/Tax/regional-tax-centers/asia-pacific-tax-centre/Documents/CountryProfiles/china-2014.pdf.

Krishna, Pravin and Devahish Mitra. (2005). "Reciprocated Unilateralism in Trade Policy." *Journal of International Economics*. 65: 461–487.

Krueger, Anne O. (1998). "Why Trade Liberalization is Good for Growth." *The Economic Journal*. 108(450): 1513–1522.

(2002). *Political Economy of Policy Reform in Developing Countries*. Cambridge: MIT Press.

"KTF Revolts Against New VAT Form." *Kashmir Times* (India). April 21, 2011.

Kuijs, Louis and Gao Xu. (2008). "China's Fiscal Policy – Moving to Center Stage." International Development Conference on Social Services, Regulation and Finance. Stanford Center. October 23–24.

Kumar, Arun. (2002). *The Black Economy in India*. New York: Penguin Books.

Kunnathoor, Peethaambaran. "AMMOI Seeks Withdrawal of 2% Excise Duty on Ayurvedic Medicines." *PharmaBiz*. January 31, 2013. Accessed March 16, 2017 at: www.pharmabiz.com/NewsDetails.aspx?aid=73464&sid=1.

Kurtz, Marcus J. and Sarah M. Brooks. (2008). "Embedding Neoliberal Reform in Latin America." *World Politics*. 60(2): 231–280.

Kyong-ae, Choi. "Korea Ranks Lowest in Tax Collection Effort." *Korea Times*. October 31, 2013.

Lagarde, Christine. (2016). "Revenue Mobilization and International Taxation: Key Ingredients of 21st-Century Economies." International Monetary Fund. Accessed March 16, 2017 at: www.imf.org/en/News/Articles/2015/09/28/04/53/sp022216.

Lal, Radhika, Steve Miller, Maikel Lieuw-Kie-Song, and Daniel Kostzer. (2010). "Public Works and Employment Programmes: Towards a Long-Term Development Approach." Poverty Group UNDP Working Paper 66. Accessed February 12, 2018 at: www.ipc-undp.org/pub/IPCWorkingPaper66.pdf.

Lam, Willy Wo-Lap. "Factions Concede on Economic Carve-up." *South China Morning Post (Hong Kong)*. November 13, 1993. Lexis Nexis.

Lardy, Nicholas. (1992). *Foreign Trade and Economic Reform in China*. Cambridge: Cambridge University Press.

(2003). "Trade Liberalization and Its Role in Chinese Economic Growth." International Monetary Fund and National Council of Applied Economic Research Conference, November 14–16. Accessed March 21, 2017 at: www.imf.org/external/np/apd/seminars/2003/newdelhi/lardy.pdf.

Interview with author. August 6, 2015, Washington, DC.

Le, Tuan Minh. (2003). "Value Added Taxation: Mechanism, Design, and Policy Issues." World Bank Course on Practical Issues of Tax Policy in Developing Countries. Accessed March 21, 2017 at: http://citeseerx.ist.psu.edu/viewdoc/download;jsessionid=E167088D7DF21BB132963D9A285B2AAA?doi=10.1.1.197.4742&rep=rep1&type=pdf.

Lee, Dwight R. and Richard B. McKenzie. (1989). "The International Political Economy of Declining Tax Rates." *National Tax Journal*. 17(1): 79–84.

"Left Parties Protest Centre's Alleged Anti-Poor Policies." *Daily News and Analysis*. March 13, 2015. Accessed March 22, 2017 at: www.dnaindia.com/india/report-left-parties-protest-centre-s-alleged-anti-poor-policies-2068579.

Leung, Esther. "Suggested Tax Incentives Could Damage Economy." *South China Morning Post*. March 24, 2001. Lexis Nexis.

Levi, Margaret. (1988). *Of Rule and Revenue*. Berkeley: University of California Press.

Levi, Margaret and Audrey Sacks. (2009). "Legitimating Beliefs: Sources and Indicators." *Regulation and Governance*. 3(4): 311–333.

Levi, Margaret, Audrey Sacks, and Tom Tyler. (2009). "Conceptualizing Legitimacy, Measuring Legitimating Beliefs." *American Behavioral Scientist*. 53(3): 354–375.

Levitsky, Steven and Lucan A. Way. (2002). "The Rise of Competitive Authoritarianism." *Journal of Democracy*. 13(2): 51–65.

Lewis, Leo. "VAT Rise Sparks Days of Riots by Migrant Workers." *The Times (London)*. October 28, 2011.

Li, Jinyan. (1991). *Taxation in the People's Republic of China*. Westport: Greenwood Publishing Group.

    (2010). "Tax Transplants and Local Culture: A Comparative Study of the Chinese and Canadian GAAR." *Theoretical Inquiries into Law*. 11(2): 655–685.

Li, Lianjiang. (2016). "Reassessing Trust in the Central Government: Evidence from Five National Surveys." *The China Quarterly*. 225: 100–121.

Li, Wei. (1997). "The Impact of Economic Reform on the Performance of Chinese State Enterprises, 1980–1989." *Journal of Political Economy*. 105(5): 1080–1106.

Lileeva, A. and D. Trefler. (2010). "Improved Access to Foreign Markets Raises Plant-Level Productivity ... for Some Plants." *The Quarterly Journal of Economics*, 125(3): 1051–1099.

Lim, Timothy. (1998). "Power, Capitalism, and the Authoritarian State in South Korea." *Journal of Contemporary Asia*. 28(4): 457–483.

Lin, Justin Y. and Mingxing Liu. (2007). "Rural Informal Taxation in China: Historical Evolution and an Analytic Framework." *China and the World Economy*. 15(3): 1–18.

Lin, Wanlong and Christine Wong. (2012). "Are Beijing's Equalization Policies Reaching the Poor? An Analysis of Direct Subsidies under the 'Three Rurals'." *The China Journal*. 67 (January): 23–46.

Linz, Juan J. (2000). *Totalitarian and Authoritarian Regimes*. Boulder: Lynne Rienner Publishers.

Lipton, Michael and Qi Zhang. (2007). "Reducing Inequality and Poverty during Liberalization in China: Rural and Agricultural Experiences and Policy Options," in Vijay S. Vyas, Surjit Singh, and Ratna Reddy (eds.), *Changing Contours of Asian Agriculture: Essays in Honour of Vijay Vyas*. Revised version of Working Paper 37. Sussex University: Poverty Research Unit, pp. 531–602.

Liu, Shuang and Sian M. Griffiths. (2011). "From Economic Development to Public Health Improvement: China Faces Equity Challenges." *Public Health*. 125(10): 669–674.

Lobell, Steven E. (2012). "Power Disparities and Strategic Trade: Domestic Consequence of U.S.–Jordan Trade Concessions," in Kristen Williams, Steven Lobell, and Neal Jesse (eds.), *Beyond Great Power and Hegemons: Why*

Secondary States Support, Follow, or Challenge. Stanford: Stanford University Press.

Lomelí, Enrique Valencia. (2008). "Conditional Case Transfers as Social Policy in Latin America: An Assessment of their Contributions and Limitations." *Annual Review of Sociology.* 34: 475–499.

Louzi, Basem M. (2007). "Assessment of Poverty in Jordan: 1990–2005." *International Journal of Applied Econometrics and Quantitative Studies.* 4(2): 25–44.

Luo, Renfu, Linxiu Zhang, Jikun Huang, and Scott Rozelle. (2007). "Elections, Fiscal Reform and Public Good Provision in Rural China." *Journal of Comparative Economics.* 35: 583–611.

Lust, Ellen. (2013). *The Middle East.* Washington, DC: Sage.

Ma, Damien and William Adams. (2013). *In Line Behind a Billion People.* United States: FT Press.

Maddy-Weitzman, Bruce and Daniel Zisenwine. (2013). *Contemporary Morocco: State, Politics and Society under Mohammed VI.* New York: Routledge.

Maertens, Miet and Johan F. M. Swinnen. (2009). "Trade, Standards, and Poverty: Evidence from Senegal." *World Development.* 37(1): 161–178.

Magaloni, Beatriz. (2008). "Credible Power-Sharing and the Longevity of Authoritarian Rule." *Comparative Political Studies.* 41(4/5): 715–741.

Magazine, Aanchal. "Corporate Tax Exemption Cuts May Start with SEZs." *The Indian Express.* February 24, 2016. Accessed February 13, 2017 at: http://indianexpress.com/article/business/budget/union-budget-2016-corporate-tax-exemption-cuts-may-start-with-sezs/.

Malesky, Edmund. (2015). "Transfer Pricing and Global Poverty." *International Studies Review.* 17(4): 669–677.

Malkawi, Bashar and Haitham S. Haloush. (2008). "The Case of Income Tax Evasion in Jordan: Symptoms and Solutions." *Journal of Financial Crime.* 15(3): 282–294.

Man, Joyce Yanyun. (2012). "China's Property Tax Reform: Progress and Challenges." *Land Lines.* Lincoln Institute of Land Policy. April.

Manage, Neela and Michael L. Marlow. (1986). "The Causal Relation between Federal Expenditures and Receipts." *Southern Economic Journal.* 52(3): 617–629.

Mandal, Ram Krishna. (2009). *Value-Added Tax in North-East India.* New Delhi: Mittal Publications.

Mansour, Mario. (2015). "Tax Policy in MENA Countries: Looking Back and Forward." IMF Working Paper WP/15/98. Accessed March 21, 2017 at: www.imf.org/external/pubs/ft/wp/2015/wp1598.pdf.

Martin, Will, Deepak Bhattasali, and Shantong Li. (2004). "China's Accession to the WTO: Impacts on China." World Bank. Accessed August 9, 2017 at: http://siteresources.worldbank.org/INTEAPREGTOPINTECOTRA/Resources/chapter+1.pdf.

Marshall, Monty G. and Ted Robert Gurr. (2016). Polity IV Project. Accessed March 16, 2017 at: www.systemicpeace.org/polity/polity4.htm.

Mascagni, Giulia, Mick Moore, and Rhiannon McCluskey. (2014). "Tax Revenue Mobilisation in Developing Countries: Issues and Challenges." European

Parliament. Accessed February 7, 2017 at: www.europarl.europa.eu/RegData/etudes/etudes/join/2014/433849/EXPO-DEVE_ET(2014)433849_EN.pdf.

Mateo, Janvic. "Businessmen Protest QC Tax Hike." *Philippine Star*. February 1, 2014. Accessed March 22, 2017 at: www.philstar.com/metro/2014/02/01/1285291/businessmen-protest-qc-tax-hike.

"Mauritius Overtakes Singapore as India's Top Source of FDI." Delhi. *India Briefing*. December 4, 2014. Accessed August 7, 2015 at: www.india-briefing.com/news/mauritius-overtakes-singapore-indias-top-source-fdi-9458.html/.

McBride, Stephen. (2015). "Neo-Liberalism in Question?" in Stephen McBride, Rianne Mahon, and Gerard W. Boychuk (eds.), *After '08: Social Policy and Global Financial Crisis*. Toronto: UBC Press, pp. 1–21.

McCarthy, Julie. "Why Do So Few People Pay Income Tax in India?" *npr.org*, NPR News, March 22, 2017. Accessed March 23, 2017 at: www.npr.org/sections/parallels/2017/03/22/517965630/why-do-so-few-people-pay-income-tax-in-india.

McDermott, Christopher. (1996). "Macroeconomic Environment and Factors Underlying Growth and Investment," in Ahsan S. Mansur and Edouard Maciejewski (eds.), *Jordan Strategy for Adjustment and Growth*. Washington, DC: IMF, pp. 13–20.

McGuire, James. (1994). "Development Policy and Its Determinants in East Asia and Latin America." *Journal of Public Policy*. 14(2): 205–242.

McGuire, James W. (2010). *Wealth, Health, and Democracy in East Asia and Latin America*. Cambridge: Cambridge University Press.

McGuire, Martin C. and Macur Olson. (1996). "The Economics of Autocracy and Majority Rule: The Invisible Hand and the Use of Force." *Journal of Economic Literature*. 34(1): 72–96.

McKinnon, Ronald. (1991). "Financial Control in the Transition from Classical Socialism to a Market Economy." *Journal of Economic Perspectives*. 5(4): 107–122.

McMaster, Nick. "China Drops Death Penalty for Tax Evasion." *Newser*. February 25, 2011. Accessed March 16, 2017 at: www.newser.com/story/112878/china-drops-death-penalty-for-tax-evasion.html.

Mehra, P. "Black Economy Now Amounts to 75% of GDP." *The Hindu*. August 4, 2014. Accessed August 6, 2015: www.thehindu.com/news/national/black-economy-now-amounts-to-75-of-gdp/article6278286.ece.

Mehra, P. and G. Shivakumar. "UPA's Flagship Schemes Face Big Funding Cuts." *The Hindu*. November 14, 2013. Accessed August 6, 2015 at: www.thehindu.com/news/national/upas-flagship-schemes-face-big-funding-cuts/article5348127.ece.

Mehta, P. B. "Protest, Softly." *The Indian Express*, Column. July 5, 2010. Accessed August 6, 2015 at: http://indianexpress.com/article/opinion/columns/protest-softly/.

Melitz, Marc. (2003). "The Impact of Trade on Intra-Industry Reallocations and Aggregate Industry Productivity." *Econometrica*. 71: 1695–1725.

Melitz, Marc and Stephen J. Redding. (2014). "Heterogeneous Firms and Trade." *Handbook of International Economics*. 4th edition. 4: 1–54.

Meltzer, Allan H. and Scott F. Richard. (1981). "A Rational Theory of the Size of Government." *The Journal of Political Economy*. 89(5): 914–927.

Meng, Qun, Ling Xu, Yaoguang Zhang, Juncheng Qian, Min Cai, Ying Xin, Jun Gao, Ke Xu, J. Ties Boerma, and Sarah L. Barber. (2012). "Trends in Access to Health Services and Financial Protection in China between 2003–2011: A Cross-Sectional Study." *The Lancet*. 379: 805–814.

Michelson, Ethan. (2012). "Public Goods and State-Society Relations: An Impact of China's Rural Stimulus," in Dali L. Yang (ed.), *The Global Recession and China's Political Economy*. New York: Palgrave, pp. 131–157.

Michielse, Geerten and Victor Thuronyi. (2010). "Overview of Cooperation on Capacity Building in Taxation." United Nations Committee of Experts on International Cooperation in Tax Matters, Sixth Session, October 18–22. Geneva, Switzerland.

Miller, Michael K. (2015). "Electoral Authoritarianism and Human Development." *Comparative Political Studies*. 48(12): 1526–1562.

Milner, Helen V. and Keiko Kubota. (2005). "Why the Move to Free Trade? Democracy and Trade Policy in the Developing Countries." *International Organization*. 59(1): 107–143.

Mkandawire, Thandika. (2006). "Disempowering New Democracies and the Persistence of Poverty." United Nations Research Institute for Social Development. Democracy, Governance, and Human Rights Programme Paper 21. January. Accessed March 21, 2017 at: www.unrisd.org/unrisd/website/document.nsf/(httpPublications)/660234231C9D6710C12571780 0248890?OpenDocument.

Mohamadieh, Kinda. (2013). *IMF's Trade and Investment Related Advice to Arab Countries: Trends and Implications*. Beirut: Arab NGO Network for Development.

Mohsin, Husam Taseen. (2016). "The Impact of China's Accession to the WTO on Tax and Customs Revenues." *International Journal of Economics and Finance*. 8(2): 81–93.

Mohtadi, Hamid and Terry L. Roe. (2003). "Democracy, Rent Seeking, Public Spending and Growth." *Journal of Public Economics*. 87(3): 445–466.

Moseti, Brian. "Kisii Traders Protest over High Taxes." *Daily Nation (Kenya)*. April 8, 2015. Lexis Nexis.

Mosley, Layna. (2003). *Global Capital and National Governments*. Cambridge: Cambridge University Press.

Mugerwa, Yasiin. "Shs300b Cut from Health to Fund Defense." *The Daily Monitor*. May 2, 2013. Accessed March 23, 2017 at: www.monitor.co.ug/News/National/Shs300b-cut-from-health-to-fund-defence/688334-1766942-wul2ak/index.html.

"Mumbai Eateries Go on Strike Against New Service Tax." *IBN Live*. April 29, 2013. Accessed August 6, 2015 at: www.ibnlive.com/news/india/mumbai-eateries-go-on-strike-against-new-service-tax-606025.html.

Murillo, M. Victoria. (2001). *Labor Unions, Partisan Coalitions, and Market Reforms in Latin America*. New York: Cambridge University Press.

Nagarajan, R. "Is Government Secretly Cutting Social Sector Budget Bypassing Parliament?" *Times of India*. December 1, 2014. Accessed August 6, 2015 at: http://timesofindia.indiatimes.com/india/Is-government-secretly-cutting-social-sector-budget-bypassing-parliament/articleshow/45331296.cms.

Naim, Moises. (1994). "Latin America: The Second Stage of Reform." *Journal of Democracy*, 5(4): 32–48.

Nakazawa, Katsuji. "Shadowy Tax Havens Inflame Chinese Power Struggle." *Asian Review.* April 16, 2016. Accessed February 15, 2017 at: http://asia.nikkei.com/Features/China-up-close/Shadowy-tax-havens-inflame-Chinese-power-struggle.

Nandy, A. "To Bring All that Black Money Back." *The Hindu Business Line.* November 17, 2014. Accessed August 6, 2015 at: www.thehindubusinessline.com/opinion/to-bring-all-that-black-money-back/article6608645.ece.

Nashashibi, Karim. (2002). "Fiscal Revenues in South Mediterranean Arab Countries: Vulnerabilities and Growth Potential." IMF Working Paper WP/02/67.

"National Solidarity System Bridges the Gap." *New African.* December 1, 2010. Accessed March 16, 2017 at: 7www.thefreelibrary.com/National+solidarity+system+bridges+the+gap%3A%20+Tunisia's+success+story..-a024873629.

Naughton, Barry. (2007). *The Chinese Economy: Transitions and Growth.* Cambridge: MIT Press.

Navia, Patricio and Andres Velasco. (2003). "The Politics of Second-Generation Reforms," in Pedro-Pablo Kuczynski and John Williamson (eds.), *After the Washington Consensus: Restarting Growth and Reform in Latin America.* Washington, DC: Institute for International Economics, pp. 265–303.

Nayyar, D. "Column: Govt's Meek Surrender on Tax Reform." *The Financial Express,* New Delhi. August 28, 2010. Accessed August 6, 2015 at: http://archive.financialexpress.com/news/column-govt-s-meek-surrender-on-tax-reform/673393.

"How to End India's Tax Terrorism" *Bloomberg View,* India. April 17, 2015. Accessed August 6, 2015 at: www.bloombergview.com/articles/2015-04-17/how-to-end-india-s-tax-terrorism.

Nazmi, Nader. (1995). *Economic Policy and Stabilization in Latin America.* New York: M.E. Sharpe.

Nelson, Joan M. (2007). "Elections, Democracy, and Social Services." *Studies in Comparative International Development.* 41(4): 79–97.

Neumann, Rebecca, Jill Holman, and James Alm. (2009). "Globalization and Tax Policy." *The North American Journal of Economics and Finance.* 20(2): 193–211.

"New Government Will Face Early Crisis of Funding." *The Nation (Thailand).* June 28, 2011. Lexis Nexis.

"New Tax Plan Sparks China Protest." *BBC News.* June 15, 2009. Accessed February 15, 2017 at: http://news.bbc.co.uk/2/hi/asia-pacific/8100766.stm.

Nichenametia, Prasad. "Andhra Nearly Broke, CM Naidu Seeks Help from Modi." *Hindustan Times.* January 22, 2015. Accessed March 16, 2017 at: www.hindustantimes.com/india/andhra-nearly-broke-cm-naidu-seeks-help-from-modi/story-kfWdX8SFRe5acKfgJkibFJ.html.

Nicita, Alessandro. (2009). The Price Effect of Tariff Liberalization: Measuring the Impact on Household Welfare. *Journal of Development Economics.* 89(1): 19–27.

Nielsen, Kaytie. "How Indians Dodged Government's 'Black Money' Clampdown." *Al Jazeera News.* February 15, 2017. Accessed March 23, 2017 at:

www .aljazeera.com/indepth/features/2017/02/indians-dodged-government-black-money-clampdown-170201095846627.html.

Nijzink, Lia, Shaheen Mozaffar, and Elisabete Azevedo. (2006). "Parliaments and the Enhancement of Democracy on the African Continent." *The Journal of Legislative Studies.* 12(3–4): 311–335.

Nomi, Tomoaki. (1997). "Determinants of Trade Orientation in Less Developed Countries." *Policy Studies Journal.* 25(1): 27.

Nooruddin, Irfan and Joel W. Simmons. (2006). "The Politics of Hard Choices: IMF Programs and Government Spending." *International Organization.* 60(4): 1001–1033.

   (2009). "Openness, Uncertainty, and Social Spending: Implications for the Globalization-Welfare State Debate." *International Studies Quarterly.* 53: 841–866.

Nooruddin, Irfan and Nita Rudra. (2014). "Are Countries Really Defying the Embedded Liberalism Compact?" *World Politics.* 66(4): 603–640.

North, Douglass C. and Barry R. Weingast. (1989). "Constitutions and Commitment: The Institutions Governing Public Choice in Seventeenth Century England." *Journal of Economic History.* 44: 803–832.

Nsour, Maen F. "Tax Evasion in Jordan – Causes, Means, and Size." *Jordan Times.* June 3, 2014. Accessed March 16, 2017 at: www.jordantimes.com/opinion/maen-f-nsour/tax-evasion-jordan—-causes-means-and-size.

Nussbaum, Martha and Amartya Sen, eds. (1993). *The Quality of Life.* Oxford: Clarendon Press.

Obeidat, Omar. "Industrialists on Tiptoes as Lawmakers Discuss Income Tax." *Jordan Times.* July 1, 2013. Accessed March 22, 2017 at: http://vista.sahafi.jo/art.php?id=836aaa4f871dbc849f27ae1b0449dd0291774e86.

OECD. (2015). "Tunisia: A Reform Agenda to Support Competitiveness and Inclusive Growth." March. Accessed March 16, 2017 at: www.oecd.org/countries/tunisia/Tunisia-a-reform-agenda-to-support-competitiveness-and-inclusive-growth.pdf.

   (2017). "Revenue Statistics." Accessed July 24, 2017 at: https://stats.oecd.org/Index.aspx?DataSetCode=REV.

"Official Says West China Sees Increasing Public Health Emergencies." *BBC Monitoring Asia Pacific.* January 2, 2006.

Ondetti, Gabriel. (2015). "The Roots of Brazil's Heavy Taxation." *Journal of Latin American Studies.* 47: 749–779.

O'Neill, Mark. "300,000 Tax Police on Way." *South China Morning Post.* November 21, 2000.

   "Tax Cuts Ahead as Revenue Soars." *South China Morning Post.* January 3, 2006.

Overesch, Michael and Johannes Rincke. (2009). "Competition from Low-Wage Countries and the Decline of Corporate Tax Rates: Evidence from European Integration." *The World Economy.* 32(9): 1348–1364.

Oxfam. (2016). "Tax Battles." Oxfam Policy Paper. December 12. Accessed March 16, 2017 at: www.oxfam.org/en/research/tax-battles-dangerous-global-race-bottom-corporate-tax.

Panagariya, Arvind. (1991). "Unraveling the Mysteries of China's Foreign Trade Regime." World Bank Working Paper 801. Accessed March 21, 2017

at: http://documents.worldbank.org/curated/en/170871468769156224/
Unraveling-the-mysteries-of-Chinas-foreign-trade-regime-a-view-from-
Jiangsu-Province.

(2004). "India in the 1980s and 1990s: A Triumph of Reforms." IMF Working
Paper WP/04/43.

Panda, M. and A. Kumar-Ganesh. (2009). "Trade Liberalization, Poverty,
and Food Security in India." *International Food Policy Research Institute*,
November. Accessed March 21, 2017 at: www.ifpri.org/publication/
trade-liberalization-poverty-and-food-security-india.

"Patanjali to Invest Rs 500 Crore for Food Processing Unit in Madhya Pradesh."
Economic Times. August 4, 2016. Accessed February 3, 2017 at http://
economictimes.indiatimes.com/industry/cons-products/fmcg/patanjali-
to-invest-rs-500-crore-for-food-processing-unit-in-madhya-pradesh/
articleshow/53545809.cms.

Patnaik, B. "Cutting the Food Act to the Bone." *The Hindu.* June 24, 2015.
Accessed August 6, 2015 at: www.thehindu.com/opinion/lead/cutting-the-
food-act-to-the-bone/article7347261.ece?css=print.

People's Republic of China. (2015). "Criminal Law of the People's Republic of
China." Accessed March 16, 2017 at: www.fmprc.gov.cn/ce/cgvienna/eng/
dbtyw/jdwt/crimelaw/t209043.htm.

Pepinsky, Thomas. (2014). "The Institutional Turn in Comparative
Authoritarianism." *British Journal of Political Science.* 44(3): 631–653.

Perlitz, Uwe. (2008). "India's Pharmaceutical Industry on Course for
Globalisation," Deutsche Bank Research. April 9. Accessed March 16,
2017 at: www.dbresearch.com/PROD/DBR_INTERNET_EN-PROD/
PROD0000000000224095.pdf.

Peters, Anne M. and Pete W. Moore. (2009). "Beyond Boom and Bust: External
Rents, Durable Authoritarianism, and Institutional Adaptation in the
Hashemite Kingdom of Jordan." *Studies in Comparative International
Development.* 44: 256–285.

PEW Research Center. (2014). "Global Attitudes and Trends: Faith and Skepticism
about Trade, Foreign Investment." Accessed February 5, 2016 at: www
.pewglobal.org/2014/09/16/faith-and-skepticism-about-trade-foreign-
investment/.

Pfeifer, Karen. (1999). "How Tunisia, Morocco, Jordan and even Egypt Became
IMF 'Success Stories' in the 1990s." *Middle East Report.* 210: 23–27.

Piketty, Thomas and Nancy Qian. (2010). "Income Inequality and Progressive
Income Taxation in China and India, 1986–2015," in Anthony B. Atkinson
and Thomas Piketty (eds.), *Top Incomes: A Global Perspective.* Oxford: Oxford
University Press, pp. 40–75.

Pillay, Amritha. "Exempt Export Profits from Income Tax." *Daily News
and Analysis.* January 5, 2011. Accessed October 10, 2017 at: www
.dnaindia.com/money/interview-exempt-export-profits-from-
income-tax-1490396.

Pinto, Francisco Roberto, Joao Verissimo Lisboa, and Paulo Cesar de Sousa
Batista. (2013). "Tax Evasion Analysis: Perceptions from Brazilian
Businessmen." *International Journal of Business and Social Science.* 4(14):
82–89.

Pinto, Jose M. (2011). "Challenges and Perspectives on the Chemical Industry in Brazil." American Institute of Chemical Engineers. Accessed March 16, 2017 at: www.aiche.org/sites/default/files/cep/20110857.pdf.

Plumper, Thomas, Vera Troeger, and Hannes Winner. (2009). "Why Is There No Race to the Bottom in Capital Taxation?" *International Studies Quarterly*. 53: 761–786.

Poirson, H. (2006). "The Tax System in India: Could Reform Spur Growth?" IMF Working Paper WP/06/93. April: 1–22. Accessed March 21, 2017 at: www.imf.org/external/pubs/ft/wp/2006/wp0693.pdf.

"Poor Infrastructure, High Taxes Deter Foreign Airlines from Investing: IATA." *DNA*, New Delhi. June 21, 2015. Accessed August 6, 2015 at: www.dnaindia.com/money/report-poor-infrastructure-high-taxes-deter-foriegn-airlines-from-investing-iata-2097523.

"Poor Suffer the Brunt of Doctor Shortage in Bhadrak." *Times of India*. March 24, 2011. Accessed August 7, 2015 at: http://timesofindia.indiatimes.com/city/bhubaneswar/Poor-suffer-the-brunt-of-doctor-shortage-in-Bhadrak/articleshow/7782716.cms.

Porto, Guido G. (2003). *Trade Reforms, Market Access and Poverty in Argentina*. Washington, DC: World Bank Publications.

(2006). "Using Survey Data to Assess the Distributional Effects of Trade Policy." *Journal of International Economics*. 70(1): 140–160.

Prasad, Eswar. (2004). *China's Growth and Integration into the World Economy*. Washington, DC: International Monetary Fund.

Prasad, Naren. (2008). "Policies for Redistribution: The Use of Taxes and Social Transfers." International Institute for Labor Studies Discussion Paper Series DP/194/2008.

Prasadi, Krishna. "Education Standards Poor in Andhra, Telengana." *Times of India*. August 25, 2016. Accessed February 22, 2017 at: http://timesofindia.indiatimes.com/city/hyderabad/Education-standards-poor-in-Andhra-Telengana/articleshow/53852337.cms.

"30 Telangana, Andhra Pradesh Towns Face Drinking Water Crisis as Demand Rises." *Times of India*. January 14, 2017. Accessed February 22, 2017 at: http://timesofindia.indiatimes.com/city/hyderabad/30-t-ap-towns-face-drinking-water-crisis-as-demand-rises/articleshow/56530094.cms.

PricewaterhouseCoopers. (2015a). "China: New GAAR Procedures Released." Accessed August 20, 2015 at: www.pwc.ch/wordpress/wp-content/uploads/2015/01/china-new-gaar-procedures-released.pdf.

(2015b). "China, People's Republic of: Corporate Tax Credits and Incentives." Accessed March 16, 2017 at: http://taxsummaries.pwc.com/uk/taxsummaries/wwts.nsf/ID/Peoples-Republic-of-China-Corporate-Tax-credits-and-incentives.

(2015c). "India: Corporate Tax Credits and Incentives." Accessed March 16, 2017 at: http://taxsummaries.pwc.com/uk/taxsummaries/wwts.nsf/ID/India-Corporate-Tax-credits-and-incentives.

PricewaterhouseCoopers and World Bank Group. (2014). "Paying Taxes 2014: The Global Picture – A Comparison of Tax Systems in 189 Economies Worldwide," The World Bank/IFC and PwC External Relations and Tax

Transparency. Accessed August 7, 2015 at: www.pwc.com/gx/en/paying-taxes/assets/pwc-paying-taxes-2014.pdf.

Prichard, Wilson. (2015). *Taxation, Responsiveness, and Accountability in Sub-Saharan Africa: The Dynamics of Tax Bargaining.* Cambridge: Cambridge University Press.

Prichard, Wilson, Alex Cobham, and Andrew Goodall. (2014). *The ICTD Government Revenue Dataset.* ICTD Working Paper 19. Brighton: International Centre for Tax and Development. Accessed March 16, 2017 at: www.ictd.ac/datasets/the-ictd-government-revenue-dataset.

Przeworski, Adam. (1991). *Democracy and the Market: Political and Economic Reforms in Eastern Europe and Latin America.* Cambridge: Cambridge University Press.

Przeworski, Adam, Michael E. Alvarez, Jose Antonio Cheibub, and Fernando Limongi. (2000). *Democracy and Development: Political Institutions and Well-Being in the World, 1950–1990.* Cambridge: Cambridge University Press.

"Punjab Hit by HP Tax Concessions." *Financial Express.* January 9, 2006. Accessed February 3, 2017 at: www.financialexpress.com/archive/punjab-hit-by-hp-tax-concessions/152775/.

Purfield, Catriona. (2004). *The Decentralization Dilemma in India, Issues 2004–2032.* Washington, DC: International Monetary Fund.

Quah, Jon S. T. (2013). "Ensuring Good Governance in Singapore: Is This Experience Transferable to Other Asian Countries?" *International Journal of Public Sector Management.* 26(5): 401–420.

Queralt, Didac. (2017). "Protection Not for Sale, but for Tax Compliance." *International Studies Quarterly.* 61(3): 631–641.

Quinn, Dennis. (1997). "The Correlates of Change in International Financial Regulation." *American Political Science Review.* 91(3): 531–551.

(2003). "Capital Account Liberalization and Financial Globalization, 1890–1999: A Synoptic View." *International Journal of Finance and Economics.* 8(3): 189–204.

Rada, C. (2010). "Formal and Informal Sectors in China and India." *Economic Systems Research.* 22(2): 129–153.

Rajaram, Anand. (1992). "Do World Bank Recommendations Integrate Revenue and Protection Objectives?" *World Bank WPS 1018.*

Ram, Rati. (1988). "Additional Evidence on Causality between Government Revenue and Government Expenditure." *Southern Economic Journal.* 54(3): 763–769.

Ramanujam, T. C. A. "Kelkar Report: Flawed 'n' Faulty." *The Hindu Business Line.* November 14, 2002. Accessed August 6, 2015 at: www.thehindubusinessline.com/2002/11/14/stories/2002111400060800.htm.

Randolph, E. "10,000 Take to Streets in Delhi for Anti-Corruption March." *The National,* Abu Dhabi. January 31, 2011. Accessed August 6, 2015 at: www.thenational.ae/news/world/south-asia/10-000-take-to-streets-in-delhi-for-anti-corruption-march.

Ranjan, Prabhash. "The Government Must Use its Majority in the Lok Sabha to Get Rid of the 2012 Amendment." *Financial Express.* April 19, 2016.

Accessed October 13, 2017 at: www.financialexpress.com/opinion/column-just-talking-not-enough/239198/.

Rao, Elizaphan J. O. and Matin Qaim. (2011). "Supermarkets, Farm Household Income, and Poverty: Insights from Kenya." *World Development.* 39(5): 784–796.

Rao, Govinda. Interview with author. June 24, 2015. Bangalore, India.

Rao, M. Govinda. (2000). "Tax Reform in India: Achievements and Challenges." *Asia-Pacific Development Journal.* 7(2): 59–74.

Rao, M. Govinda and P. Chakraborty. (2007). "Multilateral Adjustment Lending to States in India: Hastening Fiscal Correction or Softening the Budget Constraint?" *The Journal of International Trade & Economic Development: An International and Comparative Review.* 15(3): 335–357.

Rao, M. Govinda and R. Kavita Rao. (2006). "Trends and Issues in Tax Policy and Reform in India." *India Policy Forum.* 2(1): 55–122.

Rao, M Govinda and Nirvikar Singh. (2007). "The Political Economy of India's Fiscal Federal System and Its Reform." *Publius.* 37(1): 26–44.

Rapoza, Kenneth. "Tax Evasion a Way of Life in Brazil." *Washington Times.* July 13, 2004. Accessed August 9, 2017 at: www.mckinsey.com/mgi/overview/in-the-news/tax-evasion-a-way-of-life-in-brazil.

Ravallion, Martin. (2001). "Growth, Inequality and Poverty: Looking Beyond Averages." *World Development.* 29(11): 1803–1815.

Rawlings, Laura B. and Gloria M. Rubio. (2005). "Evaluating the Impact of Conditional Case Transfer Programs." *World Bank Research Observer.* 20(1): 29–55.

Ray, Suchetana and Timsy Jaipuria. "Fearing High Tax Rates, Lobbying Starts for Exemption from GST." *Hindustan Times.* August 12, 2016. Accessed February 13, 2017 at: www.hindustantimes.com/business-news/fearing-high-tax-rates-lobbying-starts-for-exemption-from-gst/story-hETwkPgS9uZJUfJo86uq2O.html.

Razin, Assaf. (1990). "Capital Market Integration: Issues of International Taxation." NBER Working Paper 3281. Accessed March 21, 2017 at: www.nber.org/papers/w3281.

"Readymade Garment Dealers Stage One-Day Strike." *Times of India.* March 15, 2010. Accessed August 6, 2015 at: http://timesofindia.indiatimes.com/city/jaipur/Readymade-garment-dealers-stage-one-day-strike/articleshow/5681011.cms.

Reimer, Jeffrey. (2002). "Estimating the Poverty Impacts of Trade Liberalization." World Bank Policy Research Working Paper 2790. Accessed March 21, 2017 at: https://openknowledge.worldbank.org/handle/10986/15611.

Rennie, David. "Chinese Peasants Fight Police in Riots over Tax." *The Telegraph.* August 31, 2000. Accessed February 15, 2017 at: www.telegraph.co.uk/news/worldnews/asia/china/1368344/Chinese-peasants-fight-police-in-riots-over-tax.html.

Rhode, David. "Musharraf Redraws Constitution, Blocking Promise of Democracy." *New York Times.* August 22, 2002. Accessed February 20, 2017 at: www.nytimes.com/2002/08/22/world/musharraf-redraws-constitution-blocking-promise-of-democracy.html?_r=0.

Riccardi, Lorenzo. (2013). *Chinese Tax Law and International Treaties*. Italy: Springer.

Richardson, Grant. (2008). "The Relationship between Culture and Tax Evasion across Countries: Additional Evidence and Extensions." *Journal of International Accounting, Auditing and Taxation*. 17(2): 67–78.

Richburg, Keith B. "China May Have Dug a Financial Hole: Stimulus Created Many Infrastructure Projects that May Not Pay off." *The Washington Post*. June 18, 2010.

Rickard, Stephanie. 2012. "Welfare versus Subsidies: Governmental Spending Decisions in an Era of Globalization." *The Journal of Politics*. 74(4): 1171–1183.

Rippee, John. "Maquiladora Workers in Ciudad Juarez Protest Pending Tax Reform Bill." *Mexico Industry News*. October 24, 2013. Accessed March 22, 2017 at: www.tecma.com/maquiladora-workers-in-ciudad-juarez-protest/.

Robinson, James A. and Daron Acemoglu. (2008). "Persistence of Power, Elites and Institutions." *American Economic Review*. 98(1): 267–293.

Robinson, James and Ragnar Torvik. (2005). "White Elephants." *Journal of Public Economics*. 89(2–3): 197–210.

Rodan, Garry. (2008). "Singapore 'Exceptionalism'? Authoritarian Rule and State Transformation," in Joseph Wong and Edward Friedman (eds.), *Political Transitions in Dominant Party Systems: Learning to Lose*. Abingdon: Routledge.

Rodlauer, Markus. (1995). "The Experience with IMF-Supported Reform Programs in Central and Eastern Europe." *Journal of Comparative Economics*. 20: 95–115.

Rodriguez, Francisco and Dani Rodrik. (2001). "Trade Policy and Economic Growth: A Sceptic's Guide to Cross-National Data." *NBER Macroeconomics Annual*. 15: 261–338.

Rodrik, Dani. (1992). "The Limits of Trade Policy Reform in Developing Countries." *The Journal of Economic Perspectives*. 6(1): 87–105.

(1997). *Has Globalization Gone Too Far?* Washington, DC: Peterson Institute for International Economics.

Rodrik, Dani, Arvind Subramanian, and Francesco Trebbi. (2002). "Institutions Rule: The Primacy of Institutions over Geography and Integration in Economic Development." *Journal of Economic Growth*. 9(2): 131–165.

Romagnoli, Alessandro and Luisa Mengoli. (2013). *The Economic Development Process in the Middle East and North Africa*. New York: Routledge.

Romer, Christina D. and David H. Romer. (2009). "Do Tax Cuts Starve the Beast? The Effect of Tax Changes on Government Spending." *Brookings Papers on Economic Activity*. Spring. Accessed March 21, 2017 at: www.brookings.edu/wp-content/uploads/2009/03/2009a_bpea_romer.pdf.

Ross, Michael. (2004). "Does Taxation Lead to Representation?" *British Journal of Political Science*. 34: 229–249.

(2006). "Is Democracy Good for the Poor?" *American Journal of Political Science*. 50(4): 860–874.

Rowley, Anthony. "Radical Rethink of Globalisation Needed to Stop Backlash." *The Business Times Singapore*. June 7, 2017.

Royal Government of Bhutan. (2005). "Bhutan National Human Development Report." Accessed February 20, 2017 at: http://hdr.undp.org/sites/default/files/bhutan_2005_en.pdf.

Rudra, Nita. (2002). "Globalization and the Decline of the Welfare State in Less-Developed Countries." *International Organization.* 56(2): 411–445.

(2008). *Globalization and the Race to the Bottom in Developing Countries.* Cambridge: Cambridge University Press.

(2009). "Why International Organizations Should Bring Basic Needs Back in." *International Studies Perspectives.* 10(2): 129–150.

Rudra, Nita and Jennifer Tobin. (2017). "When Does Globalization Help the Poor?" *Annual Review of Political Science.* 20: 287–307.

Rumbaugh, Thomas and Nicolas Blancher. (2004). "China: International Trade and WTO Accession." IMF Working Paper 04/36. Accessed March 16, 2017 at: www.imf.org/external/pubs/ft/wp/2004/wp0436.pdf.

Ryan, Curtis. (2011). "Political Opposition and Reform Coalitions in Jordan." *British Journal of Middle Eastern Studies.* 38(3): 367–390.

(2013). "Governance, Reform and Resurgent Ethnic Identity Politics in Jordan," in Abbas Kadhim (ed.), *Governance in the Middle East and North Africa.* New York: Routledge, pp. 342–356.

Sachs, Jeffrey D. and Andrew Warner. (1995). "Economic Reform and the Process of Global Integration." *Brookings Papers on Economic Activity.* 1: 1–118.

Sachs, Jeffrey and Wing Thye Woo. (1994). "Structural Factors in the Economic Reforms of China, Eastern Europe, and the Former Soviet Union." *Economic Policy.* 9(18): 101–145.

Saich, Tony. (2008). *Providing Public Goods in Transitional China.* New York: Palgrave Macmillan.

Saner, Raymond and Ricardo Guilherme. (2007). "The International Monetary Fund's Influence on Trade Policies of Low-Income Countries: A Valid Undertaking?" *Journal of World Trade.* 41(5): 931–981.

Sasoon, Joseph. (2016). *Anatomy of Authoritarianism in the Arab Republics.* Cambridge: Cambridge University Press.

Satpaev, Dosym. (2007). "An Analysis of the Internal Structure of Kazakhstan's Political Elite and an Assessment of Political Risk Levels," in Uyama Tomohiko (ed.), *Empire, Islam, and Politics in Central Eurasia.* Hokkaido University, Sapporo, Japan: Slavic Research Centre.

Saunders, Peter and Xiaoyuan Shang. (2001). "Social Security Reform in China's Transition to a Market Economy." *Social Policy and Administration.* 35(3): 274–289.

Schamis, Hector E. (1999). "Distributional Coalitions and the Politics of Economic Reform in Latin America." *World Politics.* 51(2): 236–268.

Schneider, F., A. Buehn, and C. E. Montenegro. (2010). "Shadow Economies All over the World: New Estimates for 162 Countries from 1999 to 2007," *World Bank Working Paper Series.* 5536 (July): 1–52. Accessed March 21, 2017 at: http://documents.worldbank.org/curated/en/311991468037132740/Shadow-economies-all-over-the-world-new-estimates-for-162-countries-from-1999-to-2007.

Schneider, Friedrich. (2005). "Shadow Economies Around the World: What Do We Really Know?" *European Journal of Political Economy.* 21(3): 598–642.

Schraeder, Peter J. and Hamadi Redissi. (2011). "Ben Ali's Fall." *Journal of Democracy.* 22(3): 5–18.

Schroeder, Larry and Michael Wasylenko. (1986). "A Preliminary Report on the Jordanian Tax System." USAID. Accessed March 16, 2017 at: http://pdf. usaid.gov/pdf_docs/PNABG442.pdf.

Schultz, Kenneth and Barry R. Weingast. (2003). "The Democratic Advantage: Institutional Foundations of Financial Power in International Competition." *International Organization*. 57(1): 3–42.

"Scrap Tax Incentives, Civil Society Urges Governments." *The Monitor (Kampala)*. July 29, 2011. Accessed March 22, 2017 at: www.monitor.co.ug/ Business/-/688322/1209482/-/view/printVersion/-/ry1rvjz/-/index.html.

"Sealing off Tax Loopholes." *The Business Times Singapore*. October 21, 2009. Lexis Nexis.

Sen, Amartya. (1999). "Democracy as a Universal Value." *Journal of Democracy*. 10(3): 3–17.

Sen, Siow Li. "Profits Earned by Temasek Are Returned to Community; Company Takes a Long-term View, Says its Chairman on its 40th Anniversary." *The Business Times*. March 24, 2014. Accessed February 20, 2017 at: www.businesstimes.com.sg/top-stories/profits-earned-by-temasek- are-returned-to-community.

Seshan, Ganesh K. (2014). "The Impact of Trade Liberalisation on Household Welfare in a Developing Country with Imperfect Labour Markets." *Journal of Development Studies*. 50(2): 226–243.

Shaban, Radwan A., Ragui Assaad, and Sulayman S. Al-Qudsi. (1995). "The Challenge of Unemployment in the Arab Region." *International Labour Review*. 134(1): 65–81.

Shaikh, Nasir N. (2015). "Indian Pharmaceutical Trade." *International Research Journal of Multidisciplinary Studies*. 1(2): 1–20.

Shamrat, Abu Sufian. (2016). "Electoral Reform in Bangladesh (1972– 2014): An Assessment." *South Asia Journal*. Accessed February 20, 2017 at: http://southasiajournal.net/electoral-reform-in-bangladesh-1972-2014- an-assessment/.

Sharkey, Nolan. (2004). "Tax Reform in the China Context: The Corporate Tax Unit and Chinese Enterprise." *eJournal of Tax Research*. 2(2). Accessed March 21, 2017 at: https://papers.ssrn.com/sol3/papers.cfm?abstract_id= 644015.

Sheldon, Peter, Sunghoon Kim, Yiqiong Li, and Malcolm Warner. (2011). *China's Changing Workplace: Dynamism, Diversity and Disparity*. New York: Routledge.

Sheng, Andrew. "Global Imbalances Call for Debate on Global Fiscal System." *The Korea Herald*. November 24, 2009. Accessed March 22, 2017 at: www. koreaherald.com/view.php?ud=200911240046.

Sheng, Hong and Pu Qian. (2015). *Opening Up China's Markets of Crude Oil and Petroleum Products*. Hackensack, NJ: World Scientific.

Shih, Toh Han. "China's Efforts to Curb Tax Evasion Net Extra 47b Yuan." *South China Morning Post*. March 20, 2014. Accessed March 9, 2017 at: www.scmp.com/business/china-business/article/1452672/chinas-efforts- curb-tax-evasion-net-extra-hk59b.

Shih, Toh Han. "China's Crackdown on Tax Evasion to Impact Cross-Border Transaction." *South China Morning Post*. January 5, 2015a. Accessed

March 16, 2017 at: www.scmp.com/business/economy/article/1673667/chinas-crackdown-tax-evasion-impact-cross-border-transactions.

Shih,Toh Han. "China's Tax Officials Vow 'Shock and Awe' Campaign in War against Cross-Border Cheats." *South China Morning Post.* March 6, 2015b. Accessed February 15, 2017 at: www.scmp.com/business/china-business/article/1731364/chinas-tax-officials-vow-shock-and-awe-campaign-war-against.

Shirk, Susan L. (1993). *The Political Logic of Economic Reform in China.* Los Angeles: University of California Press.

"Shiv Sena Protest over Water, Power Supply in Jammu." *Press Trust of India in Business Standard.* Jammu. July 5, 2015. Accessed August 7, 2015 at: www.business-standard.com/article/pti-stories/shiv-sena-protests-over-water-power-supply-in-jammu-115070500470_1.html.

Shu-ki, Tsang and Cheng Yuk-Shing. (1994). "China's Tax Reform of 1994: Breakthrough or Compromise?" *Asian Survey.* XXXIV(9): 769–788.

"Singapore Replaces Mauritius as Top Source of FDI in India." *Times of India.* May 25, 2014. Accessed August 7, 2015 at: http://timesofindia.indiatimes.com/business/india-business/Singapore-replaces-Mauritius-as-top-source-of-FDI-in-India/articleshow/35590304.cms.

Singh, Jatinder. (2014). "India's Automobile Industry: Growth and Export Potential." *Journal of Applied Economics and Business Research.* 4(4): 246–262.

Singh, Rajesh Kumar. "India Launches New Tax Evasion Amnesty Scheme to Unearth Unaccounted Cash." *Reuters.com.* November 28, 2016. Accessed March 22, 2017 at: www.reuters.com/article/us-india-modi-corruption-tax-idUSKBN13N194.

Slemrod, J. (2004). "Are Corporate Tax Rates, or Countries, Converging?" *Journal of Public Economics.* 88: 1169–1186.

Solt, Fredrick. (2016). "The Standardized World Income Inequality Database." *Social Science Quarterly.* 97(5): 1267–1281. Accessed March 16, 2017 at: http://fsolt.org/swiid/.

Song, Yang. (2012). "Poverty Reduction in China: The Contribution of Popularizing Primary Education." *China and World Economy.* 20(1): 105–122.

Soto, Alonso. "Brazil Extends Tax Aid to Sugar and Ethanol Sectors." *Reuters.* September 10, 2014. Accessed October 10, 2017 at: http://af.reuters.com/article/commoditiesNews/idAFL1N0RB0WQ20140910.

Srivastava, Shruti. "Coming Soon, a Sunset Clause on Tax Exemption." *The Indian Express.* October 10, 2015. Accessed February 13, 2017 at: http://indianexpress.com/article/business/business-others/coming-soon-a-sunset-clause-on-tax-exemption/.

Stokes, Bruce. (2015). "The Modi Bounce." PEW Research Center. Accessed February 14, 2018 at www.pewglobal.org/2015/09/17/the-modi-bounce/.

Stotsky, Janet. (1995). "Summary of IMF Tax Policy Advice," in Parthasrathi Shome (ed.), *Tax Policy Handbook.* Washington, DC: IMF, pp. 279–284.

"Strict Tax Enforcement to Push China's Tax Revenue to New High." *People's Daily Online.* October 17, 2006. Accessed March 24, 2017 at: http://en.people.cn/200610/17/eng20061017_312409.html.

"Study Sees India as Weak Democracy." *UPI.* May 23, 2004. Accessed March 9, 2017 at: www.upi.com/Study-sees-India-as-weak-democracy/13841085367128/?spt=su.

Surana, Suresh. "Eight Key Industry Expectations from Budget 2017." *Business Today*. January 20, 2017. Accessed February 13, 2017 at: www.businesstoday. in/union-budget-2017-18/columns/eight-key-industry-expectations-from-budget-2017/story/244489.html.

Svolik, Milan W. (2012). *The Politics of Authoritarian Rule*. Cambridge: Cambridge University Press.

Swank, Duane. (2016). "The New Political Economy of Taxation in the Developing World." *Review of International Political Economy*. 23(2): 185–207.

Swank, Duane and Sven Steinmo. (2002). "The New Political Economy of Taxation in Advanced Capitalist Democracies." *American Journal of Political Science*. 46(3): 642–655.

Takashima, Ryo. (2007). "The Impact of Trade and Factor Flows on Domestic Taxation." *International Journal of Business and Economics*. 6(1): 47–62.

Takeuchi, Hiroki. (2013). "Political Economy of Trade Protection: China in the 1990s." *International Relations of the Asia-Pacific*. 13: 1–32.

Talvi, Ernesto and Carlos A Vegh. (2005). "Tax Base Variability and Procyclical Fiscal Policy in Developing Countries." *Journal of Development Economics*. 78: 156–190.

Tanzi, Vito. (1986). "Fiscal Policy Responses to Exogenous Shocks in Developing Countries." *American Economic Review*. 76(2): 88–91.

(1989). "The Impact of Macroeconomic Policies on the Level of Taxation and the Fiscal Balance in Developing Countries." *Staff Papers International Monetary Fund*. 36(3). Accessed March 21, 2017 at: www.imf.org/external/ pubs/cat/longres.aspx?sk=16802.0.

Tanzi, Vito and Howell Zee. (2000). "Tax Policy for Emerging Markets: Developing Countries." *National Tax Journal*. 53(2): 299–322.

(2001). "Tax Policy for Developing Countries." Accessed March 16, 2017 at: www.imf.org/external/pubs/ft/issues/issues27/.

Tax Administration Reform Commission. (2014). *Tax Administration Reform in India: Spirit, Purpose and Empowerment (Third Report)*. New Delhi: Ministry of Finance, Government of India (GOI).

"Tax Concession on Ayurveda Medicines?" *NDTV*. February 14, 2012. Accessed February 3, 2017 at: www.ndtv.com/kerala-news/ tax-concession-on-ayurveda-medicines-569113.

"Tax Evaders Pay Up to $32 Million to Vietnam Gov't." *Inquirer.net*. August 3, 2015. Accessed July 3, 2017 at: http://business.inquirer.net/196377/ tax-evaders-pay-up-32-million-to-vietnam-govt.

"Tax Evasion 'Rampant' among India's Wealthy." *The National*, New Delhi. April 3, 2013. Accessed August 6, 2015 at: www.thenational.ae/news/world/south-asia/tax-evasion-rampant-among-indias-wealthy.

"Tax Exemptions for Rich Costs Government Rs 4.6L cr." *Times of India*. December 18, 2011. Accessed August 6, 2015 at: http://timesofindia. indiatimes.com/india/Tax-exemptions-for-rich-costs-govt-Rs-4-6L-cr/ articleshow/11149543.cms.

"Taxation in India: Take it Easy." *The Economist*. November 5, 2016. Accessed February 13, 2017 at: www.economist.com/news/leaders/21709546-india-risks-squandering-benefits-ground-breaking-economic-reform-take-it-easy.

Taylor, Alan. "Rising Protests in China." *The Atlantic*. February 17, 2012. Accessed February 15, 2017 at: www.theatlantic.com/photo/2012/02/rising-protests-in-china/100247/.

Taylor, Grantley, Grant Richardson, and Roman Lanis. (2015). "Multinationality, Tax Havens, Intangible Assets, and Transfer Pricing Aggressiveness: An Empirical Analysis." *Journal of International Accounting Research*. 14(1): 25–57.

"The Drive to Rid India of Black Money." *The New Statesman*, March 14, 2017. Accessed March 22, 2017 at: www.newstatesman.com/culture/observations/2017/03/drive-rid-india-black-money.

"There Should Be Minimum Tax on Ayurvedic Products: Acharya Balkrishna." *Zee Business*. November 4, 2016. Accessed February 3, 2017 at www.zeebiz.com/india/news-there-should-be-minimum-tax-on-ayurvedic-products-acharya-balkrishna-7648.

"Thousands at May Day Rally against GST." *The Star*. May 1, 2014. Accessed March 22, 2017 at: www.thestar.com.my/news/nation/2014/05/01/may-day-anti-gst-rally-kuala-lumpur/.

"Thousands Protest Trade Pact in India." *San Jose Mercury News*. April 5, 1994. Lexis Nexis.

"Thousands Protest in Ukraine over Tax Reform." *Kyiv Post*. November 16, 2010. Accessed March 22, 2017 at: www.kyivpost.com/article/content/ukraine-politics/thousands-protest-in-ukraine-over-tax-reform-video-90139.html.

Toh, Mun-Heng and Qian Lin. (2005). "An Evaluation of the 1994 Tax Reform in China Using a General Equilibrium Model." *China Economic Review*. 16: 246–270.

Topalova, Petia. (2004). "Trade Liberalization and Firm Productivity: The Case of India." IMF Working Paper WP/04/28.

Topalova, Petia. (2007). "Trade Liberalization, Poverty and Inequality: Evidence from Indian Districts," in Ann Harrison (ed.), *Globalization and Poverty*. Chicago: University of Chicago Press.

"'Total Solution Project' Will Affect Small Businesses, Say Traders." *The Hindu*. March 9, 2016. Accessed March 22, 2017 at: www.thehindu.com/news/national/tamil-nadu/total-solution-project-will-affect-small-businesses-say-traders/article8330060.ece.

Transparency International. (2016). Corruption Perception Index. Accessed February 15, 2017 at: www.transparency.org/news/feature/corruption_perceptions_index_2016.

Truex, Rory. (2017). "Consultative Authoritarianism and Its Limits." *Comparative Political Studies*. 50(3): 329–361.

Tsai, Kellee S. (2004). "Off Balance: The Unintended Consequences of Fiscal Federalism in China." *Journal of Chinese Political Science*. 9(2): 7–26.

Tubilewicz, Czeslaw. (2016). *Critical Issues in Contemporary China: Unity, Stability, and Development*. New York: Routledge.

Tuck, Laura and Kathy Lindert. (1996). "From Universal Food Subsidies to a Self-Targeted Program: A Case Study in Tunisian Reform." World Bank Discussion Paper 351. Washington, DC: World Bank.

"Tunisia: 2008–2009 Davos WEF Global Competitiveness Report Ranks Country First in Africa and Maghreb." *All Africa*. October 8, 2008. Accessed February 14, 2018 at: http://allafrica.com/stories/200810090889.html.

UNCTAD. (2015). *World Investment Report: Reforming International Investment Governance.* Accessed March 16, 2017 at: http://unctad.org/en/ PublicationsLibrary/wir2015_en.pdf.

(2016). "Target 17.1 Domestic Resource Mobilization." Accessed May 8, 2017 at: http://stats.unctad.org/Dgff2016/partnership/goal17/target_17_1.html.

UNDP. (2004). *Democracy in Latin America: Towards a Citizens' Democracy.* Argentina: Aguilar, Altea, Taurus, Alfaguara, S.A.

(2013). "Jordan Poverty Reduction Strategy." Accessed March 16, 2017 at: www .jo.undp.org/content/dam/jordan/docs/Poverty/Jordanpovertyreduction strategy.pdf.

UNESCO Institute for Statistics. (2011). *Financing Education in Sub-Saharan Africa.* Montreal: UNESCO.

(2014). Statistics Database. Accessed March 16, 2017 at: http://data.uis .unesco.org.

United Nations. (2002). "Improving Resource Mobilization in Developing Countries and Transition Economies." Accessed February 7, 2017 at: https:// goo.gl/3J6zsF.

(2008). *Public Enterprises: Unresolved Challenges and New Opportunities.* New York: United Nations.

(2015a). "Addis Ababa Outcome Document-Zero Draft." Accessed March 16, 2017 at: www.un.org/esa/ffd/wp-content/uploads/2015/03/1ds-zero-draft-outcome.pdf.

(2015b). "India and the MDGs." Accessed February 13, 2017 at: www .unescap.org/sites/default/files/India_and_the_MDGs_0.pdf.

United Nations Economic and Social Council. (2012). "Foreign Aid as a Catalyst to Improving Domestic Revenue Mobilization." Accessed March 16, 2017 at: www.un.org/en/ecosoc/newfunct/pdf/domestic_revenue_mobilisation_ june_11(july3).pdf.

USAID. (2010). "Jordan Fiscal Reform Project II." Accessed March 16, 2017 at: http://pdf.usaid.gov/pdf_docs/PBAAE537.pdf.

(2011). "Evaluating Tax Expenditures in Jordan." Accessed March 16, 2017 at: https://jordankmportal.com/system/resources/attachments/000/000/ 449/original/Evaluating_Tax_Expenditures_in_Jordan_2013_.pdf?14566 52503.

(2014a). "Jordan Fiscal Environment Assessment." Accessed March 16, 2017 at: https://goo.gl/V89WmJ.

(2014b). "Fiscal Reform Project II." Accessed at: http://pdf.usaid.gov/pdf_ docs/pdacy474.pdf.

US Department of State. (n.d.). "Uzbekistan." Accessed July 3, 2017 at: www .state.gov/j/drl/rls/hrrpt/2016/sca/265554.htm.

"Gambia, The: Country Reports on Human Rights Practices." March 4, 2002. Accessed February 20, 2017 at: www.state.gov/j/drl/rls/hrrpt/2001/af/8377. htm.

Vaishnav, Milan. "India's Taxing Tax System." *Foreign Affairs.* August 15, 2016. Accessed February 13, 2017 at: http://carnegieendowment.org/2016/08/15/ india-s-taxing-tax-system-pub-64321.

Valdes, Alberto. (1996). "Surveillance of Agricultural Price and Trade Policy in Latin America during Major Policy Reforms." World Bank Report. WDP329.

Accessed October 12, 2017 at: http://documents.worldbank.org/curated/en/877621468753259514/Surveillance-of-agricultural-price-and-trade-policy-in-Latin-America-during-major-policy-reforms.

"Valley Traders Demand Rollback of Taxes." *Kashmir Monitor (India).* June 1, 2016. Lexis Nexis.

Van De Walle, Nicolas. (1989). "Privatization in Developing Countries: A Review of the Issues." *World Development.* 17(5): 601–615.

Varshney, Ashutosh. (2000). "Why Have Poor Democracies Not Eliminated Poverty? A Suggestion." *Asian Survey.* 40(5): 718–736.

Vasal, V. and Jain, A. "Is Corporate Tax Rate High in India?" *The Hindu Business Line.* September 10, 2014. Accessed August 6, 2015 at: www.thehindubusinessline.com/opinion/is-corporate-tax-rate-high-in-india/article6397953.ece.

"VAT Implemented in 20 States Today." *Times of India.* April 1, 2005. Accessed August 6, 2015 at: http://timesofindia.indiatimes.com/india/VAT-implemented-in-20-states-today/articleshow/1066694.cms.

"VAT: Traders to Appeal to President." *Rediff Business.* New Delhi. March 29, 2005. Accessed August 6, 2015 at: www.rediff.com/money/report/vat/20050329.htm.

Vera, Ben O. de. "Lower Import Duties Seen to Boost PH Output." *Philippine Daily Inquirer.* June 26, 2014. Accessed August 9, 2017 at: www.pressreader.com/philippines/philippine-daily-inquirer/20140626/282205123974531.

Vergne, Clémence. (2009). "Democracy, Elections and Allocation of Public Expenditures in Developing Countries." *European Journal of Political Economy.* 25: 63–77.

Viet, Cuong Nguyen. (2015). "The Impact of Trade Facilitation on Poverty and Inequality." *The Journal of International Trade and Economic Development.* 24(3): 315–340.

Vikraman, Shaji. "In Fact: The Good and the Not-So-Good in the Mauritius Tax Treaty." *The Indian Express.* May 18, 2016. Accessed March 27, 2017 at: http://indianexpress.com/article/explained/india-mauritius-tax-treaty-indian-economy-2805967/.

Virmani, A. (2006). "Poverty and Hunger in India: What Is Needed to Eliminate Them?" *Planning Commission.* 1: 1–20.

"The Wrong End of the Right Debate." *The Indian Express.* August 25, 2014. Accessed August 6, 2015 at: http://indianexpress.com/article/opinion/columns/the-wrong-end-of-the-right-debate/.

"Voice Against Tax Shriller." *The New Indian Express.* March 31, 2012. Accessed August 6, 2015 at: www.newindianexpress.com/states/odisha/article464801.ece.

Von Schiller, Armin. (2016). "Business Organizations, Party Systems and Tax Composition in Developing Countries: A Comparison between Colombia and Peru." *The Journal of Development Studies.* 52(12): 1722–1743.

Von Soest, Christian. 2009. *The African State and its Revenues.* Germany: Nomos.

Vreeland, James Raymond. (2006). *The International Monetary Fund: Politics of Conditional Lending.* New York: Routledge.

Wacziarg, Romain and Jessica Seddon Wallack. (2004). "Trade Liberalization and Intersectoral Labor Movements." *Journal of International Economics.* 64(2): 411–439.

Wade, Robert H. (2004). "Is Globalization Reducing Poverty and Inequality?" *World Development*. 32(4): 567–589.

Walter, Stefanie. (2010). "Globalization and the Welfare State: Testing the Microfoundations of the Compensation Hypothesis." *International Studies Quarterly*. 54: 403–426.

Wang, Xiaobing and Jenifer Piesse. (2010). "Inequality and the Urban-Rural Divide in China: Effects of Regressive Taxation." *China and World Economy*. 18(6): 36–55.

Wang, Zhi and Fan Zhai. (1997). "Tariff Reduction, Tax Replacement, and Implications for Income Distribution in China." *Journal of Comparative Economics*. 26: 358–387.

Warrier, Maya. (2011). "Modern Ayurveda in Transnational Context." *Religion Compass*. 5(3): 80–93.

Weingast, B. R. (2009). "Second Generation Fiscal Federalism: The Implications of Fiscal Incentives." *Journal of Urban Economics*. 65(3): 279–293.

Weir, Fred. "Russia's Richest Man Arrested for Fraud and Tax Evasion." *The Independent*. October 25, 2003. Accessed May 1, 2017 at: www.independent.co.uk/news/world/europe/russias-richest-man-arrested-for-fraud-and-tax-evasion-93066.html.

Welle, Deutsche. "Global Risk Report Warns of Polarized Societies." *Daily News Egypt*. January 11, 2017.

Weymouth, Stephen. (2012). "Firm Lobbying and Influence in Developing Countries: A Multilevel Approach." *Business and Politics*. 14(4): 1–26.

White, Lawrence H. (2017). "India's Failed Demonetization Program and its Retreating Economic Defenders." September 28. Cato Institute. Accessed October 4, 2017 at: www.cato.org/blog/indias-failed-demonetization-program-its-retreating-economic- defenders.

Whiting, Susan. (2011). "Values in Land: Fiscal Pressures, Land Disputes and Justice Claims in Rural and Peri-Urban China." *Urban Studies*. 48(3): 569–587.

Wibbels, Erik. (2006). "Dependency Revisited: International Markets, Business Cycles, and Social Spending in the Developing World." *International Organization*. 60: 433–468.

Wibbels, Erik and Moisés Arce. (2003). "Globalization, Taxation, and Burden-Shifting in Latin America." *International Organization*. 57: 111–136.

Willis, Michael. (2014). *Politics and Power in the Maghreb*. Oxford: Oxford University Press.

Wils, Oliver. (2004). "From Negotiation to Rent Seeking, and Back? Patterns of State-Business Interaction and Fiscal Policy Reform in Jordan," in Steven Heydemann (ed.), *Networks of Privilege in the Middle East*. New York: Palgrave MacMillan.

Wilson, John D. (1985). "Optimal Property Taxation in the Presence of Interregional Capital Mobility." *Journal of Urban Economics*. 17: 73–89.

Winters, L. Alan and Antonio Martuscelli. (2014). "Trade Liberalization and Poverty: What Have We Learned in a Decade?" *Annual Review of Resource Economics*. 6: 493–512.

Winters, L. Alan, Neil McCulloch, and Andrew McKay. (2004). "Trade Liberalization and Poverty: The Evidence so Far." *Journal of Economic Literature*. 42(1): 72–115.

Wintrobe, Ronald. (1998). *Political Economy of Dictatorship*. New York: Cambridge University Press.

"Withdrawal of Excise Duty Demanded." *The New Indian Express*. September 22, 2014. Lexis Nexis.

Wong, Christine P. W. (1991). "Central-Local Relations in an Era of Fiscal Decline: The Paradox of Fiscal Decentralization in Post-Mao China." *The China Quarterly*. 128: 691–715.

(1992). "Fiscal Reform and Local Industrialization: The Problematic Sequencing of Reform in Post-Mao China." *Modern China*. 18(2): 197–227.

(2000). "Central-Local Relations Revisited: The 1994 Tax Sharing Reform and Public Expenditure Management in China." World Bank. Accessed February 14, 2018 at: http://citeseerx.ist.psu.edu/viewdoc/download?doi=1 0.1.1.201.8596&rep=rep1&type=pdf.

(2009). "Rebuilding Government for the 21st Century: Can China Incrementally Reform the Public Sector?" *The China Quarterly*. 200: 929–952.

Wong, R. Bin. (2001). "Tax Resistance, Economy, and State Transformation in China and Europe." *Economics of Governance*. 2: 69–83.

World Bank. (1980). *World Development Report, 1980*. August. Washington, DC.

(1991). *India. 1991 Country Economic Memorandum*, Country Operations Division: India Country Department, August 23. Washington, DC: World Bank Publication Services.

(1993). "China Budgetary Policy and Intergovernmental Fiscal Relations." Report 11094-CHA. Accessed March 21, 2017 at: http://documents. worldbank.org/curated/en/351891468216949906/Main-report.

(1996). "Bureaucrats in Business: The Economics and Politics of Government Ownership." Accessed February 16, 2018 at: http://documents.worldbank. org/curated/en/867101468780298811/Bureaucrats-in-business-the-economics-and-politics-of-government-ownership.

(2004). *India State Fiscal Reforms in India Progress and Prospects*, Poverty Reduction and Economic Management, Sector Unit South Asia Region, November 10. Washington, DC: World Bank Publication Services.

(2005). "World Development Report 2005: A Better Investment Climate for Everyone." Accessed March 16, 2017 at: http://elibrary.worldbank.org/doi/abs/10.1596/0-8213-5682-8.

(2006). "World Development Report: Equity and Development." Accessed March 16, 2017 at: http://documents.worldbank.org/curated/en/435331468127174418/World-development-report-2006-equity-and-development.

(2007). "The Revenue Implications of Trade Liberalization." Accessed February 1, 2018 at: http://siteresources.worldbank.org/PROJECTS/Resources/40940-1118776867573/revenueimplications.pdf.

(2009). "Doing Business 2010 Tunisia." Accessed February 14, 2018 at: http://documents.worldbank.org/curated/en/525941468119339889/pdf/506070WP0DB02010Box342003B01PUBLIC1.pdf.

(2012). "Poverty Trends in Uganda: Who Gained and Who Was Left Behind?" Accessed February 20, 2017 at: http://siteresources.worldbank.org/INTUGANDA/Resources/uganda-poverty-and-inequality-trends-full-policy-note.pdf.

(2013). "Bangladesh Reduced Number of Poor by 16 Million in a Decade." June 20. Press Release. Accessed February 20, 2017 at: www.worldbank .org/en/news/press-release/2013/06/20/bangladesh-reduced-number-of-poor-by-16-million-in-a-decade.

(2014). "The Unfinished Revolution: Bringing Opportunity, Good Jobs and Greater Wealth to All Tunisians." Development Policy Review Report 86179-TN. Accessed March 21, 2017 at: www.worldbank.org/en/country/ tunisia/publication/unfinished-revolution.

(2015a). "Goods and Fiscal Impact." Accessed March 16, 2017 at: http:// go.worldbank.org/0W9S7MGVC0.

(2015b). "Middle East and North Africa: Governance Reforms of State-Owned Enterprises." Report ACS15142. Accessed March 21, 2017 at: https://goo. gl/bQtKGg

(2016a). World Development Indicators Database. Accessed March 16, 2017 at: http://data.worldbank.org/data-catalog/world-development-indicators.

(2016b). "Winning the Tax Wars: Global Solutions for Developing Countries." Accessed March 16, 2017 at: www.worldbank.org/en/events/2016/04/29/ winning-the-tax-wars-global-solutions-for-developing-countries.

(2016c). "Hashemite Kingdom of Jordan: Promoting Poverty Reduction and Shared Prosperity." Report 103433-JO.

(2017). "Globalization Backlash: Should Asia Worry?" Accessed July 3, 2017 at: www.worldbank.org/en/news/video/2017/04/14/should-south-asia-worry-about-globalization-backlash.

World Bank Enterprise Survey. (2016). Accessed March 16, 2017 at: www .enterprisesurveys.org.

World Integrated Trade Solution. (2016). Accessed March 16, 2017 at: http:// wits.worldbank.org.

World Trade Organization. (2003). "Market Access for Non-Agricultural Products." Accessed March 16, 2017 at: https://ustr.gov/archive/assets/ Trade_Sectors/Industry_Market_Access/Industrial_Market_Access_in_ the_WTO/asset_upload_file437_8252.pdf.

(2017). "Members and Observers." Accessed July 3, 2017 at: www.wto.org/ english/thewto_e/whatis_e/tif_e/org6_e.htm.

World Values Survey. (2015). Accessed March 16, 2017 at: www.world valuessurvey.org/wvs.jsp.

Wright, Joseph. (2008). "Do Authoritarian Institutions Constrain? How Legislatures Affect Economic Growth and Investment." *American Journal of Political Science*. 52(2): 322–343.

Wu, Weiping. (2010). "Urban Infrastructure Financing and Economic Performance in China." *Urban Geography*. 31(5): 648–667.

Wu, Xiaogang and Zhuoni Zhang. (2010). "Changes in Education Inequality in China, 1990–2005: Evidence from the Population Census Data." *Research in Sociology of Education*. 17: 123–152.

Xiang, Li. "China Joins Int'l Effort to Fight Tax Evasion." *China Daily*, European Edition. August 27, 2013. Lexis Nexis.

Xu, Hua and Huiyu Cui. (2011). "The Revenue System of China: Past, Present, and Emerging Issues." *Journal of Public Budgeting, Accounting and Financial Management*. 23(4): 544–568.

Yackee, Jason Webb and Susan Webb Yackee. (2006). "A Bias Towards Business? Assessing Interest Group Influence on the U.S. Bureaucracy." *The Journal of Politics*. 68(1): 128–139.

Yan, Sophia. "China's Taxman Is Coming for Alibaba." *CNN Money*. April 7, 2015. Accessed August 9, 2017 at: http://money.cnn.com/2015/04/07/news/economy/china-alibaba-tax/index.html.

Yang, Dennis Tao, Junsen Zhang, and Shaojie Zhou. (2012). "Why Are Savings Rates So High in China?" in Joseph P. H. Fan and Randall Morck (eds.), *Capitalizing China*. Chicago: University of Chicago Press, pp. 249–282.

Yao, James Y., Gamal Zaki El-Masry, Padamja Khandelwal, and Emilio Sacerdoti. (2005). *Mauritius: Challenges of Sustained Growth*. Washington, DC: International Monetary Fund.

Yasar, Mahmut. (2013). "Political Influence of Exporting and Import-Competing Firms: Evidence from Eastern European and Central Asian Countries." *World Development*. 51: 154–168.

Ye, Lin. (2011). "Demographic Transition, Developmentalism and Social Security in China." *Social Policy and Administration*. 45(6): 678–693.

Yom, Sean L. and F. Gregory Gause III. (2012). "Resilient Royals: How Arab Monarchies Hang on." *Journal of Democracy*. 23(4): 74–88.

Zayani, Mohamed. (2015). *Networked Publics and Digital Contention: The Politics of Everyday Life in Tunisia*. Oxford: Oxford University Press.

Zhan, Shaohua and Joel Andreas. (2015). "Beyond the Countryside: Hukou Reform and Agrarian Capitalism in China." *Chiang Mai University Conference Paper 7*. Accessed March 21, 2017 at: www.iss.nl/fileadmin/ASSETS/iss/Research_and_projects/Research_networks/LDPI/CMCP_7-_Zhan_and_Andreas.pdf.

Zhang, Le-Yin. (1999). "Chinese Central-Provincial Fiscal Relationships, Budgetary Decline and the Impact of the 1994 Fiscal Reform: An Evaluation." *The China Quarterly*. 157: 115–141.

Zheng, Yongnian. (2013). *Contemporary China: A History since 1978*. Chichester: John Wiley and Sons.

Zhou, Yu. (2008). "Synchronizing Export Orientation with Import Substitution: Creating Competitive Indigenous High-Tech Companies in China." *World Development*. 36(11): 2353–2370.

Zhu, Xiaodong. (2012). "Understanding China's Growth: Past, Present, and Future." *Journal of Economic Perspectives*. 26(4): 103–124.

Zodrow, George R. (2010). "Capital Mobility and Capital Tax Competition." *National Tax Journal*. 63(4): 865–902.

Zucman, Gabriel. (2014). "Taxing across Borders: Tracking Personal Wealth and Corporate Profits." *Journal of Economic Perspectives*. 28(4): 121–148.

Index

Acemoglu et al. (2016), 196
Andhra Pradesh (AP)
  public services provision, 97
  tax on cow urine, 2, 35, 73
Appel, H., 44
authoritarian regimes, *see also* conservative
    regimes (ConservAuth); liberal
    authoritarian regimes (LibAuth)
  administrative quality and fiscal
    performance, 39–43, 53–54
  classification of, 7, 25–27
  corporate tax compliance, 81
  corporate tax rates and effects of trade
    tax revenues on, 82–85
  corporate taxes and less productive
    firms, 76
  domestic tax reform strategies, 7, 26–27,
    31–33, 34, 59, 193
  domestic tax revenue collection,
    post-liberalization, 36–39
  economic growth and domestic
    revenues, 43t3.1b
  hypothesis on tax revenues, 33–34
  impact on the poor of declining state
    revenues, 104–106
  liberalization and domestic tax revenue,
    hypothesis test, 44–57
  numbers of less productive firms, 87
  political factors for regime maintenance,
    25–26, 30–31, 59
  political powers of business interests, 31
  political responses to free trade, 187
  public confidence in, 59
  public goods provision, 33
  public goods provision, perceptions of
    across regime type, 62, 107–108
  regime types, 61–62
  state-owned enterprises (SOEs)
    revenues, 42–44
  tax compliance and government
    confidence among elites, 69–72

tax compliance and satisfaction with
    public goods, 62–68
tax compliance,
    post-liberalization, 68–69
tax concessions to loyalist groups,
    25–26, 30, 59
tax inspection rates across
    regimes, 87–91
value-added tax (VAT), 33

Baunsgaard, T. and Keen, M., 39–40
Ben Ali, Zine El Abidine, 171, 175–176,
    179–181
Bernstein, T. and Lu, X., 148
Bhagwati, J., 130
Bhagwati, J. and Panagariya, A., 20
black money, 23, 59
Brazil, 30, 79–80
bureaucracy quality, 17, 18, 137, 138

Carstens, Agustín, 17
Cheibub et al. (2009), 62
China
  agricultural taxes, 137
  anti-tax evasion measures, 144, 149–152
  central government and tax
    collection, 149
  coercive tax collection, 32, 148–149, 189
  corporate income tax (CIT), 143, 144,
    149, 151, 153
  dissatisfaction with public goods
    provision, 147–148, 154, 189
  domestic tax reforms, 136, 140, 153
  education spending in, 155–156, 156f8.8
  export-oriented trade regime
    development, 140–142
  government expenditure (percentage of
    GDP), 157
  healthcare expenditure, 147–148,
    155–156, 156f8.8
  industrial taxes, 138

319